LOOKING BEYOND THE ICONS

LOOKING BEYOND THE ICONS

Midcentury Architecture, Landscape, and Urbanism

RICHARD LONGSTRETH

UNIVERSITY OF VIRGINIA PRESS Charlottesville & London

University of Virginia Press
© 2015 by the Rector and Visitors of the University of Virginia
All rights reserved
Printed in the United States of America on acid-free paper

First published 2015

9 8 7 6 5 4 3 2 1

LIBRARY OF CONGRESS CATALOGING-IN-PUBLICATION DATA
Longstreth, Richard W., author.
 [Essays. Selections]
 Looking beyond the icons : midcentury architecture, landscape,
and urbanism / Richard Longstreth.
     pages cm
 Includes bibliographical references and index.
 ISBN 978-0-8139-3643-7 (cloth : alk. paper)
 1. Modern movement (Architecture)—United States. 2. Cultural
landscapes—United States. 3. City planning—United States—
History—20th century. I. Title.
 NA712.5.M63L66 2015
 720.973—dc23

                                        2014025624

For Norma Evenson
and in memory of
Jean Bony and Spiro Kostof

CONTENTS

ACKNOWLEDGMENTS

I am grateful to the many people who offered insight, advice, and support for the content of this book over the nearly thirty years that portions of its content have been written. These include Charles Birnbaum, Richard Cloes, Mark Edwards, Lisa Pfueller Davidson, Christine Madrid French, Paul Groth, Michael Jackson, the late H. Ward Jandhl, Terry Klein, Antoinette Lee, the late Steven Levin, Chester Liebs, David Lowenthal, Eugene Pasymowski, Beth Lattimore Reiter, Katherine Cole Stevenson, Richard Striner, de Teel Patterson Tiller, Michael Tomlan, Richard Wagner, and Chris Wilson. Likewise, I am indebted to those who kindly supplied me with information on specific buildings and sites, including: Mrs. Nathaniel Curtis, the late Arthur Davis, Valerie Gomez, Karen Kingsley, and Nancy Niedernhofer (for St. Frances Cabrini); the late Charles Atherton, Robert Bruegmann, Leslie Coburn, Araldo Cossutta, Paul Ivey, Kyle Johnson, Sue Kohler, Arlie Schrantz, Diane Shaw, Janet Adams Strong (for the Third Church); the late J. Carter Brown, Christine Madrid French, Thomas S. Hines, Dion Neutra, and de Teel Patterson Tiller (for the Cyclorama Building); Karen and John Culpepper, Paula Dennis, Kimberly Corwin Gray, David Hochschartner, Lauren McGovern, Paul Nowicki, Martha Spear, and Betsey Thomas Train (for North Country School–Camp Treetops); Stephen Dennis, James Goode, Ruth H. Landman, the late Carolyn Pitts, Donna J. Seifert, Kathleen Sinclair Wood (for the community garden at 3901 Connecticut Avenue); Peter Espenschied, James Goode, David Hammond, Don Hawkins, George Idelson, Ann Loikow, Christopher Martin, Diane Olsson (for Friendship Shopping Center); Michael Brooks, Peter Featheringill, Lisa Sundrla, John Sussman, Beth Lattimore Reiter, and Sarah Ward (for Broughton Street); and Cindy Keeba, Teresa Lachin, Eileen McGuckian, Dorothy Patterson, John Tyner, Mary Van Balgooy, and the students in my graduate class who undertook the initial research—Rebecca Berlyoung, Emily Burrows, Eve Errickson, Shira Goldstein, Joanna Hall, Noriko Kikuchi, Anna Klosterman, Walter Lehmann, Diana Maxwell, Ashley Roesler, Camille Smiley, Cindy Thompson, and Alden Watts (for Twinbrook).

I benefited greatly from material available from a number of archives and libraries, including American Institute of Architects Archives, Washington, D.C. (Nancy Hadley); Architectural Archives, University of Pennsylvania (William Whitaker); Architecture and McKeldin libraries, University of Maryland, College Park; Archives of the Archdiocese of New Orleans; Archives–Special Collections, College of Environmental Design, California State Polytechnic University, Pomona (Lauren Weiss Bricker); Avery Architectural and Fine Arts Library, Columbia University (Janet Parks, Jason Escalante); Chatham County–Savannah Metropolitan Planning Commission (Sarah Ward); Christian Science Publishing Society (Ed Blomquist); Gelman Library, George Washington University, especially the interlibrary loan division; Georgia Historical Society, Savannah (Lynette Stoudt); Hartford (Connecticut) Public Library; Historical Society of Washington, D.C.; Library of Congress, Prints and Photographs Division; National Gallery of Art; New Orleans Public Library; Savannah Public Library (Sharen Lee); Southeastern Architectural Archives, Tulane University; and Wilmington (Delaware) Public Library. Additional photographs were graciously supplied to me by Erica Stoller and Ryan Rothman of Esto Photographics and Emma Cobb of Pei Cobb Freed & Partners. Paul Davidson deserves particular thanks for preparing the superb drawings made for this volume.

Many of the costs incurred in procuring images and for travel were covered by a grant from George Washington's University Facilitating Fund.

My research trips were enlivened in many ways by the hospitality of Catherine and John Bishir, James A. Figg III, Bruce and Barbara Haldeman, Morrison and Fenella Heckscher, Beth Lattimore Reiter, and Virginia Miller and Bruce Wallis.

Not enough thanks can be given to Araldo Cossutta, Christine Madrid French, Paul Ivey, Suleiman Osman, Beth Lattimore Reiter, Richard Striner, Janet Adams Strong, and Michael Tomlan for reading various chapters and offering an abundance of useful suggestions for their improvement.

I am grateful to Boyd Zenner of the University of Virginia Press for the idea of this book, for allowing me to deviate from that concept, and for making the whole process a pleasure. Thanks also go to Mark Mones, Angie Hogan, and Martha Farlow for their editorial, design, and production expertise.

My wife, Cinda, as always, has been patient and supporting. I take special pleasure in dedicating this book to Norma Evenson, my graduate adviser at U.C. Berkeley, who, by example, set a very high bar, and to the memory of two of her colleagues, Jean Bony and Spiro Kostof, from whom I benefited just as much. The breadth of their inquiry, the spectrum of their approaches to scholarship, and the acuity of their intellects has been an enduring inspiration.

LOOKING BEYOND THE ICONS

Introduction

In recent years interest in architecture, landscape, and urbanism from the recent past has mushroomed.[1] Scholarship on post–World War II subjects has outstripped that on most other periods. Concerns among historic preservationists have not been far behind. Federal agencies, city and state preservation offices, and nonprofit organizations of many kinds have embraced the subject. Some private-sector groups have been founded to address the matters pertaining to the recent past and others have substantially expanded their initiatives in this sphere, sometimes with a swelling of membership as a result.[2] Major campaigns have been launched to save Boston's City Hall and Christian Science Center. MIT's Baker Hall has been meticulously restored as has Yale's Art and Architecture Building.[3] Walter and Leonore Annenberg's Sunnylands near Palm Springs is now a house museum and conference center. A substantial number of Frank Lloyd Wright's postwar houses are open to the public or are readily accessible as bed and breakfast establishments. Surveys of mid-twentieth-century resources have been done from New Canaan to Los Angeles.[4] A new generation of historians, preservationists, and many others have come to regard the recent past with unyielding dedication. On the popular front, owning a Modern house holds greater appeal than it did fifty or sixty years ago when such work was new. Likewise furniture of the period enjoys an appeal exceeding any previous time.

Why the great rise of interest? For people in their twenties or thirties, work from the postwar era seems part of a distant past, even if they grew up in suburban tracts and hung out in shopping malls. Nostalgia or an attraction to things that just predate childhood remembrance (things their parents knew when *they* were young) is no doubt a driving force at the popular level. That may explain the current love of 1950s coffee shops, for example, or of neon signs. But such personal attachment hardly explains the interest in saving monumental, concrete piles of the 1960s, which never have been and may never will be objects of popular appeal. And nostalgia cannot begin to explain the widespread migration of historians to subjects grounded in the second half of the twentieth century. The roots of the recent past phenomenon run deeper.

Among the primary reasons to explore this realm in scholarship and preservation is the remarkable richness of its legacy in all aspects of the built environment. Between 1945 and the early 1970s, the United States experienced a nearly unwavering period of economic growth. Prosperity was enjoyed by an unprecedented percentage of the population; indeed, an entirely new mass market was created, with higher levels of education and greater amounts of disposable income, leisure time, and mobility. For at least a decade after the war, European nations were in the throes of recovery. The United States had few cultural rivals. In architecture, the proliferation of talent on the home front was likewise unmatched. Not only did the country harbor the majority of great avant-garde modernists from earlier decades, including Frank Lloyd Wright, Ludwig Mies van der Rohe, Walter Gropius, Richard Neutra, R. M. Schindler, Marcel Breuer, and Erich Mendelsohn, it had also launched a new generation, many of them taught under the aegis of Gropius or Mies or who gained nurture from the example of Wright. The range of work produced by young and old alike—in expression, in character, in the use of structure and materials, in the development of space and form, and in many other respects had never been matched by earlier generations. Beyond formal and technical innovation came

an enormous spectrum of change to existing building types—schools, banks, libraries,
apartment buildings, hospitals, manufacturing
plants, among them—and the development of
new or nearly new types, including shopping
malls, airport terminals, "country" corporate
headquarters, and visitor centers. Finally, if
the social concerns that had helped propel
the avant-garde during the interwar decades
diminished somewhat during the mid-twentieth century, a concern for designing in greater
harmony with the natural environment gained
currency, following the example of figures as
different as Neutra and Wright.

The legacy is also rich in the vernacular
realm. The tens of thousands of tract houses
constructed during the postwar era that were
so bemoaned by some, in fact manifest a major
historical shift the complexion of the American
populace and its living environment, they also
represent many innovations in design, materials, and mass-production building techniques.
Considering present and future needs, they are
resources that we cannot replace in kind. Land
is too scarce and construction is too expensive
to build equivalents for the persons of moderate to middle income that continue to occupy
most postwar tracts today. Commercial buildings along the roadside and on Main streets
embodied far more than the garishness with
which many critics once dismissed them. Other
components of the landscape, from those of the
interstate highway system to those built for
defense during the Cold War likewise command
our serious attention. Many things considered
ordinary from the period are now coming to
be viewed as resources that are important to
understand and, often, to protect.

But what is the rush? Scholarship on the subject can flourish, but why not hold off on preservation campaigns for another decade or so until
public appreciation grows even wider? The concern for these resources now is justified by the
circumstances. Unlike many commercial centers or residential areas that date from the late
nineteenth through the early twentieth centuries, the survival rate of things from the recent
past can be alarmingly short. As the historic

preservation movement incrementally came to
embrace places created between the Civil War
and World War I, they were at least seventy,
eighty, or even one hundred years old. In contrast many important segments of the recent
past are defaced or destroyed within a matter
of a few decades, sometimes even less. Noteworthy landscape designs have proven especially
vulnerable in this regard, but so have the ordinary commercial buildings, for which extensive
remodeling, if not demolition, can occur after
a quarter century. The time may soon come
when noteworthy housing tracts are targeted
for higher-density development. Distinguished
singular buildings can be laid to waste as well.
Paul Rudolph's Orange County, New York, government center was seriously threatened until
recently, and his Riverview High School at Sara-
sota, Florida, demolished. Several of Richard
Neutra's most important works from the postwar years have been lost (the Maslon house in
Rancho Mirage and the former visitor center
at Gettysburg) or could well be lost in the near
future (Mariner's Medical Arts Center at Newport Beach), while his Kronish house in Beverly
Hills narrowly escaped destruction in 2012.
John Johansen's Mechanic Theater in Baltimore
and, perhaps, his Mummer's Theater in Oklahoma City are likely to be lost as well.

• • •

My concern for preserving buildings and landscapes of the recent past initially arose out of
my interest in such places as an architectural
historian. Until I was twenty, most of my attention was focused on work of the nineteenth and
early twentieth centuries. The scope began to
broaden dramatically during the summer of
1966 when I had the good fortune to work at the
office of Richard & Dion Neutra in Los Angeles.
Besides the rewarding experience of being in
that environment, I gained much from devoting
time after hours and on weekends to examining
buildings throughout Southern California, a
process greatly facilitated by the then-recently
issued architectural guide authored by David
Gebhard and Robert Winter. At that time, their
approach to listing was unusually ecumenical,

encompassing a rich selection of the pictorial eclecticism of the 1920s and 1930s, but also Art Deco and Modern architecture, the latter of which reflected the region's unsurpassed array of avant-garde design. Their book became a conceptual springboard for one I undertook of architecture in the Philadelphia area as a senior project, which, in turn, was further developed with coauthor Edward Teitelman and published in 1974.[5] During the proceeding four years, I had also acquired an interest in the ephemeral architecture of the highway spurred in part by several drives across the country and additional forays in the Northeast.[6] It was not for another decade, however, that I became engaged as an activist in preserving architecture from what was then considered to be of recent vintage, with efforts to demonstrate the historical significance of two 1930s shopping centers in the Washington, D.C., area. Subsequent endeavors resulted in safeguarding a Greyhound bus depot, an additional shopping center, a branch department store, two department store warehouses, and a Sears department store—all in Washington and from the late 1930s and early 1940s.[7] Concurrently I worked unsuccessfully on preserving an outlying business center developed between the mid-1940s and early 1950s in Silver Spring, Maryland. Along with a number of others engaged in that initiative, my hope was to provide a model for how such places could continue to make a vital contribution to their communities, just as the National Main Street Program had done with town centers of earlier vintage.[8] By 1990, my concern for the recent past broadened to encompass a wide range of postwar architecture, high style and vernacular examples alike, that had interested me as a historian for over twenty years. Much of my effort was channeled into public lectures, conference papers, and articles, as well as my graduate courses, but toward the decade's end I helped launch an effort to save Neutra's visitor center at Gettysburg.[9] My preservation activities profoundly affected my scholarly interests, which turned in the mid-1980s to commercial development from the 1920s to the 1960s. More recently I have focused on a variety of approaches to addressing post–World War II housing needs, a shift triggered in part by projects undertaken by graduate students under my direction over the past dozen years.[10]

. . .

Responding to the gracious invitation of Boyd Zenner at the University of Virginia Press to publish an anthology of writings, I decided that too many of them were freshly issued and readily available through electronic means as well as in print. Older writings were too varied in subject to form a coherent book. However, I had written enough on issues related to preserving the recent past to form part of a volume, supplemented by case studies of projects with which I have been involved since the mid-1990s. In several instances, I had prepared sufficiently detailed documents to use here with some minor modifications, including the addition of notes for several and updating references in the notes of others. The remaining projects, however, necessitated new texts. Preparing this book thus entailed a substantial amount of research, travel, and time in preparation. The focus of all this work has been on historical significance, often addressing matters that a number of cohorts in the preservation field still find difficult, even perplexing. The icons of the postwar decades—the Lever Houses and Dulles Airports, as it were—may be safe, but most of that era's legacy is far less secure.

The first section, "Style and Taste," comprising chapters 1 and 2, examines phenomena that apply to preservation practice across the board, but can be especially pernicious when assessing the recent past. Nationwide, the preservation community has accepted "style" as a basic way to categorize and also to characterize architecture. Some of the style guides upon which preservationists now rely pay scant attention to work of the recent past, but others, including the list promulgated by the National Register of Historic Places, include a half-dozen seemingly innocuous terms that apply to work of the mid-twentieth century. Among the problems generated by this tendency is that it ignores the stunningly broad range of expression found in architecture of the period. The style fixation also distorts or ignores the importance of personal style in Modern architecture. How does one characterize the work of Buckminster Fuller? Can Fay Jones's work simply be cast as Wrightian? What about that of Bart Prince? Cesar Pelli? Frank Gehry? Are Louis Kahn's buildings best explained as Brutalist? What about those by I. M. Pei? In what cubbyhole does Eero Saarinen's work fit? And what about that of his father? Preservationists who have become addicted to "style" often do not know where to begin when addressing such work. "Style" becomes a substitute for thought. The shortcomings of the system are perhaps even more pronounced when examining, say, tract houses, motels, retail facilities, or airplane hangars of the late 1950s, 1960s, or 1970s.

In contrast to style, taste is a term that preservationists shun, for invoking it overtly subsumes professional judgment. Yet, as I note in the second chapter, taste lies just below the surface and it can break into the open when it addresses the recent past. Buildings often incorrectly dubbed Brutalist seem to be particularly susceptible to outpourings of personal emotion, not just among those preoccupied by blogs and tweets as shapers of reality, but among many preservationists, who can be inclined to duck the issue because it is so controversial and the buildings so out of fashion. Without acquiring a solid, historical understanding of the work and the circumstances around which it was commissioned, its design was conceived, and the purposes it served, preservationists can all too often dismiss work because it seems strange, or perhaps even ugly, to them without admitting as much.

The second section of this volume, "Some Challenges of the Recent Past," contains four reprinted pieces addressing subjects that have seemed especially daunting to many of those preservationists who have considered them at all: the legacies of urban renewal (chapter 3), landscape design (chapter 4), suburban development (chapter 5), and shopping centers (chapter 6). A general loathing of urban renewal does not seem to have dissipated some four decades after the program's demise. This attitude is commonplace among historians as well as designers, planners, and the public at large. The third chapter makes a plea for a less biased framework, examining the enterprise anew. If some major projects are rightly destined for transformation, others have at least some components that merit serious consideration, and yet others, such as Lafayette Park in Detroit, Society Hill in Philadelphia, or the Southwest Redevelopment Area in Washington, D.C., are indeed remarkable places that should be held as long-term assets to the urban environment. Landscape design and open space more generally are key components to numerous urban renewal projects, yet are all too frequently accorded little attention for the essential role they play in site planning and, ultimately, in the character of these places. Even when the significance of landscape is acknowledged, it can be seen as of a lesser rank than the buildings to which it is so closely related. The fourth chapter, which focuses on landscape design, emphasizes these points and the fragility of Modern landscapes as a result. The outgrowth of a paper delivered at a Wave Hill conference in New York on preserving the work of major landscape architects, this chapter also seeks to broaden the parameters to include some vernacular settings of the sort that have yet to attract historical attention.

Landscape also figures prominently in the fifth chapter, on postwar suburbs. Since it was initially published a dozen years ago, a number of detailed historical studies have been issued on the subject, and preservation organizations at the national, state, and local levels have amassed copious material to stimulate interest in, and guide documentation of, such places.[11] Still, the major thrust of this literature is on the houses, not on salient aspects of planning, including the overall spatial order and the provision of public open space. And even as awareness grows about the need to protect postwar residential communities from decline and destruction, concrete efforts remain in their infancy. The pressure to alter such enclaves in adverse ways is mounting, with piecemeal destruction through "teardowns" to discussions of wholesale clearance ("suburban renewal"?) for new, denser development. The latter process will not occur where the communities remain viable and appealing, but may well take place where tracts have declined and lose their attraction to the income groups that can afford to maintain them.

Few components of the built environment pose as many challenges to preservation as do shopping centers, especially those from the postwar era. The conditions delineated in the sixth, final chapter in this section, which was initially published in 1992, have not changed. Since the 1950s, most retail development has been essentially impermanent in nature. That situation might change if merchants and real estate developers alike could be convinced that extensive, periodic remodeling is not needed to maintain customer appeal. The objective has, of course, been attained now on numerous Main Streets, in some neighborhood centers, and in a small number of high-end suburban retail complexes—most all of them developed before World War II. The same may be possible with some of the major, multiuse complexes of more recent vintage as well. Preservationists should neither dismiss the possibilities nor settle for a passive role in this arena.

The eight case studies assembled in the third and fourth sections—"Extraordinary and Unknown" and "Commonplace and Taken for Granted," respectively—demonstrate a small segment of the multitude of issues concerning historical significance. Those in the third section entail several distinguished resources of singular design that have never enjoyed the recognition they deserve. Chapters 7 and 8 examine churches of markedly different kinds, one Roman Catholic, the other Christian Scientist, in New Orleans and Washington, D.C., respectively; chapters 9 and 10 consider in turn the former visitor center at Gettysburg and a private school and summer camp complex in the Adirondacks. Those in the fourth section focus on resources of a more generic variety: a community garden and a small shopping center, both in Washington (chapters 11 and 12); the traditional retail core of Savannah, Georgia (chapter 13); and residential subdivisions in suburban Montgomery County, Maryland (chapter 14).

The intent of all these case studies is to underscore how addressing historical significance, even for seemingly simple things, is not a simple process conceptually. Equally important is to emphasize how the nature of inquiry—the questions asked, the sources pursued, and ultimately the matters addressed—can vary to a considerable degree from case to case, demanding assessment predicated on the individual circumstances rather than on formulaic assumptions. The basic *methods* of inquiry are no different for the mid-twentieth century than for any other era, but the *particulars* of inquiry must be attuned to the particulars at hand, irrespective of period.

In the cases presented here, technological prowess in the development of structure figures to a degree in analyzing St. Frances Cabrini Church in New Orleans, but two of the most important factors are the seemingly disparate ones of the nature of liturgical reform and a new interpretation of some venerated traditional building patterns in that city. Although it might not have appeared so, St. Frances Cabrini was indeed a quintessential New Orleans building, while its configuration was predicated on a global shift in the practices of Catholicism. The design of the Third Church of Christ, Scientist, is of a more universal cut. Technological refinements in concrete construction are a major consideration in examining the building; so is the significant, but the largely unknown, contribution of its designer to one of the nation's leading architectural firms of the postwar era. Artistic intent is key to understanding the former visitor center at Gettysburg not only in its physical form, but also as a key component of the expansive, layered memorialization at the battlefield park. The building must be considered from a cultural landscape perspective as well as from an architectural one. It is also necessary to understand the emergence of the visitor center as a type, of which the Gettysburg building is arguably one of the most sophisticated, pioneering examples. The ideals of progressive education are key to shaping the campus of the North Country School and Camp Treetops. Equally important is the ecumenical outlook of its designer, Douglas Haskell, who was one of the period's foremost architectural journalists and an independent thinker regarding the capacity of architecture and landscape to affect the human condition. His work also conveys the sense of freedom to pursue unorthodox solutions that characterized a number of design endeavors, by amateurs as well as professionals, in the Adirondacks since the Gilded Age. Indeed, the personal concerns of the architect figures prominently in all four cases in section three, underscoring the centrality of individualism in mid-twentieth-century design.

The small community garden in Washington was a wholly vernacular landscape, the product of multiple tenants in the apartment house behind which it stood. Subject to ongoing changes, this place nevertheless maintained an overriding sense of continuity. Here, the process and what it meant to those who were so engaged are arguably more important than the physical entity at any given time. The significance of the Friendship Shopping Center, less than a mile away, stems in part from the locally pioneering practices of the commercial real estate firm that developed it and additionally as a now rare embodiment of popular notions of modernism during the early postwar era. The need to consider change over time is central to understanding Savannah's Broughton Street, when work introduced after World War II that, like the Washington shopping center, was of a thoroughly mainstream modernist cut, but also represented one of the most important episodes in the corridor's development. Finally, Twinbrook, in Rockville, Maryland, demonstrates the value of examining house tracts on an individual basis, not just as examples of the generalized tendencies characteristic to postwar suburban development. Here, the builder's role was especially important, but so, too, was that played by the new occupants, who were proactive in creating a strong sense of community in both tangible and intangible ways.

Most of the examples analyzed in the eight case studies have generated controversy. Style and taste were the enemies of St. Frances Cabrini Church, which was disparaged because it was not rendered in one of the "styles" that ostensibly distinguish the city's architecture. The state preservation office did not know how to classify it, as if classification according to one of National Register "style" terms was necessary in order for the building to have any standing in its historical assessment. As a result, in my report I included a preamble on the salient attributes of Modern architecture, which, like Beaux-Arts architecture or Arts and Crafts architecture, entails a broad set of values and priorities—an approach, an outlook, and conventions (towards the making of form, space, composition, and character) that should be understood in the abstract, not in terms of narrow categories. Taste was also a key factor. Bloggers derided the building as being akin to something along a commercial strip (which should not be assumed to be a derogatory statement, but in this instance was intended as such)—a hideous excrescence, the destruction of which would be welcomed. More importantly, the archdiocese, while never stating as much, seems to have considered the building in detrimental terms. Absent its congregation as a result of Hurricane Katrina, the church remained intact but without internal defenders. The site, on the other hand, was considered optimal for the relocation of Holy Cross School, a distinguished institution, the leadership of which decided not to rebuild in the devastated Lower Ninth Ward. Though the school needed a chapel and St. Frances Cabrini could have been economically rehabilitated to serve the purpose, it was demolished for an insipid interpretation of 1870s building formerly occupied by the school.[12] The Section 106 review, triggered by FEMA funding for the project, succeeded in preserving only a few small panels of stained glass.

The situation was somewhat similar with the Third Church of Christ, Scientist. In this instance, the building became too large for its dwindling congregation, whose members were no longer enamored with it and were unwilling to lease the spaces for outside activities that could have sustained it. The matter was complicated by the fact that the connected Christian Science Monitor Building and the entire property were owned by the Mother Church in Boston, which wanted to downsize its operation and sell what was becoming an ever-more valuable parcel of land. In order to pursue options other than demolition, the Committee of 100 on the Federal City submitted a landmark nomination in January 1991. Soon thereafter, the D.C. Preservation League joined the initiative. Neither Third Church nor Mother Church representatives proved amenable to discussion of alternatives to demolition; however, the landmark hearing was postponed several times at their request in order to leave the door open for a resolution. The hearing was not held until 2007, by which time the Mother Church had sold the property to a developer who wished to erect an office building that would include modest quarters for the Third Church. Landmark status was granted. Nonetheless, the District government, whose mayor publicly favored more intense development, ruled that action constituted economic hardship for the church. As of March 2013, the building stood vacant, and a new scheme for the site received the Historic Preservation Review Board's approval.[13] Twelve months later, the complex was demolished. For more than a dozen years, the building has been repeatedly condemned in the court of public opinion.[14] Even members of the D.C. Preservation League criticized its leadership for defending such an ostensibly unattractive building, and the local chapter of the American Institute of Architects refused to endorse the landmark application. The complex was demolished in March 2014.[15]

The effort to preserve Neutra's visitor center at Gettysburg was an equally protracted affair and a markedly complex one. The building had become too small to serve all of its original functions and was deemed an ill-suited environment for the cyclorama painting it housed. (Whether modifications could be made to the building that would rectify that situation was never substantively addressed.) The building adjoins one of the historically most important areas of the battlefield, a relationship that was an integral part of its original siting by the National Park Service, but now was considered an encroachment. The siting also ran counter to battlefield "restoration" plans prepared under the aegis of the park's superintendent, who hated the building and publicly derided it.[16] As a preemptive move, he secured a finding from the state historic preservation officer that the building was

not eligible for the National Register of Historic Places (an astounding determination) and also received the blessings of the president of the National Trust for Historic Preservation, who is a Civil War buff.

Once the building's impending fate was made public, preservation efforts were mounted by myself on behalf of the Society of Architectural Historians, later by the Recent Past Preservation Network, and throughout by Neutra's son Dion, who had worked on the project. After National Register eligibility was secured at the federal level in 1999, a National Historic Landmark nomination was prepared and overwhelmingly approved by the Park Service's internal review body, only to be summarily dismissed by the agency's Advisory Board at the year's end. The stonewalling apparently occurred due to apprehension that saving the building might undermine what Park Service officials considered a precedent-setting project to create a new visitor center funded by the private sector, but there was also the widely held belief that, however distinguished a design it might be, the Neutra building was intruding on hallowed ground. That was the conclusion of members of the Advisory Council on Historic Preservation, who reviewed the case as part of the Section 106 process months before the National Historic Landmark hearing. Demolition was impeded in part due to a suit by the Recent Past Preservation Network. Even though the superintendent and his supporters have all left their positions, Park Service officials announced in January 2013 that the building would be demolished for a pseudo restoration of battlefield site. Less than two months later, the property was cleared (fig. I.1).[17] The agency's failure to understand the significance of the building as an integral and indeed important part of the memorial landscape that so distinguishes the battlefield has resulted in the loss of a major Cold War–era component as well as an exceptional work of architecture. Indeed, the Park Service's intractability in this case calls in to question the viability of its traditional role as the federal government's standard-bearer in historic preservation matters.

In contrast, all parties involved with North Country School and Camp Treetops embrace

FIG. I.1. Demolition of Visitor Center and Cyclorama Building, Gettysburg National Military Park, 1959–62, Richard J. Neutra and Robert E. Alexander, architects. (Photo Matthew Amster, March 2013)

the legacy of their campus and have taken pains to protect it. Most buildings have experienced remarkably little change; much of the landscape likewise remains intact. As institutions, school and camp evolve while maintaining a strong sense of continuity with the principles and practices of their formative years. At the same time, the demands of even modest growth, of new instructional methods, and, perhaps, of changes in building code requirements all hold the potential to affect the historic attributes of the campus in adverse ways. Sustained recognition of what makes the place so distinctive and distinguished will be essential for its future protection.

The tenants of the apartment house at 3901 Connecticut Avenue pursued local landmark status for both the building and its community garden, located at the rear of the property, when the owner made plans for a large new complex where the garden and surrounding woodland stood. In this instance, however, the D.C. Historic Preservation Office staff member assigned to the case did not seem to grasp the anthropological framework in which the garden's significance was necessarily cast. His negative report on this component of the property assessed it

in terms perhaps applicable to designed landscapes, but not to one shaped by multiple, nonprofessional parties over time and one where a sense of continuity coexisted with a more or less continual state of minor physical modifications. In March 1996, the day following the hearing, the owner had the garden destroyed.[18]

No one ever seems to have embraced the Friendship Shopping Center save for the convenience it afforded for goods and services. However, the local Advisory Neighborhood Commission, a quasi-public, quasi-private-sector group charged with forging connections between citizens and municipal government, initiated a landmark nomination for the complex in 2002. The threat was to prevent development many nearby residents considered far too dense for an already busy traffic and business corridor that transects a number of Washington's most affluent neighborhoods. While some parties charged that the ANC was abusing the preservation process, such couplings have long helped preservation's cause nationwide. Locally, proponents of creating the Georgetown historic district in the early 1950s did so in part out of fear of encroachment by new apartment buildings. Residents of Cleveland Park, adjoining the Friendship Shopping Center, sought historic district status for their neighborhood as a defense against intense development of several large residential properties and also in the commercial node along Connecticut Avenue. But advancing preservation in this way is only valid if the resources in question merit protection on historical grounds, which I believed to be the case with the shopping center. The landmark hearing was never held because the ANC was able to secure assurances from the property owner that the land would remain at a low density. The complex continued to operate for another decade, during which time area residents and new property owners have battled anew over the scale of a proposed mixed-use development.[19] Accord was reached in 2012, and the buildings were demolished by the year's end. Unfortunately, saving the shopping center on historical grounds never attracted much support, reflecting the low regard in which such work of the postwar era is generally viewed. Preservation has granted a new lease on life to thousands of buildings designed for retail purposes from the early nineteenth through the early twentieth centuries. Will we leave nothing of counterparts created during subsequent decades for future generations?

Postwar commercial buildings fronting Savannah's Broughton Street, which had been the city's foremost retail corridor until the 1970s, once appeared to be headed for destruction as well, but have been rescued thanks to a new appreciation for the episode in that downtown's development they represent. Through the 1990s, they suffered from an attitude that is all too common in places renowned for their historic architecture. The venerated legacy dates from the eighteenth and/or nineteenth centuries, perhaps even from the early twentieth; "new" buildings are seen only as intrusions, sorry contrasts to the splendid work left by earlier generations. The case of St. Frances Cabrini was adversely affected by this attitude, and Broughton Street's "modern" buildings had a number of detractors, including some preservationists. The city's preservation officer had a more inclusive outlook. In 1999, she asked me to prepare a report on postwar buildings along the street and in several other parts

of Savannah's enormous historic district. My research revealed that many of these resources represented a significant period of downtown growth. Far from being indicators of decline, they stood as emblems of substantial long-term investment that was sustained between the late 1940s and early 1960s. The report has had a beneficial impact. In its ongoing revitalization, Broughton Street demonstrates over a century of growth and change. What has occurred there should serve as a model for other communities.

Longstanding residents of Twinbrook respect their neighborhoods, and the civic engagement that characterized the development's early years persists in many quarters. Still, some newcomers are unaware of, or have little concern for, this heritage. No community stays desirable by default; without ongoing citizen commitment it will in all likelihood decline at some point. In its location, moreover, Twinbrook is susceptible to pressures for new development of a much higher density. It lies adjacent to a D.C. Metro station and not far from Rockville's burgeoning town center. To some advocates of smart growth, Twinbrook is a prime candidate for rebuilding, yet to do so would entail the loss of a quiet, spacious, leafy environment that cannot be created anew for middle-income households in a major metropolitan area. One of the things that made places such as Twinbrook significant in the first place remains a strong basis for its preservation.

. . .

Additional case studies could be introduced to expand the range of building types, design attributes, social concerns, and geographic coverage. Were this a book devoted to presenting the heritage of the recent past generally these matters would command attention. But they are superfluous here because the intent is to provide examples of in-depth historical analysis to the kind of thinking that is important if retaining resources that are unrecognized and often are unpopular is to be consummated or at least given a respectable chance. Fifty case studies would yield more information, but not more guidance on a process that is necessarily different in each instance, tailored to the particularities of the resources at hand. Furthermore, all of the resources examined here are, coincidentally, in places that are associated with older pasts; none are viewed as centers for innovation in architectural or landscape design during the second half of the twentieth century comparable to, say, metropolitan Boston, New York, Chicago, San Francisco, or Los Angeles, nor are any of them places where newness is omnipresent such as Miami Beach, Houston, or Phoenix. Finally, the fact that over half of these resources have been destroyed and that this action occurred in places, or by parties, well known for their distinguished preservation records speaks to the situation that, despite all the advances that have been made in safeguarding the recent past, the challenges remain numerous and formidable.

I STYLE AND TASTE

1   The Problem with "Style"

"Style" is irresistible, or so it seems. Architects and other designers have discussed both past and contemporary work in stylistic terms since the late eighteenth century. The delineation and analysis for stylistic properties have been central concerns of art history for almost as long. By comparison, other categorical constructs have been given much less exposure. The concept of type based on building form is quite a recent development, derived from methods employed in the social sciences. This approach to classification was initiated in the 1930s; it has only enjoyed widespread scholarly use since the late 1960s and, with few exceptions, remains outside the realm of popular literature.[1] Type based on building elements connoting function is of course a much older idea, the origins of which date from the same period as those of style. Classification by this means received considerable attention from architects associated with the French academic tradition. Since World War II, a growing number of scholars have studied the history of individual building types, yet an emphasis on function has rarely been a conspicuous part of writing intended for a general audience. (Much to its credit, in the mid-1980s the National Trust published popular histories of the city halls and rural schools, as well as a concise lexicon of common building types.[2]) Technical classification systems have remained almost exclusively within the province of the engineer and the serious students of industrial archaeology. The language and indeed the concerns of this realm may seem the most obtuse to the layperson.[3] Style is the obvious choice for the individual who wishes to learn something about the subject.

The enormous growth of popular interest in architecture during recent years—an interest that has encouraged and in turn has received added impetus from the historic preservation movement—has not surprisingly generated an abundance of published material on "style." Guides to architectural styles began to appear in the late 1960s. The initial venture was written by the architectural historian Marcus Whiffen, who noted in the preface that his project stemmed from teaching undergraduates with little historical background and no training in architecture. Equally important, as a wildlife enthusiast, he sought to create an architectural equivalent to Roger Tory Peterson's *Field Guide to the Western Birds*. Whiffen soon realized that an analogous work was impossible "because nature and art are not amenable to the same method of classification."[4] Buildings or any other objects, in other words, are not designed in a manner comparable to the reproduction of species. Yet he ignored his own admonition, using "style" as a surrogate for species. The idea proved infectious: Style guides have proliferated. Scores of regional and local studies include and often emphasize "style." Preservation newsletters issued by state offices and nonprofit organizations have joined the march with serial features. "Style" never had it so good.

By offering fodder so enthusiastically received, preservationists may feel that they have made significant advances in nurturing public support for their cause. Ample ammunition exists to defend this rationale. Architectural history is a complex and, for the novice, a perplexing field. Nevertheless, grassroots interest has swelled and many preservationists believe

This chapter initially appeared in *The Forum*, Bulletin of the Committee on Preservation, Society of Architectural Historians, 6 (December 1984): whole issue. It is reprinted here with minor modifications to the text and the addition of notes.

they must sustain that interest by using terms the public can understand. From this perspective, a letter to the editors of *Historic Preservation*, in all likelihood reflecting thoughts shared by thousands of subscribers, sums up "style's" immense popular appeal: "I want to express my appreciation for 'What Style Is It?' I have often looked for a book showing architectural styles so that I would learn to identify them easily. The ones [books] I have seen go into so much detail and have pictures of details so that the woods are lost for the trees."[5]

The preoccupation with "style" does not end at the popular level. "Style" has infiltrated the working sector of preservation, becoming a stock tool of the trade in numerous survey and documentation programs. "Style" sections can be found on many state and local survey forms, and a similar component will soon be an integral part of forms used to nominate properties to the National Register.[6] In some circles, "style" has become the focus of architectural history to the point that one graduate course in American work places "special emphasis on the applicability of style recognition."

The fact that style guides, inaugurated to assist the novice, have become important texts for architectural history as it is practiced in preservation should serve as a warning signal. Few people in the preservation field would knowingly tolerate, let alone encourage, using amateurish techniques for development strategies, legal statues, design criteria, or materials conservation standards. One reason for this disparity may be that history of any sort appears to have ever-less bearing on preservation's priorities. If one has a somewhat clouded view of the past, it does not necessarily inhibit a successful preservation effort. The movement has always received much of its impetus from the concerned citizen, and even today many of its leaders have no more than a general knowledge of architectural history. Thousands of buildings have been saved because people cared about them, not because concerned individuals or groups had a profound understanding of architecture. Such rationalizations can be persuasive, but only up to a point. A lack of sound historical perspective can open the door to needless distortions of the past in rehabilitation and restoration work—a tendency that is occurring on a larger scale than many people care to admit. Furthermore, overemphasizing "style" can encourage preservation's advocates and supporters alike to think of architecture in a superficial way, which in turn could jeopardize the movement in years ahead. In countless cases, buildings have been advanced because they are excellent examples of thus and such "style" or assailed because they are not. Indeed, failure to pass the "style" test has led to the failure to protect any number of buildings nationwide. Some of the underlying reasons why second-rate architectural history is bad for the discipline are closely tied to those that make it bad in the public arena.

I have placed "style" in quotes because what generally passes for style in this context is often debased and sometimes a fallacious version of concepts that have been used by scholars for generations. Style is not a thing; it is composed of ideas developed to facilitate the interpretation of physical qualities; that is, to understand its meaning. There never has been a consensus on the definition of style. During the early 1950s, in what is still one of the best essays on the subject, Meyer Shapiro reviewed no less than seven approaches to stylistic classification that had been advanced by art historians during the nineteenth and twentieth centuries. Each approach, he concluded, had strengths but also weaknesses; a redefinition or new, consistent theory of style was needed. Shapiro reiterated that despite traditional differences in approach, one can posit common attributes: style comprises more than conventions of form; it entails "a system of forms with a quality and a meaningful expression through which the personality of the artist and the broad outlook of the group are visible" and is "a vehicle of expression within the group, communicating and fixing certain values of religious, social, and moral life through the emotion suggestiveness of forms." Furthermore, styles can encompass the "qualities shared by all the arts of a culture during a significant span of time."[7]

Style thus may be very particular, connoting strong characteristics in the work of one person (e.g., Michelangelo, Le Corbusier) or of a small group (e.g., the creators of the Court Style or Art Nouveau). Style can also refer to broad and generalized tendencies occurring over many decades or even centuries, as is indicated by terms such as Gothic, Renaissance, and Baroque. Pertaining to phenomena of vastly different scales and involving intangible as well as tangible qualities, the ideas that style represents are complex and not easily confined to neat boundaries.

Additional factors must be considered when addressing the matter of style. Although the term may have value when applied to the work of certain key artistic personalities, it does not follow that the products of all or even most people are best understood in this way. Likewise, some groups may have a distinct style, but others may not. Finally, style used in the broadest sense is not monolithic; it refers to important characteristics—some would say *the* most important characteristics—but not all aspects of a given era. It must also be remembered that scholarly conceptions of style were formulated in the nineteenth and early twentieth centuries to analyze a select range of work that was considered to be of an especially high caliber. The periods under study were also well removed in time and were purportedly more homogeneous in their artistic content. Stylistic concepts were not devised to address the then-prevalent practice of eclecticism, which, in its use of references to numerous historical precedents and its pursuit of varied expressive modes, was quite unlike the then-perceived qualities of earlier periods. Nor could style concepts have anticipated modernism, which has been just as multifaceted in its complexion, albeit in markedly different ways.

With modernism, too, came hostility toward the very idea of style. When Henry-Russell Hitchcock and Philip Johnson employed art historical methods to define one of modernism's thrusts, which they believed was becoming a new International Style—a universal manner of expression destined to flourish for years to come—the initiative was derided by members of the very circle it sought to canonize. While Hitchcock noted in his preface to the 1966 reprint edition (the first one to attain broad circulation) that the term now enjoyed widespread use (although not by architects), he also stressed how much more multifaceted Modern architecture had become even a decade after the tome was originally published.[8]

The modernists' emphatic rejection of style has no doubt had an impact on the concerns of art and architectural historians during the past several decades. Even as Shapiro delineated the need for fresh thinking on the nature of style, young scholars were less and less interested in the matter. That withdrawal is succinctly reflected in another letter to *Historic Preservation*, this time from the architectural historian Christian Otto at Cornell University. He criticized the "What Style Is It?" series then being published in that magazine not because of its authors' interpretation of style, but because of the fact that style was being featured: "I am dismayed to see *HP* begin a series on architectural styles. Almost a century ago, our history laundry was rinsed in stylistic analysis by the German art historian Wölfflin [Heinrich Wölfflin developed a new approach toward stylistic analysis; he did not invent the process himself]. As he and his students handed down this wet wash its messy underside became apparent. Neither they nor anyone since has been able to avoid vagueness in stylistic categories. And the process of categorization has been based on suspect methodology, with the notion of 'development' in the Darwinian sense. The architectural conditions can be studied by means of other interesting and informative lines of inquiry—the history of ideas, a psychological analysis of art and creativity, or the social context of architecture, addressing such concerns as patronage, purpose, personality and meaning. In pursuing these questions, historians are grappling with the richness and complexity of their discipline."[9] Thus as grassroots interest in architecture was swelling, many historians who believed style had become an academic imbroglio turned to new avenues of exploration. Nineteenth- and twentieth-century architecture has been intensely studied by scholars during the past several decades, but seldom with much emphasis on stylistic classification, which in any event is not well suited to the material.

In order to create a "complete" guide to American architecture, one that would purportedly cover all the bases comparable to field guides to birds, flowers, trees, and the like, the authors have had to devise a system based on fragments. Many of the terms employed by art historians, such as Perpendicular or Northern Baroque, did not apply. Whiffen and his successors could rely on a scattering of terms frequently used to identify certain phases, movements, or interludes—some of the nomenclature long-standing (e.g., Gothic Revival, Queen Anne); others new (e.g., Shingle Style). An approach of this nature may have some merits. Few people would dispute the convenience of being able to refer to a building in such well-established terms as Mission Style or Art Deco, knowing that others will have a general idea of what that means. Much territory remained uncharted, however, lacking both thorough research and appropriate names, so that a host of additional categories had to be created de novo to fill in at least some of the obvious gaps. While Whiffen tried to exercise some restraint in this sphere, most of his successors were less cautious. The whole process appears to have been expeditious and pragmatic, responding to an immediate need: there are numerous buildings that possess certain obvious characteristics and, therefore, can be given a name, which is called a "style." Does an architectural quilt pieced together in this manner constitute an informative whole, clarifying intricate issues in a consistent way?

Without extensive study of the period itself, without the focused rethinking of style concepts that Shapiro advocated, without even a consistent methodology, style guides give the reader little substance. Basic questions probably have not been raised and certainly they have not been answered. How is style best defined for work of the past two centuries? Should categories be broad, narrow, or both? What are the advantages and disadvantages in each case? Is style a concept best limited to major works or can it be applied to all architecture? Are existing terms such as Federal, Italianate, or Arts and Crafts appropriate within the context of an inclusive system? What should we be learning about this work, and how can style assist us? Do we in fact need style, or is it best relegated to the annals of history, as Otto suggested?

Among the problems that arise when "style" is feely concocted is encouraging an impulse to create even more categories without much thought as to what collective purpose they serve. From the start, the style guides have tended toward hair-splitting divisions. There are attempts, for example, to distinguish between "Italian Villa" (in the U.S.?) and "Italianate" (a tower seems to be the essential difference); between "Italian Villa," "Renaissance Revival—Roman Tuscan," and "Renaissance Revival—North Italian"; or between "Beaux-Arts Classicism," "Second Renaissance Revival," and "Neo-Classical Revival."[10] Yet even such thin slicing has yielded a patchy selection. Efforts to broaden the coverage have produced a plethora of new ingredients in the architectural gumbo. A regional study offers "National Park Style" and a "Half Modern Style," in addition to "Modernistic Style." In another instance a vaguely Richardsonian building is designated "Celtic Norman or Hiberno-Romanesque style," and a genre of rather conventional houses from the early twentieth century are in the "Shirtwaist Style."[11] One local survey provides no less than seventy-five options under "style."

From the start, too, the guides have been inconsistent in the way "style" is derived. Some categories are based on an architect's personal style: "Wrightian," or "Miesian." In other instances, "style" comes from popular, generic terms that are most useful in connoting an idea: "Bungalow," or the more clinical "Bungaloid." All restraint has been abandoned in some recent publications. A few of the categories used in two of them will suffice to make a point: "Shaker" style, "Shanty" style, "Cottage" style, "False Front" style, "Fantasy" style (which includes the Brown Derby and Bruce Goff's work), "Rammed Earth" style, "Mobile Home" style, "Prefabricated" style, "A-Frame" style; and "Edwardian Villa," "Georgian Revival–Romanesque," "Beaux-Arts Manhattan," "Millionaire's Colonial," "Tudor Nouveau" (Maybeck!), "American Prelude," "The Natural House," "The Regional House," "The Articulated House," "The Essential House," "The New Roof," "The In-Joke."[12]

The confusion is heightened by the fact that each successive style guide offers some new variations on (or substitutions for) the terms propagated by its predecessors. The Park Service is seeking to control this taxonomic melee by initiating thirty-eight standardized stylistic classifications for National Register listings. Yet some divisions retain a derivational inconsistency and are redundant: "Commercial Style," "Chicago Skyscraper." Moreover, a very large number of examples will inevitably have to be dumped into the amorphous realm of exceptions: "Other, No Style."[13]

Another fundamental problem resulting from the absence of a clear method in these books is that they tend to ignore underlying commonalities of a given period that can entail shared values, ideas, and intentions in design, and shared characteristics in the way form, space, scale, and ornament are handled. For all phases of eclecticism, these commonalities transcend the specific historical references used. A Gothic villa by Richard Upjohn bears much greater affinity to an Italianate one by John Notman than to buildings by Leopold Eidlitz or William Potter, let alone ones by Ralph Adams Cram or James Gamble Rogers. Yet the fact that such work makes reference to that of the Middle Ages can be the overriding consideration in style guides: one volume includes work by both A. J. Davis and Frank Furness under "Gothic Revival." Furthermore, new terms are introduced such as "Late Gothic Revival," which implies that the legacy of Cram and his followers is best characterized as the final phase of a "style" begun a century earlier. At the same time, there is at best only vague indication that designs such as those by Cram, Charles Platt, and Paul Cret possesses numerous qualities that are closely related.[14]

An even more disturbing pattern emerges when the products of European colonists are grouped with work done in the early twentieth century that, to a limited degree, drew on colonial imagery. In one book, San Estevan at Acoma, a designs by Irving Gill, and the exotica of Palm Beach from the 1920s all fall under the heading of "Spanish Colonial."[15] Fundamental differences not only in intent, planning, materials, and expression, but also in culture are ignored. If such factors are not central determinants of style, what are? One does not have to peruse the guides for long to discover the surrogate.

The idea that style equals decoration and selected motifs is implicit in these books, and sometimes the analogy is made in such a matter-of-fact way that the authors must assume most people will take it for granted. One volume begins with a chapter entitled "Style: The Fashions of American Houses," explaining that "most surviving American houses were not folk houses but are styled; that is, they were built with at least some attempt at being fashionable." Fashions may come and go, but it is intimated here that they also come back again and again—a process that has been occurring for centuries. After the introduction of genealogical roots—"Ancient Classical, Renaissance Classical, Medieval, Modern, and Other"—the text proceeds to schematize connections. Thus the Farnesina, Westover, an Italianate suburban villa, a large country residence by Delano & Aldrich, and a developer's "Colonial" tract house emerge as members of the same group. The family trees are then cross-pollinated with chronological periods, creating hybrids such as "Eclectic Houses," which in this case does not include work of the pre- and post–Civil War eras, but does encompass that by of Frank Lloyd Wright, R. M. Schindler, and Walter Gropius. "Modern" houses postdate 1940, as do two other categories, "Neoeclectic" and "Contemporary Folk."[16]

Form and materials can also contribute to fatuous linkages. Several guides include a separate "style" category for octagonal buildings. In one case a "theory" is introduced, although never explained, that the false fronts common to numerous wood-frame buildings erected during the second half of the nineteenth century are direct descendants of the stepped gables found on work in New Amsterdam. A few pages later, "The Log Tradition and Pioneer House" category presents dugouts and sod buildings along with almost anything constructed of logs, including some of the enormous residential camps in the Adirondacks.[17]

Style as ornament, style as motif, style as fashion, style as materials—all suggest that style is but a garnish, applied independent of any underlying thought or order, and that it is subject to change at the slightest whim. Add a portico and the work becomes Neo-Classical, an *espadaña* and a little stucco and it is Mission Style, a mock thatch roof and it is Tudor. To be sure, motifs used as so many interchangeable parts can be found in all phases of eclecticism. J. C. Loudon's influential *Encyclopedia* (1833) diagrammed how the same basic box could be dressed in many historical "jackets" according to the client's taste. A. J. Davis boasted that he could design houses for persons planning to build in Llewellyn Park in any mode they desired: "American Log Cabin, Farm House, English Cottage, Collegiate Gothic, Manor House, French Suburban, Swiss Chalet, Swiss Mansion, Lombard Italian, Tuscan from Pliny's Villa at Ostia, Ancient Etruscan, Suburban Greek, Oriental, Moorish, Round, Castellated."[18] But Davis and other talented colleagues of his generation knew better, for they also shared an overriding concern for creating varied manners of expression to reflect programmatic factors such as size, function, site, and cost. While the repertoire of historical references was greatly increased by the end of the century, leading architects became quite explicit that this inclusivity was not tantamount to practicing in dozens of styles. To claim otherwise would indicate that their primary objective was replication. Whatever may be Romanesque, or Georgian, or Spanish Colonial about them is subsidiary to what is new when one considers all aspects. Conversely, most style guides probe no further than parts of the surface. They seldom include interiors and, with one exception, almost never provide plans. When virtually all the context and most of the architectural fabric are ignored, "style" is left a lonely and trivial thing.

Style guides are probably used most by people who wish to learn more about the buildings in their locale, and yet these books pay little attention to the myriad differences that exist from one part of the country to another. Documenting locational variations fully would be far beyond their scope. Nevertheless, when the very existence of such variety is discounted, readers can get the impression that "styles" coated the nation in more or less uniform waves and even infer that a place is architecturally impoverished if it is not well represented by a large number of "styles."

A related danger is the perpetuation of the idea that pure "styles" comprise the prevalent tendencies in architecture and, by extension, are the most important ones. Much significant work designed by architects with a strong personal style is omitted from this schema. More onerous for preservation work is the embrace of "purity" in style, an idea implicitly defined by the style guides as if design that does not conform to some artificial construct is of a lesser caliber. The very word underscores the style guides' reliance on a biological analogy run amok, suggesting that buildings are comparable to species or minerals. Moreover, no matter how these guides define a given "style," they give almost no indication that "pure" examples are very much the exception.[19] This is especially true when examining popular design. The most casual study of urban and rural areas will confirm that most of what has been built falls outside the strict confines of the usual categories. One book takes a stab at explaining "stylistic mixtures" by noting that sometimes "styles" were "blended" in the original design and that on other occasions the result stems from remodeling.[20] This section constitutes eight out of more than five hundred pages, intimating that regardless of reasons for "blending," the product is of peripheral concern. One might also deduce from style guides that nonconforming work is inferior. Both their structure and content encourage people not to look at whole buildings, but to stalk features that match those in the illustrations.

If "style" is a poor guide to Main Street, it can get one hopelessly lost in industrial quarters, amid working-class neighborhoods, along the highway, or on the farm. In such places "style" has often little or nothing to do with the salient architectural qualities, and attempting to apply such labels can only distort or debase the work at hand. One recent effort to include vernacular examples simply results in the creation of more meaningless categories such as "Folk Victorian—a style . . . defined by the presence of Victorian decorative detailing on simple folk house forms, which are generally much less elaborated than the Victorian styles they seek to mimic."[21] In another case, work related to industry and transportation is placed at the end of the volume under the title "Utilitarian." Windmills, bridges, factories, barns, railroad stations, lighthouses, diners, steel mills, oil derricks, and a host of other types are gathered together not only because they fall outside the standard view of genteel architecture, but also because they are not readily classified by "style."[22] Yet when the bulk of a text *is* stylistically organized, the exceptions are given an odorous tinge. Although it is not nearly as blatant, such relegation to the back of the architectural bus echoes the once-common attitude Europeans had toward non-Western cultures. Many editions of Sir Banister Fletcher's *History of Architecture* (1896), for instance, introduced the concluding section, devoted to "The Non-Historical Styles," by stating: "A History of the world's architecture would be incomplete if we did not pass in review not only those allied and progressive styles which we have designated as Historical, but also those other styles—Indian, Chinese, Japanese, Central American, and Saracenic—which remain detached from Western Art and exercised little direct influence on it, and which we therefore term Non-Historical." (Fletcher, incidentally, considered "constructive" aspects of architecture to form the essence of style: "In the East decorative schemes seem generally to have outweighed all other considerations;" this aspect comprises the "essential difference between Historical and Non-Historical architecture.")[23]

It is ironic that books written with the admirable intention of encouraging people to look at the architecture around them employ a technique that ignores so much and depicts the rest in a manner that gives little insight on its historical significance. One pathetic result of this approach is to have an extensive survey of a community conducted and perhaps even published with the main emphasis on "style." A rich local legacy is devalued in the process, for the things that are there become important not so much for what they tell us about architecture, society, or place, as for the degree to which they can be stuck into so many contrived pigeonholes.

Style, like type, can be useful as long as its conceptual parameters are kept consistent, simple, diagrammatic, and responsive to modification. If style is applied to the architectural mainstream, it should be treated as a hypothetical model based on some evidence, tested in the field, and altered as the situation warrants. All such categorical systems are but a beginning; once digested they may afford an instructive point of departure for the intricate realm of the real stuff. When placed in a proper perspective, style can indeed further one's understanding; as an end unto itself, this creature merely intensifies the quagmire. There is nothing simple about the history of architecture, but its aspects—including style, structure, systems, function, patronage, and symbol—can be presented in a clear, straightforward language that the public finds engaging. To accomplish this balance is no small challenge; it is, however, an imperative one. The integrity of the discipline as it is practiced in the historic preservation field is at stake, and so is the subject matter. When people eventually get tired of looking for this or that embellishing motif, will they understand that our architectural heritage is comprised of more than a collage of "styles"?

2   Taste versus History

Taste is a term seldom used in the historic preservation field. Most people so engaged shun the word, for it suggests amateurish endeavors driven by personal preferences rather than widely accepted practices shaped by professional disciplines. In short, taste stands for the old days when efforts were largely avocational, the pursuit of aficionados and dowagers. Things are different now. Historic preservation has come of age.

Yet however much lip service is paid to objectivity and professionalism, however profuse the jargon in which decisions are explained, taste lies just below the surface of numerous preservation efforts. Taste, which can be predicated on individual affinities or collective connoisseurship, codified in the case of preservation, by projects and images sanctioned by at least some leaders in the field, continues to exercise a profound influence on what we preserve and how we preserve it. Sometimes the relationship is subtle; often it is overt. Taste can subsume, forever altering the historical record and public perception of the past. Taste can destroy the past so that little if anything of consequence is preserved. While preservationists may deny the specter of taste, its presence is real, its mischief all around us.

Of course, one can argue that historic preservation is never wholly divorced from taste. Many aspects of the field depend upon value judgments. Every survey project is shaped by individuals' views of what is important. The processes of saving historic resources and of repairing, restoring, and finding viable uses for them are especially resistant to formulas. No matter how objective one seeks to be, it is impossible to avoid actions predicated on contemporary outlooks. Ultimately, preservation will reflect our own era as well as the past.

Fair enough. Yet a fundamental difference exists between decision-making based upon well-founded knowledge and analytical techniques on one hand and that grounded in personal or popular opinion on the other. Historical significance is determined from a corpus of facts and from methods of interpretation that are generally accepted by scholars. It cannot only be substantiated, it can be explained clearly and persuasively in the public arena as well as in the professional one. Historical significance provides a solid foundation both for identifying resources and for determining which among their attributes must be retained to ensure their continued integrity. Taste, on the other hand, is by its very nature relative; its validation can come only from others who happen to share the same view. No clear yardstick, factual or interpretative, can be crafted to yield a sequence of coherent, rational findings. Decisions predicated on taste may be couched in language suggestive of detachment and objectivity, but once such justifications are identified for what they really represent, the entire premise can be easily refuted. Furthermore, since tastes vary and frequently change, a decision-making process guided by taste is inherently unstable even if the results are not contested at the outset.

The impact of taste is not hard to find in the choices made about what is worthy of preservation. Snobbery, fueled by taste, is widespread and sometimes even dominates the process. As a result, only things judged to be the "best"

This chapter initially appeared in the National Trust for Historic Preservation's *Forum Journal* 8 (May–June 1994): 40–45. It is reprinted here with minor modifications to the text and the addition of notes.

are singled out for attention in any number of instances. More than one state historic preservation office has adhered to an unofficial policy of selecting but one or two of the "best" examples of their kind for the National Register: Is it really among the "best" (e.g., largest, most ornate, least altered) Greek Revival country houses in our state? We have over a dozen buildings by Frank Lloyd Wright in our state; is this among the "best" (i.e., most widely recognized in publications)? We can't save *all* the Carnegie libraries statewide, but we can recognize two, perhaps three, of the "best" (i.e., most stylistically consistent or perhaps most unusual). Whole communities and even whole parts of some states have been written off as being of little value, with resources that simply do not measure up to the "best." Just what is deemed the "best" may vary, but often what the individuals in authority find pleasing to the eye plays a determining role.

By its very nature, such thinking excludes most of the built environment. However, even when not pursued in the extreme, this approach favors resources that are considered rare, unconventional, or even exotic over those deemed commonplace. Exceptional things indeed deserve attention, but it can be just as important to protect broad patterns of development, for they, too, are salient distinguishing features of place and more than anything else may afford a sense of continuity with the past. They can provide the essential context through which the more singular landmarks derive meaning.

No matter how comprehensive survey and evaluation programs seek to be, they often remain subject to lingering biases driven by taste. Buildings, for example, are frequently assessed for this or that motif. An ornate commercial block of the 1880s or 1920s is more likely to elicit interest than an unadorned one, simply for that difference. The whole basis upon which such work is assessed may have little to do with current practices in architectural history, but instead focus on aesthetics. Even then, aesthetic qualities are seldom delineated with sophistication. Rather than analyzing the formal design attributes—form, space, scale, materials, de-

tailing, and the like—that give a building its expressive character, such assessments generally rely on style guides, which reduce architectural interpretation to a formulaic sampling of motifs.[1] Among the many problems with this approach is that it intimates the existence of "pure" style—an entity that can be quantified as well as qualified—as if components of the built environment were analogous to natural species. Many historic resources thus can be ignored or their significance degraded because they are not "pure" examples. Equally unfortunate, resources can be stereotyped, recognized for a few "features," which may be comparatively incidental, rather than for those attributes that make the work important. The late-nineteenth-century schoolhouse, for example, may be revered not for what it may tell us about the interplay between national tendencies in design and local patterns in building, not for what it may reveal about rising standards in the public education system, not for what it may have symbolized as a mark of progress for the neighborhood, nor for its longstanding role as a community center, and certainly not for how it may embody racial segregation practices, but instead as one of East Petunia's "best" surviving examples of this or that "style."

The preoccupation with appearances affects perspectives on building types as well. Utilitarian functions often get short shrift unless the property in question possesses strong visual features associated with high-style traditions. The early-twentieth-century power plant may be venerated foremost because its exterior suggests a grand classical building, while the trolley barn nearby is less esteemed because it is so "plain." Equally pernicious are stereotypical assumptions about type. The neighborhood cinema of the late 1930s may be judged relative to the grandest film palaces of a decade earlier, even though changes that occurred in the motion picture industry during the intervening years—widespread production of feature-length films with sophisticated sound tracks, for instance—render the comparison irrelevant. A veteran preservationist challenged the validity of designating a department store warehouse in Washington, D.C., a local landmark because it was built later than, and looked different from, wholesale facilities with which he was familiar in St. Louis. The building's key role in a changing retail operation and the distinct attributes it possessed as a result did not enter into the predetermined equation.[2]

Ancillary or support functions are likewise victims of taste and often are simply taken for granted. For example, listing of farm, ranch, and plantation houses with scant mention of outbuildings, let alone landscape features, remains common. The railroad station is described in exhaustive detail, without examining the infrastructure—tracks, bridges, signals, baggage sheds, loading docks, sidings, and the like—of which it is a part, or analyzing its role as a catalyst for development of the surrounding precinct. In such cases, the building is comparable to the motif—the tree upon which all eyes focus while the forest is not seen.

Taste also dismisses certain functions as irrelevant to preservation, irrespective of their historical significance. The very idea of protecting a gas station or a shopping center sends some preservationists into mild convulsions because such types are assumed to be detrimental to the landscape—the sort of thing preservation should be against. Never mind the individual distinction some examples may possess. Never mind the impact they have had on patterns locally. Never mind the profound changes to commerce, human activity, and urban structure they represent. Never mind, in short, the historical significance they possess. They are simply in bad taste.[3]

Age poses a further set of problems. In this realm, taste is shaped perhaps less by aesthetic biases than by antiquarian ones. The older a remnant of the past, the more preservationists tend to venerate it, even though no historiographical method uses age, in itself, as a measure of significance. Yet in some eastern and southern parts of the United States feelings can still run strong against much of the twentieth century. Elsewhere, too, many properties dating after World War II, or even earlier, are routinely held to a higher standard than those of earlier eras. The basis for such an outlook is seldom articulated, but is rooted in the belief that "old" is inherently better than "new." Many preservationists whose attitude toward a more distant past is quite inclusive nevertheless abandon their perspective at a certain timeline. Taken to its logical end, this view is tantamount to stating that once upon a time people knew how to build "right." A large portion of this legacy is worth preserving. But then, at some unspecified moment, the faultless past became the failure-ridden present. How such cataclysmic decline occurred, or whether in fact it really *has* occurred, are matters not given much thought. "New" is simply in bad taste.

Although it is never stated as such, taste carries a pronounced class prejudice. Preservationists have long embraced the legacy of the middle class as well as that of the rich. Yet the farther down on the income scale, the less value preservationists are likely to assign to a resource. Most environments traditionally associated with the working class and with the poor are ignored or, at best, accorded marginal significance. A neighborhood of modest row houses built for factory workers around the turn of the twentieth century, for example, may well be deemed less "architecturally" distinctive than an upper-middle-class suburban enclave of the same era to the point of not warranting designation. Why? The dwellings are not as large; they are of nearly identical designs; they have few embellishments; they were not the work of a well-known architect. The setting is not a pastoral landscape, but a tightly gridded sequence of streets. Similarly, this neighborhood may be dismissed as less "historically" significant because no individuals of note lived there. The role of skilled labor in the nation's stunning industrial growth and in the concomitant growth of vast urban areas; the persistence of tradition in retaining the single-family house as the basic unit for persons of moderate means despite the spiraling expansion of cities; the considerable attention given to improving both the efficiency and the commodiousness of such dwellings—these and other basic historical issues may not even lie within the preservationist's realm of thought.

A telling indicator of taste's prominence in the field is the continued use of separate—albeit ostensibly equal—categories of "architectural" and "historical" significance, as if architecture has no past and history no physical dimension. Such a division may have been understandable in the mid-1960s given then-prevailing views of the past; however, it seems trivializing as well as archaic with the changes that have occurred to historical and related disciplines over the last five decades. Architectural history, cultural anthropology, cultural geography, folklore, historical archaeology, social history, and urban history among other fields have contributed to a more holistic approach, one that reveals the salient connections between tangible and intangible realms.[4] To be sure, some properties are primarily significant for their physical attributes, and some others foremost for their associational ones, yet seldom are the two wholly divorced from one another. How can one understand the significance of a great department store building such as that of Marshall Field in Chicago without knowing about the rise of large-scale retail operations, the intensifying centralization of trade in urban cores, or the widespread social appeal of these palaces of consumption? How, conversely, can one fully grasp the struggles and determination of eastern European immigrants without experiencing the tenements or the isolated farmsteads in which many of them lived? As long as "architectural" remains a code word for aesthetic and "historical" for a miscellany of other things, preservationists often will miss many of the salient points.

Another sad reflection of how history has been devalued in recent years is the growing habit among preservationists of referring to listed properties as "historic" and to everything else as "non-historic." Besides the fatuous implication that the listing process—national, state, and local—has been thorough and complete, this jargon carries Orwellian overtones of manipulatively altering the past to suit unspecified ends of the present. Many resources are condemned as "non-historic" even if they possess a considerable degree of historical significance. Moreover, "historic" in this context may have little to do with historicity; it becomes a code word for settings of a certain type designed to attract a specific audience. "Historic" is a theme, a "look"—very fashionable, in the best of taste.

A direct correlation exists between the role of taste in evaluating and in protecting the past. Change, it is argued, is necessary if this or that resource is to have a viable existence in the future. But to an alarming degree, change is often driven by taste as much as by economic and other practical imperatives. A primary reason for this approach is the belief that preservation is foremost a method of improving communities—environmental enhancement, as it were—rather than a means of protecting the past on its own terms. If, the unstated assumption goes, we are powerless to create "good" places anew, we are somehow always capable of improving upon the "better" ones created by our forebears. Preservation initiatives can and should improve the settings in which they occur through renewal or by adding a welcome stability. But when "enhancement" becomes the overriding objective, there is seldom much respect for the past, only the use of it as a pretext for a new agenda in which historic fragments are conspicuous tokens.

The legacy of taste in preservation is abundant from recent decades. Countless blocks of revitalized commercial districts boast brick sidewalks they never previously possessed. Light fixtures and street furniture are more elaborate and numerous than would have been conceivable in the past. Street trees and other forms of ornamental landscaping are so extensive that they dominate vistas during summer months even though such elements were almost never found in these precincts at any previous time. "Non-conforming" storefronts—that is, almost anything done after 1940 or even after 1930—are summarily removed. So are building signs and whole buildings that do not fit the theme. The cumulative change is far more extensive and indeed radical in effect than the most freewheeling church restorations of the nineteenth century in Europe. Most "enhancements" of this kind are not necessary. Worth Avenue in Palm Beach and Rodeo Drive in Beverly Hills, retail centers that command some of the highest leases per square foot in the country, are bereft of the "historic" look.

Individual properties may fare little better. Some preservationists appear to bend over backward to delineate how *little* of a building or site is actually "historic" in an effort to seek compromise with developers. The rationale used by a preservation official to sanction a multistory addition atop the low-slung mass of a listed movie theatre was that the roof was not "historic" because it was not seen from the street. Additions and alterations alike are frequently judged as to whether they are "good" or "bad" design, quite independent of their potential impact on the resource in question. More than one nonprofit preservation group has denatured a vintage building in its possession through a well-intentioned attempt to provide a model for adaptive use. Never mind, the look is "historic." Everybody agrees it's in good taste.

All things possess some degree of historical significance, however meager it might be. Properly done, preservation provides the framework by which one may select from the past, prioritizing significance in a reasonably consistent and meaningful way. The integrity of method is vital, for preservation's greatest contribution to society is enabling people to gain insights on the past that are real and to do so in ways that written, pictorial, and other forms of communication cannot duplicate. Part of this past is distant, removed in time and often in space from the present world. A much larger share of the past is recent; it was built or at least was still new within living memory, the product of one's parents' or grandparents' generations. Here, the intrinsic worth lies in fostering a sense of continuity, in striking a balance with change, in gaining perspective on the present, in knowing that some of the things one creates have value over time.

The past is the most powerful instrument preservationists have, for it possesses enormous capacity to move and motivate people of differing persuasions. History is not just the province of the specialist, not just a subject of arcane discussions in cloistered settings. It can engage and persuade review boards, developers, the public, even politicians, when presented well. Determining historical significance is not just a perfunctory exercise conducted to meet federal requirements; it is a guidepost for all stages of preservation work. Historicity is what distinguishes preservation from all other pursuits in shaping the environment. Without it, preservationists have little save their wits . . . and taste.

II   SOME CHALLENGES OF THE RECENT PAST

3   The Difficult Legacy of Urban Renewal

Perhaps no term associated with the American landscape is fraught with more pejorative connotations than "urban renewal." Although the federal program bearing that name ended in the early 1970s, the phrase remains in common parlance, almost always in reference to something that should not have occurred ("This city suffered from widespread urban renewal") or something unfortunate that might occur ("That project would be as devastating as urban renewal"). The term evokes myriad negative references—to the wholesale destruction of neighborhoods we would rush to preserve today; to forced relocation and, with it, community dissolution, primarily affecting low-income minorities; to large-scale development, with cold, anonymous-looking architecture that is wholly incompatible with the urban fabric around it; to vast, little-used pedestrian plazas; to boundless accommodation of motor vehicles, including freeway networks destined to augment, rather than relieve, congestion, and immense parking garages that dwarf all that is around them. How could we, as a society, have ravaged our cities and towns the way we did, critics continue to charge. The prevailing view remains that, like war, urban renewal affords only lessons in what we must avoid.

The historical reality is, of course, much more complicated. While many of the stereotypical castings have some foundation in fact, our perspective also has been shaped by myths and half-knowledge. The urban renewal program is often conflated with that for public housing, for example. Advocates for the latter became reluctant allies of urban renewal, but

the two programs had entirely different origins and objectives; initially their backers were at odds with one another—a relationship that was never entirely rectified.[1] Urban renewal was also not primarily a case of federal officials dictating practices to communities. The heads of local agencies initiated and framed the projects they wished to undertake; the federal role had more to do with enforcing regulations, which, for better or worse, were developed to ensure a reasonable level of professionalism in planning and other relevant functions that were part of the process. These regulations carried a considerable amount of baggage, to be sure. Federal standards and prejudices probably affected the shape of *every* urban renewal scheme in various ways. Moreover, the immense amounts of money in the federal highway program and decisions at the federal and state levels as to where those highways would go in the inner city had an enormous impact on what areas became targeted for urban renewal. Still, the ball was in the court of local authorities to determine the basic form, character, and functions of a project as well as to select the consultants, designers, planners, and developers who would translate initiatives from a rough idea to a concrete proposal, thence a reality. Some of the best-known and most influential urban renewal projects, such as Gateway Center in Pittsburgh (begun 1950), Penn Center in Philadelphia (begun 1956), and Charles Center in Baltimore (begun 1958), were indeed entirely local undertakings, with no federal involvement in any defining aspect of their plans. The federal legislation that framed and facilitated urban renewal—provisions in

This chapter initially appeared in CRM: The Journal of Heritage Stewardship 3 (Winter 2006): 6–23, and is reprinted here with minor modifications.

the housing acts of 1949 and, especially, 1954—was the result of strenuous lobbying by locally based business interests. Whatever was done to the core of American communities during the 1950s and 1960s was the result of local agendas, not those of some Big Brother.

Urban renewal was initially the creation of downtown property owners and business interests, who, beginning in the 1930s, sought to stem what they saw as a steadily advancing tide of blight, which if left unchecked would eventually destroy the lifeblood of the city. Blight was defined as an erosion of commercial property value, and the worst of it purportedly lay on the periphery of downtown. Deteriorated housing and outmoded, small-scale commercial and industrial plants in particular were seen as serious hindrances to downtown growth. Land was difficult to acquire for new development and access routes. Blight also tarnished the image of downtown, discouraging investment. Business interests may have propelled the issue of blight to the fore, but they found strong allies among planners and many people concerned with public policy who believed that blight fostered crime and other social ills. In the formative stages of urban renewal their collective argument was remarkably simplistic: remove blight and the problems of people who had resided in those areas would dissipate as well.

Compounding the problem of declining land values was the ever-increasing movement of the middle class to the urban periphery and the emergence of new facilities in those outlying areas to serve them. Many feared that even if blight was removed, the impetus to build new projects of a scale sufficient to reinvigorate in-town areas would be insufficient when they had to compete with affluent outlying districts. Piecemeal solutions would prove ineffectual, the argument ran; only sizable undertakings could yield significant change. Comprehensive planning and the power of eminent domain were the essential instruments to retrieve the urban core. A long gestation period led to the federal laws that gave local authorities the tools to regenerate the multifaceted, dominant role the central district had long enjoyed in large towns and cities nationwide.

Urban renewal thus tended not to occur in places where property values were high—in the retail and office cores of cities—but rather in places close-by so as to enable expansion and/or modernization of what were deemed vital core components. Projects thus included office buildings and hotels, convention halls, government centers, institutional complexes such as hospitals and universities, and cultural facilities such as theaters and concert halls. Equally important was the creation of large new residential areas tailored to middle- and upper-middle-income households to bolster patronage of downtown places and to revive the desirability of living in the urban core. Sweeping improvements to transportation infrastructure, almost all of which catered to motor vehicles, were also viewed as key projects. Limited-access highways were deemed essential to facilitate access to downtown, as were capacious parking garages to serve new and existing development alike. Tracts near downtown and sometimes farther afield were designated for many wholesale, warehousing, and light manufacturing functions housed in "antiquated" core plants so that the land they occupied could be cleared for more profitable uses. Only toward the end of the period, around the mid-1960s, as the decline of downtown retailing accelerated, did plans emerge in some cities to recast such a significant core function in a radical way.

Most cities and many towns throughout the United States undertook some form of urban renewal activity during the quarter century following World War II. Portions of some major metropolises, including Boston, Philadelphia, Baltimore, Pittsburgh, Detroit, Chicago, St. Louis, Kansas City, Denver, Los Angeles, and San Francisco, were substantially changed as a result. Numerous smaller cities from Tucson to New Haven, Sacramento to Sheboygan, were likewise altered. No single movement in American city building has resulted in more sweeping changes, although boom periods in urban development such as those that occurred during the 1920s and 1980s led to a multitude of individual initiatives whose collective scale and impact often exceeded those of urban renewal.

Quantitative yardsticks aside, the scope and

nature of change induced by urban renewal—from in-town living to the proliferation of urban freeways, and from large-scale displacement to accelerated decrease in the very activities identified for rejuvenation—continues to affect the ways in which we inhabit and use cities. Given such factors, the significance of urban renewal in the history of American cities cannot be denied. But what about the *physical* significance of this phenomenon from a historical perspective? Is the landscape of urban renewal imbued with attributes that merit its preservation? Until recently few people cared to address the issue. Dismissing the whole episode as an aberration in the material as well as in the social and sometimes even in the economic arenas was seldom called into question. The time has come, however, for a fresh, more detached perspective. Urban renewal bestowed upon communities some places of lasting value, which can be appreciated if we consider them apart from the mental baggage we have acquired. Doing so entails challenges of several kinds.

Addressing the issue of preservation for urban renewal sites has been particularly encumbered by recollections of what such projects replaced. Hundreds of Victorian houses in San Francisco's Western Addition, and hundreds of an earlier vintage in Southwest Washington, D.C., were among the many thousands of buildings in quarters that would have been considered prime historic districts by the 1970s had they not been leveled under the aegis of urban renewal. Preservationists frequently fought against urban renewal; some of their organizations were formed in order to oppose the wholesale clearance that came to be closely identified with that program. Arguably much of the impetus for the National Historical Preservation Act came from those who feared wholesale destruction of the past if urban renewal programs remained unchecked. An equally repugnant aspect of urban renewal in the minds of many people was the uprooting of neighborhoods whose residents did not have the knowledge, money, or clout to fight back effectively—people who, as the sociologist Herbert Gans demonstrated early on, had stable, nourishing communities even if they lived on meager incomes.[2]

However regrettable, neither the destruction of building fabric nor of communities should detract from the historical significance of what was developed in their wake. Innumerable components of the landscape have replaced ones that we would venerate were they standing today. The Empire State Building (1929–31), to name an obvious example, rose on the site of the original Waldorf-Astoria (1891–93, 1895–97), which was a key prototype for recasting the urban luxury hotel in the late nineteenth century and a defining work for its architect, Henry Janeway Hardenbergh, who continued to be instrumental in the development of that type. Indeed, much of Gilded Age Fifth Avenue was replaced by stores, office buildings, and other commercial piles now venerated. Crown Hall at the Illinois Institute of Technology (1955–56), one of the most important buildings designed by Ludwig Mies van der Rohe and an icon of Modern architecture worldwide, replaced the Mecca (1891–92), a remarkable apartment building constructed around twin, multistory atria.[3] Advocates of the Colonial Revival regarded the Victorian legacy as detritus and recommended remodeling or destroying it at every opportunity, but that position does not detract from the significance of their own work.

Nor can the social displacement caused by wholesale clearing in urban renewal, however onerous it was, undermine the determination of significance today. Countless historic sites have tainted pasts in this respect. Central Park displaced a sizable squatter population and its creation was propelled to a substantial degree by the quest for high-end residential development around it. Many loft buildings prized today began their lives as sweatshops. Perhaps the most egregious legacy in this realm is that of the Southern plantation, which by the early eighteenth century depended upon human chattel for its very existence. Plantations should not be venerated because of slavery, and slavery must be a part of the interpretation irrespective of how little concrete evidence remains, yet this past does not reduce the material significance of the main house and other contributing components of the landscape that survive.[4] In a parallel way, what urban renewal projects replaced should always be remembered in some cases, but should not give cause for rejecting the potential value of what came thereafter.

Another prejudice that needs to be cast aside is ineligibility due to age. Few urban renewal projects broke ground before the mid-1950s; most were underway through the 1960s or later. The fact that many are less than fifty years old, however, should not inhibit their study and evaluation. The projects that clearly merit such inquiry from a historical perspective are almost certainly ones that possess exceptional significance within the *local* context, the threshold for National Register listing. Some examples are arguably of national significance as primary manifestation of important tendencies in design and urbanism of the period. Irrespective of the level of significance, such work generally had a profound impact on the communities in which it was executed. Today, many of these endeavors are vulnerable to changes that may not be for the better. Ignoring the issue under the guise of the standard fifty-year rule is to dismiss a historical phenomenon of obvious magnitude.

Taking stock of the historical significance of urban renewal is urgently needed because the resources in question are fragile. As has long been the case, the heritage of the recent past seems dated, even antiquated, certainly unfashionable, different from and even counter to the ways in which we prefer to design places today. At the same time, this legacy is insufficiently old in the minds of many people to be designated as historic. Urban renewal projects are especially vulnerable to modification since they generally entail complexes or even whole neighborhoods. Thus *both* buildings *and* the environment in which they are set are susceptible to unsympathetic changes.

The tenuous position of urban renewal's legacy is underscored by looking through the lens of landscape design. Preservationists as well as numerous other contingents all too frequently consider these ensembles primarily as buildings, with site and landscape design unrecognized or undervalued. Moreover, the copious amounts of open space that characterized such work of the period is all too often now seen as a blank slate for denser development. Why

retain an expansive plaza when the space could host a new office tower? Ignoring the landscape dimension runs directly counter to the framework in which numerous examples were conceived, where landscape architecture was an integral, often underlying component of the entire scheme. Open space allotted in generous amounts that today might be castigated as wasteful was considered to be as important to the design concept as the buildings in numerous instances. A misunderstanding of this perspective and a tendency to criticize the results because they are different from what would be done today rather than a serious consideration of the objectives and values that such work represents have led to an alarming rate of destruction of mid-twentieth-century landscape designs, many of them developed as part of urban renewal projects, and promises to threaten many more in the near future.[5]

Presumptions aside, pursuing a rigorous historical assessment will usually entail no small degree of original research, for systematic, scholarly investigation of the subject remains in a nascent state. There is no shortage of material from the period. The scope and policies of urban renewal were well chronicled in its own day by planners, sociologists, political scientists, and journalists, among others.[6] Issues were debated and many projects critiqued in architectural and other professional journals. Newspaper coverage in the communities affected was extensive. The archives of some local redevelopment agencies have been preserved, but few have been catalogued; many others are lost. Yet no matter how extensive and accessible the record, it requires substantial amounts of time to review, let alone digest.

Historical interest in urban renewal has increased considerably in recent years, but the resulting studies tend to be broadly based, addressing policies, practices, and their social and political consequences, with scant attention paid to the physical realm.[7] Scholarly interest to date also has focused more on the shortcomings of the program than on any strong points. A negative profile particularly applies to the relatively few published case studies that afford substantive analysis of urban renewal's physical dimensions. Probably the most copious work of this kind is David Schuyler's examination of Lancaster, Pennsylvania, which documents the ravaging of the commercial center for a new complex that was in part a functional failure. While of great value for the insights it yields and the detail with which it examines the pitfalls of the process, the text can also reinforce the stereotypical view that urban renewal was a pervasive disaster.[8] Work needs to be done on endeavors that led to more beneficial outcomes.

Begging focused investigation, too, are the biographies of key figures involved: public officials such as William Slayton, commissioner of the Urban Renewal Administration; Richard Lee, mayor of New Haven; and planners such as Edmund Bacon of Philadelphia or Edward Logue of Boston. Little is available on the developers who played a major role in a number of cities and whose work, in turn, helped define the nature of that done in many other places. William Zeckendorf perhaps ranks among the most extraordinary and unorthodox of these individuals, but many others such as Herbert Greenwald and James Scheuer, as well as corporations such as Reynolds Aluminum and Tishman Construction, warrant further examination.[9]

No matter how bountiful the sources, much of the challenge in assessing urban renewal projects lies with their multiple characteristics and the unevenness with which their objectives were realized. Examination needs to be on a case-by-case basis, with projects analyzed as individual endeavors within a local framework, as well as part of a national phenomenon. The difficult complexion of some projects is well illustrated by New Haven's Church Street Redevelopment Area. Intended to propel the city center into regional dominance as a retail and office hub, the complex suffered at the outset from never having a master plan shaped by business needs, from a piecemeal layout, and from an inward-looking orientation that perceptually isolated it from neighboring blocks.[10] Although it has often been criticized as a transplanted regional shopping mall, Church Street possessed little of the detailed, program-driven planning that characterized such complexes.

Despite predictions of swift realization, the

project took a decade (1957–67) to execute, causing no small degree of disruption to and displacement of the business community in the process. There is no question that Church Street is historically significant, but some of that significance lies in its example as a scheme that was poorly planned, fell short of its goal to revitalize the business core, and enjoyed a relatively brief live as a viable operation. Today [2006] open land exists where one of the anchor department stores stood; the companion emporium, built by Macy's, has been vacant for some years. A long-moribund, disconnected interior mall lies in the third block, called Chapel Square. The somber, neglected appearance of the ensemble only underscores its tarnished legacy (fig. 3.1).[11]

Under the circumstances the separation of determining significance and determining treatment may be unusually pronounced. If significance is indisputable, what about retention? Some may contend that the whole endeavor falls far short of a priority for preservation and

FIG. 3.1. Church Street Redevelopment Area, New Haven; Macy's department store, Abbott, Merkt & Company, architects and engineers, 1962–64 (now demolished), in left foreground; Chapel Square, Lathrop Douglass, architect, 1964–67, in center foreground. (Photo Richard Longstreth, 2004)

indeed might best be replaced by more site- and need-sensitive development. Yet Chapel Square itself was not only an early large-scale, mixed-use project (shops, offices, hotel) designed by a leading commercial architect in New York of the period (Lathrop Douglass); its spaces are readily adaptable to other functions. Its laconic modernist design is a good representative of its genre and has been a substantial part of the skyline facing the New Haven Green for decades. To the west of Chapel Square lies another component worth further scrutiny, the Temple Street Parking Garage, designed by the internationally renowned modernist Paul Rudolph, who was then dean of Yale's School of Architecture (fig. 3.2). The structure is a work of great originality —a bold, sculptural transformation of a utilitarian arrangement devised to accommodate the movement and storage of cars efficiently. At the same time, it presents a foreboding face to the businesses on the opposite side of the street for a two-block stretch.

Relating well to adjacent urban fabric was seldom a concern among those who shaped urban renewal projects and thus should not be a major factor is evaluating their historical significance. Hartford's Constitution Plaza (1959–63), for example, was developed on then-marginal commercial land as a gateway to downtown and a substantial addition to its office, hotel, and parking capacities (fig. 3.3). Unlike Church Street, it had a strong master plan and represented one of the most ambitious undertakings of its kind from the era. The system of plazas, walkways, and planted open space that gives the complex its pervasive unity was a major work of Sasaki, Walker Associates, then among the most prominent landscape architecture firms in the country; a signature building, for the Phoenix Mutual Life Insurance Company, that was designed by the distinguished New York architects Harrison & Abramovitz; and a hotel designed by another firm of national standing, New Orleans–based Curtis & Davis.[12] Constitution Plaza remains an important business center for the city, but its limited range of functions and the absence of residential areas nearby mean that its expansive spaces remain

FIG. 3.2. Temple Street Parking Garage, Temple Street between North Frontage Road and Crown Street, New Haven, 1959–62, Paul Rudolph, architect. Perspectival rendering, 1963. (Prints and Photographs Division, Library of Congress, LC-DIG-ppmsca-03539)

FIG. 3.3. Constitution Plaza, bounded by Harkey, Talcott, and Grove streets and Columbus Boulevard, Hartford, Connecticut, 1959–63, Sasaki, Walker & Associates, landscape architects; Phoenix Mutual Life Insurance Company Building, 1960–64, Harrison & Abramovitz, architects, in background. (Photo Richard Longstreth, 2002)

unpopulated after business hours and, since they lie a story or more above street level, the immediate environs lacks much pedestrian activity at any time.

Functionally and physically, Constitution Plaza has worked as an ensemble, and preserving anything less than the entire complex would undermine that integrity. But how should one approach the less cohesive legacy of Church Street? Can only a portion of what survives be justified for preservation even though the complex was conceived, however poorly, as a single entity? Does such partitioning run counter to sound preservation practice even though it is hard to assign high priority to a building such as the former Macy store. Macy's decision to participate, which did not occur until 1962, saved the project from oblivion and represented a milestone in that firm's expansion program. When it opened two years later it was

not only the first full-fledged department store from New York to operate in New England, but also the second-largest emporium in the state. Nevertheless, retaining the building's exterior in anything approximating its original form is problematic given its huge, windowless mass and the absence of demand for so large a retail facility in that location.

Fragmentation may be an undercurrent even when a project had a cohesive, well-considered plan and coherent execution. Baltimore's Charles Center not only ranked among the most ambitious schemes to enlarge a city's commercial core; it became a poster child for large-scale redevelopment generally, even though it was conceived and executed independent of the federal program. The master plan, developed under the aegis of planner David Wallace, offered a conspicuous exception to the norm in the degree to which it interwove old and new fabric.[13] The initial building, One Charles Center (1960–62), was designed by Mies van der Rohe. A prominent member of New York's architectural avant-garde, John M. Johansen, designed the Mechanic Theater (1965–67), a facility intended to bring major cultural activities to the heart of downtown. Other components were of less distinguished design, but unlike Constitution Plaza, Charles Center as realized never imparted the sense of a strongly unified ensemble. Indeed, the effect is more of an assemblage of discrete undertakings. Should preservation thus focus on the most significant parts rather than the whole? Has the ensemble lost a key contributor to its integrity because the skyway system (fig. 3.4), which never lived up to expectations, has been mostly dismantled? Conversely, should Charles Center not only be considered as a single entity, but also as part of a much larger renewal effort, including the Convention Center and the Inner Harbor, for which it served as a catalyst?

Many downtown urban renewal initiatives consisted of multiple projects conceived as components of a long-range master plan. The functional relationships among these undertakings were considered to be central to the viability of the whole and often of the parts as well. The building of new office towers, the argument ran, would not live up to expectations unless the street and highway network was improved. New cultural facilities would not have sufficient draw unless housing was created nearby for a substantial population with disposable income—a population also needed to sustain the office developments. Even a large tract far afield designated as a site for a new mass distribution center could enter the equation because it would replace aged facilities in town so they could be cleared for housing or new commercial

FIG. 3.4. Charles Center, bounded by Charles, Saratoga, Liberty, and Lombard streets, Baltimore, mostly 1958–67, David A. Wallace, principal planner, with Kostritsky + Potts of the Planning Council of the Greater Baltimore Committee; RTKL, coordinating architects and planners. General view showing a portion of the now mostly demolished skyway system. (Photo Richard Longstreth, 1971)

buildings. Clearly, evaluation of any given component should take the overall planning context into account, but to what degree should preservation objectives be tied to the entire spectrum of work in a community? To what degree, in other words, should a given urban renewal project be treated as an entity in its own right and to what degree should it be regarded merely as a part of an integrated plan? Is the latter approach practical or even desirable given the scattered array of sites and the varying degrees to which projects were realized and met their objectives?

The answer to such questions, of course, depends upon the particulars. One of the major urban renewal projects in Sacramento, for instance, was Capitol Mall, which transformed the blocks between the river and the state house from an agglomeration of marginal commercial facilities to ranges of public- and private-sector office buildings that were viewed as being far more appropriate for the primary approach to the government center. While the project was effectively realized, the near-contemporary one to extend the retail core along adjacent blocks to the north yielded few concrete results. A series of ambitious plans failed to materialize beyond the conceptual stage. A pedestrian mall and a large, isolated department store that was not an outgrowth of any master plan were the principal products of an effort that extended for over a decade.[14]

Even though current design preferences should never influence the assessment of work from a historical perspective, taste persists as an influential, if not always acknowledged, undertow, especially when addressing work of the recent past. Boston's Government Center (1964–70) well illustrates the difficulties in allaying taste prejudices despite the fact that the scheme was strong and much praised when it was new. Replacing the Scollay Square area tangent to the financial district, Government Center was anchored by a grand plaza, which was compared to those of St. Peter's in Rome and St. Mark's in Venice.[15] No less sweeping a gesture was made by the city hall, which rose in the northeast sector of the plaza and was heralded for the bold new language of monumentality it brought to the public realm. Both components

were by the then-young architectural firm of Kallman, McKinnell & Knowles and were won in competition predicated on an urban design plan developed by I. M. Pei & Associates (fig. 3.5). To the west rose the John F. Kennedy Federal Building, one of the last designs by Walter Gropius, founder of the Bauhaus, whose tenure at Harvard's Graduate School of Design had a profound impact on architectural education and practice in the United States. Beyond lay a spectrum of other facilities, including the State Service Center by Rudolph, all contributing to an ensemble that ranks as an unusually powerful design of the era.

Yet the City Hall and plaza, in particular, have long been vilified as foreboding places. The plaza is typically damned as a barren sea of pavement, lacking any elements that would give it life. City Hall's impact is equally perverse in the minds of many observers, reading more as an impenetrable bastion than a harbor of democratic governance. It is hard to find the entrance and one's destination beyond. Inside, no less than out, the atmosphere is cast as the antithesis of a welcoming public place. How does one respond to these deeply held views among so many of the people who frequent the premises or work there? Can these issues be addressed without compromising the design's integrity? *Should* they be addressed or is the design of sufficient import to justify its full retention, as in the case of Philadelphia's once equally vilified City Hall (1871–1901)?

Examining residential redevelopment under urban renewal may prove easier in certain respects, for program initiatives tended to result in schemes that were not only of strong and coherent design, but also were appreciated by their constituencies. At the same time, these projects generally represented avant-garde views of community design that created settings very different from traditional neighborhoods. Unlike areas that extended the commercial core, where the existing street configuration could seldom be modified to any great degree, new housing tracts tended to be somewhat farther afield in places where the matrix was reconfigured to suit the modernist canon. Thus superblocks became the norm, penetrated only

FIG. 3.5. City Hall Plaza, Government Center, bounded by Tremont, Cambridge, New Sudbury, and Congress streets, Boston, site plan, 1961–62, I. M. Pei & Associates, architects; City Hall, 1962–68, Kallmann, McKinnell & Knowles, architects, on left. (Photo Richard Longstreth, 2006)

by small streets and cul-de-sacs, with through traffic kept to the periphery. The presence of motor vehicles was indeed minimized. The traditional American pattern of parking the car close or adjacent to the dwelling was abandoned for more remote lots that often were screened from view. Enclosed, even underground, parking garages also were utilized. All these arrangements facilitated devoting large amounts of open space to pedestrians.

Site planning was closely tied to building design. The row house, which had fallen from favor among the middle class by the second quarter of the twentieth century, was revived—and rechristened the town house to enhance its marketability—to render the area occupied by buildings as compact as possible.[16] Houses were generally accorded small private yards; most of the open space was communal, another feature that ran directly against long-prevailing patterns. The arrangement of housing clusters, as they were called, was done in ways to encourage community interaction. Open spaces were frequently varied somewhat in their dimensions

and components, and the houses could differ in size, have staggered setbacks, and/or have varying details to avoid the sense of monotony associated with earlier row house neighborhoods. Often, too, houses were interspersed with apartment towers, which were not the traditional chunky blocks with embellished fronts and utilitarian sides, but rather were freestanding towers that maximized exposure to natural light as well as to views for all the dwelling units.

In another pronounced departure from tradition, urban renewal housing complexes tended to be inward looking, without necessarily having a strong presence when viewed from the principal streets. Their public face, in other words, may not be nearly as engaging as their private one. The inner sanctum was enhanced through landscape design. As some of the primary examples of large-scale development forged on the principals of modernist urbanism, the projects attracted many of the nation's foremost landscape architects, who used them as opportunities to refine their ideas. Today, these landscapes have reached maturity and often have sustained little or no substantial alterations, making them distinguished and significant examples of the period.

Prominent modernist architects were attracted to these projects for the same reasons. As a result, numerous cities have major residential projects of high caliber. The numerous exceptional enclaves of this genre include Portland Center by Skidmore, Owings & Merrill and Lawrence Halprin & Associates (1966–71) in Oregon; St. Louis's Plaza Square by Harris Armstrong and Hellmuth, Obata & Kassabaum (1960–61); San Francisco's St. Francis Square by Marquis & Stoller and Halprin (1963–65); Minneapolis's Cedar Square West by Ralph Rapson (1968–73); and Chicago's Hyde Park by I. M. Pei and Harry Weese (1957–61). Mies van der Rohe, together with his close associates, planner Ludwig Hilberseimer and landscape architect Alfred Caldwell, designed Detroit's Lafayette Park (1956–68) for Herbert Greenwald, the maverick Chicago developer who became a leading sponsor of

avant-garde design. Even with later additions by others, the ensemble represents the most fully formed manifestation of the three original designers' internationally influential urban vision (fig. 3.6).[17]

An equally ambitious residential undertaking of this kind occurred in the Southwest Redevelopment Area of Washington, D.C., which between 1959 and 1972 emerged as a precinct of ten housing projects as well as a number of individual buildings. Intended as a model for the urban renewal program, the enterprise included work by an array of young talent. The first complex helped propel its architect, Chloethiel Woodard Smith, into the national limelight as a leader in the housing field. Two other distinguished Washington firms—Charles Goodman and Keyes, Lethbridge & Condon—also made major contributions that received widespread acclaim (fig. 3.7). Pei, Weese, and Morris Lapidus contributed as well. Major portions of the landscape were designed by Daniel Urban Kiley,

FIG. 3.6. Lafayette Park, Lafayette Avenue and Rivard Street, Detroit, 1956–60, Herbert Greenwald, developer, Ludwig Mies van der Rohe, architect, Ludwig Hilberseimer, planner, Alfred Cauldwell, landscape architect. General view showing the relationship between the row houses, main drive, and the first high-rises. (Photo Richard Longstreth, 2005)

FIG. 3.7. Tiber Island, bounded by 4th, M, and N streets, S.W., Washington, D.C., 1963–65, Berens Companies and Charles H. Tompkins Company, developers, Keyes, Lethbridge & Condon, architects, Eric Paepke, landscape architect. (Photo Richard Longstreth, 1991)

Sasaki, Walker & Associates, Robert Zion, and Wallace, McHarg, Roberts & Todd. Few other places rival the degree to which the brave new world of urban life envisioned by modernists was manifested with such richness and variety.[18]

Such projects attracted many households who likewise harbored a view of community that differed from the norm—one that was grounded in engagement and activism. Their neighborhood was not just a domestic sanctuary, but a staging ground for change. Many embraced racial diversity, at least to the degree that the cost of purchasing these dwelling units allowed. Often the projects were the first in their cities to be planned from the start as racially integrated. Many residents considered themselves to be pioneers whose commitment to the city was nurtured by the desire to make urban life a better experience. Decades later that spirit can still be found and has in some cases led to steps that will ensure protection. Surrounded by decay, Lafayette Park was recently listed as a local historic district in response to a residents' ini-

tiative. Threat of overdevelopment has spurred discussion to take similar steps in Washington. Although now considered to be dated and even "failed experiments" by some planners, these communities have remained viable places to live and indeed are enjoying a revival among a new generation, who find both the physical environment and the community it shelters an appealing alternative of conventional market housing.

If urban renewal's residential projects did suffer from a failed agenda, it was that they seldom served their intended role as catalysts for additional revitalization, but instead remained oasis-like enclaves. The major exception was Philadelphia's Society Hill (officially called Washington Square East; ca. 1960–75), which set preservation as a top priority. In the great majority of urban renewal endeavors, existing fabric was seen as something best eliminated. Occasionally a remnant of the early nineteenth century was judged to be of sufficient historical significance to be retained. These vestiges of a distant past were either left to stand in isolation, affording a striking contrast to everything around them, as with the Basilica of St. Louis, King of France, at the Jefferson National Expansion Memorial in St. Louis (1831–34); or, less often, were woven into a new context, as with Wheat Row in Southwest Washington (1794–95), which became part of a large new row house and apartment complex.[19] Even in a rare case where the existing stock of the Southwest was acknowledged to have some historic merit, authorities believed that a sufficient market did not exist for rehabilitation of that scale. Work of that order then underway in Georgetown and in Alexandria was believed to be saturating the meager demand that existed for old houses.

In Society Hill, by contrast, massive retrieval of historic fabric was employed for the first time as an instrument to spearhead urban revitalization. Abundant dwellings, as well as churches and a few other building types, all dating from before the mid-nineteenth century, remained there, affording an incomparable urban landscape. Although most of this fabric had long deteriorated as low-rent rooming houses and small-scale commercial facilities, it was ear-

marked as the key inducement to turn the precinct into one of choice among households of substantial means. Society Hill was to a large degree the conception of Edmund Bacon, director of the Philadelphia Planning Commission, who believed the area should also be a showcase of Modern design. Through the work of Pei as well as of such prominent locally based firms as Mitchell/Giurgola and Louis Sauer, Society Hill bucked the then-prevailing trend of having infill buildings in a historic district feign the appearance of period pieces. Equally unusual was Bacon's plan to retain all streets and alleyways *and* weave into this grid a subtle network of pedestrianways and plazas—designed by the landscape architecture firm of Collins, Adelman & Dutot—that were places to foster community interaction. Society Hill was a benchmark in demonstrating that preservation could be a powerful tool in revitalizing cities and that old and new design could be compatible (fig. 3.8).[20] The project also spawned what remains a growing field of investment in historic properties over many blocks beyond to the west and south. Society Hill was one of the rare cases where the

FIG. 3.8. Washington Square East (Society Hill) redevelopment area, realized design begun late 1950s; Edmund Bacon and others, planners, Collins, Adelman & Dutot, landscape architects. View of neighborhood park. (Photo Richard Longstreth, 2002)

renewal activities there became contagious. Importantly, the period of significance extends through the 1960s in the historic district nomination approved by the Philadelphia Historical Commission several years ago.

The issues involved in addressing urban renewal projects are hardly new. They rise to the fore constantly in preservation when evaluating resources of many types and especially when examining districts and such complexes as institutional campuses. The underlying challenge is to approach the task with an open mind, checking one's assumptions at the door, as it were, and acquiring a strong base of knowledge of pertinent source material. The concept of cultural landscape is particularly valuable for examining the legacy of urban renewal because of the emphasis it gives to multifaceted parts as well as to the processes of change over time. This concept, too, foregrounds the significance of *designed* landscapes, while placing them in larger physical and cultural contexts. The widespread prejudices against urban renewal and much of the legacy of the second half of the twentieth century generally must be set aside in order to assess the real significance of such initiatives. Our cities and towns changed dramatically during the postwar era and we can ill afford to dismiss all those transformations out of hand.

4   The Last Landscape

Landscapes of the recent past are, too often, the last considered and the most threatened. As nearly the last things we have done, they are often the first things we believe must be done again. The last landscape frequently is cast as one of errors, functional and aesthetic, before it has had the time to acquire a substantial past of its own.[1] From the preservation perspective, no greater challenge exists. But it is a challenge worth addressing for a number of reasons.

The basic arguments are essentially the same for preserving both architecture and landscape architecture from the second half of the twentieth century. First, this period benefited from a stunning array of artistic talent, with the maturing of pioneer modernists and the emergence of a new generation as well. Thomas Church, Garrett Eckbo, Paul Friedberg, Lawrence Halprin, Dan Kiley, Hideo Sasaki, and Robert Zion are among the figures who created designs of extraordinary character that received widespread recognition nationally and internationally when they were created. The post–World War II legacy is at least as strong as any other period in landscape architecture from the standpoint of conceptual originality and formal sophistication.

Second, the period was one of sweeping change in settlement patterns, when the fundamental characteristics of metropolitan structure experienced dramatic changes. The extent of low-density, decentralized, and eventually also multinucleated forms of development became much more pronounced than had previously been the case. The United States was by far the most important crucible for these changes and landscape design played a central role in many instances, for it was the setting that established the ambient character so essential to the appeal of such places as alternatives to the urban norm.

A primary manifestation of this shift was the regional shopping mall, whose creators sought to bring the advantages of the downtown centralized business configuration within easy reach of middle-class households that now lay near the urban periphery. The result, of course, was anything but urban in character. The initial archetype for the mall was in fact the then-prevailing, idealized view of the traditional New England town green, whose appeal lay as much in a purported capacity to foster social interaction as in its bucolic character.[2]

As the shopping mall idea took hold, these places became an important proving ground for applying new ideas in landscape architecture to the public realm. Even with budget constraints, as Sidney Shurcliff complained about at Shopper's World near Framingham, Massachusetts (1948–51), complexes with copious amounts of central open space afforded a then-rare opportunity to adapt some of the new ideas introduced in private gardens to a larger scale and broader use.[3] Lawrence Halprin produced one of the most fully developed and sophisticated examples for Old Orchard Shopping Center northwest of Chicago (1954–56), where the concept of an informal, but highly active, interplay of form and space was carried into the layout of the complex itself (fig. 4.1).[4] But there were

This chapter initially appeared in *Preserving Modern Landscape Architecture II: Making Postwar Landscapes Visible*, edited by Charles Birnbaum, with Jane Brown Gillette and Nancy Slade (Washington, D.C.: Spacemaker Press, 2004), 118–25, and is reprinted here with minor modifications. Additionally, the original concluding section was cut, as its content is more fully developed in chapter 9, and the concluding paragraphs herein are more fully developed.

many other less-adventurous manifestations where the concept of bringing the garden into the marketplace was nonetheless crucial to establishing the character of the complex from a marketing no less than an aesthetic standpoint.

A second major sphere of innovation was the suburban corporate headquarters, or what now is often called the corporate estate, where a function that had been key to defining the city center since the mid-nineteenth century experienced sweeping changes in form and location.[5] Often the work of renowned architects and landscape architects as well as repositories of noteworthy assemblages of art, these latter-day villas were not, however, completely private bastions. In some cases, as with the Connecticut General Life Insurance Company near Hartford, Connecticut, by Skidmore, Owings & Merrill (1954–

FIG. 4.1. Old Orchard Shopping Center, Skokie Highway between Gulf Road and Harrison Street, Skokie, Illinois, 1954–56, Loebl, Schlossman & Bennett, architects, Lawrence Halprin & Associates, landscape architect; since altered. (Photo Hedrich-Blessing, 1956. Architectural Archives, University of Pennsylvania, by the gift of Lawrence Halprin)

57), their grounds were readily accessible to the public and played a significant role in defining place amid the low-density residential tracts that lay around them (fig. 4.2). Connecticut General was a seminal work in this regard, one that had a profound impact on the conceptualization of such complexes for several decades. Equally celebrated were the grounds Sasaki designed to complement Eero Saarinen's John Deere headquarters in Moline, Illinois (1958–64).[6] In both examples, the picturesque English park of the late eighteenth and early nineteenth centuries provided the conceptual springboard, but the designs are essentially new in their breadth and simplicity of effect. At the same time, when compared to contemporaneous designs for shopping malls, these schemes underscore the multifaceted nature of landscape architecture of the period and the ability of the profession to respond in new, creative ways to essential differences in programmatic demands.

A third sphere is residential development. Some very innovative work occurred in terms of both site design and the treatment of individual properties. Hollin Hills in Fairfax County, Virginia, developed mostly during the 1950s, is a prime example. For a sizable subdivision it was unusual in its respect for the terrain and existing woodlands as well as for its uncompromisingly Modern houses (fig. 4.3). Several landscape architects contributed to the scheme over time, including a young Dan Kiley.[7] The ecological concerns nascent at Hollin Hills became a formative component of the site plan for the Sea Ranch (1962–67), one of the most unusual residential enclaves to be realized in the United States during the twentieth century. Here Halprin and his architect-collaborators, MLTW and Joseph Esherick, developed a dynamic and decisively new approach to relate buildings and landscape, clustering the former near existing hedgerows and abutting mountain woodlands to minimize the visual impact on the overall natural setting—an approach that continues to resonate as a model for rural development (fig. 4.4).[8] Beyond such well-known examples, there are probably more distinguished, singular postwar residential developments than we realize in the United States.

FIG. 4.2. A portion of the Connecticut General Life Insurance Company offices, Cottage Grove Road and Hall Boulevard, Bloomfield, Connecticut, 1956–57, with the extensive public grounds surrounding the building; Skidmore, Owings & Merrill, architects and landscape architects. (Photo Richard Longstreth, 2000)

The much greater mainstream of suburban residential development generally did not involve architects or landscape architects of note, but the results also beg our attention. At no time in American history was the opportunity so prevalent for so many people to obtain a slice of the American dream—a freestanding, single-family house with a capacious yard. For millions of Americans, many of whom were just entering the middle class, postwar housing tracts represented a seminal change in their living environment.[9] They also represented a major shift in metropolitan form, the full effects of which we are only beginning to comprehend. The Levitt community of Belair-at-Bowie near Washington, D.C., begun in the late 1950s, is a good example of many tracts where site design remained an important attribute. What occurred in such cases was a skillful adaptation of naturalistic planning principles that had been refined in the layout of elite suburbs prior to World War II to more limited sites and economical circumstances (see figs. 5.1 and 5.2). The mass-produced approach to residential development that Levitt & Sons was instrumental in advancing was often the subject of derision among professionals and critics, but from the consumer's standpoint these tracts represented nirvana, and as they mature it is imperative to take fresh stock in their considerable merits. They are irreplaceable resources where the landscape as much as—perhaps more than—the buildings define the character of place.

The framework presented thus far contributes to arguments for significance, but what about the need for preservation? Some observers see all the attention to the recent past as artificially rushing the process, but they ignore the sobering reality that many components from the recent past are seriously threatened. Shopper's World is gone. Old Orchard is remodeled. After a protracted campaign, Connecticut General's building has been saved, but much of the grounds have been redeveloped. Sea Ranch's pathbreaking site plan was changed years ago. The Levittowns of the nation survive underappreciated and sometimes still vilified, their value as habitat ignored or snubbed in many circles. In a society that continues to experience substantial growth and well as change, and one that is ever more prone to disposability, we can no longer afford to wait for several generations

FIG. 4.3. Hollin Hills residential development, Fort Hunt Road, Fairfax County, Virginia, 1948–61, Robert Davenport, developer, Charles M. Goodman, architect, Lou Bernard Voight, Dan Kiley, and Eric Paepecke, landscape architects. (Photo Richard Longstreth, 2000)

FIG. 4.4. Sea Ranch residential development, State Route 1, Sonoma County, California, site plan 1962–67, Oceanic Properties, developer, Lawrence Halprin Associates, landscape architects, Joseph Esherick and Moore Lyndon Turnbull Whitaker, architects. (Photo Richard Longstreth, 1975)

to elapse before we focus on preserving landscapes of the post–World War II era.

From this standpoint, a few types of landscape design seem reasonably safe. The museum garden is one exception, but even these can be subject to change when the significance of their design is not fully understood or appreciated. A good example is afforded by Philip Johnson's Roofless Church in New Harmony, Indiana (1959–60), which has always been under the tutelage of a foundation (fig. 4.5). The importance of this design, at least as a work of architecture, is understood, but in recent years the main interior court, which was predominantly paved, has been altered to one that is primarily lawn, markedly changing the effect and the relationship between this space and the fields beyond.

The same fragility holds true for private gardens. The original owners almost always remain superb stewards, but when the property changes hands, the garden is often the first thing to be altered or even destroyed. Perhaps it is just neglected, but the impact can be much the same. Gardens are very personal things and that special relationship increases their fragility in the long term. Many from the postwar era are lost.

Public parks might seem better protected. Historically changes to such places tended to be made in increments over time, and often those changes are now seen as contributing to the richness of the whole. Even changes deemed less than enhancing have tended to be piecemeal and generally reversible. But today, change seems to be more comprehensive and final: the existing landscape is eradicated and an entirely new scheme put in its place. Such has been the case in recent years with Dan Kiley's block at Independence Mall in Philadelphia (1963) and Halprin's Skyline Park in Denver (1970–76) (fig. 4.6).[10] Both were lauded projects in their day; both became cast as liabilities by the next generation; both will never have a chance for reassessment with lives of less than forty years. Such decisive change is often justified on the basis of functional obsolescence. Kiley's portion of Independence Mall, for example, was hampered by two other blocks of less sophisticated design created by others, and the ensemble was

FIG. 4.5. Roofless Church, North Street, New Harmony, Indiana, 1959–60, Philip Johnson, architect; now altered. (Photo Richard Longstreth, 1965)

so large and poorly sited that it served little purpose. The Kiley block was a superb design by all accounts, but it never had a user constituency. Halprin's Denver plaza was well positioned in the city center, but was seen as harboring undesirables where high-end development was cultivated—its loss a needless one.

The challenge of function looms large with many projects of the recent past, none more pointedly than the urban mall. Pedestrianways such as that which Victor Gruen and Garrett Eckbo designed at Fresno, California (1960–64), were seen as being components of a cure for decline in central business districts, making the core again competitive with shopping malls on the periphery (fig. 4.7).[11] More recently, however, these projects have been perceived as contributing to downtown's downward spiral. Citi-

FIG. 4.6. Skyline Park, Arapahoe Street between 15th and 18th streets, 1970–76, Denver, Lawrence Halprin & Associates, landscape architects; demolished 2003. (Photo Richard Longstreth, 2003)

three-block Commercial Street Mall (1963–65) was the first to be realized in a town.[13] Capitalizing on a now unusual and evocative environment, combined with a sound tenant structure and marketing strategy to encourage revitalization, is precisely what preservation has done with success on hundreds of Main Streets nationwide over the past twenty years. Malls *can* be successful in certain cases, especially in university towns. Examples by Halprin in Charlottesville, Virginia (1972–76), and by architects Shapiro Petrauskas Gelber in Burlington, Vermont (completed 1982), are good illustrations of the fact that it is not the concept but the way in which it is developed and tied to the patterns of the community that are the crucial factors.[14]

Underlying all the threats to the recent past is a lack of recognition. Few people outside the profession know so much as the names of leading landscape architects. All too often properties are admired, even studied, on the basis of their architecture, while the landscape component is marginalized. This tendency is fostered by the fact that good landscape design often does not call attention to itself. The results can seem elegant, fitting, and natural, but observers do not think about how these places got that way or who was responsible for that resolution. As in any field, recognition entails understanding, and here the challenge is formidable indeed. Since the 1970s enormous advances have been made in our knowledge of the history of twentieth-century landscape design in the United States, but much more needs to be done in scholarship and advocacy.

One way to foster the process is more integrative study—that is, looking at architecture, landscape architecture, or, for that matter, planning not as discrete entities, but as part of a larger whole. Here the concept of landscape, as J. B. Jackson advanced it, or cultural landscape, as it is often called today, can serve our purposes well. Through this process, we can learn more and present a compelling case for preservation. A cultural landscape approach certainly enriches the meaning of all types of development.[15] While viewed as a landscape design, for example, Halprin's Freeway Park in Seattle (1970–74) derives much of its impact from

zens have generally applauded when their Main Streets have been reopened and all vestiges of malling disappeared. But should this scenario be universal? Calls for preserving the first executed example in the United States, designed in 1959 by Gruen for Kalamazoo, Michigan, were unsuccessful, but it is doubtful that the modifications that ensued or indeed that any design solution in itself will bring life back to what has become a moribund area.[12] Might not, however, Fresno's Fulton Mall—which was among the most artfully designed, is of major historical significance as a national prototype, and remains virtually intact—be skillfully marketed as a singular place that becomes an effective component of a new downtown revitalization program? Perhaps, too, the pedestrian mall could again function as a draw in smaller communities such as Atchison, Kansas, where the

FIG. 4.7. Fulton Mall, Fulton Street between Tuolumne and Inyo streets, Fresno, California, 1960–64, Victor Gruen Associates, architects, Eckbo, Dean, Austin + Williams, landscape architects. (Photo Richard Longstreth, 2004)

FIG. 4.8. Freeway Park, Sixth Avenue and Seneca Street, Seattle, 1970–74, Lawrence Halprin & Associates, landscape architects. (Photo Richard Longstreth, 1981)

FIG. 4.9. Motel court, U.S. Route 441, Ocala, Florida, ca. late 1950s–early 1960s. (Photo Richard Longstreth, 2001)

FIG. 4.10. Motor House (Woodlands) motel, off State Route 125Y, Williamsburg, Virginia, 1956, Department of Architecture, Colonial Williamsburg, architects and landscape architects; mostly demolished 2001. (Photo Richard Longstreth, 1997)

FIG. 4.11. J. B. Jackson house, La Cienega, New Mexico, 1965, J. B. Jackson, designer. (Photo Richard Longstreth, 1998)

a defiant relationship with the broader urban context—the canyons of skyscrapers that abut it and the cacophony of the subgrade channel for motor traffic it mitigates (fig. 4.8).[16]

The same can be said within the vernacular realm, which is of immense importance in understanding any era, but all too often receives little attention when it is still perceived to be new. The tended and sometimes secluded ambience of the motel landscape of the 1950s and 1960s offered a sense of relief and relaxation after hours of driving through disorderly highway corridors (fig. 4.9). Such places were generally not part of an integrated design; their landscape features were more likely the result of individual decisions by the owner—sometimes made at the time of construction and in consultation with the architect and/or builder, and in other instances, made subsequent to the building's completion. They are seldom considered consequential and even more rarely valued as historic, but they are significant contributors to what once was a major pattern in the development of overnight accommodations—one that was more relaxed and individualized than most options today and hence stands as an important episode in the history of tourism in the United

States.[17] Landscape can also be a manifesto, as at the 1956 Motor House, a motel complex created by the Colonial Williamsburg Foundation, that stood in silent protest against the commercial strip, which many architects, landscape architects, and planners viewed as blighting communities coast-to-coast (fig. 4.10). Here the motel was located apart from the highway, in its own grassy, semiforested setting that enhanced its role as a tranquil retreat set within walking distance of the museum town.

From this perspective, landscape is greater than the sum of its parts, but without landscape design the whole cannot be comprehended. Imagine, for a minute, how anyone could attempt an analysis of J. B. Jackson's house near Santa Fe (1965) without addressing its landscape components in detail (fig. 4.11).[18] Complementing the residence, the landscape is a sophisticated yet seemingly simple and direct play of formal and informal elements that evoke tradition while eluding specific precedent. As a place, it is an utterly fitting oasis in a semi-arid region, yet is utterly unlike any historical patterns in that region. Like the Motor House, it can be read as a protest, in this case to the scenographic theatricality of the historicizing "Pueblo" architecture that became pervasive in northern New Mexico by the 1960s. How self-evident, we assume, because of the formative role Jackson had in our thinking about landscape, as well as an extraordinary character he imparted to the scheme. But the same can be said of many other places. The holistic nature of many residential properties designed by Richard Neutra is a good case in point. The Edgar Kaufmann house in Palm Springs (1946–47) embodies Neutra's concern for, and knowledge of, landscape design (fig. 4.12). Here, in what was then an open desert setting, he also created an oasis, but one of an unusual order. Boulders were manipulated to provide a berm for privacy, but also to afford an extraordinarily rugged enunciation of the underplayed portal to the inner sanctum, where manicured grounds rest amid a ring of desert flora. Perhaps not since Henry Hobson Richardson's boulder-encrusted Ames gate lodge (1880–

81) in North Easton, Massachusetts, had large stones been used by an architect with such élan. But, of course, with Neutra, house and nature stand in dynamic contrast, the machine precision of the building resting amid an impressionistic use of plant material. Each loses much of its meaning without the other. Yet Neutra's use of landscape has been for the most part given only passing note by scholars.[19]

Taking landscapes seriously is well worth the effort. Landscape design, high-style and vernacular, has been a central defining component of post–World War II development, and it is central to understanding the nature of the places in which many of us work, live, and seek refuge. If we do not focus on preserving our landscape heritage from the recent past, we will have little real sense of the richness places created during the second half of the twentieth century have possessed.

FIG. 4.12. Edgar Kaufmann house, 470 W. Chino Canyon Road, Palm Springs, California, 1946–47, Richard Neutra, architect and landscape architect. (Photo Julius Shulman, 1947. © J. Paul Getty Trust. Used with permission. Julius Shulman Photography Archive, Research Library at the Getty Research Institute [2004.R.10])

5   The Extraordinary Postwar Suburb

Extraordinary is among the least likely adjectives that would come to most people's minds in describing the vast residential tracts developed throughout the metropolitan periphery coast to coast between the late 1940s and the mid-1960s.[1] Virtually from the start, this epochal shift in the nation's settlement patterns was castigated as oppressively ordinary and mundane. Architects, planners, sociologists, journalists, and the intellectual community in general branded such development as a despoliation of the landscape with cookie-cutter "boxes," the whole exuding a monotony that was dehumanizing and capable of breeding social, even mental, dysfunction. The phenomenon, many observers charged, was a horrendous speculative free-for-all that was destined to become a wasteland in short order.[2]

As with numerous forms of popular culture that emerged after World War II, a conspicuous disparity existed between the viewpoint of critics and consumers. Attacks on the burgeoning subdivisions tended to focus on appearances, expressing points of view that were to no small degree snobbish and revealed a lack of understanding of the forces that shaped these environments as well as of the concerns of the middle- and moderate-income families that flocked to them in droves. But however off the mark, it is the criticism that nonetheless lingers in the minds of many preservationists who realize they may soon have to survey and evaluate such places. How can things once so vilified now be identified for protection? The thought may linger, too, that historic preservation's rise as a national movement in the 1960s was in part predicated on the assumption that it was rescuing older residential areas that were far superior in design and character to the ostensibly "tacky" suburbs then blanketing the countryside. How can the two now be considered on a more or less even playing field? Indeed, can the tracts of the 1950s ever be justifiably equated with the Georgetowns or Oak Parks of the nation? The newer places possess none of the rich variety of architecture, or so it seems, and few individually distinguished buildings that are present in many forebears.

Compounding the uneasiness many preservationists may feel in addressing the postwar suburb is the fact that the individuality absent at the inception has often been achieved in later years by remodeling. Thus altered, the fabric flies in the face of traditional notions of integrity in preservation. Finding a house in Levittown, New York, for example, that possesses most of its original features is challenging (fig. 5.1). With many examples, the character has been greatly modified; in numerous cases, too, it has been transformed beyond recognition. With this extent of change, what are the salient historical attributes that remain—just what is it that should be preserved? And if changes to date are pervasive, how does one assess proposed changes in the future?

But perhaps the biggest psychological barrier to the preservationist's embrace of postwar suburbs is their size. Tracts may entail hundreds, sometimes thousands, of houses—an enormous quality to single out for protection, particularly if that measure leads to ongoing review of proposed changes at the local level. When the components of a tract—street layout, yard size, and house models—are standardized, with only minor variation block after block, does all of the

This chapter initially appeared in the National Trust for Historic Preservation's *Forum Journal* 15 (Fall 2000): 16–25, and is reprinted here with minor modifications.

FIG. 5.1. Remodeled houses, Ashley Lane, Levittown, Nassau County, New York, 1947–51, Levitt & Sons, developers, designers, and builders. (Photo Richard Longstreth, 2009)

development have to be designated? Might not a sampling be sufficient?

The problem with all these reservations is that they are based on a vague and unsubstantiated outlook rather than on the thorough historical analysis that must be the basis of any successful, long-term preservation strategy. Preservationists have readily accepted historical frameworks for the civil rights movement and even the Cold War as a foundation for documenting and in many cases preserving sites. But, perhaps because of all the critical baggage from past decades, they have been much more reluctant to take a careful look at the postwar suburb on its own terms. The omission is all the more unfortunate since there is now a respectable corpus of scholarly literature on the subject.[3]

When examined from a historical perspective, considering not only relationships to previous settlement patterns but also to subsequent ones, the postwar suburb is far more significant a phenomenon than is generally realized. Never before in the history of habitation in the United States or any other country was such a large share of the population able to afford quarters that were as convenient, private, and spacious—both indoors and out (fig. 5.2). The longstanding dream of owning a freestanding,

single-family house set in a capacious yard, with ample space for individual pursuits, became available to millions of Americans who theretofore had known much more limited possibilities. In the process, both living and landscape patterns were modified to a profound degree. The multiplicity of these developments is major facet of their significance.

For persons of moderate to middle income, housing choices during the first half of the twentieth century might include a single-family residence, but generally one of modest proportions. In urban areas, many of these dwellings were attached or semidetached (fig. 5.3). When it existed, yard space was generally limited to a small area in front and a utilitarian one at the rear, with narrow strips separating the house from its neighbors. For a large contingent of the working population, homeownership was not an option; renting space in a walk-up flat, an apartment building, or a rooming house was the only feasible means of securing shelter. The postwar tract house was often larger and more convenient than comparable quarters of previous decades; it was also filled with new amenities and had easy connections to the out-of-doors. But the most dramatic departure from the norm lay with siting practices. Property size ranged from twice to several times prewar standards. Now the long side of houses generally ran parallel to the street. The front yard was expansive in comparison to earlier years; the rear yard seemed even more so and was now primarily reserved for recreational uses. As vegetation matured, the overall effect was more of a garden setting than an urban one, a characteristic previously confined to a comparatively small number of enclaves developed for the well-to-do.

The postwar suburb was made possible by a variety of converging factors. The period was one of unusual and sustained prosperity; by 1955 the gross national product was double that of 1929. In contrast to prevailing patterns in earlier years, skilled labor and management reached accords whereby salary and benefit increases were tied to rising productivity and demand, availing a sizable portion of the blue-collar workforce with unprecedented amounts of leisure time and disposable income. Industrial decentralization intensified, placing hundreds of thousands of additional jobs

at the urban periphery. White- and blue-collar households alike had accumulated an unusually large amount of capital through saving during the Second World War, giving them funds they could only have dreamed about in the Depression. The population was swelling, with a huge new generation of young, upwardly mobile families seeking places that were conducive to raising a family. This demand confronted an acute shortage of housing due to the paucity of residential construction since 1930.

Orchestrated incentives played a central role in shaping the nature of postwar residential development. Through the Federal Housing Administration (FHA), Veterans Administration, and other agencies, the U.S. government took aggressive steps to encourage new house construction and homeownership. As a result, little or no money was required for down payments; mortgages were structured for extended periods at low interest rates. At the same time, the FHA insured mortgages taken by builders, greatly facilitating the availability of funds

FIG. 5.2. Street scene, Belair-at-Bowie, Prince George's County, Maryland, 1959–68, Levitt & Sons, developers, designers, and builders. (Photo Richard Longstreth, 1999)

FIG. 5.3. Semidetached houses, Mander Street, St. Louis, ca. 1920s. (Photo Richard Longstreth, 2000)

from lending institutions. Many housebuilders had entered the world of volume production during the war. Bolstered by experience and capital as well as by the economy and government incentives, a number of them began to operate on a far larger scale than they had previously. Building in volume reduced unit cost, but also required an abundance of inexpensive land. Ample acreage of this sort existed on the urban fringe, since most prewar development was still predicated on access to public transportation and thus formed relatively compact extensions of the city. Moreover, local officials usually encouraged new construction by rezoning tracts and providing schools, access roads, and even some infrastructural improvements at little or no cost to the builder. Builders capitalized on these circumstances and on the accelerating rate of automobile use, realizing that people would depend entirely on their vehicles for transportation if that reliance afforded them a better domestic environment.

The scale of postwar house construction far exceeded earlier levels. Probably no single builder came close to the extent of work undertaken by Levitt & Sons, whose developments on Long Island and in Bucks County, Pennsylvania,

alone totaled over 33,000 dwellings. Still, a number of colleagues now commonly built tracts of hundreds of houses rather than the dozens that would have previously been considered sizable. This scale fundamentally altered the relationship of individual residences to their neighborhood. Whereas prewar houses were characteristically viewed as part of a larger, evolving district or community that was created by multiple parties over a sustained period of time, the new tracts seemed like communities unto themselves—close to, perhaps, but still apart from other developments.

In part because of its size, the postwar suburban tract was frequently the product of comprehensive or at least some detailed planning, to a far greater degree than most earlier counterparts. For inspiration, builders took cues from the high-end residential developments that proliferated during the 1910s and especially the 1920s.[4] FHA subdivision guidelines had a direct impact as well. Without that agency's approval, builders could not get their mortgages insured. But had the thrust of these guidelines substantially departed from patterns with which the real estate industry was familiar, it is likely they would have had markedly less influence.

As it was, the fact that FHA planning models often correlated with key features of earlier elite enclaves probably did much to enhance their application. The new work that resulted not only accorded the automobile overwhelmingly dominance as the mode of transportation, the tracts were either differentiated from contiguous parts of the metropolitan area or lay some distance removed from any built-up section. Most were given their own names and a layout that was inward-looking. Natural terrain was generally respected; on more than a few occasions, existing trees were selectively saved and open space preserved for recreational uses. Roadways tended to be curvilinear in response to topography, but also to enhance a sense of variety and to remove through traffic. Indeed, streets were generally configured to discourage the passage of vehicles that were not destined for a house in the immediate vicinity. The matrix fostered allusions to rural settings, particularly when landscaping matured, furthering perceptual disassociation with urban precincts.

The most obvious difference between the large tracts of the postwar era and older ones developed for the affluent was the relatively small size and standardization of house design, which was the aspect that gave rise to so much derision among critics. The premise was faulty, however. Comparable shelter designed for persons of moderate to middle income in previous eras—the row houses and bungalows of the early twentieth century, for example—were no less homogeneous. At the same time, postwar tracts proved more conducive to individuality in other, unanticipated ways that were not as easy to realize in the limited confines common to earlier middle-market dwellings. Many postwar house plans stressed openness and informality, with an accompanying new sense of flexibility in spatial use. Those attributes extended to the yard as well, where space was equally accommodating to passive and active uses (fig. 5.4). Enough room existed so that extra vehicles (including boats) could be stored, shop and yard equipment housed, gardens cultivated, play equipment installed, or terraces, decks, and porches extended. The backyard became a pri-

vate domain to an extent that only a relatively small percentage of the population had previously known. Indoors and out, the arrangement was conducive to additions and modifications—really individualization—based on fluctuating family size, personal interests, and increased means, among other factors. Far more than was the case in earlier periods of building, the tract house and yard became malleable entities that could express the needs, tastes, and aspirations of their owners.[5]

The distinguishing features of postwar suburban tracts, of course, establish the basis for priorities in any preservation effort. Since the multiplicity of the pattern, the scale of many of the developments, and an ambience of totality through planning are foremost characteristics, the notion that saving this kind of resource can be achieved by retaining a token slice of the whole should be dismissed as being a poor solution, just as it is in any other case where a unified entity is parceled into bits. This maxim holds especially true for the properties in question, given the prevailing sense of open, verdant, informal setting that is so important an attribute. Besides the assemblage of individually owned lots, those parcels set aside for supporting uses—educational, religious, recreational, and commercial—are a key part of the equation. As in any historic district, the whole is greater than the sum of its parts, but here the whole is a landscape, broadly defined, that includes much more than a collection of buildings.

As for the individual properties, when customizing has become an important mark of a development, then it should continue as an ongoing process, yet within parameters that prevent the results from eroding the sense of the greater whole. Such an approach requires a serious rethinking of conventional notions of physical integrity in preservation, but it is, like them, predicated on distinguishing characteristics of significance. Those characteristics must be carefully researched and clearly delineated before any guidelines for treatment are developed. Furthermore, this approach should also include raising the awareness of residents about the value of the original qualities of their houses and yards and about how to introduce

FIG. 5.4. Rear yards in residential development, Wheaton, Maryland, ca. 1950s. (Photo Richard Long-streth, 2002)

modifications that are complementary to them in the way well-developed historic district guidelines do at present. Yet restrictions should not preclude property owners from electing to take another course if they so choose. In this way, a central trait of the postwar suburb's evolution would not be eliminated, while the basic features of the ensemble would be preserved.[6]

Still the question remains, why should preservationists concern themselves with the postwar suburb at all? Why rush the process, particularly when it necessitates some changes in approach and the number of properties is so vast? The answer is simple. These settings demand our attention not just because they represent an extraordinary chapter in the history of the built environment, but also a finite one. By the late 1960s, new steps were being taken in large-scale residential development, spurred by escalating land values and construction costs among other factors. Except for dwellings targeted at upper-income levels, tracts tended to have higher densities than their immediate pre-

cursors. The row house, rechristened the town house, was introduced to outlying areas, not so much as a dwelling of preference as one of economic necessity. The proliferation of interstate highways tended to foster a greater hierarchy of property values and also to bring greater levels of commercial development, some of which emerged as large business centers. The idea that the "average" American family could afford to live in sylvan repose was still perpetrated in real estate advertisements, but became ever less a realistic objective. These trends have intensified during the forty years that have elapsed since then. We cannot entertain the thought of building a postwar suburb today; it would be much too expensive, especially for the middle market that comprised the original clientele. What has long been taken for granted is now an irreplaceable resource.

The postwar suburb is also a threatened resource, although it may not seem that way upon casual observation. Like earlier residential developments, these places tend to face a pivotal point in their lives after the generation that initially occupied them leaves. Assuming no circumstances exist to stimulate premature dispersal, that time span can run between thirty to fifty years.[7] If a new generation of occupants buys into the community with the aim of long-term investment in their houses, then a new, constructive cycle is begun. If, however, perceptions of the community turn negative—a condition real estate appraisers refer to as "stigma"—if newcomers see their purchases simply as hand-me-downs, unwanted by young counterparts to their previous occupants, the area can decline. This phenomenon has little to do with the caliber of the physical fabric. Hundreds of thousands of early-twentieth-century dwellings in cities today are decaying, sometimes to an advanced degree, even though they are far more solidly built than new construction, have well-crafted details, provide commodious accommodations, and afford easy access to a variety of business and recreational locations.

The downward cycle will continue to occur in place after place unless there is intervention. Preservation has proven itself for decades to be among the most effective long-term methods of breaking the pattern of decline and giving new life to valuable assets. But in recent years preservation has failed to expand and encompass anywhere near the extent of places it should address. For every new historic district, many times the number of blocks continue to suffer neglect. This failure stems in part from the public stereotype that preservation is an elite pursuit, concerned with aesthetic niceties, not social necessities. To rectify the situation, preservation needs to assume the mode of conserving nonrenewable resources. The incalculable costs of losing great quantities of our urban fabric, as we do today, need to be emphasized in economic and social terms, not just in the somewhat arcane ones that so often hold forth when it is proclaimed, for instance, that one of a community's best examples of some so-called "style" is threatened.

The postwar suburb is an ideal staging ground for new initiatives that can broaden preservation's agenda because so many of these places are still well maintained and appreciated by their residents. The time is at hand to capitalize on this sentiment and take active steps with communities to ensure that the next wave of residents will understand the value of their acquisitions and invest fully in their future. The challenges are significant because now, like many points elsewhere in the past, the next generation represents a demographic shift and may be led to believe they are only getting second or third best, that theirs is a "used" house whose economic life has become quite limited.

Substantial pressure also may soon exist for more intense development. The postwar suburb long ago ceased being on the urban periphery. Most examples remain intact, but the time may not be too far distant when all that space consumed by yards could be seen as wasteful and pressure mounts to put it to higher and purportedly better uses.

The postwar suburb is a resource that we cannot afford to squander. If we fail to address the issue, it will be tantamount to admitting that much of our residential fabric, no matter how historically significant and no matter how well built, is essentially disposable matter. The comparatively small oases that are historic districts and others predominantly occupied by the affluent will last for generations, renewed by reinvestment at regular intervals, but the great majority of places are destined for a shorter, less productive lives. What does this perpetual state of impermanence say about our cities and about us as a society? Are we capable of doing better? Can we conserve what our parents, grandparents, and even great-grandparents labored to create? Preservation has shown that we can at a modest scale. Just like the housebuilders after World War II, we need to broaden our horizons and expand the scope of operation to have a really decisive impact on the way people live.

6   The Lost Shopping Center

Americans have held a rather pragmatic attitude toward shopping centers since the inception of the type's emergence as a common form of retail development during the post–World War II era. Complexes that drew crowds when they opened and remained magnets of trade for some years thenceforth now lie fallow. After years of declining use, they await either demolition or complete transformation without much public awareness, let alone concern. These were places that served as retail surrogates for the city center, but with none of the same sense of identification or attachment. They are settings the public takes for granted as having outlived their usefulness. No matter how ambitious or important the facility once was, the relic is now viewed as disposable.

The situation is not unalterable, however. Preservation has an almost infinite capacity to change the way people think about the world around them. Prevailing attitudes toward the shopping center once applied to many other forms of the built environment that are now venerated. Among the most obvious examples is the more traditional form of linear commercial development that exists along thoroughfares in communities nationwide. During the 1930s, while many examples were still of recent vintage, "Main Street" became a term of ridicule among architects, planners, retailers, and real estate developers. By the 1940s, if a commercial district was said to be going "Main Street" in the retail trade, it meant that it had ceased to function as a desirable shopping area. Preservation helped to reverse that attitude, not just toward late-nineteenth-century town centers in the heartland, but also toward less ornate neighborhood centers in major cities nationwide. Preservation has further demonstrated that such places can continue to play a worthwhile function in the community. Indeed, one of the most consequential lessons from the successes of the National Trust's Main Street Program and its now numerous offspring is that retail facilities do not have to be extensively remade every generation or so in order to remain competitive.

The need to apply this strategy to more recent work is pressing because most of it is not going to remain otherwise. Traditional Main Streets have survived for one hundred or even one hundred and fifty years. They may become tattered and abused, but the large bulk of their original fabric remains conspicuous and can be a very persuasive element in eliciting popular support. But try to find counterparts from the 1940s or 1950s that remain in comparably recognizable form; most have either been extensively altered or destroyed. The shopping center, and the whole phenomenon of mid-twentieth-century commercial development, need not be a lost resource, one that will vanish with the generation that built it. If the purpose of preservation is to vouchsafe a sense of continuity with significant aspects of the past, we cannot afford to lose a component so central to our collective experience. There is no question that the shopping center is a very important part of our history, as significant in the commercial sphere during the twentieth century as the vertically organized office building or the horizontally organized manufacturing plant. The imperative is to recognize the nature of its significance, and to take active steps to ensure the retention of noteworthy examples.

This chapter initially appeared in *The Forum*, Bulletin of the Committee on Preservation, Society of Architectural Historians, 20 (October 1992): whole issue, and is reprinted here with minor modifications.

The possibilities afforded by such efforts are very promising if initial endeavors give any indication. Just as shopping centers frequently served as catalysts for development when new, so they can stimulate constructive redevelopment today. The earliest such instance of which I am aware occurred during the 1970s and early 1980s with the Nob Hill Business Center (1946) in Albuquerque (fig. 6.1). Neither the complex nor the commercial corridor of which it is a part, along what was once U.S. Route 66, had changed that much. But the area was increasingly neglected and headed for accelerated decay or for new development that would effectively eradicate its past. The preservation alternative proved not only that the restored building could once again function as a magnet for activity, but also foster an ongoing campaign to revitalize the whole precinct. Heritage has become a primary determinant of Nob Hill's economic future.[1]

The resistance to preserving a shopping center initially can be widespread and intense among preservationists no less than among the business community, simply by virtue of the way people tend to view the building type. In Washington, D.C., the Park and Shop (1930) had long been neglected by its owner, who intended to eventually use the land for much denser devel-

opment. Imminent threat of demolition came in 1984 and was not fully resolved until 1991 (fig. 6.2). The issue of building density, far more than the attributes of the building, coalesced neighborhood support for retaining the complex. Yet a number of local preservationists took a dim view of the endeavor, believing that there was nothing historic to save—a viewpoint guided by personal taste and assumptions rather than by knowledge.

As it turned out, the complex proved to be extremely important as the earliest example of any consequence in the United States to fuse the drive-in concept with that of the fully integrated neighborhood shopping center. Considered from a national perspective, the Park and Shop ranks among the most historically significant commercial properties in the metropolitan area. Once the proponents of preservation could delineate in a meticulous way why the complex was so important, the city's Historic Preservation Review Board responded positively. Later, there was no problem securing landmark designation for one of the Park and Shop's first successors, the Massachusetts Avenue Parking Shops (1936), which is among the most intact examples in the metropolitan area in terms of its fabric, tenant mix, and neighborhood setting.[2]

FIG. 6.1. Nob Hill Business Center, Central Avenue, N.E., Albuquerque, New Mexico, Louis Hesselden, architect, 1946. (Photo Richard Longstreth, 1986)

FIG. 6.2. Park and Shop, 3507–23 Connecticut Avenue, N.W., Washington, D.C., 1930, Arthur Heaton, architect; additions 1991 (at right), Bowie-Gridley, architects. (Photo Richard Longstreth, 1991)

The matter of use is central to such undertakings; unless these complexes can remain economically viable, it is unlikely they will be saved. Adaptive use may aid the process, but the best solution is continued use of the building and of the car lot, which is such an integral part of the scheme. Some snickering occurred over the assertion that the latter component of the Park and Shop was historic. Some mandarins of taste repeatedly expressed the urge that this expanse of "unattractive asphalt" be "improved"—with brick paving, with trees, with flower beds, with tables, with kiosks; that is, with what had become the conventional repertoire of the festival market place. Many preservationists do not like to be told that turning a historically significant car lot into a garden can be as egregious as turning a historically significant garden into a car lot, but when the space itself is significant, the change renders it an utterly misleading, false statement about past.

A phenomenon that had an important affect upon efforts to save the Park and Shop was the concurrent revival during the 1980s of the neighborhood shopping center idea in the retail and real estate development industries. Now unflatteringly and incorrectly referred to as strip malls, many of these complexes are the same size and configuration as their progenitors from the 1930s and 1940s. This correspondence suggested that when the location and market were favorable, old examples could serve current purposes just as well as new ones. An important by-product of such an approach is that tenants need not be limited to the sort of peripheral specialty shops that characterize so many preservation projects in the commercial sphere. Fortunately, Douglas Jemal, the developer who undertook the rehabilitation of the Park and Shop in 1991, was able to secure tenants purveying everyday goods and services—not the exact mix that characterized the neighborhood center over half a century ago, but one that is similar in its routine trade orientation. In both this respect and in its historically sensitive appearance, the complex can provide instructive lessons for owners of commercial properties in the adjacent blocks, which are part of the same historic district.

The relationship between appearance and operation is well illustrated by several of the large shopping centers constructed during the interwar decades. The first such project, one that had a profound influence on its successors, was the Country Club Plaza in Kansas City, Missouri (begun 1922).[3] It has long been a trade magnet throughout the greater metropolitan region and also has achieved the status of a city institution—a place that must be visited when in the area. The Plaza's great popularity in part stems from its ornate physical plant. This was a place conceived as a civic fixture and one so unlike the norm that people would want to go there on account of its distinctiveness. But looks are not everything. The physical character of Westwood Village in Los Angeles (begun 1929) was closely patterned after the Plaza. Most of its original buildings remain intact and the location is still a superb one; however, the place has suffered greatly from lackluster management, which has in turn affected the nature of tenancy. Something of the same fate was occurring at Highland Park Village in Dallas, another offspring of the Plaza also begun in 1929.[4] Here, however, a new owner has turned the situation around by capitalizing on the high caliber of the original design, so that the complex is now functioning in a way that parallels its early years. While not the primary factor in generating patronage, the appearance of a place can be an important component when it is an integral part of a sound merchandising strategy, one that takes full advantage of the particulars of the situation.

The extent of the challenge and of the dilemmas faced in such work are well illustrated by the regional shopping mall, which make the difficulties encountered with the Park and Shop seem modest by comparison. Like such large-scale forebears as the Plaza, the regional mall has traditionally functioned well. Some examples also were designed to be memorable places that would foster social interaction as well as trade.[5] Malls entail huge investments in construction and maintenance, and retailers believe that they require substantial renovation every fifteen to twenty-five years if they are to remain competitive. When this practice is not implemented, it is an indication to real estate interests of the need to undertake an entirely different kind of development. In a number of instances, the demographics of an area have changed so that the shopping center is rendered of little or no value (fig. 6.3). In other cases the shopping center has been outdistanced by the competition in nearby locations such that it has become redundant.[6] In yet other situations, the value of the land has become sufficiently great to warrant development of a much higher density. Irrespective of the circumstances, it is now very hard to find a shopping mall or other form of shopping center of any substantial size that was built before the 1970s and has not experienced major alterations. Change has always characterized commercial districts, but it has never before been so integral to the program, so systematic, and so frequent—in short, so thoroughly pervasive. These circumstances mean that even if consumers love a mall, and no matter how important a place it is in their lives, they will likely never come to identify with it as they may a town center. Rather it will be more analogous to a prized automobile, which one assumes must be traded in after it has reached a certain age.

This analogy is not quite right, because unlike "classic" cars, "old" malls are not appreciated as such. A poignant example is afforded by the Parole Plaza just outside Annapolis, Maryland (1960–62) (fig. 6.4). Before this mall was demolished in 2004, fewer and fewer people went there; many merchants had left and none wanted to take their place. There were still a number of good tenants, but the complex had ceased to be a place where people chose to shop. The complex was cast not just as an impediment to progress, but as a potential blighting influence on the community. How could one save a shopping center like Parole Plaza? Its operational success was dependent upon major retailers. How could one convince the leadership of a department store or specialty chain that the place should be restored? How could one convince lending institutions, even in the best of economic times? How could one convince a crit-

FIG. 6.3. East Hills Shopping Center, Robinson Boulevard, Pittsburgh, 1959–60, Charles Roberts, architect; demolished ca. 2002–4. (Photo Richard Longstreth, 2001)

ical mass of the consuming public that this was not a dreary place, but a special environment worth passing down to future generations? Where could one even begin? We have no models, no examples that can be used to illustrate how, if one takes a given course, the outcome may be predicted. From almost any perspective, the venture would seem like a risk of such magnitude that anyone who would even conceive the idea would be summarily dismissed as a member of the lunatic fringe.

When the scale of an undertaking is so large and no precedent exists for projects of its type, a constructive outcome may only be possible when the whole endeavor seems unthreatening from an economic standpoint; that is, when the project does not prevent actions that appear to be much more lucrative. It helps, too, if the project is not too costly and if most of the work that needs to be done is cosmetic. That is how, for example, the Paramount Theatre in Oakland,

California (1930–31), one of the last of the movie palaces to be built, was restored in 1972–73, only some forty years after its completion and at a time when its exuberant Art Deco design was for the most part unappreciated.[7] Indeed, just a few years before, the notion of preserving a redundant, 3,400-seat movie palace of any sort seemed folly from a practical standpoint, and even devotees of the type presumed that most examples would soon disappear. Once the Paramount was restored, however, preserving such a leviathan seemed an eminently sensible way to secure a performing arts center when a strong market for such a facility was identified. One did not have to denature the historic fabric, as was done slightly earlier at Pittsburgh's Heinz Hall; restoration was just as sound an investment.[8]

Perhaps a good candidate for a parallel course of action existed with Shopper's World in Framingham, Massachusetts. Completed in 1951, it was the second regional mall to be realized anywhere and the outgrowth of a project that was unprecedented when it took form in 1946. The architect, Morris Ketchum, was a seminal figure in the early development of the type, and its principal planning consultant, Kenneth Welch, was equally important in establishing the methods by which such facilities became major retail magnets.[9] Shopper's World was the only example from the first generation of regional malls to have survived into the 1990s without significant changes. Historically, it is a work of transcendent importance. From a current real estate development perspective, of course, Shopper's World was a hopeless antique, and it is not surprising that plans began to coalesce in the 1980s to replace the facility. As important as the complex was to the history of architecture, it would do preservation no service to have mounted an all-out offensive once redevelopment plans were well along. No matter how effectively conceived the preservation initiative, it is doubtful whether much would be gained in the end. However, had the poor economic climate continued for an extended period, particularly in the real estate field, an opportunity just might have arisen whereby the existing complex, much like the Paramount, could have been cast as a frugal and engaging alternative to new construction. A large number of retail facilities, including one other regional mall, operate in the same precinct, so that the best marketing initiative might have been not to try to compete on their terms, but to take advantage of the differences and to turn age from a liability to an asset.

Opportunities to preserve shopping malls of the 1950s and 1960s in something approximating their original state have all but vanished. Perhaps it is necessary to go off the beaten track to find a safe proving ground for what remains an unorthodox venture. One such place is Los Alamos, New Mexico, where a virtually unique

FIG. 6.4. Parole Plaza, Solomon Island and Riva roads and Forest Drive, Parole, Maryland, 1960–62, Evantash & Friedman, architects; demolished 2004–5. (Photo Richard Longstreth, 1992)

FIG. 6.5. Los Alamos Center, Los Alamos, New Mexico, ca. 1947–48, W. C. Kruger & Associates, architects. (Photo Richard Longstreth, 1991)

surviving example can be found of the immediate precursors to the regional mall, which were built between the mid-1930s and mid-1940s (fig. 6.5).[10] At that stage, the mall concept was not the child of business interests, but rather of planning reformers, who saw it as one of many necessary ways to separate pedestrian from vehicular traffic and foster a sense of social interaction in community design. The shopping center at Greenbelt, Maryland, was the first of these experimental endeavors; several others were constructed by the federal government during World War II in cases where the private sector could not be induced to build much-needed shopping facilities for defense housing projects. Los Alamos was both the largest and the last of these federally sponsored works, constructed shortly after the war's end.

By 1991, the Los Alamos shopping center remained, but with a high vacancy rate.[11] The distances one had to walk between stores and from one's car may have seemed too great for some consumers, although these were much less than what has long been the standard at regional malls. Many residents appeared to be indifferent to a shopping environment that was seques-

tered and park-like, and activity along the strip nearby was booming. But such circumstances do not pose an insurmountable hurdle. Where there is not much pressure for change and where competitive emporia are some distance removed, with the right tenants and some creative merchandising, one might again make the complex a hub for the community. Such a project also holds the potential to attract tourists, for whom there are few readily accessible vestiges of those years that made the town world famous.

While these scenarios are purely speculative, they need not be taken as wishful thinking. The opportunity still exists to focus on some key complexes developed during the 1970s and 1980s that are major examples and that can probably continue to thrive without major alterations. The Galleria in the Post Oak district of Houston (1969–71, et seq), for example, pioneered the concept of a shopping mall organized on multiple levels along a skylighted pedestrianway, much like the great arcades of the nineteenth century.[12] The complex also broke new ground in its mix of uses, combining major office, hotel, and recreational facilities with the retail center (fig. 6.6). There may be opportunities, too, to retain less singular complexes—ones representing broad patterns in shopping center development—that are situated in places where the pressures for change are not great. The issue at hand is a fundamental one. Can we understand and appreciate the significance of commercial places created after the early twentieth century? If we have that capacity, can we protect important examples, or will this whole episode of our history become something known to future generations only through pictures and words?[13] Can we think of such retail development as more than a short-term phenomenon? Can, indeed, preservation broaden its impact on current development practices—not by fostering some bogus look or atmosphere—but inculcating the idea of developing properties as long-term investments so that their sense of worth is inherent and self-perpetuating?

FIG. 6.6. Galleria, 5015 Westheimer Road, Houston, 1969–71, Gerald Hines, developer; Hellmuth, Obata & Kassabaum, architects; with later additions. (Photo Richard Longstreth, 2000)

III EXTRAORDINARY AND UNKNOWN

St. Frances Cabrini Church, Liturgical Reform, and Historical Association

For New Orleans, St. Frances Cabrini Church is extraordinary as an example of religious architecture, as an example of design and structural innovations, and as an example of the work of Curtis & Davis, the architecture firm that created it (fig. 7.1). In its sophistication, richness, and complexities, including a pronounced dichotomy between the worship space and the exterior, the building ranks among the most significant examples of post–World War II architecture in that city. St. Frances's intrinsic merits and the considerable body of recent scholarship related to examples of religious architecture in the United States enable this church to be examined within a national context as well.

What most of its practitioners and proponents simply referred to as Modern architecture from the 1920s into the 1970s was predicated on broad principles anchored in a search for form, expression, and meaning that was appropriate to the contemporary world. Part of that agenda entailed the rejection of overt references to any period of the past, differentiating this new approach to design from the various strains of eclecticism that had characterized Western architecture since the late eighteenth century and from the classical tradition that had a considerably longer legacy. Modern architecture *could* and often *did* entail oblique ties to the past, as many of its practitioners admired earlier, generally preindustrial, and vernacular traditions of both East and West. But the language of Modern architecture, or avant-garde modernism, was one of abstraction. "Honesty" in the Ruskinian sense was no less important. Materials should express their inherent prop-

erties. At the same time, the structural "honesty" propagated by E. E. Viollet-le-Duc in the mid-nineteenth century was also embraced; materials and the structural systems they comprised should be frankly expressed and could often become a basis for expression. Finally, form and structure should be predicated on function—utilitarian and symbolic. To accommodate contemporary needs, proponents believed, planning should be free from conventional patterns; openness and flexibility would replace the supposed strictures of symmetry and enclosure. New conceptions of form, structure, and materials usage could all serve this function-driven program to create an architecture that was wholly responsive to society, and indeed to manifest society's ideals and aspirations as well as its basic requirements.[1]

The advocates of this modernism were virulently anti-"style," which they equated with eclecticism. In 1932, the Museum of Modern Art's director, Alfred H. Barr Jr., and his assistant, Philip Johnson, along with a guest curator, the architectural historian Henry-Russell Hitchcock, sought to codify what they believed was a maturing, new equivalent to Romanesque, Gothic, or Renaissance architecture: "Modern Architecture"—the title they gave to the exhibition and its catalogue. That same year, Hitchcock and Johnson also published a book that elaborated their thesis, entitling it *The International Style*. That term, however, was vehemently refuted by the architects it lionized. Moreover, avant-garde modernism continued to evolve with increasingly conspicuous variety. When the book was reissued in 1966, Hitchcock

This chapter initially was prepared in January 2007 as part of a URS Group report for FEMA, per the Section 106 review process, and is reprinted here with minor modifications. The church was demolished later that year.

FIG. 7.1. St. Francs Cabrini Church, 5500 Paris Avenue, New Orleans, 1961–64, Curtis & Davis, architects; aerial view, school at right; demolished 2007. (Photo Frank Lotz Miller, ca. 1964. © Curtis & Davis Office Records, Southeastern Architectural Archive, Special Collections Division, Tulane University Libraries)

admitted in the new foreword that his and Johnson's efforts over thirty years earlier had identified a moment, but hardly the broad phenomenon of Modern architecture.[2]

From a historical perspective, scholars now understand that Modern architecture has comprised numerous thrusts—a fact reflected in the profusion of literature that continues to be issued on aspects of the phenomenon globally. Perhaps nowhere was such diversity more pronounced than in the United States during the post–World War II era. This nation had become the world's most powerful, but also its most prosperous. The sweeping generational change that occurred after the war was defined not only by a new mass market, but by people of many persuasions that embraced some form of modernity as emblematic of ascendancy—personal and national.[3] Although it never became

truly popular, avant-garde modernism flourished under these circumstances, with an ever-increasing array of manifestations. Just considering the most recognized "form givers," as the leaders of Modern architecture frequently were called at that time, indicates the remarkable breath of expression—from Frank Lloyd Wright to Ludwig Mies van der Rohe, from Richard Neutra to Buckminster Fuller, from Pietro Belluschi to Marcel Breuer, from Edward Durrell Stone to Bruce Goff, from Walter Gropius to Minoru Yamasaki, from Philip Johnson to Louis Kahn, from Gordon Bunshaft to Eero Saarinen, from Charles Eames to Victor Gruen.[4]

This diversity encompassed more than varied forms of personal expression; it entailed outlooks, methods, theoretical frameworks, and cultural concerns. Underlying this spectrum of design pursuits lay a stunning array of talent that no other country could begin to match during the postwar era. That period ranks among the most innovative in American architecture, when fundamentally new approaches to developing form and space, to the use of structure and materials, and to resolving new and existing programmatic demands were undertaken in a remarkable variety of ways. Far from being understudied, the postwar period has been the subject of some of the most intense and rigorous research in recent decades. A large corpus of scholarly work now exists upon which to place the output of that period in a proper historical context, even if the work in question has not itself been subject to scrutiny.[5]

The Parish

Established in 1952, St. Frances Cabrini parish was named in honor of the first American citizen to be canonized by the Roman Catholic Church, in July 1946. Maria Francesca (St. Frances Xavier) Cabrini (1850–1917) was renowned for her tireless work in founding nearly seventy schools and orphanages throughout the United States, South America, and Europe. Mother Cabrini, as she was widely known, was also the patron saint of immigrants. The circumstances of the parish's founding typified those of the post–World War II era, when large housing tracts were constructed on theretofore sparsely developed land at the metropolitan periphery. These new residential areas manifested long-held dreams among their inhabitants, affording more spacious, comfortable, and well-appointed living quarters than many of their middle-class and prosperous blue-collar forebears had ever known. At the same time, such tracts lay far removed from existing services. The intense drive to establish new houses of worship in these outlying areas stemmed not only from the fact that existing churches and synagogues were far removed, but also out of a desire to create true community centers at a time when places for social interaction outside the home were few in new outlying areas.[6] For Roman Catholics, this concern was all the more pronounced due to the central place of the school in their faith.

From the start, St. Frances Cabrini was conceived as a campus; a ten-acre lot was purchased for school, church, and other facilities, including a rectory and administration center. Located in the Oak Park neighborhood in the Gentilly section of New Orleans, the church drew in large part from subdivisions that had been recently developed or were then in the course of development. Temporary quarters for worship, comprised of two Quonset huts, were assembled on the site in July 1952. The first unit of the school was set to open in September of the following year. The pastor was Monsignor Gerard Frey (1914–2007), a native of New Orleans. Ordained in 1938, Father Frey had been director of the Confraternity of Christian Doctrine since 1946. He became bishop of Savannah, Georgia, in 1967 and of Lafayette, Louisiana, six years later, retiring in 1989. When the original St. Frances Cabrini church edifice opened for services, the parish had between four hundred and five hundred families. Funds for this and subsequent projects were all raised by the parishioners, whose "extraordinary efforts," according to their pastor, also included doing some of the finish work and erecting a temporary cafeteria to serve the school.[7]

One thing about the fledgling compound that was far from typical, however, was the avant-garde design of the school and the other buildings that would later be erected there. In seeking an architect, Father Frey consulted with the head of the Orleans Parish school district, who recommended the still-young firm of Curtis & Davis. Father Frey was receptive to their approach. The resulting design was received enthusiastically by the parish and was an early step in its architects' ascendancy to national prominence. It won a coveted National Honor Award from the American Institute of Architects (AIA) in 1954 and four years later was selected as part of an exhibit for the International Congress of Modern Architecture (CIAM), held in Moscow that year, "to show the Russian people as well as the delegates . . . that America is a land of constant change and experiment."[8]

Curtis & Davis

When they founded their firm in 1946, Nathaniel Cortlandt Curtis Jr. (1917–1997) and Arthur Quentin Davis (1920–2011) were armed with impressive credentials. Curtis's father, Nathaniel senior (1881–1953), was a pioneering architectural educator in the South, starting at the University of North Carolina in 1904, moving to Alabama Technical Institute three years later, and arriving to serve as the first professional head of Tulane's School of Architecture in 1912. After a brief absence, he returned to New Orleans in 1920 to become chief designer for Moise Goldstein, who headed one of the city's largest practices, and to resume his instruction at Tulane, retiring from both positions in 1945.[9] He was also a continual source of inspiration for his son. The younger Curtis entered Tulane's architecture school in 1936, just prior to the shift from its traditional, Beaux-Arts-inspired methods to more modernist ones, a change he enthusiastically embraced. During much of that time, he gained practical experience working for Goldstein. After doing construction work in the U.S. Navy during World War II, Curtis rejoined Goldstein's office before setting up his independent practice. While younger, Arthur Davis had been a classmate at Tulane. He worked for several large New Orleans firms and, during the war, as a field representative for Albert Kahn and Eliel Saarinen in Michigan. Following naval service, he received a master's degree from Harvard University's Graduate School of Design, which was then considered the foremost program in Modern architecture.[10]

Despite their training, Curtis and Davis experienced substantial difficulties in establishing an economically sound practice. Much of the problem stemmed from an unwavering commitment to avant-garde modernism. From the start, the young partners proclaimed that they would accept no commissions unless they could be developed in this vein ("contemporary architecture" was the term they initially used). In a city so steeped in tradition and so conservative it its architectural tastes, such design was generally regarded with suspicion at best, and as heretical by many parties. Throughout much of the South, indeed, Modern architecture was only rarely accepted until the 1960s.[11] The first several years were lean ones for the partners. By 1949, however, the firm of Curtis & Davis began to establish itself as a viable operation, and six years later it boasted twenty-one employees. "The appearance of the venerable city of New Orleans," the editors of *Fortune* noted in a profile of Curtis & Davis that year, "has been changed more by [these] two young architects than by anything else since fire swept the Vieux Carre in 1794."[12]

Curtis & Davis continued its ascendancy, securing commissions for schools, churches, medical facilities, and motor hotels, among other building types. Curtis's design for the New Orleans Public Library (1956–58) was widely acclaimed, winning a design award from *Progressive Architecture* and an Honor Award from the American Institute of Architects (fig. 7.2). In a retrospective account, a reporter for the *New York Times* cast it as a precedent-setting work nationally for libraries that seemed open, accessible, and inviting to the public at large. Locally it was heralded as the one truly distinguished design in the then-new civic center.[13] Other landmark buildings in the urban core followed, most notably the Rivergate exhibition hall (1964–68; demolished 1994) and the Louisiana Superdome (1967, 1971–75). In many other parts of the city, too, the office produced an array of distinguished commercial, institutional, and residential buildings.[14] Well before the firm was disbanded in 1978, it had acquired preeminent status in the city and surrounding region. That reputation has persisted. In 1999 Curtis and Davis were cast in the *Times-Picayune* as "the James Galliers [Senior and Junior] of the epoch. Like the seminal architect[s] who defined Neo-Classicism for New Orleans in the last century . . . Curtis and Davis have defined heroic-scale Mod for New Orleans in this century." Three years later, a plaque was installed in the Superdome honoring Curtis as an "architect of genius," concluding, "Thank you for a Monumental accomplishment.—THE PEOPLE OF LOUISIANA." At the time of his posthumous nomination for the Louisiana AIA Medal of Honor, colleagues described Curtis as "probably the most prominent member of our profession in Louisiana," and "an icon of modern architecture in Louisiana," noting that the "design quality of his firm ... was legendary."[15]

Soon after they began to receive commissions, Curtis and Davis embarked on an aggressive program to publicize their work. At a time when architects were ethically bound to refrain from advertising, the principal means of advancing one's career was through exhibitions, publication of work, and awards. As early as 1950, the firm's designs were presented in the leading national architectural journals, thereafter appearing frequently in *Architectural Forum*, *Architectural Record,* and *Progressive Architecture* through the 1960s. Seven prestigious Progressive Architecture National Design awards and an equal number of National AIA Honor awards were given to Curtis & Davis between 1954 and 1964. Their houses received the National Award of Excellence four times between 1956 and 1960 and won three comparable citations from *House & Home.* Over time, they amassed more than eighty awards given by regional, state, and local organizations, many of which were not Louisiana-based.[16] After being in practice for just over a dozen years, both Curtis and Davis were inducted into the AIA's College of Fellows in 1961 and 1959, respectively.[17]

National publicity and professional stature helped the firm secure major commissions outside the region, some of them abroad. In 1956, the Department of State's Office of Foreign Building Operations commissioned Curtis & Davis to prepare plans for the U.S. Embassy in Saigon as part of that agency's program to show the best in American design talent abroad. The following year, the Paris-based, internationally prominent journal *Architecture d'aujourd'hui* featured Curtis and Davis among twelve promising young U.S. architects in a worldwide survey. In 1960, work began on the $31-million medical center for the Free University in Berlin, which was likewise seen as a showcase of American architectural prowess.[18] At home, IBM, a corporation committed to fostering high design standards in

FIG. 7.2. New Orleans Public Library, 219 Loyola Avenue, 1956–58, Curtis & Davis, architects. (Photo Richard Longstreth, 2011)

its buildings, secured plans from Curtis & Davis for offices in Shreveport, Mobile, and Trenton (New Jersey), and for a major facility in Pittsburgh. A much-praised sequel to the New Orleans Public Library built in Worcester, Massachusetts, and a hotel in Hartford, Connecticut's Constitution Plaza, were among the numerous other out-of-state projects realized by the mid-1960s.[19] By that time, too, a New York office was established, with others subsequently set up in Los Angeles, London, and Berlin. Probably no other Southern-based architectural firm had ever attained such broad geographical practice or attracted so much national recognition.

As a strategy for the firm, Curtis and Davis embraced innovation in their projects whenever possible. No house style emerged because the partners and their associates alike resisted becoming subjected to such convention. A lengthy profile of the office published in *Interiors* emphasized that the principals "follow no easy formulas. Each job, particularly each job in a new category [i.e., a building type with which they had not previously worked], is undertaken with a great deal of research into specialized problems. Obvious design solutions are questioned; pat answers discarded for new approaches, new solutions.... Dissent is encouraged and discussion is frequent. . . . Research, experimentation, innovation, and trials are as important to their design work as actual planning and specifying."[20]

Much of that energy was channeled in the organization of space, as at the Thomy Lafon School (1952–53; demolished 2011) (fig. 7.3), where classrooms were raised on pilotis and corridors were eliminated to conserve outdoor recreation space on a constrained site—a configuration that also recalls the raised main floors enveloped by open galleries of the region's large, French Colonial plantation houses. The scheme attracted national attention, not just for its arresting appearance, but also for its pragmatic, climate-sensitive arrangement—all developed for low-income African American children at a time when educational facilities available to them usually offered few amenities.[21] Replacing what was considered one of the worst prisons in the country, the Louisiana State Penitentiary at Angola (1953–55) broke new ground and attracted national attention in providing forty gradations of prisoner groups, divided by age, behavior, severity of offense, race (in a still segregated society), and other factors—all in a dispersed plan of airy, small-scale, economical pavilions. The horizontal arrangement, too, was praised for the clarity of its spatial organization at Lakewood Hospital at Morgan City, Louisiana (1955–56).[22]

Curtis & Davis proved equally adept at structural innovation. Sometimes the solution was a minimalist one, governed by a tight budget. At St. Frances Cabrini School, for example, the structure was reduced to steel columns supporting lightweight steel trusses, the perimeter enclosed by sliding glass doors, glass jalousies, and brick end walls. At the Immaculate Conception Church in Marrereo (1956–58), a New Orleans suburb, the sanctuary was enveloped by an enormous roof of lightweight, pie-shaped panels of structural steel preassembled onsite and lifted into place.[23]

Later work was more structurally audacious. The firm abandoned a precedent of over seventy years by eliminating the skeletal frame in its thirteen-story IBM Building (1961–63) in Pittsburgh's Gateway Center redevelopment area. Here the structure was comprised of the central utility core's casing and the lattice-pattern, steel-truss exterior walls, each of which rested on only two supports (fig. 7.4). Developed by the distinguished, Seattle-based structural engineer John Skilling (1922–1998), working closely with the architects, the scheme allowed steel to be employed with unusual efficiency, providing an unbroken interior space of 54 by 27 feet on each floor. Skilling subsequently adapted the concept for the Twin Towers at the World Trade Center in New York (1963–76; destroyed 2001).[24] Curtis & Davis developed an entirely different system for the twenty-four-story Louisiana National Bank headquarters in Baton Rouge (1965–68), where eight enormous exterior columns carried much of the load.[25] The firm again teamed up with Skilling for the Rivergate exhibition hall, devising a novel use of prestressed reinforced concrete for a thin-shell (4½-inch) roof formed by curvilinear barrel

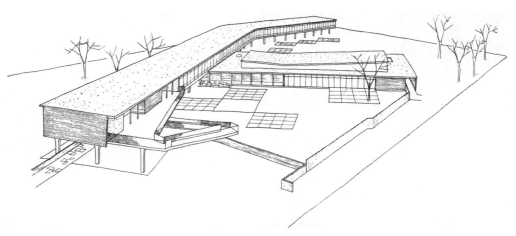

FIG. 7.3. Thomy Lafon School, 2601 7th Street, New Orleans, 1952–53, Curtis & Davis, architects; demolished 2011. (*Architectural Forum*, April 1953, 132)

arches held in place by a post-tension system that allowed an unprecedented span of over 250 feet between supporting, tapered columns (fig. 7.5).[26] The Louisiana Superdome, designed by a team with Curtis as project director, was not only the largest domed structure in the world; it had an unusual degree of flexibility in its seating, which could be configured for conventions, basketball, hockey, and other events as well as for football and baseball games. Here the dome, with a surface area of nine acres, was comprised of a complex lamella system of skewed steel trusses forming a diamond pattern—the resulting web held in place by an enormous tension ring set above the supporting columns.[27]

Given the firm's engagement in creating innovative, sometimes bold, structural solutions, their concurrent concern for the historic character of the city might seem surprising. Yet maintaining a sense of continuity with tradition was a strong lynchpin of their approach. Curtis's father wrote a pioneering history of early New Orleans architecture in 1933 and had been intimately involved in preserving some of the city's landmarks, as well as serving on the state committee of the Historic American Buildings Survey.[28] His focus on impressions—on the character of the city and quest to identify the components that were central to that character—had a lasting impact on his son. Indeed, the firm took pride in showing how many of their designs drew from local precedent—an unusual practice among the avant-garde. Early on the partners realized that emphasizing their reinterpretation of New Orleans vernacular building traditions helped win over potential clients who might be prone to consider Modern architecture too radical an approach for the buildings they wanted. Visual links to a venerated past could indeed help persuade people to accept a Curtis & Davis design that in other respects represented more pronounced departures from convention than they might allow under different circumstances. But these ties were born not just out of personal interest or out of an astute marketing strategy; they were founded on practicality, addressing climatic conditions that were often oppressive, sometimes before air-conditioning could be made an integral part of the building's systems. In discussing method, Davis remarked: "We find that [this] sincerity of approach is appreciated by our clients, but, in many instances, they become absorbed by the same spirit and not only become better clients because of this, but demand better buildings."[29]

In response to the local climate, screens, arcades, pilotis, and patios all became common features of Curtis & Davis buildings. Yet the use of these elements never lapsed into cliché or a purely aesthetic device in large part due to the project-specific rationality of their use. Patios, for example, became an integral component of

FIG. 7.4. IBM Building, 60 Boulevard of the Allies, Pittsburgh, 1961–63, Curtis & Davis, architects. (Photo Frank Lotz Miller, ca. 1963. © Curtis & Davis Office Records, Southeastern Architectural Archive, Special Collections Division, Tulane University Libraries)

the firm's residential work at an early date (fig. 7.6). While inspired by the rear courts of houses in the Vieux Carre, they were used to maximize cross ventilation and a sense of spatial openness as well as to give privacy on constrained sites. Moreover, these enclosed outdoor spaces were treated in a variety of ways in their materials as well as in their relationships with paths of circulation and with the indoor spaces beyond. Collectively, as a result, this work avoided being merely variations on a theme.[30] Curtis & Davis also used courtyards to varied effect in public buildings, such as the Medical Plaza complex (1959–60), where they became esplanades connecting offices, or at the New Orleans Public Library, where they afforded cloistered retreats that also allowed large amounts of natural light to penetrate two levels of interior space. Screens assumed a variety of forms—as operating metal louvers at the Lakewood Hospital; as open-ended, intricately detailed metal filigree at the New Orleans Public Library (an updated version of the city's profuse iron porches and balconies); as rhythmically patterned clay tiles enframed as horizontal layers at the Caribe Building (1957–58).[31] Irrespective of the elements used, Curtis & Davis's work was generally imbued with a varied palette of materials, textures, and colors that suggested the sumptuousness of

FIG. 7.5. Rivergate exhibition hall, Canal and Poydras streets and Mississippi River, New Orleans, 1964–68, Curtis & Davis, architects; demolished 1995. (Photo Frank Lotz Miller, ca. 1968. © Curtis & Davis Office Records, Southeastern Architectural Archive, Special Collections Division, Tulane University Libraries)

effect found in so much of the city's nineteenth-century architecture, from the Vieux Carre to the Garden District. This new work at once recalled and contrasted with its urban environment, collectively adding to the rich layers of the city's development in a multifaceted way.

As part of this distinguished legacy, the church of St. Frances Cabrini ranks among the most significant, for it is among the most synthetic of the firm's strongest design attributes. It is innovative in plan and no less so in structure. At the same time, it is deferential in scale and character to the residential community in which it stands. Finally, the building is imbued with a character that renders it a quintessential embodiment of the special qualities that have long distinguished New Orleans. This response is made in a stunningly singular way that renders St. Frances Cabrini a unique landmark of

FIG. 7.6. Curtis house, 6161 Marquette Place, New Orleans, ca. 1962–63, Curtis & Davis, architects. View of living room and adjacent patio. (Photo Richard Longstreth, 2011)

distinction in the city. Perhaps only the New Orleans Public Library, in very different ways, matches the coalescence of qualities found here. As was characteristic of Curtis & Davis's work, pragmatic concerns served as the springboard for the solution. With the design of the new house of worship for St. Frances Cabrini these concerns emanated to a significant degree from the drive for liturgical reform in the Roman Catholic Church.

Liturgical Reform and Church Architecture in the 1950s and 1960s

The liturgical reform movement within the Roman Catholic Church spanned over half a century. Prior to his death in 1914, Pope Pius X pressed for substantive changes in the liturgical function. After World War I, the concern for reform was more intensely pursued, especially in Germany, and after World War II became widespread in northern Europe.[32] Central to this effort was the belief that the clergy and the ceremonies they performed needed to reengage with the congregation. For a millennium, Christian celebration had become overritualized, the argument ran, with the segregation of clergy and congregation ever more pronounced. To change this situation, many believed that the Church needed to return to earlier practices when the congregation more actively participated in services. To affect these changes, the altar should not be at the end of a long chancel but rather in a sanctuary that was open to the nave, with the priest facing his flock while conducting the service. The linearity of traditional basilican and cruciform plans likewise tended to remove the congregation; arrangements that facilitated proximity of all congregants to the altar should be developed instead. Many Catholics in the United States were slow to embrace such ideas, but the need for change had gained considerable momentum by the late 1950s. Even in this country, then, the reform measures of Vatican II did not originate with that conclave, but were rather codified there.

Modern architecture was seen among advocates of liturgical reform as a potentially great liberating device. A traditionalist approach to design only perpetrated what they held to be archaic ritual. Edward Sutfin, a prominent priest and scholar, and Maurice Lavanoux, editor of the New York–based *Liturgical Arts,* emphasized that "even if we could duplicate a medieval cathedral, stone by stone, we would still be unable to relive the spirit of its age. Our copy would be no more than a curiosity . . . rather than living architecture." Otto Spaeth, a founder and past president of the Liturgical Arts Society, was even more blunt: in a historicizing church, he noted, the "clear implication is that God does not exist today; he is made out to be a senile old gentleman dwelling among the antiques of his residence, one whom we visit each week out of sentiment and then forget since he obviously has no relation to the normal part of our lives." But advocates were of two minds about a radical change in architectural expression. "Modern art," cautioned Bishop Robert Dwyer of Nevada, "has developed in a prevailing atmosphere of secularism, and has been predominantly concerned to create forms which reflect only too clearly the functionalism of industry and the extreme personalism of the artist." Likewise, attempts to break from tradition simply by pursuing designs that looked different were condemned. Creating dramatic effects with "crazy sweeping roofs, tall narrow windows," and the like, observed one critic, were "tricks [that] do not represent a true expression of our Christian vision."[33] If bold new approaches were based primarily on aesthetic concerns of the designer then the product would be ill-suited to the underlying, spiritual purpose of reform.

Instead, change must be driven by the liturgy. "Many of our building problems," Sutfin and Lavanoux argued, "can be solved by a return to first principles based upon the liturgy—that is, art in its relation to, and in the service of, the living liturgical community," adding, "the historically traditional norms set forth in pontifical rites for liturgical functions give sufficient indication for an architecture basic to the expression of the *Civitas Dei* [City of God] without thereby determining any particular type of style of building."[34] Enumerating the imperatives of reform, Bishop Dwyer asserted: "*We have to think of a structure designed for the altar, rather than the altar designed for the structure.*" The "altar of sacrifice" should be "the immediate focus of the family of Christ gathered around it and participating in its divine action." "The client," wrote architect Patrick Quinn, "is the Mystical Body of Christ, and if architecture is to provide a place with which such a client can identify Itself, he must understand it fully." A "passing acquaintance with the ritual form of the ceremonies" would not suffice. The hierarchy of spatial order was a key factor in the equation. The baptistery, "symbolizing man's entry into Christ," should be second only in importance to the altar. Furthermore, circulation patterns should be predicated on communion and processions at Easter, Christmas, and other holy occasions, not just on facilitating routine access and egress. The manipulation of light should underscore this liturgical order. The architect's responsibility, James Cardinal Lercaro concluded, was to "understand well the elements of sacredness. . . . primarily sincerity expressed in the clear and thorough line of the design and in the adherence to it of all structural and decorative elements. Any tinseling, any overstructure, any deceitful or artificial effects . . . betray a lack of sincerity."[35]

Yet the new church should not be a Spartan thing. "The liturgy," cautioned one observer, "is often in danger of being intellectually considered," and thus interpreted by architects "only in its coldly objective and impersonal aspect. We feel this," he continued, "in many 'functional' churches, where the festive character of the celebration is not properly favored," with "everything around the altar, and in the nave . . . too dryly systematized." "The liturgy," he concluded "is a very rich, complex, organic reality. It needs a setting of great simplicity, but also of genuine freedom and calm beauty." Too much emphasis was generally given to the exterior of the church, to give it a public face of power and beauty, but this was really a "medieval idea." The new church should be a "real human house," that "calls the faithful together and takes them out of the routine of everyday life in order to introduce them into a world whose rules and values—without being totally abstracted from the world of material realities—are altogether new and different." Thus the church was in fact a home—"home of the celebration, home of the community, home of the Eucharistic presence."[36]

To advance their objectives, advocates of liturgical reform stressed a reintegration of the arts in church edifices. Catholic houses of worship, critics charged, had long been beleaguered by poorly designed, ritualistic paraphernalia—meaningless echoes of the rich artistic embellishment that had made churches of earlier periods whole. For at least a century, critics maintained, church art had been debased by the factory, "where the baroque and pseudo-baroque prototypes of statues and paintings of Christ, the saints, and Old Testament characters are stiffened or made yet more sickly sweet by the process of machine mass production"—a process in which the "final horror . . . has been achieved by the use of plastics and tricky gadgetry." These "lifeless banalities" should be replaced by "the works of contemporary genius." Father Pierre Marie-Alain Couturier, who had spearheaded such a campaign in France, intoned that "for more than a century, imagination . . . has remained completely outside of, and alien to, the Church. Life withdrew from the Church." Life today, he continued, lies "among those who are . . . the true masters of living art. . . . when rebirth is in question, one needs life which is as vigorous as the preceding decay has been long and profound. . . . lesser talents would never suffice." Such work should play a central role in the program. To balance the simplicity of Modern architecture, Lavanoux advised, sculpture, stained glass, metalwork, and other means of iconographic expression should be developed as integral parts of the scheme: "All the arts [should be] brought into play to infuse the whole with that warmth which makes a church truly the House of God." At the same time, others cautioned, the results should be "sober," without excessive display of stained glass, frescoes, sculpture, or tapestries. Too often such fittings could overwhelm the altar or even the worship space in its entirety.[37]

The means by which the ideas of liturgical reform should be manifested architecturally were, not surprisingly, subject to differing interpretations. At a time when many Catholic parishes in the United States were leery of venturing too far into unknown realms and the design of many Catholic institutions was undertaken by members of that faith who specialized in such work, the Benedictine Order set important precedents with several, much publicized projects: St. John's Abbey Church in Collegeville, Minnesota (1958–61), designed by Marcel Breuer; St. Mary and St. Louis Priory Chapel at Crevecoeur, Missouri (1957–62), designed by Hellmuth, Obata & Kassabaum (HOK); and the Church of the Priory of St. Gregory the Great in Portsmouth, Rhode Island (1957–61), designed by Pietro Belluschi.[38] Among the architects, only Belluschi had experience in designing houses of worship, but most of that work was for Protestant denominations and was part of a broad, general practice. Each firm was chosen for its excellence in design and its responsiveness to the Benedictines' reform agenda. The three buildings also underscored the spectrum of approaches that could positively manifest the imperatives of liturgical reform.

Trapezoidal in plan, with a seating capacity of 1,700, St. John's was enclosed by a series of gargantuan, tapered concrete bents, connected to form a bearing wall—all pirouetting on beams supported by triangular masonry piers—a structural tour de force inside and out. Fronted by a commensurately gigantic and sculptural campanile, the complex ranks among the most monumental and insistently abstract works of religious architecture of the period. The much smaller St. Louis Priory Chapel was also designed using structure as a basis of expression, with a circular plan, altar at the center, and enclosed by two tiers of fanning, thin-shell, parabolic arches, affording a sense of lightness and transparency. By contrast, Belluschi eschewed conspicuous plays of structural determinism in his churches, while he sought abstractly to anchor them to tradition through his use of form and materials. At the Portsmouth chapel he used a centralized plan defined by alternating, inward-curving stone walls and wood partitions. The space was framed by a simple post-and-beam system supporting an octagonal drum of stained glass window strips and wood infill—the whole conveying an effect of both simplicity and richness. All three houses of worship shared an underlying commonality: exterior form was a direct result of the spatial configuration and the materials used to achieve it inside.

Roman Catholic cathedrals and parish churches constructed during the 1950s tended to be much more reserved in expression and conservative in plan and sometimes in imagery as well. For nearly a decade after World War II, many new Catholic houses of worship were designed in a historicizing vein that differed little from work of several decades prior.[39] The National Shrine of the Immaculate Conception in Washington, D.C. (1954–59) employed a "Byzantine and Romanesque" design developed in 1919; the Cathedral of St. Mary Our Queen in Baltimore (1957–59) was an updated rendition of English Gothic.[40] Modernity was sometimes embraced in a vein that advocates of Modern architecture derided as "modernistic"—a variation on classicizing Art Deco work of the 1930s. Described as "truly timely, truly Catholic," the Cathedral of St. Joseph in Hartford, Connecticut (1959–62) (fig. 7.7), was an exuberant amalgam of this somewhat streamlined classicism and medievalizing elements, while the Sacred Heart Cathedral in Salina, Kansas (1951–53), was a massive, sculpted rendition of the great terminal grain elevators of that region.[41] Mainstream views toward church art likewise remained conservative, finding fundamental spiritual as well as aesthetic fault with the work of the avant-garde.[42] A few parish churches had broken from the fold in both their arrangement and imagery, but they often tended to be cast somewhat in the mold of large public auditoria, a tendency many reformers deplored because of its secular overtones. Many others adopted at least some aspects of avant-garde modernism in their appearance, but remained traditional in their plans.[43] As a result, Albert Christ-Janer and Mary Mix Foley included no postwar U.S. examples in their *Modern Church Architecture* of 1962, then the most detailed and broad-based volume on the subject.[44] By that time, some change was beginning to occur. Maurice Lavanoux seems to have been especially partial to Breuer's work.

Additional examples he selected for his influential *Liturgical Arts* magazine nonetheless, tended to be much more reserved—elegant rectangular boxes imbued with a lyrical minimalism, perhaps inspired by recent examples in Germany and Switzerland where liturgical reform was well established.[45]

Aside from the Benedictine chapels, all three still under construction in 1960, little precedent existed for a Catholic parish church in the United States that would fully embody the spirit of liturgical reform when the design of St. Frances Cabrini commenced. Indeed, completed examples from any denomination, the configuration of which was appropriate to its liturgical program, were relatively few.[46] As with any period of fundamental change, without a recognized paradigm, the responses continued to be

FIG. 7.7. Cathedral of St. Joseph, 140 Farmington Avenue, Hartford, Connecticut, 1958–62, Eggers & Higgins, architects. (Photo Richard Longstreth, 2008)

of a highly varied nature well after the acceptance of liturgical reform became widespread. That situation was not necessarily a detrimental one, as an informed observer noted a decade later: "Today's church is a full orchestration of all the elements that create a living, moving symphony of forms, no longer frozen in dogma and ritual, but released in the warm light of the new era. In this light, the apparent vagueness of the Vatican directive has been a master stroke in ensuring, hopefully for all time, the continuing totality of the church interior."[47] In developing the design for St. Frances Cabrini, the circumstances were ripe for Curtis, as partner-in-charge, to break new ground.

The Church Edifice

The site for St. Frances Cabrini was determined by Curtis & Davis when preparing plans for the school. Designing the church edifice began in earnest around the latter months of 1959 or the early months of 1960 as overcrowding in the temporary quarters became severe. The preliminary scheme was unveiled in May 1960 and given the first round of approval by the Archdiocesan Building Commission that August. A drive to raise $640,000 for the $1,000,000 project was launched by Father Frey, who enlisted some five hundred of his parishioners in the campaign. Nearly half the target amount had been gathered by the following March, as development of the working drawings neared completion. Two months later Father Frey was authorized to accept a revised low bid of $924,000; construction began shortly thereafter.[48]

When the building was dedicated on 21 April 1963, Monsignor Henry C. Bezou declared in his sermon that it bespoke "authority, clarity, and simplicity." "Authority," he explained, "is evident in the church's strong lines, clarity in its light interior, which contrasts with the dark churches of old." On the last point, he elaborated: "We need simplicity in our churches. There is so much pretense in today's world; there are so many false facades, so much meretricious decoration and cheap veneer. Simplicity is achieved in this church because all lines lead to the altar, pillars are absent, side altars are in separate rooms and all the clutter and cheap commercial statues, lamp stands, and shrines have given way to the simple, striking basic furnishings." Archbishop John Patrick Cody pronounced it the "Cathedral of the Lakefront," adding: "Many times I have knelt at St. Peter's Basilica at the Ecumenical Council my mind wandered across the sea and I wondered how this building would look when complete. It is a thing of beauty."[49] Indeed, all parties involved appear to have been immensely pleased with the product. Church and local newspapers stressed that the design was state of the art in its manifestation of liturgical reform practices, allowing a seated congregation of 1,200 people to be no farther than 102 feet from the altar, half the distance commonly found in worship spaces of comparable capacity. Some twelve months previous, the Church Architectural Guild of America had given two of its eight annual awards for design excellence to the scheme and to Curtis & Davis's earlier Immaculate Conception Church. In 1964 the worship space of St. Frances Cabrini was the opening illustration in a cover story on new directions in church architecture in *Fortune*. Most important, the maturing parish now had a permanent home that stood as an area landmark, with a worship space that underscored the intimate relation between the members and the instruments of their faith.[50]

According to Arthur Davis, the first studies for the church were developed along relatively conventional lines. Father Frey, however, urged Curtis and his project associate, Sidney Folse, to revise their approach so that it might be fully in the spirit of the ongoing move toward liturgical reform.[51] The new scheme was a pronounced departure and indeed an unorthodox one in church design of the period. The plan is not in the shape of a modified Greek cross, a circle, or a polygon—then the standard alternatives to a longitudinal configuration—but rather like an auditorium, fan-shaped, here with its central axis set at forty-five degrees to the square formed by the enclosing walls (fig. 7.8). Consciously or otherwise, Curtis's basic organization is akin to that found in numerous Protestant churches, especially Congregational and Methodist ones, from the late nineteenth century that were part of the evangelical drive to bring congregants in closer to the minister and service rituals.[52] Curtis's design, however, is quite unlike such predecessors in avoiding other theatrical analogies: it does not have a sloping floor, a large gallery, or an altar set on a stage. Nor does the interior suggest civic auditoria of more recent years.[53] In contrast to the vast spaces associated with large auditorium-plan churches, the seating area at St. Frances Cabrini was given a sense of intimacy by being subtly divided into three "naves," each with a central aisle and with common side aisles between them. The elongated hexagonal arrangement of pews in each nave allowed them to converge at the sanctuary while opening space for confessionals toward the rear. Each nave is entered through its own three portals in a screen of wooden slats and plexiglass infill that separates the worship space from the entry corridor, which, in turn, forms an arc spanning the north and east sides of the building (fig. 7.9). The baptistery lies on the main, diagonal axis with the altar, underscoring its key liturgical role.

Each nave is spatially defined by a thin-shell, shallow, barrel-vaulted, concrete roof that mirrors its pew configuration (fig. 7.10; see also fig. 7.8). The shells come close to convergences near the altar at one end and, at the other, two of the shells extend beyond the worship space to form shelters for the principal entries. The shells pivot on four concrete columns set at the widest portion of the nave, with six smaller tie columns placed just beyond the screen enclosing the worship space. With two of the four support columns integrated with partition side walls, the worship space seems virtually uninterrupted. The use of these shells stemmed in part from Father Frey's request that a memory image of the Quonset huts, of which he and his flock had grown fond over the preceding decade, be a significant part of the design. Their arcuated form could enhance the acoustical properties of a large space, but this system also enabled a sizable area to be spanned with minimal visual intrusion at a reasonable cost and with a maximum degree of structural efficiency. Furthermore, the shells fostered a sense of spatial drama. Not only was their polygonal configuration unusual, so was the extent of their cantilevers, projecting with a slight incline some 64 feet outward and rising at a much more acute angle toward the altar.

At the time of its conception, the use of thin-shell concrete construction was still unusual for a church and for most other building types in the United States. Unlike a true barrel vault, which requires closely spaced vertical supports along its edges, the shell form acts like a beam and therefore is capable of long spans. The curvature minimizes the amount of materials used and, as a result, the structural load that requires support. The inherent logic in concrete shell construction, coupled with the plasticity it enabled in both form and space, made it a favored system among champions of avant-garde design. Yet at the time St. Frances Cabrini was designed, most applications in this country had been for airplane hangars, industrial plants, and other utilitarian buildings. The exploration of thin-shell concrete construction for civic, institutional, and religious buildings remained at an early stage.[54] The boldly cantilevered version developed for St. Frances Cabrini was quite unusual nationwide and unique in New Orleans when it was conceived in 1960. In all likelihood, it was adapted from one created a quarter century earlier by Eduardo Torroja (1899–1961), among the most famous structural engineers of the twentieth century, for his iconic Zarzuela Hippodrome in Madrid (1935).[55]

At St. Frances Cabrini, a separate structure, no less dramatic in effect and economical in design than the fan of cantilevered shells, is the "tower base" that defines the sanctuary, consisting of four tapered concrete arches in the shape of splayed parabolas that converge to form a domical cap above the altar (fig. 7.11). This latter-day baldachin, in turn, provides the base for a needle-like steel spire that rises 135 feet to form the most conspicuous exterior component of the building. The internal effect is accentuated by a third structure that envelops the sanctuary around its sides and rear as a semicircular, coffered concrete slab tied to the baldachin and supported by fourteen round columns, most of which rise behind an intricate metal screen that also fronts the choir and organ. Yet a fourth

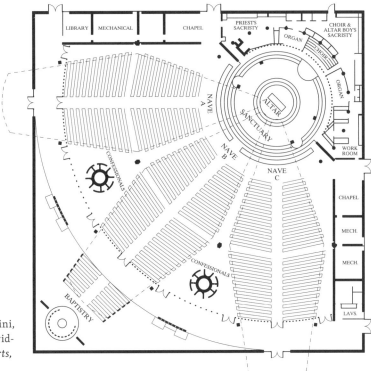

FIG. 7.8. St. Frances Cabrini, plan. (Drawing by Paul Davidson, 2013, after *Liturgical Arts*, February 1965, 55)

FIG. 7.9. St. Frances Cabrini, nave and sanctuary from entry corridor. (Photo Frank Lotz Miller, ca. 1964. © Curtis & Davis Office Records, Southeastern Architectural Archive, Special Collections Division, Tulane University Libraries)

FIG. 7.10. St. Frances Cabrini,
sanctuary, looking toward nave.
(Photo Frank Lotz Miller, ca. 1964.
© Curtis & Davis Office Records,
Southeastern Architectural
Archive, Special Collections Divi-
sion, Tulane University Libraries)

structural system consists of concrete beams that are tied to the shells' main support columns and to the outer walls. These beams support the flat roof that extends between the shells. Curtis and Folse worked closely with John Skilling in developing this unusually complex structural ensemble. As with many other architects, they appreciated the engineer's technical prowess, but also his instinctive ability to think like a designer and to seek bold solutions that would meet programmatic objectives.[56] Yet despite the prominence of its structural attributes, the design was not structurally driven. Rather structural solutions were devised to address the symbolic, spiritual, and practical needs of the congregation. Here the goals of liturgical reform—a freestanding altar upon which the entire worship space was focused, connectivity between the clergy and congregation, a sense of community (with the church as the house of God and of His children), a sense of shelter and quietude and of separation from the outside world—were all important consider-

ations. "The result," Curtis wrote in retrospect, was "an honest expression of the activities that occur within, utilizing a forthright statement of the structural system[s] and the materials employed. It was a church unlike any that had been built before."[57]

In meeting these objectives, the design also sought to integrate work in allied arts throughout the premises, commensurate with that objective of the liturgical reform movement. The semicircular bronze screen enframing the altar, comprised in part of elongated crosses, is matched by a more opaque one defining the baptistery at the opposite end of the principal axis (fig. 7.12). There, extending to a circular skylight, bars alternate with fins performed in abstract patterns that suggest fish. A large mahogany figure of Christ triumphant—not crucified—the creation of a woodcarver from New Iberia, Louisiana, was suspended above the altar. The stained glass, by contrast, was ordered from the Paris studio of Maurice Max-Ingrand, a long-renowned manufacturer.[58] All of these embellishments reflected the concerns of liturgical reform; they remained subordinate to the altar, the worship space, and the activities that are housed in accordance with the priorities of that reform. The importance of such work nevertheless was underscored when the diocesan building committee, which held the responsibility of financial oversight, demanded that goldleafing the underside of the baldachin be eliminated to reduce costs. The subtle, luminous effect of gold leaf was considered to be so important, however, that several members of the Curtis & Davis office and a number of parishioners joined forces after hours to execute the work themselves.[59]

For all its responsiveness to the imperatives of liturgical reform, St. Frances Cabrini was a decidedly singular design. Unlike most Catholic and other houses of worship that embraced avant-garde modernism of the period, it did not have a single, dominant structural system, but several that were related in a complex manner. Defying more than clarifying how the building was held solidly in one piece, the assemblage of structural components ran against the prevailing predilection for visual rationality.[60] Likewise, the exuberance of arcuated, cantile-

vered, and coffered slab forms, accentuated by art, affords a sense of sumptuousness that challenged the reform trend for restraint. While abundant natural light was a nearly pervasive concern for houses of worship at that time, St. Frances Cabrini's exterior sources of illumination were muted by comparatively small window areas of stained glass, limited to those places enframed by the outer ends of, and to small strips beneath, the shells. All these characteristics contributed to a sense of mystery and awe—a church that was at once intimate and welcoming, vigorous and sensual.

The effect was too much for Lavanoux, who found the interior "a bit gaudy," adding in a rather patronizing way that perhaps the "weather in New Orleans may have something to do with the architectural exuberance of this church, in contrast to the order, discipline, and liturgical *sense* of [Breuer] churches in Michigan and Minnesota."[61] While Lavanoux preferred the muscularity of Breuer's work or the somewhat repetitive lyricism of HOK's St. Louis Priory, he sensed, but did not understand, how St. Frances Cabrini was a subtle, sophisticated embodiment of the interweaving of emotions,

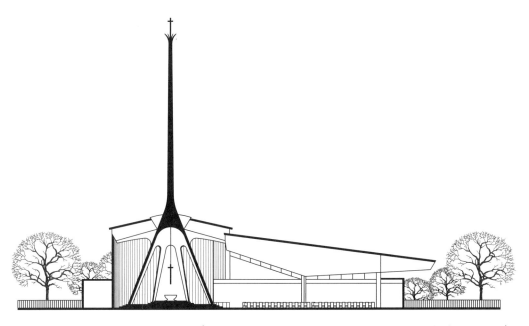

FIG. 7.11. St. Frances Cabrini, section. (Drawing by Paul Davidson, 2013, after print in author's possession)

FIG. 7.12. St. Francis Cabrini, baptistery. (Photo Frank Lotz Miller, ca. 1964. © Curtis & Davis Office Records, Southeastern Architectural Archive, Special Collections Division, Tulane University Libraries)

sentiments, and passions that have long characterized New Orleans culture. Writing thirty years earlier, Curtis's father observed: "The composite face of New Orleans is an old face and a young face, worn, and some think repellent, in places, but fair and sweet and good to look up in others. But whether worn or fresh it is an interesting face, a face of charm and character."[62] St. Frances Cabrini was all new—strikingly new—yet suggested the complexities of the city's "charm and character" perhaps as much as any other twentieth-century building.

Not the least of those complexities was the dichotomy between indoors and out. The vast majority of Modern churches utilized structure as a basis for expression on the exterior as well as on the inside. Among architects and the general public, probably the most celebrated—and controversial—example was the design by Walter Netsch of Skidmore, Owings & Merrill for the Air Force Academy Chapel near Colorado Springs (1955–63), consisting of seventeen "spires" of six interlocking tetrahedrons each.[63] But irrespective of denomination, locale, or materials employed, structure as the leitmotif of the new house of worship was a pervasive tendency in the United States and in many places abroad as well. Sometimes the effect was delicate and transparent, as with Lloyd Wright's iconic Wayfarer's Chapel (1946–51) in the Palos Verdes district of Los Angeles, where an intricate redwood frame and large expanses of glass rose on a rugged, mountainous site transformed into a lush garden. Richard Neutra's Community Church at Garden Grove, California (1960–62), was scarcely less transparent, but shaped as a great, hangar-like hall of steel and glass. On the other side of the equation was Breuer's St. Francis de Sales in Muskegon, Michigan (1964–66), a windowless citadel of massive, self-supporting reinforced concrete hyperbolic paraboloids (see fig. 8.15).[64] Sometimes interior structural expression provided the skeleton for an exterior that emphasized form, as with Wallace Harrison's First Presbyterian Church in Stamford, Connecticut (1955–58), where an unbroken surface of slate shingles rests over a multifaceted web of reinforced concrete ribs. Eero Saarinen did just the opposite at the North Christian Church in Columbus, Indiana (1959–64), where on the exterior six steel beams, rising at a thirty-degree angle from a hexagonal concrete base, converge to support a needle-like spire, while the worship space, set in a concrete bowl, gives no clue of its overhead structural supports.[65] Saarinen, too, pursued a course where form itself, without any adventurous use of structure, established the character for houses of worship inside and out, beginning with his celebrated Kresge Chapel at the Massachusetts Institute of Technology (1950–55). An anomalous approach was taken by Louis Kahn, who wrapped the worship space of his First Unitarian Church in Rochester, New York (1959–69), with enclosures of subordinate functions to give the whole an emphatic sense of massiveness and monumentality.[66]

The approach Curtis & Davis took departed not only from those of their most prominent colleagues, but also from virtually all architects who designed houses of worship. On the outside St. Frances Cabrini gives little indication of its structural complexity—the upper portions of the shells, two of which boldly project, rising over the roofline to shelter the entries, and the spire well behind being the principal signs. On all four sides, the building is presented as a tall (15 feet, 7 inches) tapestry-like wall of brick, interrupted only by wood (later steel) entry doors that are slightly recessed from the wall plane. Most of the wall expanse is enlivened by projecting brick flankers and headers arranged in interlocking geometric patterns that vaguely suggest Greek crosses, but bear no overt religious symbolism (fig. 7.13). At the corners, these projecting bricks extend the full height of the wall much like classical quoins. The doors mesh with this texturing, their considerable size mitigated by five tiers of narrow window lights. The transom above is a seamless continuation, enunciated by a series of projecting, T-shaped light casings. The pervasiveness of textured

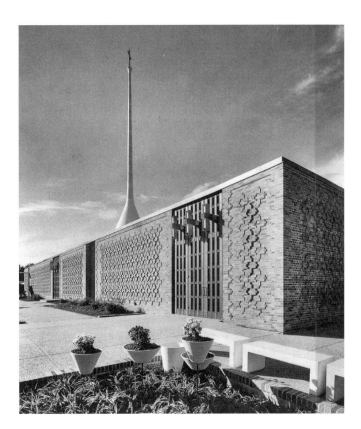

FIG. 7.13. St. Frances Cabrini, south face. (Photo Frank Lotz Miller, ca. 1964. © Curtis & Davis Office Records, Southeastern Architectural Archive, Special Collections Division, Tulane University Libraries)

surfaces is not only the antithesis of the aggressive structural forms above and behind, but breaks down the scale of one of the largest Catholic church buildings in the city and helps relate it to the environs.

A high, unbroken masonry wall might seem like a peculiar way to relate a building to a residential neighborhood, but not in New Orleans. Walled inner courts were an aspect of the Vieux Carre that Curtis's father especially admired, and they had become a common attribute of many Curtis & Davis houses (fig. 7.14). Here, for the House of God, the wall is grander in its scale and richer in its texture, but one with which people could easily relate through other local buildings. The city's large Catholic churches of the mid-nineteenth century were especially admired by the elder Curtis, who observed that "as examples of the organic expression of brick architecture these edifices are hardly equaled by any elsewhere in the United States, and are fairly comparable to the latter fifteenth century brick churches of Rome." He was especially partial to the adjacent churches of St. Alphonsus (1855–57) and St. Mary's Assumption (1858–60), erected for Irish and German parishioners, respectively, in the Lower Garden District.[67] The brickwork of the latter is especially vibrant, its weaving of iconography and abstract patterns evocative of what the younger Curtis would

design at St. Frances Cabrini (fig. 7.15). The contrast between the linear, monochromatically articulated exteriors of St. Alphonsus and St. Mary's on one hand and their sumptuous, baroque interiors on the other strikes a further parallel with the external-internal dichotomy of St. Frances.

Walls of whitewashed brick were also a hallmark of the most celebrated early New Orleans cemeteries, separating sacred ground from the residential communities that grew up around them (fig. 7.16). The elder Curtis sought to reclaim their artistic stature amid twentieth-century skepticism, focusing on the craft of tombs and metalwork, as well as the design strengths of such features as the chapel at Campo Santo of St. Roch.[68] Any connections between St. Frances Cabrini and this array of venerated nineteenth-century precursors probably would not have been conscious among the parishioners, but these precedents had the capacity to make people regard the church as a part of the greater community, rather than as some abstract, alien intrusion. The only other noteworthy instance where a high perimeter wall was used in a remotely comparable way was by Philip Johnson for his Roofless Church in New Harmony, Indiana (1958–60; altered), which was likewise designed to be compatible with the adjacent residential blocks, in that

FIG. 7.14. Service court of house, 818 Bourbon Street, New Orleans, probably late eighteenth–early nineteenth centuries. (Photo Frances Benjamin Johnson, 1937–38; Prints and Photographs Division, Library of Congress, LC-DIG-csas-01203)

case, of a nineteenth-century rural community. At New Harmony, however, the wall is rendered more as an abstract plane, enclosing an open, landscaped court that allows worship to occur in many parts and in many forms (see fig. 4.5).[69] In a very singular way, St. Frances Cabrini became a landmark, not just because of its size and distinctive form, but because it was an oblique suggestion of local traditions amid a community of newly constructed ranch houses.

Conclusion

In being part of the first wave of Catholic parish churches with a configuration predicated on the principals of liturgical reform; in its use of a singular plan and bold, innovative structure to achieve that end; in its equally distinctive dichotomy between indoors and out that allows a large building to complement its humbler surroundings; and in its varied, indirect references to the historical traditions and character of its city, St. Frances Cabrini is an exceptional building. In this intricate array of attributes, it is clearly different from the substantial corpus of other churches erected during the postwar

FIG. 7.15. St. Mary's Assumption Church, 901 Josephine Street, New Orleans, 1858–60, attributed to Albert Diettel, architect. Detail of side elevation. (Photo Richard Longstreth, 1974)

FIG. 7.16. St. Louis Cemetery, 425 Basin Street, New Orleans. Exterior wall. (Photo Richard Longstreth, 2007)

era in New Orleans and its environs, including Curtis & Davis's own Immaculate Conception and, farther afield, Our Lady Queen of Heaven Church in St. Charles, Louisiana (1968–71).[70] Among a number of noteworthy designs for churches in greater New Orleans during the postwar era, none approaches either the complexity or the originality of St. Frances Cabrini nor the sophistication with which those qualities are executed.[71] When considered within the context of the oeuvre of its firm—widely regarded as the preeminent one in the region from the mid-1950s into the 1970s—the church ranks among the most accomplished works, integrating as few other examples do a number of characteristics that distinguish Curtis & Davis designs. Finally, in a city renowned for its architecture, but where most twentieth-century examples are noteworthy as reflections of broader, national tendencies, St. Frances Cabrini stands in a league of its own. It was clearly informed by outside currents in Modern architecture no less than by those in liturgical

reform, yet its interpretation of these tendencies is without parallel and is closely tied to the cultural traditions of the city.

In its singularity, complexity, richness, and dichotomies, St. Frances Cabrini offers a parallel with Bernard Maybeck's First Church of Christ, Scientist, in Berkeley, California (1910–11). The latter building, too, possesses an interior defined by structural adventurousness, enveloped in an exterior that gives no indication of what lies beyond and instead defers to its once pervasive residential environs. It, too, was little known outside of its region for many years. Not until Jean Murray Bangs (Mrs. Harwell Hamilton Harris) began to reclaim Maybeck's reputation in the 1940s did the church begin to attain wider recognition. Since the early 1970s, it has become widely considered a landmark of twentieth-century architecture—not for its acuity in rendering generally accepted patterns and not as a pioneer, setting a precedent that would enjoy considerable influence, but for its distinctiveness, its own intrinsic merits.[72]

8 The Power of Reserve

A Christian Science Complex in the Heart of the Nation's Capital

Designed in 1967–68 and constructed over the next three years, the Third Church of Christ, Scientist, and the attached Christian Science Monitor Building constitute an ensemble of extraordinary architectural distinction for Washington, D.C.—a design that is unusually rich in its development of form, detail, materials, and space (fig. 8.1). It was the creation of I. M. Pei & Partners, one of the nation's most prominent architectural firms of the second half of the twentieth century. Although far less well known nationally, and even locally, than that firm's more or less contemporary East Building at the National Gallery of Art (1968–78), the church complex evinces that same kind of sophistication and refinement—a reserved monumentality that nonetheless engages the human scale; a bold, sculptural abstraction that also speaks to its environs comprised of older, classical and classicizing buildings; a textural richness that at once seems rugged and is imbued with a sense of subtlety and precision.[1] The church received almost no critical attention when it was built, nor has it in historical accounts of Pei or of religious architecture, and remains among the firm's least known works. Araldo Cossutta (b. 1925), the partner in charge of the design, left the firm two years after the scheme was completed, and seldom again achieved the level of recognition accorded to his work while he was in that office.[2] However, such circumstances should not obscure the intrinsic design qualities of the Washington complex.

The Firm

During the decade prior to the commission for the Christian Science Church complex, the architectural firm responsible for its design had experienced a dramatic ascendancy.[3] Its unusual origins proved to be both a challenge and an asset to that rise in stature. In 1948, Ieoh Ming Pei (b. 1917) left the rarified world of Harvard's Graduate School of Design (GSD), then generally considered by members of the avant-garde to be the finest architecture program in the country, and joined Webb & Knapp, a New York real estate company that was in the early stages of its transformation into one of the nation's largest and most adventurous large-scale development enterprises under the aegis of its president, William Zeckendorf (1905–1976). Among the myriad unconventional steps taken by Zeckendorf was to hire a young architect of exceptional promise and charge him with establishing a department that would design projects in-house. Zeckendorf wanted to produce buildings that matched his own visionary inclinations—buildings that would not only set a high standard in design, but also in efficiency and economy. Six years later, Pei created a professional identity under the name of I. M. Pei & Associates, with himself, Henry N. Cobb (b. 1926), and Eason Leonard (1920–2004) as "partners," but they continued to work exclusively for Zeckendorf as employees of Webb & Knapp.[4] The developer's financial problems

This chapter is based in part on prepared testimony delivered before the District of Columbia Historic Preservation Review Board on behalf of the Committee of 100 on the Federal City and the D.C. Preservation League on 1 November 2007. While landmark status was granted, a subsequent ruling declared the case of the Third Church's congregation to be one of economic hardship. Plans for a new office building, with quarters for the congregation incorporated, were conceptually approved in 2012, and the existing complex was demolished in March 2014.

FIG. 8.1. Third Church of Christ, Scientist, and Christian Science Monitor Building, 900–910 Sixteenth Street, N.W., Washington, D.C., 1968–71, I. M. Pei & Partners, architects. General view looking northwest. (Photo Richard Longstreth, 1991)

were among the factors that led to an amicable termination of the relationship in 1960, at which time Pei's firm was officially established. Working as a developer's architect for over a decade carried a stigma in the eyes of many colleagues and critics. At the same time, the experience gave the partners and their staff dexterity in politics, community relations, financial management, and solving complex urban problems with clarity and purpose that most architectural firms lacked.[5]

Major commissions received in 1961 for the National Center for Atmospheric Research in Boulder, Colorado, and in 1964 for the John F. Kennedy Library, originally to be in Cambridge, Massachusetts, helped propel the firm into the national spotlight. The housing and commercial projects the firm designed for Zeckendorf had long been covered favorably in the architectural press, but the recognition grew wider and stronger as Pei and his associates demonstrated their capacity to create designs of an

exceptionally high caliber for a range of prestigious institutional building types.[6] Observers praised the firm's capacity to practice on a large scale—numbering around 175 employees by 1971—and still create consistently distinguished architecture of a kind generally associated with smaller offices. The fact that design was the top priority for all the principals attracted a talented pool of subordinates. Staff loyalty was strong because each project was assigned its own workforce from start to finish. Unlike many large firms, Pei's continued to accept relatively minor commissions, in part so that new recruits could become more directly involved in their development. A range of expertise was also cultivated, with accomplished planners, interior designers, and other specialists as part of the team.[7]

Pei was clearly the leading figure; as senior partner, he set the tone for how the office operated and his prowess in securing clients was essential to expanding the operation. He also received the professional and public recognition; his partners were anonymous in that regard. At the same time, Pei shared design responsibilities with his senior colleagues on a more or less equal basis. For most of the firm's first twenty-five years, commissions were divided between himself, Cobb, and Cossutta, who joined the office in 1956, became an associate three years later, a full partner in 1963, and, toward that decade's end, was given charge of the Third Church project.[8]

By the early 1960s, a house style was clearly developing in broad terms, distinguished by bold, sculptural forms, activated by plays between mass and void, and given an air of authority by the generous use of masonry, generally exposed concrete, or stone veneers, rendered with elegant precision in form no less than in detail. Yet the range of solutions and the resulting character of the work was considerable, stemming in part from the priority given to solving the practical and symbolic needs of each project on its own terms and in a way that was sensitive to the setting, rather than purveying favored conventions. The strong personalities of each of the three design partners also likely contributed to the diversity of output, but it remains difficult to discern which partner was in charge of a given project by the physical evidence alone.[9] The importance of the firm as a triad of design partners, managed by an equally committed fourth partner (Leonard), and bolstered by a top-flight staff—as if it were three firms under one roof—operationally integrated and balancing independence and harmony in its creative endeavors, was reflected in the titular change to I. M. Pei & Partners in 1966.

The Architect

Among the design partners, Cossutta was probably the most independent in his inclinations. Virtually from the time he joined the office, he became an important catalyst, whose embrace of concrete launched an approach that gave the firm's work a clear identity, distinguishing it in technical and economic spheres as well as in the aesthetic one. Born on the Island of Krk in the former Yugoslavia, Cossutta was the son of

a prosperous importer. The town in which he grew up dated to Roman antiquity, vestiges of which were still in evidence. Even as an adolescent, Cossutta wanted to become an architect, inspired, in part, by the multiple layerings of building fabric in his own community. At the University of Belgrade, he took architecture courses and, through friends, was exposed to design and other facets of French culture, for which he acquired a particular affinity. Continuing his studies at the École des Beaux-Arts in Paris, which he entered in 1947, became a foregone conclusion in Cossutta's mind.[10] His time at the academy was grounded in the atelier of André Lurçat, who since the 1920s had ranked among France's leading avant-garde modernists. Cossutta's interest in concrete had been stimulated by the example of Auguste Perret, a pioneering architect in the use of that material since the turn of the twentieth century who was still seen as a luminary in France after the Second World War. But the transformative experience was working in the office of Le Corbusier for several months in 1949, during which time the Unité d'Habitation at Marseilles (1946–52) was the major project at hand. The visceral corporality of that design, where structure, form, and character were fused in a monumental web of exposed, rough-textured, reinforced concrete soon was heralded not only as a significant turn in the work of its designer, but in Modern architecture generally.[11] By example rather than by style, the Unité and the sophisticated use of concrete in France generally had a profound impact on Cossutta's work.

After completing his studies at the École, Cossutta entered the GSD, receiving a master's degree in 1952. From his perspective, the two programs were optimal complements to one another. The emphasis given to formal design considerations, especially composition, at the École was matched by the focus on technical and other practical spheres at Harvard. He did not approve of the team approach emphasized by Walter Gropius, the program's director, nor did he embrace the Miesian vocabulary, as Pei and Cobb had done, that, more than Gropius's, framed the design discourse at the GSD.[12] Nonetheless, he would become increasingly adept at structural innovation. After graduation he entered the New York–based firm of Hare & Hatch, whose partners were Modern architects of considerable ability. While there Cossutta was given charge of designing the U.S. Embassy and Chancellery in Tegucigalpa, Honduras, as well as the student center at Valparaiso University in Indiana.[13] The opportunity to join a firm undertaking larger-scale work was irresistible, however. In January 1956, Cossutta heard that Pei was looking for another designer, went for an interview, and was hired.

Three years out of graduate school, Cossutta found himself in charge of designing the 1,000-room Hilton Hotel in Denver, part of the Courthouse Square project, which Zeckendorf had been attempting to realize since the late 1940s. Ulrich Franzen, who had prepared some schematic proposals for the hotel, had recently left

the office to start a practice of his own. Cobb and Pei were immersed in other projects; the hotel was placed in Cossutta's hands. Over two years elapsed before construction began; however, the hotel's design was developed in more or less its final form by June 1956. It differed markedly from the January 1955 proposal, which called for a Miesian slab sheathed in steel and glass. Cossutta retained the basic form, but he elongated it, emphasizing the slab's thinness.[14] He also stipulated a veneer of narrow, precast concrete panels enframing windows that extended floor to ceiling (2 by 8 feet). The verticality of these units counterpointed the slab's blocklong extent, while echoing the attenuated form of the end walls (fig. 8.2). At the same time, those walls were not treated as solid veneers, as they were on the General Assembly Building of the United Nations headquarters in New York (1947-52),

FIG. 8.2. Hilton (now Adam Mark) Hotel, Sixteenth and Court streets, Denver, 1956, 1958–60, I. M. Pei & Associates, architects, Webb & Knapp, developers. (Courtesy Pei Cobb Freed & Partners, New York)

but as load-bearing elements used for wind bracing, expressed as enframing elements for a projecting vertical band of windows that provided a classicizing balance to the screen-like long walls. The precast concrete panels were made from sand and rock aggregate sifted from the soil excavated on site, giving the exterior a reddish-brown color readily found in rock outcroppings near the city.[15]

When it opened in 1960, the Denver Hilton was a singular fusion of the Miesian idea of precision and transparency and the Corbusian one of ruggedness, but executed in a way that seemed very different from the obvious prototypes: the Unité d'Habitation and Mies van der Rohe's 845–860 Lake Shore Drive apartments in Chicago (1949–51). For the first time, arguably, the firm had produced a major building that was as distinctive as it was distinguished; certainly it was more singular in its expressive character than Pei's Mile High Center (1952–56) a block away or Cobb's Place Ville Marie in Montreal (1957–62).[16] Nationally, the hotel was also a pioneer it its use of concrete for a finely finished exterior. When Modern architects in the United States had turned to masonry as a primary finish material for the cladding of residential buildings, they generally used brick or, in small-scale projects, sometimes stone. Le Corbusier's embrace of concrete as the essence of architectural expression had yet to gain much acceptance among his American counterparts in the mid-1950s. By the time the Denver Hilton opened, the situation was rapidly changing through the work of Marcel Breuer, Louis Kahn, Paul Rudolph, Eero Saarinen, and Josep Lluís Sert, among others. Still, the scheme put the Pei firm on the front lines of a rapidly evolving technology and aesthetic, a position the office would continue to hold for over a decade.[17]

That role stemmed in part from the revelation that the precast panels used at the Hilton were about twice as strong as a comparable component of the reinforced concrete frame. Why, Cossutta queried, should the sheathing be stronger than the structure? Precast panels, of course, could not be used as structural components for a building of any height, but it was the form of the Hilton's window-encasing units that

gave them their strength. Cossutta developed the idea of an integrated concrete structure, where the exterior walls were load bearing and also provided wind bracing, for the University Apartments in the Hyde Park district of Chicago (1957, 1959–61), the design of which was more or less finalized by July 1957.[18] The idea received considerable discussion in the office, and Pei seized upon it in rethinking his design at Kips Bay Plaza in New York (1958–63).

In June 1957, Zeckendorf took over the Kips Bay urban renewal project, for which both he and Pei were determined to buck the ubiquitous pattern of local high-rise housing: chunky towers with reinforced concrete frames and brick veneers.[19] The site plan was developed by the following April with two elongated slabs, much like the Denver Hilton in profile, but sheathed almost entirely in glass. Over the next year, the scheme was recast with exterior concrete honeycomb walls similar to those designed by Cossutta.[20] For Hyde Park, Cossutta intended to get the desired smooth, seamless surface effect by employing fiberglass form liners, a new development in concrete technology. In New York, however, the building code required using wood forms, which posed considerable challenges for getting the same smooth surfaces. Zeckendorf underwrote the costs of an extended period of on-site experimentation with test panels to arrive at an economical system of pouring that would be competitive with conventional construction, and went so far as to purchase his own construction company when bids for the job from established contractors were too high. Probably by virtue of its scale and prominent location, Kips Bay was hailed as the breakthrough project—a stunning fusion of structure and aesthetics that was also practical as well as cost-effective.[21] Pei repeated the technique at Society Hill Towers in Philadelphia (1958, 1960–64). Through these projects, the firm had a portfolio that established its own strong identity by the early 1960s.[22]

Cossutta's approach to using concrete became increasingly innovative during the years that followed. A telling indicator of his trajectory was afforded by the Green Building at MIT's Earth Sciences Center (1961–64), on which he and Pei worked together and which was also the first major commission the firm received apart from Zeckendorf.[23] The initial design of 1960 called for a slim, twenty-story tower supported by concrete piers at either end that housed support functions and carried the floors, each defined as a floor-to-ceiling reinforced concrete truss on the exterior. The rationale for this bridge-like solution was that it allowed the floors to be used interchangeably for seminar and lecture rooms, offices, and laboratories without the encumbrance of structural piers, but it proved too expensive. The revised scheme reverted to the concrete honeycomb of the earlier apartment buildings, where the structure was less adventurous, but also more decorous, with a classicizing composition (fig. 8.3). From the start Pei had wanted the design to complement the great classical complex of connected buildings that was developed for the university when it moved to Cambridge in 1916.[24] The structure was fully exposed, absent any other external components. Even the windows were without metal frames, being slipped into slits in the structural grid that encased them instead. Only the sloping, precast windowsills—integral components of the composition that were vital contributors to giving the main faces their scale and character—were nonstructural. The elegance of effect was enhanced by using fiberglass formwork for the concrete, which Cossutta had first employed at the University Apartments, and which enhanced the smoothness and precision of the surfaces. Inside, too, the structure was fully exposed, the forty-eight-foot-long beams aiding in imparting a sense of clarity to the spaces. The building was, in Cossutta's words, "all muscle and no fat."[25]

As was the case with Kips Bay, the firm experimented with a number of variations on the concept of an all-structural exterior supporting column-free space inside. Pei asked Cossutta to develop the same structural system for, but without changing the appearance of, the plans for Bushnell Plaza in Hartford, Connecticut (1963, 1967–69) and the American Life Insurance Company Building in Wilmington, Delaware (1966–70). Cossutta himself used it on a much larger scale for the unrealized Eaton Centre

FIG. 8.3. Green Earth Sciences Building, Massachusetts Institute of Technology, off Ames Street and Memorial Drive, Cambridge, Massachusetts, 1961–64, I. M. Pei & Associates, architects. (Photo Richard Longstreth, 2012)

in Vancouver (1964–67). Pei also employed the concept for Hoffman Hall at the University of Southern California (1963–67), and Cobb created a striking variation in his pentagonal, thirty-story World Trade Center in Baltimore (1968, 1973–77), with sixty-foot window bands set between the five faceted piers.[26]

Cossutta carried his pursuit of an architecture bereft of "fat" further when he took over the design development of L'Enfant Plaza in Washington, D.C. The firm's involvement with the site dated to 1954, when Pei developed a schematic master plan encompassing most of the Southwest Redevelopment Area. More detailed plans were made over the years that followed for a key component, the Tenth Street Mall, which linked Independence Avenue with the waterfront. L'Enfant Plaza formed a major, cross-axial space. Responding to a significant change in grade, the mall acted as a bridge, arching over railroad tracks and a multi-lane freeway. Zeckendorf's financial trouble led him to relinquish his interest in the project in 1964. The following year it was taken over by a local developer, who retained Pei's firm to prepare the final plans for both L'Enfant Plaza and the mall that connected it to the city. Cossutta, who had been working on the general plan since 1959, developed the revised scheme, which was completed by the fall of 1962, giving a new urban focus on land sandwiched between railroad and freeway. Three years later, work resumed on the design with stringent economic limitations. The developer, E. R. Quesada, a retired Air Force general and former head of the Federal Aviation Administration, wanted an additional floor for each of the four commercial buildings that defined the central space, without increasing their height.[27]

In refining his plans, Cossutta broke with the honeycomb concrete grid to create two unusually elegant office buildings, with exteriors that celebrated their columnar grids (fig. 8.4). That grid's dimensions were, in turn, based on those of the concrete waffle floor slab, the exposed underside of which served as housing for light fixtures. Partitions extended from floor to ceiling, reducing the transfer of noise that commonly occurred through hung ceilings. Rather than having air ducts set below the floor slab, Cossutta created a double floor. Above the thin concrete slab was an even thinner cavity that allowed air to be diffused throughout the space rather than through ducts that averaged ten inches higher. Topping the cavity was a corrugated metal grid that served both as subflooring and space where wiring and cables could be placed (fig. 8.5). Besides providing maximum flexibility in the use of floor area, the solution saved a substantial amount of space, enough to meet the requirement of an additional floor.

The "fat" of the conventional suspended ceiling had been eliminated. Cossutta ruminated how systems had, in his view, overcome architecture, increasing its cost and its inefficiency: "The architect's traditional grasp of his buildings as a unity was dislodged by waves of swift technological upheaval. Structural engineering became untouchable, mechanical design incomprehensible, and the manufacturers of building products showered architects with such an array of materials . . . that they succeeded in confusing the profession and confining its freedom of action." He then added: "Instead of dealing with the essential of space, structure, and proportion, architecture became entranced with veneers, skin construction, with intricacies of the latest ceiling system, or inventing more ingenious ways of covering up the gadgetry and handiwork of engineers." The L'Enfant Plaza buildings could be elegant because of the savings derived from this integrative approach. As he noted, technological advances had added greatly "to our well-being. The problem [is] to keep those advantages and return to the integral beauty that architecture is capable of. The material that . . . best solves that problem is concrete [because it allows] monolithic sculptural shapes of lasting beauty . . . with a primal feeling that rivals the great masonry buildings of the past."[28] The chance to manifest these ideas fully came with the commission for the expanded Christian Science Center in Boston.

The Christian Science Center was the sort of project about which architects may often dream, but seldom, if ever, get to realize: a large complex, prominently sited in a major city, with ample budget and a client that encouraged creativity and was committed to seeing the work through in more or less a single building campaign.[29] The program entailed a significant expansion of the First Church of Christ, Scientist, compound, including a new administrative headquarters for the national and international operations of the church; enlargement of publication, education, and broadcasting facilities; a sizable Sunday school building; an entrance portico for the church edifice; underground parking; and copious amounts of open space accessible to the public. Space needs, which markedly increased as the project was under study between 1963 and 1966, propelled its development, but the church leadership's desire to reestablish a strong image of their institution, one now imbued with a modernity that would resonate with a new generation

FIG. 8.4. Office building, L'Enfant Plaza, Tenth Street, off Independence Avenue, S.E., Washington, D.C., 1962, 1965–68, I. M. Pei & Partners, architects. (Photo Richard Longstreth, 2010)

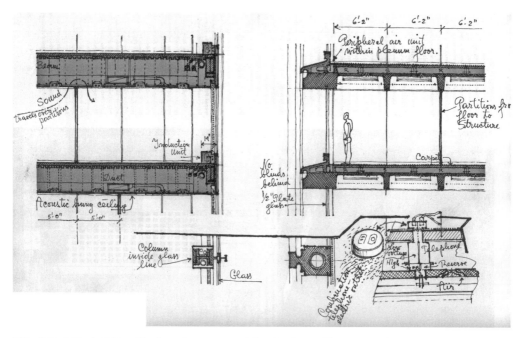

FIG. 8.5. Office building, L'Enfant Plaza, sectional sketches by Araldo Cossutta diagramming relationship between structure and systems (right) in comparison to conventional arrangement (left), ca. 1966. (Courtesy Aradlo Cossutta)

of the faithful, was perhaps the most important factor. In addition, the neighborhood had
been deteriorating for some years. Part of the
church's plan was both to protect the premises
that included the denomination's first house of
worship and to give new life to the surrounding community. The enterprise was, in essence,
a private-sector, not-for-profit urban renewal
plan conceived on a scale commensurate with
that of Boston's Government Center (for which
Cobb and Pei had developed the master plan in
1961–62) and only somewhat less ambitious than
the adjacent Prudential Center (1959–64).

More or less finalized by June 1966 and completed seven years later, Cossutta's scheme ingeniously weaves the previously disjointed group,
consisting of the Mother Church—the original
edifice (1893–94) and its extension (1903–6)—
and the Christian Science Publishing Building (1932–34) into a new ensemble and, for the
first time, into the fabric of the city (fig. 8.6).[30]
The anchoring component is a long plaza, enormous even by the standards of a time when such
open space proliferated in urban projects. But

unlike many spaces of the period, this gives a
sense of vitality and meaning to the ensemble.
Central to that effect was Cossutta's decision
to fill the space with a shallow reflecting pool,
700 feet long and 100 feet wide, that captures
the buildings around it and the skyline beyond
while establishing clear, linear paths of pedestrian movement, and, at the same time, serving
the practical function of cooling tower for the
complex's air-conditioning system. Enframed
by all the buildings in the complex and a tree-
lined, geometric garden designed by the distinguished landscape architecture firm of Sasaki,
Dawson, DeMay Associates, the plaza at once
evokes the grandeur of a ceremonial court and
the tranquility of a cloister, conjuring associations as varied as St. Peter's Square and the
Alhambra, without the slightest inference of
historical allusion. The layered, particulate
mass of the Mother Church extension, burst-
ing with a veritable catalogue of Italian Renaissance motifs, now dominates the scene as it had
never done on what been a constrained site.
The space is clearly one with the church. At the

FIG. 8.6. Christian Science Center, Massa-
chusetts and Huntington avenues, Boston,
1966–73, I. M. Pei & Partners, architects,
Vincent Ponte, planner, Sasaki, Dawson,
DeMay & Associates, landscape architects.
General view showing Administration
Building (left), Colonnade Building (right),
Sunday School and Conference Building
(center, rear), and Mother Church (right,
rear). (© The Christian Science Publishing
Society. Reprinted with permission)

same time, the space's dynamic thrust, accentuating the diagonal intersection of surrounding street grids and punctuated by Cossutta's three buildings, which serve as strong visual foils to the Mother Church, animates the experience in way that is as public as it is quintessentially urban.

Each of the three buildings Cossutta designed for the ensemble possesses its own distinct character that, in the tradition of the École des Beaux-Arts, derives from its function, but also speaks to the ensemble and the urban environs. The twenty-eight-story Administration Building, its mass a more sculptural and irregular variation on MIT's Earth Sciences Center, is positioned at one end of the plaza to serve as a beacon for the complex. Across the pool, the five-story Colonnade Building, 525 feet long, was designed to house print and broadcasting media facilities, exhibition spaces, and a reading room, among other functions—all fronted by a range of giant piers aligned to the opposing street grid and capped by a latter-day entablature comprised of a plain base, open "frieze" and bulbous, projecting "cornice" (Cossutta referred to it as a "hat"), behind which lay television studios. The emphatic horizontality of this somewhat classicizing reinterpretation of Le Corbusier's Assembly Building at Chandigarh, India (1958–62), adds an important component of visual control for the varied sequence of buildings and the immense, scaleless mass of the Prudential Tower rising behind it. By contrast, the four-story Sunday School and Conference Building affords a low-key but decisive terminus at the pool's far end, its upper-floor auditorium a curving projection that returns the eye to the Mother Church.

Cossutta summarized his concerns in designing the ensemble with a theatrical analogy: "We cannot make our actors speak. We have only inert materials to work in. They can communicate only through form. We place them on the stage to support and emphasize one another. . . . They cannot all say 'Look at me.' Some must look toward others." Elsewhere he exchanged that analogy for a biological one: "The clarity of the composition stems from the fact that our buildings are well-toned muscles in an overall anat

omy. You don't see any stratification between architecture and structure; only synthesis; only element leading to element without any apparent separation." All three buildings had exteriors comprised entirely of structure and glass. Both the Administration and Colonnade buildings had open, columnless interiors. And all benefited from his integration of floor slab and support systems. Writing for *Architectural Forum*, critic William Marlin observed that for all their robust presence, the buildings looked less heavy than comparably sized curtain-wall ones, noting "that which is clear tends not to weigh heavy on the human senses," and Cossutta's "'pours' . . . are nothing less than poetic, but also nothing less than pragmatic."[31] In his lyrical synthesizing of urbanism, architecture, and technics, Cossutta produced one of the firm's greatest projects.

The Church

Cossutta's work on Boston's Christian Science Center led to his commission for the church complex in Washington, but only as a result of complicated circumstances. In 1947, the Mother Church purchased a sizable house built in 1887–88 for Horace Gray, a Supreme Court justice. The dwelling was prominently sited at Sixteenth and Eye streets, N.W., one block north of Lafayette Square and two blocks from the White House. Three of the city's leading hotels lay close-by. The Gray house was among the last vestiges of what had been one of the city's most fashionable neighborhoods. The Christian Scientists acquired both the house and the property that enveloped it on two sides, occupied by a late-nineteenth-century hotel, with the intent of eventually building their international headquarters there. In the meantime, they invested a considerable sum in renovating the house for their Publication Committee's Washington office, displays, and the Christian Science Reading Room—all key components of the church's educational mission. The hotel was eventually demolished for a more lucrative source of revenue: parking. Whatever thoughts may have lingered about constructing an international headquarters on the site were finally put to rest during the 1960s, as plans for expanding the Boston center coalesced.[32]

The Third Church had no direct ties to the Sixteenth Street property. Since its formation shortly after World War I, the congregation had occupied three downtown locations. It was firmly lodged in an 1883 building at Thirteenth and L streets, N.W., purchased in 1926, but its members decided to sell the property at what was likely a handsome profit to the Scripps-Howard newspaper syndicate in 1967. Utilizing an apartment house auditorium as makeshift quarters, the congregation faced a dilemma in securing a desirable location for permanent quarters in the city center where land values were continually escalating. By that time, the Mother Church sought to consolidate its operations, bringing those at the former Gray house together with the Washington bureau of the *Christian Science Monitor*, which had been in the National Press Building for nearly forty years. The prime site on Sixteenth Street, however, was substantially larger than the Mother Church required. Rather than pursuing the lucrative course of developing an office building that filled the zoning envelope and leasing most of the space to other parties, the church leadership opted for having a stronger urban presence by allocating a good portion of the property to one of the seven congregations in Washington. All were adequately quartered in residential neighborhoods save the Third Church. Grouping the two was the logical outcome.[33] The Mother Church might not have a world headquarters in Washington, but it would have a multifunctional complex—the Christian Science Center in miniature—conspicuously situated on one of the city's most prestigious streets.

The character of the envisioned complex was hardly a foregone conclusion, however. When the denomination experienced rapid growth in urban areas during the early twentieth century, many Christian Science churches were designed in a distinctive idiom, with a centralized plan, embellished with Roman classical motifs, often capped by a saucer dome; however, the Mother Church never proscribed a specific repertoire of physical attributes.[34] Still, most congregations avoided drawing from Gothic and Georgian

precedents that were associated with the most tradition-oriented Protestant denominations. A decisive shift occurred during the 1930s, when many Christian Science congregations joined with Protestant denominations of virtually all stripes to embrace a Colonial Revival idiom ultimately derived from the Wren-inspired buildings of the Anglican Church in the American colonies prior to the Revolution.[35] Three of the four Washington Christian Science congregations that developed new quarters after World War II chose designs cast in a Colonial Revival vein.[36]

For its first purpose-built quarters, the Third Church's congregation commissioned studies of a similar kind. Over a dozen schemes were prepared by an architect member of the congregation and by Leon Chatelain Jr.—all to no avail. Members were divided into numerous camps, advocating various strains of traditionalist or modernist approaches.[37] Little guidance was available to the congregation. Writing on the behalf of the American Institute of Architects' Committee on Religious Buildings in 1963, Milton Grigg remarked that "it is unfortunate that the [Mother Church] has not prepared fuller material to supplement the very brief and inadequate general statement bulletin," adding: "This lack of a pooling and sharing of experience normally made available by other denominations imposes serious demands and requirements for detailed study both on the part of their building committees and their architects."[38] Without a minister and indeed without much of a hierarchy, but with multiple, diverging, and strongly held views, a congregation could founder. Probably when it became evident that the Third Church was making no headway, the Mother Church for all intents and purposes took charge of the entire project. The operation was orchestrated by Carl B. Rechner, who had been a prominent real estate developer in Kansas City and an active member in the Church for nearly forty years. At the urging of the *Christian Science Monitor*'s editor in chief, who was a fervent believer advancing high standards for Modern architecture and planning, Rechner moved to Boston in 1963 to take charge of realizing the Christian Science Center. It was he who hired

Pei's firm and was the enlightened client that Cossutta needed to create such an exceptional design. Cossutta was an obvious choice for the Washington complex from Rechner's perspective. Enough members of the Third Church were pleased with the architect's presentation to them and understood Rechner's position in the Mother Church's hierarchy so that the project thenceforth proceeded without difficulty.[39]

The Design

Although the Washington complex echoed on a modest scale the multiple functions of the Christian Science Center, its character and overall effect are markedly different, without the slightest suggestion that it is a satellite facility of the magisterial Boston compound or indeed for the same client. These distinctions arose from the commitment by Cossutta and the Pei office generally to have the factors specific to each commission—symbolic, aesthetic, and practical—and the nature of its site be the guiding forces of resolving the design. One reason the Boston Center, and perhaps many other commissions, was given to Pei was the firm's practice of only enumerating the nature of problems it would address rather than presenting a conceptual design at the interview with a potential client.[40] Both the Boston and Washington buildings have no "fat." Structure and surface are one; structure and systems are integrated. Otherwise, the latter is distinct, and among houses of worship of the era the Third Church stands as an original and distinguished solution.

The constraints and opportunities of a narrow, corner site in a prime, downtown location, as well as the two fundamentally different demands of quarters for the congregation and the Mother Church, were key to the design of the complex. Visually, the church building appropriates the corner of the property and the swath of public land beyond, its octagonal form enhancing its sense of centrality and command of the environs as a freestanding object (fig. 8.7). This urbanistic role, no less than the fundamental form and scale of the Romanesque Baptistery in Florence, served as a conceptual springboard for the strong, geometric mass Cossutta gave to

the church.[41] A correspondence exists, too, in a linearity of wall surface, although Cossutta, like other modernists of his and the previous generations, almost always drew from the past obliquely, interpreting historic sources with a vocabulary that seemed entirely of the present. The massiveness of the church building is underscored by the dearth of openings in, or protrusions from, its sheer walls. Far from unrelieved, however, these surfaces are rich with the texture of highly crafted formwork, as well as the whale remnants and expansion joints of its concrete walls. The ribbon windows of the Christian Science Monitor Building further contribute to the sense of surface linearity, while affording an arresting contrast as nearly unbroken, banded voids (see fig. 8.1).

Church building and office building form an integral whole established in part by a uniformity of materials and construction, but also by the dialogue of their dissimilarities in form and character, a relationship underscored by the principal elevations of each component facing the other in counterpoint (fig. 8.8). The triangular, landscaped green set between them also fosters this sense of wholeness through contrast—its configuration bifurcates the two components rather than tying them together. When seen in plan, this play of elemental geometric shapes—octagon, triangle, and rectangle, none of which is aligned to the others—recalls the then-radical studies in abstract form painted by the Bauhaus faculty during the 1920s and early 1930s, most specifically those of Lázló Moholy-Nagy—an aesthetic that was still present at Harvard when Cossutta was there.[42] A play of opposites in form and space was sometimes used to create a sense of dynamic tension in complexes designed by the firm, as with Cobb's Academic Center at SUNY Fredonia (1962–70).[43] At the church complex, however, opposition charges the two major components with a formalizing strength that enhances their prominence amid a dense urban setting comprised of larger buildings.

The church complex is in reality a single construction, the two aboveground components joined below grade by an extensive basement containing spaces for utilities, storage, and parking (fig. 8.9). The separation of church and

FIG. 8.7. Third Church, entrance front. (Photo Richard Longstreth, 1991)

office buildings and the distinct visual identities they are bestowed in the public realm underscore their fundamentally different purposes. Dualities also enhance the progression of space inside the church edifice. The glazed entry enunciates the sharp contrast between indoors and out. From a lobby that is at once spacious and cavernous, stairs extend on either side, at the building's perimeter, up through narrow, very tall, skylighted shafts to the worship space (figs. 8.10 and 8.11). The contrasts in this sequence are abrupt, imparting along the way an aura of mystery, then majesty. Configured in the more or less square, meetinghouse form, with an expansive, U-shaped gallery, the auditorium is simultaneously grand and tranquil, solemn and embracing, internalizing and spiritually uplifting (fig. 8.12). Flooded with light filtered from above through peripheral shafts, the space vividly conveys the sense of sanctuary, apart from the world—a place of solitude, of quiet dignity conducive to reflection, but also a place of gathering, of community, and

of regeneration. In keeping with the denomination's worship spaces, it is bereft of traditional churchly embellishments; simplicity and dignity prevail. The only added elements are quotations from the Bible and from Mary Baker Eddy's writings. Here, quotations, organ screen, and, below, the dais that holds a place for the reader's desk and the soloist form an integral composition, emphasizing the importance of both readings and music to the service. Ceilings of light, enlivened by Cossutta's concrete waffle slabs, seem to float in a space enframed by skylighted shafts at two ends, underscoring Eddy's belief in light as an expression of God's omnipresence. Thrusting into the main space, the reader's desk is intimately related to the surrounding pews. The whole arrangement is conducive to the interaction that occurs at Wednesday evening meetings, with testimonials by members of the congregation as well as the reading of lesson-sermons and the fervent singing of hymns. Services on both Sundays and Wednesdays, Grigg noted, were "emphat-

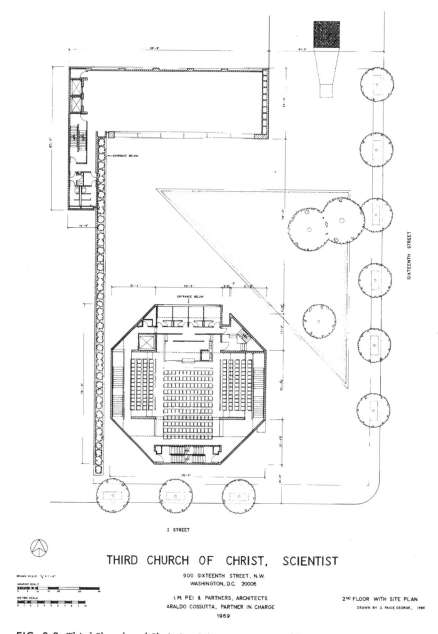

THIRD CHURCH OF CHRIST, SCIENTIST

900 SIXTEENTH STREET, N.W.
WASHINGTON, D.C. 20006

I.M. PEI & PARTNERS, ARCHITECTS
ARALDO COSSUTTA, PARTNER IN CHARGE
1969

2ND FLOOR WITH SITE PLAN
DRAWN BY D. PAIGE GEORGE. 1985

FIG. 8.8. Third Church and Christian Science Monitor Building, floor plans at second level. (U.S. Commission of Fine Arts)

ically of an auditory and communal form."[44] The seating capacity of around 425 people, more than twice the size of the congregation at that time, appears to have been determined by anticipated growth as well as yearly use for regional conclaves.[45]

These elements—the centralized mass of sheer, reinforced concrete walls; a symmetrical plan, with the entry placed at the "rear" from a plaza and away from the streets that define two of its boundaries; the cavernous lobby; the narrow, ascending paths of entry, opening onto a

dramatic, embracing, top-lighted worship space
—all recall one of the icons of Modern architecture and twentieth-century religious buildings, Frank Lloyd Wright's Unity Temple in Oak
Park, Illinois (1905–8) (fig. 8.13). Cossutta greatly
admired the building and its architect, believing that the configuration was optimal for the
kind of space he desired. If the similarities are
not coincidental, the differences are also pronounced. The scale and simplicity of the Third
Church's auditorium bespeak a clarity and monumentality that is quite unlike the complex,
embellished intricacies of Wright's design. The
space is more readily perceived as a whole from
all vantage points. The paths of circulation are
also more direct.[46] These differences stem to a
large degree from the rational order with which
Cossutta strove to imbue his buildings. Here
vertical components of the structure were all
walls—defining the perimeter and also key components of the auditorium (see figs. 8.8 and 8.9).
The results aptly reflect Cossutta's remark several years before undertaking the project: "We
[the firm] want to achieve a structural integrity
in which the building itself, not the furnishings,
is the most important part of the interior."[47]

Unlike many Christian Science churches, the
Sunday school, a central part of the denomination's spiritual program, was not relegated to
the basement, but given a penthouse directly
above the auditorium. Cossutta conceived this
lofty position, with window walls opening onto
planted terraces and capturing views of the
city beyond, to make the space an especially
enticing one for the youth that Christian Science congregations were so concerned with
nurturing. It is also the most informal space in
the building. The Third Church, like all others
in the denomination, hosted no weddings or
funerals. There was no parish hall, no spaces
given to social interactions of the sort that
were becoming ever-more important in facilities for many religious groups during the mid-
twentieth century.[48]

Contexts

Like much of the Pei firm's work, the church
complex is carefully related to its physical
context and fulfills the congregation's desire
at that time of having a building that would be
befitting of its important site two blocks from
the White House.[49] While in nearly all of its
particular aspects the design affords a contrast

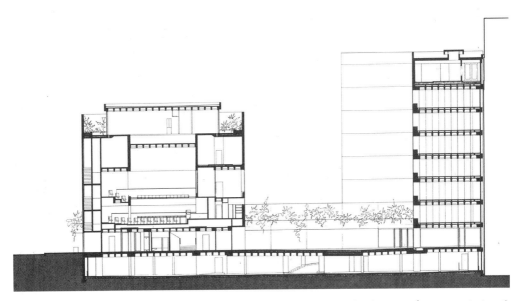

FIG. 8.9. Third Church and Christian Science Monitor Building, longitudinal section. (U.S. Commission of Fine Arts)

FIG. 8.10. Third Church, entrance lobby. (Photo Richard Longstreth, 1991)

FIG. 8.11. Third Church, stairway connecting lobby to auditorium. (Photo Richard Longstreth, 1991)

FIG. 8.12. Third Church, auditorium. (Photo Plamen Gorchev, ca. 1971, Gorchev & Gorchev Photography)

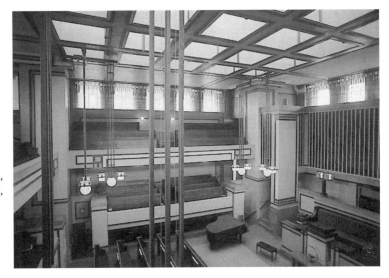

FIG. 8.13. Unity Temple, 875 Lake Street, Oak Park, Illinois, 1905–8, Frank Lloyd Wright, architect. Auditorium from second gallery. (Photo Richard Longstreth, 2003)

to many neighbors on Sixteenth Street, most of them constructed during the four previous decades as office buildings or hotels, that contrast is manipulated to enhance the richness of the streetscape (see figs. 8.1 and 8.7). The church punctuates its corner, a role reinforced by the plaza, which, in turn, makes the Christian Science Monitor Building seem larger than its modest actual dimensions. At the same time, the concrete's soft, yellowish-gray color directly ties the ensemble to the buildings around it. The complex speaks to the range in form and scale of buildings along the street absent any overt kind of reiteration; it stands firm as one of many layers that contribute to the texture of a whole which can only be created over time. Pei also achieved this equilibrium with consummate eloquence in relating the National Gallery's East Building to its grand classical neighbors in the Federal Triangle and on the Mall—most specifically to the main block of the museum, with sharply contrasting sequences of expansive mural wall surfaces, accentuated by sharp breaks in form (fig. 8.14).[50]

The Pei office has had significant ties to Washington since its earliest stage as in-house designers for Zeckendorf, with his sweeping, and largely unrealized, plan for redeveloping the Southwest quadrant of 1953–54, and continues

to do work of consequence in the region, such as the Air Force Memorial in Arlington, Virginia (2003–6). The array of projects ranges from a modest residence for William Slayton (1959–60) to the mammoth Ronald Reagan Building and International Trade Center (1989–98), for which James Ingo Freed was the partner-in-charge. With the possible exception of Freed's Holocaust Museum (1987–93), the collective legacy has been largely overshadowed by the East Building, which, since its completion over thirty years ago, is widely recognized not only as one of Pei's greatest accomplishments, but also as one of the finest museum designs of the second half of the twentieth century.[51] While the Third Church complex does not attain so rarified a stature, it does compare favorably with a number of other prominent buildings constructed in the nation's capital during the late 1960s and early 1970s that emphasized corporeality with massive forms, often in exposed concrete. At a time when relatively few notable works of Modern architecture could be found in the District, particularly among major public, institutional, or commercial buildings, the advent of this work represented a major shift in local patterns. The federal government was a major patron, with the General Services Administration's responding to President Kennedy's call for excellence in fed-

FIG. 8.14. East Building, National Gallery of Art, Pennsylvania Avenue, 3rd and 4th streets, N.W., Washington, D.C., 1969–78, I. M. Pei & Partners, architects. View from Constitution Avenue looking southwest. (Photo Dennis Brack, n.d.; Courtesy National Gallery of Art and Dennis Brack)

eral building design by commissioning a number of the nation's leading architects. Marcel Breuer's building for the Department of Housing and Urban Development (1963–69) ranks among the most distinguished, but there were a number of other examples created during a time of large-scale federal expansion. The Forrestal Building by Curtis & Davis (1963–66), the J. Edgar Hoover Building by C. F. Murphy & Associates (1969–72), the Smithsonian Institution's Hirshhorn Museum by Gordon Bunshaft of Skidmore, Owings & Merrill (1966–74), and Air and Space Museum by Hellmuth, Obata & Kassabaum (1972–76) all figure prominently in the urban core.[52] The private sector contributed as well, perhaps most conspicuously at Georgetown University's Lavinger Library by John Carl Warnecke (1968–70). The Third Church complex is far more modest in scale and more private than public in its functions. Such obvious distinctions aside, it ranks among the most carefully crafted, ingeniously ordered, and spatially sophisticated buildings in the city erected during the century's third quarter. Its visual power emanates from an authoritative elegance of form, space, and material that enables a bold statement through an economy of means.

The complex should also be considered as part of an impressive array of religious edifices along the grand avenue it faces, Sixteenth Street, N.W., beginning, at the southern end, with St. John's Episcopal Church, the initial portion of which was designed by Benjamin Henry Latrobe in 1815.[53] The most intense church-building activity along this corridor occurred from the turn of the twentieth century through the 1920s with work of historicizing character, including the Swedenborgian Church of the Holy City (1894–95), the Universalist National Memorial Church (1928), and the First Baptist Church, erected after World War II in a modern Gothic manner. All Souls Church (1923–24) and the Mount Pleasant M. E. Church (1926–27) alluded to Roman temples, while the Fourth Church of Christ, Scientist (1928–29), presented a cool amalgamation of ancient Greek and Roman motifs. Northern sections of Sixteenth Street include newer houses of worship, some historicizing and others conspicuously modernist, such as Ohev Shalom-Talmud Torah Congregation (1958–60).[54] Among religious properties of the latter category throughout Washington, the Christian Science Church complex really has no comparison. Most examples are oriented to residential neighborhoods and were designed along entirely different parameters. None approaches the exceptional design attributes with which the Third Church complex is imbued.

That complex does, however, merit comparison with a number of modernist churches in other parts of the country that were celebrated in their time by both the architectural and liturgical presses, such as Breuer's St. John's Abbey in Collegeville, Minnesota (1958–61), and St. Francis de Sales in Muskegon, Michigan (1964–67) (fig. 8.15).[55] Breuer's structurally inventive, muscular use of reinforced concrete as a basis for expression was far more assertive, even to the point of theatrics, and markedly less responsive to the specifics of physical context than the work of Cossutta and Pei. Indeed, concrete structure was frequently developed as a means of formal exhibitionism in churches of the period, generating an array of arresting angular and curving shapes.[56] The Christian Scientists were disinclined to such display. Still, the Third Church seems more reserved than Paul Rudolph's now demolished Christian Science Organization Building at the University of Illinois (1964–66) or even Harry Weese's Seventeenth Church in Chicago (1964–68) (fig. 8.16).[57] The latter, especially, invites comparison since it, too, lies in a dense urban center. Responding

to a site that is irregular and more constrained than the Third Church's, Weese developed a fan-like auditorium that occupies most of the lot area at the second level. This space is encased in a great, nearly semicircular drum of concrete, the prominence of which is accentuated by the vigorously expressed concrete frame that supports it below and a no less emphatic frame for the polygonal roof, which in turn is punctuated by a circular skylight housing. The monumental effect of this relatively small building holds its own through contrast with the forest of surrounding skyscrapers. Like the Third Church, the Seventeenth is all muscle; however, its character responds to markedly different physical circumstances. But it is not the setting alone that generated the church's character. Commensurate with the exterior, the worship space projects a sense of drama in both its configuration and its key components, recalling the auditorium plans of evangelical churches of the late nineteenth and early twentieth centuries (fig. 8.17).[58] Here, power emanates through theatrics, in contrast to the Third Church's power through reserve.

While a detailed analysis of modern religious architecture in the United States has yet

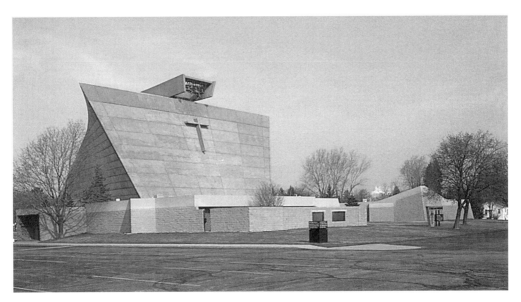

FIG. 8.15. St. Francis de Sales Church, 2929 Mccracken Street, Muskegon, Michigan, 1964–66, Marcel Breuer and Herbert Beckhard, architects. (Photo Richard Longstreth, 2000)

FIG. 8.16. Seventeenth Church of Christ, Scientist, 55 E. Wacker Drive, Chicago, 1964–68, Harry Weese & Associates, architects. (Photo Richard Longstreth, 2010)

to be undertaken, enough prime examples are known to assess the Third Church complex as a distinguished, original, and indeed highly singular design—certainly at the local level, but arguably at the national level as well. Unlike most of the prominent examples of the period, it eschews structural exhibitionism—inside and out—for a more restrained, but no less vibrant, manipulation of form that at once emphasizes mass *and* surface. It offers lyrical response to its program and to its setting. It offers homage to tradition while being of a thoroughly modern cast. Yet unlike so many buildings of its era, this one has not been reduced to the ranks of a period piece. Its numerous attributes are intrinsic; they transcend time and place. This is a design that will likely foster awe, wonderment, inspiration, and spirituality for generations to come. It is of a caliber that will make it an enduring monument to the human faith in God and the extraordinary power with which that faith can be expressed.

FIG. 8.17. Seventeenth Church, auditorium. (Photo Richard Longstreth, 2010)

9 A Modernist's Tribute to Lincoln and Remembrance of the Civil War

Richard Neutra's Visitor Center at Gettysburg

The Visitor Center and Cyclorama Building, as it was officially called when it opened in 1962 at Gettysburg National Military Park, has had a difficult history.[1] Within a decade of its completion, the building proved inadequate to meet the needs of the growing throngs of tourists it was intended to accommodate. Key functions were moved to other quarters in 1974. By that time, some National Park Service officials were becoming skeptical about the building's location, near a pivotal spot in the battlefield. Portions of the building's fabric were performing poorly, in some instances probably due to inadequate maintenance, in others due to systems that were perhaps too fragile or too quickly antiquated. The building was scarcely a quarter century old when plans arose to demolish it, "restore" the land upon which it rested, and consolidate visitor, archival, and administrative functions in a much larger new facility that would be discreetly situated away from the heart of the 1863 engagement.

The disdain with which Park Service decision-makers came to view the Cyclorama Building completely obscured its significance in the history of national parks and for the Gettysburg battlefield in particular. The edifice also stands among the pioneering examples of a new building type, developed by the Park Service in order to bring an unprecedented level of interpretation to its properties. The building indeed ranks as the most ambitious as well among the most distinctive examples of that type constructed during the post–World War II period (fig. 9.1). It not only represents a major undertaking to render one of the nation's premier battlefield sites more comprehensible but stands as the most significant addition to that battlefield's landscape since the early twentieth century, and embodies a poignant view from the Cold War of the lessons to be learned from that epic confrontation and its aftermath. It is one of the most sophisticated, fully developed examples outside the residential sphere of the work of Richard J. Neutra (1892–1971), an international leader in Modern architecture during the twentieth century and among the defining figures in avant-garde modernism in the United States for over three decades. Finally, the Cyclorama Building ranks with a handful of others as a work of exceptional modernist design commissioned in the United States by federal agencies during the decades following World War II.

A new visitor facility for Gettysburg was conceived as early as the 1940s, but was not pursued in earnest until the inauguration of the Park Service's Mission 66 program in 1956. Soon thereafter, agency architects undertook preliminary studies.[2] The Los Angeles architectural firm headed by Neutra and Robert E. Alexander (1907–1992) received the commission for the project in 1957 and completed its preliminary scheme the following April. Design development, which entailed a number of substantive changes, extended until the mid-months of 1959. Construction began that November, and the facility was opened to the public in January 1962.[3] Besides visitor information services, the

This chapter is based in part on my contributions to a National Historic Landmark nomination that I prepared with Christine Madrid French on behalf of the Society of Architectural Historians in 1999. The building lay vacant for several years before its demolition in the early months of 2013 despite a fifteen-year preservation campaign.

FIG. 9.1. Visitor Center and Cyclorama Building, Gettysburg National Military Park, 125 Taneytown Road, Gettysburg, Pennsylvania, 1959–62, Richard J. Neutra and Robert E. Alexander, architects; aerial view, 1962; demolished 2013. (Author's collection)

building housed park administrative offices; a library; a museum; a 200-seat auditorium; a rostrum, facing both the auditorium and a tangent, open-air seating area; an observation platform for viewing one of the enormous cyclorama paintings of Pickett's Charge created by Paul Philippoteaux in 1881–84; and an outdoor observation deck for viewing the battlefield. When most orientation and museum functions were moved in 1974 to the nearby Rosensteel Building, acquired from the private sector to meet far higher levels of visitation than the Neutra building could accommodate, the latter facility nonetheless continued to serve public and administrative functions for the park until its closure in 2008.

Mission 66 and the Visitor Center Concept

Mission 66 was a public works program of massive dimensions, entailing the expenditure of over $1 billion from when Congress made the first appropriations in 1956 until its conclusion ten years later, on the fiftieth anniversary of the Park Service's founding. Conceived and implemented by Conrad L. Wirth (1899–1993), who became the agency's director in 1951, Mission 66 was predicated on rectifying the setbacks that resulted from significant cutbacks in funding that were initiated when the United States entered World War II and maintained for over a decade thereafter. When adjusted for inflation, Park Service allocations were actually less in 1955 than they had been in 1939. At the same time, national park visitation had soared after the war and continued to increase steadily, reaching 56 million in 1955, more than three times that of 1940.[4] Rising public use of the parks was spurred not only by higher amounts of free time and disposable income, but also by greater use of automobiles and improved highways. Whereas a substantial portion of visitors had come to the parks by train in previous decades, the new reliance on motor vehicles put added pressure on already overtaxed facilities. These problems were exacerbated by the absence of New Deal programs—the Works Progress Administration and the Civilian Conservation Corps—that had contributed immeasurably to new construction and maintenance in the parks during most of the 1930s.

The consummate New Dealer, Wirth had a strong background in recreation planning, beginning with the Park Service in 1934 and continuing under a cooperative agreement with the Bureau of Reclamation in 1941. After seeing Park Service appeals for increased annual appropriations repeatedly turned down by Congress, Wirth developed a new strategy comparable to that used for dam building or what would soon be crafted for constructing interstate highways. A large-scale public works program, focusing on physical development and extending over a decade, could engage political support, especially since it would enjoy economies of scale and a predictability that would facilitate projects taking several years to realize. After devising Mission 66 in-house, with a small cadre of associates, Wirth secured the support of President Eisenhower and the Congress. Despite his strong political connections, Wirth could not move Congress to pass a bill covering the entire program; however, legislators were receptive from the start, passing generous appropriates each year and eventually giving Wirth more than the $787 million for which he originally asked.[5]

Much of the political appeal of Wirth's approach lay in the way he fused public works with public benefit and with protecting the parks. By the mid-1950s, the deterioration of the national park lands had become sufficiently pronounced to prompt widespread coverage in the popular press, depicting conditions as scandalous. Writing in *Harper's*, a respected journalist sardonically proposed "Let's Close the National Parks," arguing that it was the only viable means of preventing harm to these places until adequate monies for their improvement could be secured.[6] In framing his arguments, Wirth not only emphasized how "masses of people" were leaving the parks "with curiosity unsatisfied and enjoyment and appreciation

incomplete" because of inadequate facilities and personnel "to help them know and comprehend what it is they see," but argued that this deficiency carried serious repercussions, asserting that "the way we use leisure will determine the kind of Nation we are tomorrow." For Wirth, the national parks presented a "unique paradox." "To the extent we preserve them," he intoned, "and use them for their own inherent noncommercial, human values, to the same degree do they contribute their part to the economic life of the nation." Increasing visitation should not be controlled with quotas, as *"the parks belong to the people and they have the right to use them."*[7] Indeed, visitor enjoyment was the best means of protection. With the proper planning, the development of adequate facilities, and inducements to "spread" visitation within the parks and over longer periods of time, these places would be improved *and* preserved. With Mission 66, the two objectives went hand in hand. The Park Service was widely viewed as a model agency in the heady days of development during the 1920s and, through federal aid programs, maintained that prestige over the next decade. With Mission 66, Wirth believed that reputation would be restored.

The scope of the program was unprecedented for the Park Service and was indeed among the most significant federally sponsored postwar national building projects. New construction included 110 visitor centers, 221 administrative buildings, 36 service buildings, 1,239 units for employee housing, and 584 comfort stations. Numerous vehicular and pedestrian bridges were part of the program, as were myriad improvements to the roads themselves. The Park Service acquired 78 additional park units under the program, an increase of almost 40 percent over the 180 parks held in 1956. Boundary revisions and purchases of private in-holdings, coupled with the new parks, represented a 1,653,000-acre increase in the land held by the agency.

Because of its proximity to major population centers, its adjacency to a town with numerous tourist accommodations, its relatively small size, and its extensive road system, the park at Gettysburg did not require the massive infrastructural development needed at much larger and more remote units that had been designated for their natural attributes. However, Gettysburg did share a basic need with others parks, irrespective of size and location: an adequate place for visitors to receive information about the park. That need was indeed the more acute at Gettysburg and other battlefield parks because very little historical understanding could be gleaned from the physical environment. Tourists could derive at least some pleasure from observing the natural wonders of a Yosemite or Grand Canyon, but surveying the gently rolling fields and woodlands of Gettysburg yielded scant information about the events that occurred there. For many years, the National Museum, prominently located near the park and heralded by billboards, attracted travelers, a number of whom mistook it for a Park Service facility. One visitor wrote: "Following our road map, which included a sectional map of the city of Gettysburg, we arrived at 'The National Museum' expecting to find the usual high standards we've come to expect of fine National Park Service organization and preservation of treasured historical and natural wonders throughout the country. Imagine our reaction to find the 'Museum' to be privately owned and commercialized to the 'nth' degree, in a manner totally unfitting to bear the 'National' title."[8] The Park Service's offices of design and construction developed the visitor center program to address this pressing need.

The Park Service deserves much of the credit for developing the visitor center as a portal that introduced the public to a historical or natural site—a concept that has become integral to the interpretation of places since the Mission 66 program. The idea for such a place did not originate with the Park Service, however, but with by another federal agency, the Tennessee Valley Authority. From the TVA's inception, selling the American public on the necessity of so large a government intervention became an integral part of the program, and, once realized, its great projects were designed to accommodate substantial public visitation. While relatively small, TVA visitor centers were strategically placed, affording panoramic views not just of the great dam and hydroelectric plant structures, but of the landscape they had transformed. Like the engineering they celebrated, these facilities were bold, abstract masses that exuded modernity—in arresting contrast to vast majority of architecture throughout the region (fig. 9.2). Their interiors were no less striking, with bold pictorial and graphic displays, theatrically presented, that focused on both technological achievement and the agency's broad agenda for social betterment.[9] Given the widespread publicity the TVA's physical works received from the late 1930s into the postwar period, it is hard to believe it would not be fresh in the minds of at least some Park Service planners as they embarked on their own sweeping construction program.

Conceptually, the Park Service visitor centers did break new ground in the scope of functions they entailed, combining ones that theretofore had been dispersed, were often inadequately housed, and sometimes did not exist at all. Having a central place where qualified personnel could provide information on the park, give directions, and otherwise address questions from the public constituted a core service. Additional insight could be gained from interpretative facilities—an auditorium where an introductory film was shown and special programs were staged and a museum where models, artifacts, maps, and other objects were presented. Visitor centers generally included a small shop, where material related to the park could be purchased. Public restrooms were an essential component, one that had been overlooked to a remarkable degree in many parks. The park's administrative quarters would also be housed at the visitor center, ensuring it would be the locus of activity for park rangers and, in some cases, licensed guides who could assist the public. Often, the visitor center provided a vantage point from which to view key aspects of the park. Finally, these buildings sometimes included an area where the weary could sit and relax before continuing on their trip. Programmatic development of the visitor center began in 1954 and was completed three years later, just as Mission 66 was getting underway. Not surprisingly, the new building type became an emblem

FIG. 9.2. Visitor Center and Control Building, Watts Bar Dam, Rhea County, Tennessee, 1942, Roland Wank, chief architect, TVA. (Photo Richard Longstreth, 1982)

of the whole initiative—the one most conspicuous for, and useful to, the public and the one Park Service personnel saw as the centerpiece of each unit, a place that in their view assumed civic overtones and symbolized a renaissance in stewardship. The visitor center emerged as a fulcrum for activity throughout the park system.[10]

Like their TVA predecessors, Park Service visitor centers were as new in appearance as they were in their public role, absent the historicizing qualities that characterized the latter agency's buildings from the interwar decades.[11] Whether carrying allusions to regional building traditions in, for example, Virginia or New Mexico, or developed in a more generalized rustic idiom, work from that earlier period had been highly evocative of place in the public's mind. With Mission 66, the architectural vocabulary was not only of a thoroughly modernist cut, but also eschewed the monumentalizing attributes of its TVA counterparts. Less massive forms, more interplay between exterior and interior

spaces, a greater reliance on natural materials, and, overall, a less official-looking character were hallmarks of Mission 66 visitor centers. The use of materials and responses to topography and climate could reflect the location obliquely, but were not part of a region-specific mode as earlier Park Service buildings generally had been. The agency's embrace of modernism was gradual, beginning in the 1940s, yet with little construction occurring until Mission 66, the change seemed abrupt and dramatic.

The shift was grounded in practical considerations. Without the abundant, "free" labor force provided through New Deal programs, and given the rise of construction costs during and after World War II, the price tag of building in a traditionalist vein was prohibitive. The size of some buildings, major visitor centers especially, did not lend itself to using historical modes, and by the 1950s the massiveness of many TVA structures had become passé. Perhaps most important was the fact that the Park Service's own architects considered the adoption of Modern architecture the only logical course of action given contemporary conditions. Cecil Doty, chief designer at the Western Office of Design and Construction, who began his career working in a traditionalist vein and who became a key figure in the development of the visitor center, remarked in retrospect: "We couldn't help but change. I can't understand how anyone could think otherwise, how it could keep from changing."[12] From the Park Service's perspective the efficiency, innovation, and simplicity found at the new visitor centers and other Mission 66 buildings embodied values with which the agency itself wished to identify in the postwar era.

The Cyclorama Building as an Emblem of Mission 66

The Cyclorama Building was among the very largest and programmatically most ambitious of the new visitor facilities constructed as part of Mission 66.[13] The need to house and suitably present Philippoteaux's painting, a rare surviving example of the cycloramas created during the nineteenth century, was a central reason for this stature.[14] Equally important was the standing of the park as one of the most significant battlegrounds in the United States and the large number of visitors it attracted. Park Service leaders wanted the facility to be a showpiece for the battlefield, for Mission 66, and for the agency itself. Beyond official statements touting the building's distinction, their intent is evident in the fact that one of the nation's foremost designers, whose offices were far removed from the site and from the Park Service's Eastern Office of Design and Construction (EODC) in Philadelphia, was secured to provide the plans and supervise construction. Many of the visitor centers and other buildings realized as part of Mission 66 were designed by Park Service staff. Many others were undertaken in association with private-sector architectural firms located relatively close to the site.[15] While a number of these firms enjoyed a degree of local prominence, none came close to the widespread, international recognition enjoyed by Neutra. Major projects were awarded to distinguished firms,

most notably Anshen & Allen of San Francisco, Mitchell/Giurgola (then Mitchell, Cunningham & Giurgola) of Philadelphia, and Taliesin Associated Architects of Spring Green, Wisconsin, and Scottsdale, Arizona. At the time of commissioning, however, the Neutra office was the only one involved in Mission 66 to be widely recognized as a national leader.[16]

Neutra's reputation appears to have been the central factor in the decision by Park Service officials to engage him for the job. John Cabot, the EODC's chief architect, may well have made the selection. Later he would advise colleagues that "the cheapest investment is to hire the very finest design talent available." But Neutra had also caught the attention of Wirth, who wrote to the architect shortly after he had been asked to undertake the project, extolling his "perceptive analogy in viewing the National Park Service program as an anti-toxin to the increasing pressures and complexities of our industrialized civilization."[17] Neutra professed surprise at being selected; however, he may well have lobbied the Park Service for work, just as he did with other government agencies.[18] He may also have been known to some of those involved with Mission 66 from his service as a design juror in the competition for the Jefferson National Expansion Memorial in St. Louis a decade earlier. But none of these circumstances would have prompted Park Service officials to break from their prevailing practices on this occasion unless they sought an exceptional design, one that would stand as the flagship of the program.

The Building as a Component of the Park

Besides its importance to the National Park system generally, the Cyclorama Building possesses considerable significance in relation to the development of the park at Gettysburg. As visitation skyrocketed after World War II, many tourists experienced difficulty in understanding how the vast array of commemorative and historic elements that lined many of the park's roadways related to the epic confrontation itself. Park resources suffered from inadequate display and improper maintenance. The cyclorama painting, measuring approximately

360 feet long and 26 feet high, was displayed in a silo-like 1913 structure, which the Park Service acquired in 1941 (fig. 9.3). The building was utilitarian in character, without heating or adequate lighting. Park management offered no interpretive programs on the history of the artwork or the episode it depicted. In 1956 the park's historian noted that "there is urgent need for museum development at Gettysburg, especially for a building to properly house, preserve, and interpret the great cyclorama painting . . . and through the media of exhibits to better explain and interpret the events which happened here."[19]

Park Service officials intended the Cyclorama Building to rectify the situation—to offer a dignified and accurate interpretation that made the conflict comprehensible and thus bring life to the historic landscape. Well before the building was designed, its site was selected as the optimal one for achieving that objective. The location, at the edge of Ziegler's Grove, allowed visitors to see the park from more or less the same vantage point that Philippoteaux had chosen for his painting—near the apex of the Union lines on Cemetery Ridge and the scene of Major General George E. Pickett's infamous assault on the third, decisive day. Furthermore, the site's elevation provided some of the best, unobstructed views of the park as a whole. While placing the visitor center "right on top of the resource," just like the TVA visitor centers, runs counter to current practices within the agency, it was a carefully considered and strongly held position among Park Service historians and senior officials in the postwar era for enhancing the experience at Gettysburg and a number of other sites.[20]

Neutra took advantage of the location to dramatize the visitor's encounter with the site and with the presentation of its history. Instead of the static composition conceived by Park Service planners in a preliminary scheme of 1957, the realized building possesses a dynamic relationship with the setting.[21] Movement to and through the facility is circuitous rather than direct, composed purposely to enhance the drama of viewing the painting and experienc-

FIG. 9.3. Original cyclorama building, Baltimore Avenue, Gettysburg, 1913; demolished ca. 1962. (Photo Thaddeus Longstreth, 1962; author's collection)

ing the historic landscape beyond (figs. 9.4 and 9.5). An oblique and seemingly casual approach path leads to the lobby, which originally housed the information center and has the most forthright arrangement in the sequence. The path to the viewing platform for the painting, by contrast, is abrupt and unanticipated. From the rationally organized, light-filled lobby, movement proceeds through a relatively narrow and noticeably dimmer passage to a circular museum, with exhibits set in the outer wall. In the middle of this seemingly subterranean space lies a complex interplay of concrete columns and stainless steel tubes, which enframe the spiral ramp that leads to the cyclorama painting's observation platform (fig. 9.6). The slight incline of the ramp and the progressively darker space it penetrates, combined with the cage-like character of the tubes that encircle it, further divorce the experience from the everyday world left behind. The painting is presented not as in a museum but as a theater set (fig. 9.7). The space was left mostly dark until visitors arrived and a narrated sequence with light and sound began. Following the presentation, the audience had to retrace their steps as far as the second level, exiting to a glazed upper lobby, thence outside to a long, straight ramp from which the battlefield landscape unfolds (figs. 9.8, 9.9., and 9.10). Both internal and external paths seek to engage the site as an integral part of the experience, providing a sense of immediacy as well as drama that could not be meaningfully duplicated elsewhere in the park. Much like the then-contemporary television documentary series narrated by Walter Cronkite, "You Are There," the arrangement facilitated interpretation by placing visitors in the center of the action. At the same time, in its form, space, and paths of movement, the building is far from a literal statement. With the exception of the painting and exhibits, the presentation is abstract, encompassing experiences that subtly echo the broad expanses and the hilly terrain of the battlefield beyond.

The Cyclorama Building was conceived not just to house the painting, exhibits, visitor services, and administrative offices—that is, not just a facility—but also a place to commemorate Abraham Lincoln's Gettysburg Address. This function is accommodated in the most conspicuous part of the building, under the drum on the east side, contiguous to, but differentiated from, the museum. Here, there was no literal marking, but a flexible space and the most pronounced interplay in the entire scheme between indoors and out (fig. 9.11). Whereas the experience of the battle occurs in two distinct and emphatically different settings—inside, a literalistic depiction of the past; outside, a pastoral presentation of the present—this gathering area possesses a strong sense of spatial unity. Sliding glass and metal walls enable the lower section of the drum, the adjacent auditorium, and the exterior terrace and the lawn beyond to become a single space, all focusing on a rostrum. The intent was have a harmonious setting of natural and man-made components where leaders from around the globe could pay tribute to the ideals embodied in Lincoln's Gettysburg Address.

As an immigrant from Austria via Germany who embraced the democracy of his adopted country, Neutra considered the commission among the highest honors he could receive. For him, the most important aspect of the project was not commemorating the battle, but celebrating the idea of union. Like many others, the architect saw Lincoln as a hero, and he always referred to the building as the Lincoln Memorial, rather than the Cyclorama Building or Visitor Center. But the memorializing role was not to Lincoln the man, as was the monument in Washington, D.C. Instead, Neutra conceived the building as a memorial to ideals that were as urgent to uphold in the present as they were nearly a century before. This was to be a "Shrine for one Free World," where the challenges of the Cold War could be addressed before the public just as Lincoln had done during the Civil War. In 1959, Neutra wrote that here people could listen to world leaders talk "for one minute, forty seconds. . . . about the ideals of mankind which must endure," extolling that "mankind is the greatest union, which must be preserved over the sovereignty of any political area. . . . None of [those entities] must be allowed to become cause for mankind to perish from the earth. Mankind rules. The Greater Union becomes significant on a shrunken globe. The same issue is still with

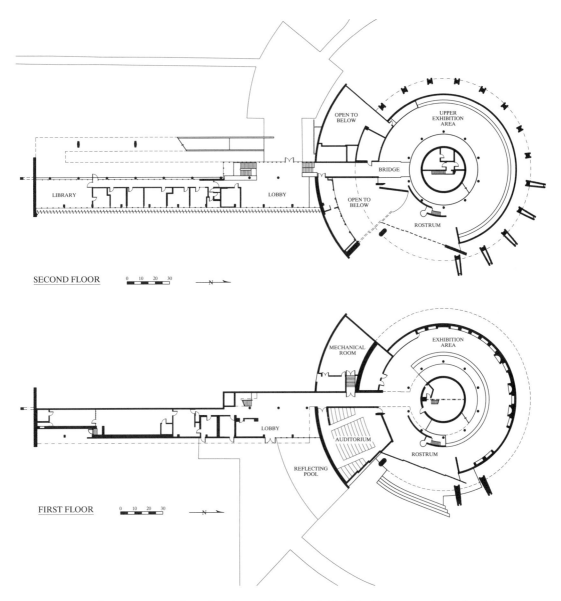

FIG. 9.4. Cyclorama Building, floor plans in 2004. (Drawing by Paul Davidson, 2013, after *Richard Neutra 1960–66: Buildings and Projects*, 158–59, and HABS PA-6709-sheet 4)

us and will probably be with us for generations to come, but Lincoln was not a victor-speechmaker. He was a prophet and his grand text still resounds."[22]

Neutra's scheme thus testifies to a newer, mid-twentieth-century view of crisis and conflict and to the post–World War II generation's perspective on the value to be inherited from Gettysburg. For those who had experienced battle firsthand (Neutra fought in the trenches with the Austro-Hungarian army during World War I), there was no need or desire for a literal landscape. Indeed, the benign setting that Gettysburg had become may have been seen as more appropriate. The late 1950s was not a time to take stock not in battle, but to reflect upon how, under

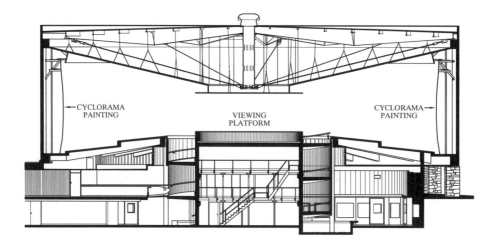

CYCLORAMA
PAINTING

VIEWING
PLATFORM

CYCLORAMA
PAINTING

LONGITUDINAL SECTION

FIG. 9.5. Cyclorama Building, section. (Drawing by Paul Davidson, 2013, after *Richard Neutra 1960–66: Buildings and Projects*, 158, and HABS PA-6709-sheet 15)

FIG. 9.6. Cyclorama Building, museum and ramp to viewing platform. (Photo [1962] © Lawrence S. Williams, Inc. Photography; courtesy ENV Archives–Special Collections, California State Polytechnic University, Pomona)

FIG. 9.7. Cyclorama Building, viewing platform and cyclorama painting, 2004. (Historic American Buildings Survey, Prints and Photographs Division, Library of Congress, HABS PA-6709-69)

FIG. 9.8. Cyclorama Building, exit bridge from ramp. (Photo Richard Longstreth, 2005)

the threat of atomic holocaust, people might peacefully coexist. Unfortunately, the building's essential role as a locus for such reflection never was realized amid the unceasing rise in visitation. These circumstances, however, do not lessen the significance of the concept of this building as an embodiment of idealism in an era fraught with uncertainty—a concept fully manifested in the physical fabric if not in the events that occurred on the premises.

The multiple meanings of the Cyclorama Building and the sophistication with which they

FIG. 9.9. Cyclorama Building, upstairs lobby, showing ramp to observation deck. (Photo [1962] © Lawrence S. Williams, Inc. Photography; courtesy ENV Archives–Special Collections, California State Polytechnic University, Pomona)

FIG. 9.10. Cyclorama Building, ramp to observation deck. (Photo Richard Longstreth, 1967)

FIG. 9.11. Cyclorama Building, auditorium with sliding doors open to speaker's rostrum and outdoor amphitheater. (Photo [1962] © Lawrence S. Williams, Inc. Photography; courtesy ENV Archives–Special Collections, California State Polytechnic University, Pomona)

are realized made it the most consequential addition to the park since the memorialization projects of the nineteenth and early twentieth centuries. Virtually from the cessation of battle, the ground on which that conflict took place began to experience an unprecedented level of veneration. The Gettysburg Battlefield Memorial Association was formed in 1863 to preserve the site, but that objective actually entailed manipulating the landscape, with the construction of monuments and roads by which strategic places could be easily visited. After the Grand Army of the Republic gained control of the association in 1879, the transformation of the battlefield into what was viewed as a national cemetery intensified. Acquisition by the federal government and the subsequent transfer to the War Department in 1895 led to more embellishments—memorials, tablets, observation towers, and roads. By 1922, the park contained 2,350 acres boasting 839 monuments, 81 bronze statues, some 1,500 tablets, and over 400 pieces of artillery scattered over 59 miles of roadway.[23] In an era of intensive memorialization, no other battlefield—indeed no other place—approached the degree to which Gettysburg was festooned with objects intended to evoke the valor and sacrifice of those who fought and the awesomeness of the engagement itself. The battleground road system, quite independent of historic routes or paths of moving troops, was designed much like that of a nineteenth-century urban park, where the public could observe a landscape passively (fig. 9.12).[24] The great array of commemorative monuments similarly reflect the conventions of iconic representation of the period; most are dedicated to participating regiments, not to the officers who led them (fig. 9.13).[25] By the early twentieth century, as Southern states became increasingly involved in the process, the War Department started to acquire land that was key to their positions, so that the park came to embody reconciliation as well as conflict. At the apex, the Cyclorama Building rises as a monument, not in

FIG. 9.12. Sickles Avenue, Gettysburg National Military Park, showing the scale of one of the early carriage drives as laid out ca. 1885–86; landscape since altered. (Photo Richard Longstreth, 1998)

FIG. 9.13. Gettysburg National Military Park, looking south across Cemetery Ridge toward Little Round Top, with Pennsylvania State Memorial (1909–10) in left background. (Photo Richard Longstreth, 2004)

FIG. 9.14. Gettysburg National Military Park, view from Little Round Top looking north toward Cemetery Ridge, with the Cyclorama Building in center background behind the Pennsylvania State Memorial. (Photo Richard Longstreth, 1998)

the traditional mode of a formal tribute, but in a more modern sense as a place for understanding and reflection (fig. 9.14). In this way it embodies values of its generation and marks them as vital contributors to the park's evolution.

Richard Neutra

The Cyclorama Building not only stands as one of the most distinguished structures erected in a national park during the second half of the twentieth century, but also as one of the finest public buildings in Neutra's oeuvre.[26] Neutra came to the United States in 1923 after studying architecture in his native Vienna and working for the great German modernist, Erich Mendelsohn, in Berlin. Two years later he moved to Los Angeles where he entered into a loose collaborative association with another brilliant Viennese émigré, R. M. Schindler, and then began to practice on his own. By the decade's end Neutra achieved international fame, principally through his arresting design for the Philip

Lovell "Health" house in Los Angeles (1927–29), but also through schemes such as the competition entry, done with Schindler, for the League of Nations headquarters (1927). Among the champions of avant-garde modernism, he was considered a leading protagonist in the United States—one of the most sophisticated and technically adept. His election as the U.S. delegate to the International Congress on Modern Architecture (CIAM) was an early indication of the widespread standing he enjoyed as a central figure in the Modern movement. Through the 1930s, 1940s, and into the 1950s, Neutra's stature continued to rise. His work received widespread publicity at home and abroad, earning him numerous national and international honors. Anthologies of Modern architecture published after World War II generally placed him in the pantheon of great architects—Frank Lloyd Wright, Le Corbusier, Ludwig Mies van der Rohe, Walter Gropius, and Alvar Aalto—who had defined the movement and had given it direction, purpose, and meaning.[27]

Neutra's reputation remained strong overseas, where he continued to be venerated on several continents during the 1960s after his career experienced somewhat of an eclipse at home. More recognition in the United States came following his death in 1971. Six years thereafter, Neutra was awarded the American Institute of Architects' Gold Medal, the profession's highest honor at that time. In 1982, he became one of the few architects whose work was the subject of a large retrospective exhibition at the Museum of Modern Art in New York.[28] Although he never taught on a regular basis, he was lionized by several generations of architecture students worldwide. While it remains to be fully assessed, his impact on design globally was, without question, enormous.

Large-scale projects in the commercial, institutional, and governmental spheres were of great interest to Neutra from the beginning of his practice.[29] Like most other pioneering modernists, however, he received few commissions of these kinds during the early decades of practice. His approach no doubt seemed too radical to many people in a position to offer such work and his office was too small to handle major projects. Moreover, Neutra considered himself an artist, not a businessman. Through the 1940s, most of his realized designs were for residences, and it was thus as a residential architect that much of his fame emanated. Public buildings, especially for institutions, began to form a significant part of his practice in the 1950s after the formation of a partnership with the more business-minded Robert Alexander and the expansion of the office staff. Much of this work, executed between the mid-1950s and early 1960s, consisted of schools, university buildings, and small office complexes. Irrespective of type, the great majority of these buildings were located in Southern California.[30]

Much as the Guggenheim Museum had for Frank Lloyd Wright, the Gettysburg project provided a rare opportunity for Neutra to design a prestigious public building on a prominent site in the eastern United States, one that would attract large numbers of people. These circumstances, in addition to the special nature of its program, prompted Neutra to lavish an unusual amount of attention on the scheme.[31] Examining the results in retrospect, the building stands as one of unusual distinction in the architect's oeuvre. Not only was the commission one of the most prestigious of Neutra's half-century-long career, the design ranks among the most adroit and compelling expressions of his personal style to be realized in the public arena.[32]

On the exterior, the design is a superb example of Neutra's flair for arranging masses in dynamic, even theatrical, opposition (figs. 9.15 and 9.16). He was adept at developing this relationship in lyrical ways on a domestic scale, but often found it difficult to achieve for buildings serving more public functions due to the challenges of scale, as well as constraints of location, use, and sometimes budget. At Gettysburg, the open, sloping site was a great advantage, as was the duality of purpose. Housing the Philippoteaux painting demanded a massive, cylindrical form. Neutra kept this form as a purely abstract one—inside and out—giving no sense of the structural gymnastics needed to keep the viewing area unencumbered. From the exterior, the concrete walls of the drum appear to float; the piers that support them are set at right angles and sheathed in fieldstone, suggesting disconnected or fragmented planes. Working with the engineering firm of Parker, Zehnder & Associates, the Neutra office devised a system of "bicycle-wheel" trusses, comprised of tapered steel girders and wire cable bridge strands bolted to the concrete walls and tied to a steel tube in the center. Unlike stadiums and other round structures of the period, the system does not rely on compression, but rather the strength of the steel girders to give the whole its structural integrity.[33] But despite the adventurous nature of the solution, it remained completely out of sight, so that the sensation of the viewing platform is somewhat akin to being suspended in space (and time) amid the cyclorama painting, dramatically presented through a carefully choreographed lighting sequence.

The drum as an abstract, "floating" form provides the visual anchor for the curvilinear extensions, from which they connect to the

FIG. 9.15. Cyclorama Building, east face. (Photo Thaddeus Longstreth, 1963; author's collection)

FIG. 9.16. Cyclorama Building, west face. (Photo Thaddeus Longstreth, 1963; author's collection)

outside world and from which, too, the administrative wing shoots out toward the heart of the battlefield. The long ramp that parallels this wing enhances that dynamism not only in form, but also through the movement of visitors to the observation deck (figs. 9.17; see also fig. 9.10). So, too, does the selection of contrasting materials—concrete, fieldstone, glass, and aluminum. Drum, ramp, and louvers (screening the offices) all contribute to the bold, abstract quality of the building. These and other elements are rendered as discrete sculptural objects. Key building components are tied together through implicit, kinetic compositional relationships—like a Constructivist painting—rather than by more traditional methods of articulation and hierarchical arrangement. Achieving an overall sense of unity through this technique was a continual challenge to modernists, particularly when working at a large scale. Neutra not only succeeded, but also gave the design a feeling of monumentality, so important to the building's purpose, that generally eluded him and many colleagues of his generation. That the Cyclorama Building achieves a strong physical presence without lapsing into cliché or thinly veiled traditional patterns, and that it does so in a way that at once contrasts with and complements the battlefield, makes it an exceptional public building of the period as well as one of major importance in Neutra's work.

The potent, abstract qualities of the Cyclorama Building are developed in response rather than in opposition to nature, which Neutra, more than most architects of his generation, saw as the wellspring of design.[34] In contrast to Wright, he never pursued an abstract language based on natural forms. Instead, he strove for a reconciliation of natural and artificial realms through complementarity. The Cyclorama Building was designed as a counterpoint to the rolling pastoral landscape all around. The scheme fits its site, enhancing it and transforming it at the same time. Like bank barns of the region, the great mass is set into the sloping ground, an arrangement that allowed both main levels to have a direct connection to the outdoors.[35] Unusual attention was paid to the laying of the stone walls in a manner directly inspired

FIG. 9.17. Cyclorama Building, observation deck from roof of drum. (Photo Thaddeus Longstreth, 1962; author's collection)

by those of a barn in the general vicinity, so that they would appear at home in their setting.[36] The visual impact of the massive drum was tempered with slight vertical projections of concrete left from thin spaces between form boards. Seen from Ziegler's Grove, the pattern echoes that of the tree trunks. The drum's bulk was further mitigated by an exterior coat of Thoroseal, a liquid sealant, that yielded a soft, white finish that was sprayed with mica to help dematerialize the wall surface.

Relationships with nature are manifested not just in the manipulation of form and materials, but also through movement and water. The louvers along the upper story's east elevation were designed to move automatically in response to sunlight, protecting the offices and public spaces within, but also creating an exterior that changes with the time of day and weather conditions (fig. 9.18).[37] A reflecting pool placed on the roof served as a cooling agent in summer and also helped dematerialize the building from the observation deck, bringing reflections of sky, clouds, and trees to the immediate foreground. At one end, this body of water cascaded into a smaller pool on the auditorium roof, thence into a reflecting pool by the main entrance that, in turn, extended the building's presence onto the land by the gentlest, most ethereal of means.[38] Neutra used such elements on a number of projects, but seldom on so large a scale and with such engaging effects. Here sunscreens (the ramp provides this function on the west side) and water are fully integrated parts of the building, imparting a kinetic quality to its presence.

Inside, the design is no less an unusually poignant manifestation of Neutra's concern for architecture's potential to affect the human outlook. He viewed the whole progression into and through the building as a means of eliciting a series of responses among visitors. Movement was indeed carefully, if unobtrusively, choreo-graphed, in contrast to most visitor centers of the period, where space often invited multidirectional paths of movement. From the rational clarity of the lobby, to the more somber character of the museum, to the increasingly mysterious ascent to the darkened viewing platform (calculated to emphasize the horrors of war), to the seemingly tenuous "escape" route halfway down the ramp over a grated "bridge" to the light-filled upper lobby—the sequence was planned to leave an indelible impression upon those who experienced it (see fig. 9.8).[39] Architecture, then, was not to assume a neutral role as a mere background for exhibits, but an active one that engaged participants fully and had an impact on their perspective. At the same time, the means to accomplish this objective was more through atmosphere than conspicuous presentation of form or spatial effect. In this way, Neutra regarded the project as his rejoinder to the Guggenheim. While he had known Wright since the mid-1920s and, unlike many colleagues, had remained a friend, Neutra's

FIG. 9.18. Cyclorama Building, main entrance and administration wing, with reflecting pool in foreground. (Photo Thaddeus Longstreth, 1962; author's collection)

views on design were substantially different. For Neutra, the Guggenheim stood as an excessive example of abstract form overriding the functional requirements of the program.[40] His solution, in contrast, was to achieve dramatic impact more obliquely, with a manipulation of effects that would be absorbed, but not necessarily in a conscious way, by visitors. Inside and out, the building is far from a background piece; at the same time, the experience of going through it was intended to have a psychological impact, not an emotional one. If the design was crafted as a latter-day memorial, it was also devised as a theater, albeit one that would scarcely be recognized as such.

Federal Architecture

Finally, the Cyclorama Building stands among the most outstanding examples of Modern architecture commissioned by a federal agency in the post–World War II era. While embraced by some conspicuous segments of the corporate world during the first ten years after the war, avant-garde modernism remained unappreciated in the majority of government circles.[41] The most notable exception was the Department of State's embassy building program of the 1950s, for which many of the nation's leading young modernists, as well as some members of the older generation, received commissions.[42] Neutra participated in that program, and while his embassy in Pakistan ranks as an important example of his work, it never saw its intended use when the capital was moved from Karachi to Lahore near the time of its completion.[43]

Given the prevailing conservatism of most government agencies, a program such as the State Department's could never have been realized in the United States itself. The United Nation's headquarters in New York (1947–52), orchestrated by Wallace K. Harrison, received extensive and generally favorable coverage in the professional and popular press alike, but it failed to have a significant impact on the design of government office complexes in the United States.[44] In other segments of the federal arena, the major exception was the master plan of the

U.S. Air Force Academy near Colorado Springs, Colorado (1954–62). Skidmore, Owings & Merrill received the commission in large part due to the firm's size, business orientation, and ties with the U.S. military as well as the client's desire that the primary training ground of this newly created branch of the armed forces have a powerful, distinctive image associated with technology and the future.[45] The Federal Aviation Administration took a similar step in commissioning Eero Saarinen to design Dulles International Airport in Fairfax County, Virginia (1958–64), as a model facility for commercial jet transportation and as a new transportation hub for the national capital region.[46]

The other primary exception came from the National Park Service, beginning with the entry chosen in the competition for the Jefferson National Expansion Memorial in St. Louis (1947–48), for which Neutra served as a design juror.[47] Shortly before Saarinen's magisterial Gateway Arch began to be realized (1959–66), the Park Service commissioned Anshen & Allen, Mitchell/Giurgola, and Neutra & Alexander for Mission 66 projects. That program differed from the State Department's overseas building campaign, however, in that it reserved only a few commissions for architects with prominent reputations.

The Cyclorama Building stands as one of the very few cases in which a federal agency chose to present Modern architecture developed to an extraordinarily high standard as an example of enlightened government views and practices during an era when the United States arguably became the world's architectural leader in the residential, institutional, and commercial spheres. The building exudes the optimism, faith, and courage of a generation that sought to take bold, decisive steps to improve the world it had inherited. Neutra's design was constructed as a showpiece—the best in modern design, housing state-of-the-art visitor and interpretive facilities calculated to bring a new perspective to one of the nation's premier historic sites. Few works in the public sphere of that period can measure up to it.

Aftermath

At the time of its completion, the Cyclorama Building was favorably received by the press and by park visitors. The *New York Times* reported: "Park Service personnel look forward to greatly increased contact with the public now that the Visitor Center has opened. For the past forty-three years, their offices have been buried in the Gettysburg Post Office building with the result that not more than a fifth of the travelers to the battlefield have had any contact with the service's historians and rangers. Now it is anticipated that at least four-fifths of future visitors will be able to meet and question the Park Service people about the historic areas they are touring." An article written one year later describing centennial activities at the battlefield added that "the handsome new $1,000,000 Park Visitor Center . . . should be the first port of call for all visitors. Already this spring, it has clocked 4,000 persons in one day, and 10,000 are expected on some days this summer. The building . . . seems likely to become one of the showplaces of the National Park System."[48]

Writing for the *Washington Post* in 1964, in a piece entitled "The Park Service Dares to Build Well," the distinguished architecture critic Wolf Von Eckardt exclaimed, "It is quite a surprise to find one of the most handsome modern buildings in this general area on, of all places, the Gettysburg battlefield." He praised the design for being "quietly monumental but entirely unsentimental," with its "big white cylinder, which resounds in the landscape like a somber drum beat." The Pittsburgh-based journalist and architectural historian, James Van Trump, provided the only account, aside from Neutra's own, to delineate the commemorative importance of the building, concluding that "here is a functioning monument. . . . The pantheon of heroes, the circle of history, has taken on a new

FIG. 9.19. Visitor Center, Wright Brothers National Memorial, U.S. Route 158, Kill Devil Hills, North Carolina, Mitchell/Giurgola, architects, 1958–60. (Photo Richard Longstreth, 2004)

dimension."[49] But Von Eckardt and Van Trump were virtually alone in their enthusiasm among the voices for the architectural community. While coverage of Neutra's work in U.S. architecture journals had been extensive from the 1930s into the early 1950s, later work received scant attention, and the Cyclorama Building was not featured at all. Some note was made in a few foreign and regional journals, but with little more than basic facts.[50] To many architectural observers in the 1960s, Neutra's work seemed somewhat archaic, employing a vocabulary that had been cutting-edge a generation earlier, but no longer held currency. Ironically, Romaldo Giurgola's Visitor Center at Kitty Hawk, the one other design in the Mission 66 program of comparable caliber, was seen as heralding a vibrant, new tendency in architecture at the time of its completion, just as Neutra's building appeared to be the last hurrah of an earlier era (fig. 9.19).[51]

In 1970, the American Institute of Architects (AIA) recognized the outstanding design of Mission 66 structures in the realm of federal architecture, bestowing an "Institute Honor Citation of an Organization" to the National Park Service for "Achievement in Architecture and Planning." The nomination, submitted by the Washington-Metropolitan Chapter of the AIA in 1969, commended the Mission 66 building improvement program for its emphasis on nationwide planning in the parks, including the preservation and restoration of 459 historic structures and the design and construction of new park facilities. The nomination singled out the visitor centers for their "architecturally innovative" and diverse designs created "not only to provide valuable service to the public but to enhance the [park] surroundings and, on occasion, to memorialize a momentous event."[52] By that time, however, the Cyclorama Building had already fallen from Park Service favor. Unknown by many, underappreciated by others, Neutra's prized monument to Lincoln and his adopted country only began to attract national attention in the 1990s, when the effort was launched to save it from destruction.

10   Douglas Haskell's Adirondack Legacy

The Understated Campus of North Country School and Camp Treetops

Situated on the edge of the High Peaks of the Adirondack Mountains, seven miles south of Lake Placid, New York, the campus jointly occupied by the North Country School and Camp Treetops is an extraordinary landscape (fig. 10.1). It does not appear that way upon first glance, however. Passing alongside a small farm that was incorporated into the complex, the entry drive is inauspicious. The buildings are scattered and suffused by trees, shrubs, fields, and rocks in ways that suggest development over time with little thought given to a coherent whole. There is indeed scant sense of a campus in the myriad forms that term has taken for boarding schools, colleges, and universities over the past two centuries. Yet closer inspection indicates randomness never entered the equation. The placement of buildings reflects careful attention not just to views but also to prevailing winds and to the sun's path year-round. The manipulation of plant material likewise fosters rich, unfolding sequences of broad vistas and small, intimate outdoor spaces that are attuned to the climate as well as to the eye. All this work in fact spanned several decades—not according to an ambitious master plan, but rather to a consistent, well-reasoned approach to design. And the results were indeed intended to look as if the process had been an unconscious one—as if it had all just happened. From the 1930s until the 1970s, this landscape was foremost the work of Douglas Haskell (1899–1979), who with his wife, Helen (1906–1991), owned the property. Haskell's work was done not just in response to the rugged setting he relished; it was intended to embody the spirit of the institutions it served. As with many educational settings, ped-agogy provided a basis for three-dimensional expression.

Career

Looking at the campus, one would be hard-pressed to believe it was created by a man who, during the post–World War II era, was hailed as one of the most important architectural journalists of the twentieth century. No one had worked in that sphere longer; few could match the extent of his knowledge of architecture and urbanism, and fewer still could rival the degree to which he framed how these spheres were chronicled and critiqued for the profession and the public. Although Haskell wrote to engage a broad audience, he is almost entirely unknown today, in part because unlike his friend Lewis Mumford or younger journalists such as Ada Louise Huxtable he never wrote a book and his pieces in the popular press were mostly produced in the first two decades of his career. Thereafter, editorships with the two most prominent architectural journals of the mid-twentieth century occupied much of his time and diminished somewhat his prominence as a critic.

Haskell came from a long line of intellectuals and independent thinkers. The son and grandson of Congregationalist missionaries, he was born in Macedonia, then part of European Turkey, amid a multicultural, often fractious environment. The agricultural school his father helped start in 1902, focusing on practical instruction with strong moral and religious underpinnings, offered a potential island of stability. But after his mother died from com-

This chapter is based in part on a short article published in *Newsletter*, Adirondack Architectural Heritage, 14 (Winter 2005–6): 1, 3–6.

FIG. 10.1. North Country School and Camp Treetops, N.Y. Route 73, Lake Placid, New York, aerial view looking west, showing original section of main building, 1937-38, Douglas Haskell, designer, Henry S. Churchill, associate architect (lower right); addition, 1942, 1946-47, Douglas Haskell, designer, probably Henry Churchill associate architect (center); Glass House (Walter Clark house), 1944, Harwell Hamilton Harris, architect, Russell S. Johnson, associate architect (left, center); with Camp Treetops (above), Round Lake (upper left), and numerous young evergreen trees planted under Haskell's direction. (Photo ca. late 1940s; Haskell Collection, Avery Architectural and Fine Arts Library, Columbia University)

plications in childbirth the following year, Haskell's life became unsettled and family ties strained. Against his wishes, he was sent to boarding school in Germany at age nine, acquiring fluency in a language that would serve well his later interest in avant-garde architecture. After attending high school in Ohio while living with relatives, he entered Oberlin College, where his father and many others in his family had gone. The imperatives of social awareness and responsibility that pervaded the institution reinforced and focused values that Haskell had learned since childhood. Majoring in political science, with a minor in art, he became a leader among students debating salient reform issues of the day.[1]

After graduating from Oberlin in 1923, Haskell ran a student exchange tour to Germany, where his interest in design was piqued by a visit to the Bauhaus, then at Weimar, and conversations with its faculty. That interest gradually expanded when, upon returning, he moved to New York, writing for a liberal, college-oriented weekly, *The New Student*. The experience convinced Haskell that not only would journalism allow him to pursue his myriad intellectual interests but that it was the ideal vehicle for him to advance ideas. Towards the late 1920s, architecture emerged foremost among those interests. In 1927 he joined the staff of a new journal, *Creative Art*, for which he wrote a perceptive analysis of Frank Lloyd Wright's buildings, a piece that began a lifelong friendship between the two men. Haskell unsuccessfully applied for a more permanent position at *Architectural Record* in 1929, but was able to work there as an associate editor for a year. During the next decade he wrote extensively on a freelance basis and authored the first regular column on architecture for *The Nation*. That series lasted until 1942, when he joined *Record*'s staff full-time. Seven years later, he became senior editor of *Architectural Forum*. During his fifteen-year tenure with that magazine, he developed it into the most insightful and wide-ranging periodical in the field—addressing the concerns of builders, real estate developers, and clients, as well as of architects. No rival publication came close to matching its breadth, insights, and acuity of criticism—then or since.[2]

From an early date, Haskell's writings revealed an unusually complex and sophisticated view of architecture. His background fostered an approach driven by cultural concerns. Architecture, broadly speaking, was an outgrowth of the human condition, shaped by social, economic, and political forces. The art of architecture stemmed from its capacity to address human needs, not in an elementary, deterministic way, but rather in one that creatively utilized form, space, and technology. For Haskell, the way in which buildings were put together afforded a key to understanding their meaning and significance. Among Americans, he was a pioneer in grasping the importance of European avant-garde architecture, but he departed from many contemporaries in rejecting a full embrace in the United States of what Henry-Russell Hitchcock and Philip Johnson had deemed the International Style. For Haskell, the European avant-garde of the 1920s and early 1930s represented a beginning, not a consummation, of a broad tendency that could imbue American architecture with a much needed vitality and purpose, while, in the process, being transformed by national, even regional, circumstances. His outlook was pluralistic: Modern architecture would assume many guises. And while numerous observers believed Frank Lloyd Wright's achievements

were in the past, Haskell viewed him as a potent contemporary force well before the architect reentered the national limelight in the mid-to-late 1930s.

As his journalistic career matured during the Depression decade, Haskell probed into a rich spectrum of subjects. Mass-produced housing became a major interest; developing new, large-scale manufacturing methods, he believed, provided the only means through which all citizens could attain decent shelter. The house trailer and the automobile offered fundamental lessons of how such production could be framed. The human value of housing was explored in what decades later would be termed a post-occupancy evaluation of Ernst May's celebrated Römerstadt Siedlung in Frankfurt. The synthesis of architecture and engineering in the service of economic development and social reform rendered the structures of the Tennessee Valley Authority exemplars of American modernism. He was also engaged by aspects of nineteenth-century vernacular architecture he saw in towns and by recent roadside developments in a cross-country trip he made along U.S. routes 40 and 66. Several years earlier, he was captivated by the epic way the interiors of Radio City Music Hall exuded an atmosphere of theatricality.[3] The range of exploration continued to broaden after World War II, as the contents of *Architectural Forum* under his editorship indicate. Among the numerous realms where Haskell proved a maverick was the then-still-fledgling efforts to preserve significant examples of twentieth-century architecture, most notably with campaigns to save Grand Central Station in New York and Wright's Robie house in Chicago.[4] While catholic in his journalistic pursuits, Haskell approached all subjects in a precise, rational, and systematic manner that he equated with scientific inquiry. Sensory issues were addressed with the same seriousness as economic, technical, or social ones.

Few people were also so well connected to leaders in the field. Besides his friendship with Wright, Haskell was close to the architect Clarence Stein and the planner Henry Wright, pioneering leaders in the drive for reform in community design. The latter commissioned Haskell to assist him in writing and then to edit his *Rehousing Urban America* (1935), a landmark text on the subject.[5] Accolades bestowed upon him by colleagues in later years suggest admiration was as widespread. Supporting his nomination for fellowship in the American Institute of Architects, which was granted in 1962, Henry Kamphoefner, dean of a leading architecture school, remarked that Haskell "has done as much to increase the stature of the profession and to elevate the professional image of architecture in American society as any person now living." The Washington architect Chloethiel Woodard Smith was no less effusive about "his brilliant and though-provoking analyses," adding that, "we in the profession have benefited immensely from his profound understanding and tireless efforts . . . toward the realization of great architecture." Shortly before his death in 1979, the AIA bestowed him with a medal in recognition of his by-then-legendary journalistic achievement, lauding his belief in architecture "as a concept 'of man working upon the whole of his environment to put it into habitable, workable, agreeable, and friendly shape'—'a moral force' for architecture, an 'advocate.'"[6]

Haskell believed his major contribution to the field was as an outsider, someone who could examine architecture's many facets without the biases of a practitioner. Nonetheless, the lack of experience in "doing" architecture—the process of conceiving a design, of developing it to the stage where it could be constructed, and of overseeing its realization in concrete form—became a source of some frustration. Only through that experience could one write with authority not just about design and construction, but about what Haskell saw as the full integration of the two spheres, whereby how a building is put together is fundamental to its design concept. His remote, private world in the Adirondacks soon afforded the opportunity to test his skills. To aid his venture, Haskell turned to an architect friend in New York, Henry Churchill (1893–1962), who had worked for Stein and Wright, and whose concern for human values were closely aligned to Haskell's own.[7] But the realized work leaves no doubt that it embodies Haskell's ideas

and indeed his yearning to experiment in ways that might become models. Like many seasonal buildings in the region, Haskell's campus also evolved as a singular and very personal statement while embodying ideas he considered to be of far broader value.[8]

Camp

Haskell's introduction to the Adirondacks was serendipitous. To augment income from his employment at *The New Student*, which was limited to the academic year, he joined the staff at Camp Treetops as a driver and maintenance man in 1925. Founded five years earlier by a Columbia University philosophy professor, Donald Slesinger, and his wife, Dorothy, Treetops was a pioneering children's camp intended to advance the progressive ideas of the educators John Dewey and William Kilpatrick. Instead of the regimented structure based upon those of the military, religious institutions, or boarding schools that characterized the majority of such camps, Treetops had a more relaxed routine that centered on individual strengths and interests. Intellectual and artistic pursuits balanced physical ones. As a result, the staff was comprised mostly of adults who brought specific skills—ranging from mathematics to cabinetmaking, psychiatry to industrial design—to the job, rather than college students, many of whom were selected for their athletic prowess. The camp also broke from convention in being coeducational, accepting children of all religious beliefs, and, after World War II, becoming racially integrated as well.

Slesinger liked Haskell and his new bride, Helen, who visited on several occasions, and both returned the following year as counselors. The Haskells had met and fallen in love while at Oberlin, and in 1924 she followed him to New York, where they were married. Trained in physical education, Helen Haskell soon became immersed in the broader realm of a progressive approach to teaching young children. While her husband wrote, she commuted to Rosemary Junior School in Greenwich, Connecticut, a prominent outpost for such progressive education. Treetops was a perfect fit for the couple. In 1928, they became codirectors with the Slesingers, and the following year, when Donald Slesinger followed his mentor to the University of Chicago, the Haskells took charge. With the aid of Daniel Buckley, whose children had attended Treetops, they purchased the camp in 1933.[9]

After assuming directorship, Douglas and Helen Haskell brought more structure to the camp routine, but only as a means of strengthening the agenda the Slesingers had initiated in an experimental, evolving manner. Camp size was limited to fifty children to ensure that personal attention was afforded to them all and to avoid the regimentation often used as a means of controlling larger groups. Most of the time, each child could pursue activities of his or her own choosing and select the counselor to serve as a guide. There were no fixed schedules for activities and no established teams for athletic endeavors. Matching the focus on individual development was a growing emphasis on collective activity that would enhance the sense of a closely interactive, nonhierarchical community. The key figures in this program were Helen's sister Leonora (1905–2004), who arrived in 1932, and her husband Walter Clark (1905–1981), who came two years later. The Clarks were likewise committed to progressive education and taught at Hessian Hills School in Croton-on-Hudson, New York, another well-known institution of its kind. Among the innovations they introduced at Treetops was manual labor as part of the regimen, capitalizing on an under-utilized farm that had been developed on the property during the late nineteenth and early twentieth centuries. The program was designed to inculcate responsibility and self-reliance in children at an early age. With chores modeled on those traditionally part of the upbringing of rural youth, an experience Walter Clark knew firsthand from childhood, the intent was also to connect campers to a way of life they would never know, being raised in urban and suburban environments. During the 1930s, too, activities beyond the campus were increased, with an array of day and overnight expeditions in the High Peaks.[10]

School

The summers spent at Treetops were sufficiently enriching for the Clarks that they soon began to contemplate starting a boarding school for children of ages from six to fourteen. The Haskells offered a portion of their 160-acre tract. Using the land more intensely would help defray costs and new facilities would enable the camp to expand into two discrete units, providing a more physically sheltering environment for a "junior" division. Designing those facilities would allow Douglas Haskell to "do" architecture, avoiding professional fees and achieving maximum richness of educational environment at minimal cost. Given both couples' limited assets, financing proved a problem. Local bankers were willing to provide a mortgage on only an eighth of the projected construction cost. Turning to their families, friends, parents they had gotten to know while at Hessian Hills, and Jack Kaplan, a rich industrialist who was grateful for his children's experiences at the camp, they managed to raise the necessary funds.[11]

For pedagogical reasons, the Clarks wanted a single building, where life and learning were integrated and where they and their staff lived under the same roof as their charges. The basic rationale, Haskell later wrote, was to break down "the hard-and-fast distinction between education as 'discipline' and the private room as 'escape.'" Combining functions was also a measure of economy since students could clean up after outdoor activities without requiring the separate accommodations commonly found in gymnasia.[12] The Clarks also were predisposed to Haskell's views on architecture, which differed markedly from those of the doctrinaire, avant-garde Swiss émigré William Lescaze and his patrician partner George Howe, who had designed the Hessian Hills School (1931–32) and whose masterwork, the Philadelphia Saving Fund Society Building (1929–32), Haskell had criticized as overly bound to European design sensibilities.[13] Completed in the late fall of 1938, Haskell's wood-frame building in the Adirondacks was markedly low-key in appearance, somewhat domestic in character but less assuming than many houses of comparable size

FIG. 10.2. Main building, North Country School, southeast face. (Photo Ezra Stoller, ca. 1939; Ezra Stoller © Esto)

FIG. 10.3. Main building, North Country School, northwest face. (Photo ca. 1939; Haskell Collection, Avery Architectural and Fine Arts Library, Columbia University)

(figs. 10.2 and 10.3). The scheme, he wrote, was designed to "impart some of the rugged feeling of the woods," but with "all the elements . . . reduced to their simplest terms." Part home, part workplace, part base for a venturous outdoor life that was integral to the curriculum, the building's elements were "not . . . studied for their 'effect' but for their effectiveness in performing their functions well."[14]

The understated visual character of the North Country School building was matched by a sense of intimacy and warmth inside. Tailored to a climate that is generally colder than most places in the northeastern United States and has few hot days during the summer, the plan was oriented to give maximum solar orientation in winter, with two classrooms and the shop and sleeping quarters enjoying a southern exposure. As a result, the heating bills were sufficiently low to preclude fuel rationing during the war. Prominently placed in the large entry hall, which doubled as an informal gathering place, and in the adjacent dining-assembly room were two enormous, shallow fireplaces designed in the Rumford tradition to maximize heat dispersal—emblems of the rugged yet nurturing environment the Clarks cultivated (fig. 10.4). Fun entered the equation as well. To counter the children's tendency to slide down banisters, Haskell designed stair rails as thin piping, but provided slides on the opposite side. Similarly, to preclude rooftop escapades, the chimney doubled as a climbing tower, with a "crow's nest" around the perimeter—another vivid enunciation of the school as a child's world (see fig. 10.2).[15] Two decades later, Haskell underscored the pedagogical importance of such a seemingly whimsical feature: "A [child] could fall [from these 'climbing trees'] in a mean way, but by that time we were committed to a policy of having risks. We want to have a place where there *are* risks, and let the children learn how to avoid them."[16]

The Clarks' reputation as educators and the demand for safe haven during World War II led to a rapid rise in enrollments. Haskell designed a small dwelling (Little House, now known as Woods House) for additional staff and pupils

in 1942. Sited across from the entrance to the school, this new component lay on higher ground and its orientation to the existing building seemed to suggest that the two components had occurred by happenstance. The house was as unpretentious as its predecessor. Its character, however, was entirely different due to Haskell's experimental design, which simplified framing by using a continuous row of studs, spaced two feet apart without breaks for windows. While it remained an anomaly, Haskell developed the system in the hope it could be manufactured in a plant less expensively than the panel systems then favored by many architects for prefabricated construction.[17] Any visual connotations of the structure's potential for mass production, however, were contravened by the large planks of horizontal siding, left irregular at the lap edge—a regional mannerism known as barnstorm siding developed by an Adirondack builder several decades earlier (fig. 10.5).[18] This structural configuration allowed window units to be placed at any level and in any com-

FIG. 10.4. Main building, entry hall, as viewed from stair landing. (Photo Ezra Stoller, ca. 1939; Ezra Stoller © Esto)

bination within the frame, enabling unusual configurations that likely proved a source of surprise and delight to their young occupants (fig. 10.6). Here Haskell's concern for architecture achieving integral relationships between construction and design, between practicality and individuality, between clarity and illusion, even whimsy, were expressed with originality and élan.

Camp Treetops also served as something of a laboratory where Haskell experimented with building techniques that he saw as eminently suitable for a child's environment but also might lead to broader applications in design and building. Probably around the same time he prepared plans for Little House, Haskell devised several open-air cabins—the Corn Crib, Hanging House, and Wing House. While varying in detail, each sought to maximize usable space while minimizing the ground area covered by canting stock wood-framing components outward and tying them to the roof to form a rigid frame (fig.

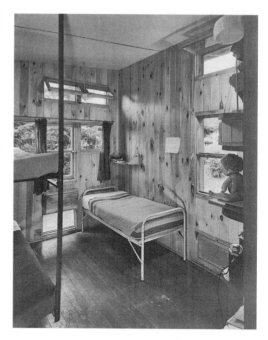

FIG. 10.6. Little house, bedroom. (Photo Ezra Stoller, ca. 1942–43 Ezra Stoller © Esto)

FIG. 10.5. Little House, North Country School, Douglas Haskell, designer, 1942; addition by Haskell, 1949, 1958; since altered. Northeast face, with entry porch. (Photo Ezra Stoller, ca. 1942–43 Ezra Stoller © Esto)

10.7). These modest structures manifested their designer's probing for new ways to achieve efficient, flexible, low-cost shelter. His decade-old interest in mass production was now furthered by the exigencies of wartime construction in remote locations, many of them with severe climates. Drawing in part from Native American patterns of shelter, Haskell believed Quonset huts offered lessons that could be adapted to postwar housing needs. These building systems also remind Americans that European architectural traditions were new in North America as compared to many centuries of building by indigenous peoples—practices that were often more environmentally responsive and economical than those imported across the Atlantic. As these forms should be venerated, so they should serve as a conceptual springboard for wholly new solutions. "Once wooden (or metal) arches are accepted for household use," he wrote in 1943, "there is open a veritable new continent of structural exploration." Haskell's cabins altered the continuous-arched form of the Quonset hut to achieve what he intended to be comparable results.[19]

FIG. 10.7. Wing House, Camp Treetops, Douglas Haskell, designer, ca. 1943. (Photo Richard Long-streth, 2010)

North Country School's continued growth following the war led to an addition to the main building (designed 1942, built 1946–47) that more than tripled its space (fig. 10.8).[20] Structurally a separate, freestanding building, connected by an enclosed bridge, the new facility again combined academic spaces at ground level with sleeping rooms for students and staff above. It also contained more specialized spaces, including a library, with an infirmary on the second floor and an observation deck on the roof. Directly opposite lay a combination gymnasium, theater, music hall, dance studio, meeting space, and ceremonial center, with administrative offices and music room to one side (fig. 10.9). The exterior treatment emphasized the building's multifaceted nature. The library was rendered as a latter-day silo, subtly evoking the farm's importance in the school's regime, but also suggestive—certainly in a child's imagination—of a fortified turret (fig. 10.10). The turret was further intended to complement the gymnasium, which was a surplus Quonset hut, its curved form tempered by clerestory and end windows.

Silo, Quonset hut, climbing trees, and other parts of the building were rendered as a collage, which was most fully developed at the new main entrance. That approach appears as little more than a utility porch, complete with racks for skis and other outdoor gear on the wall, unceremoniously attached to the side of the Quonset and abruptly terminated by the enclosed bridge from the earlier building. Above, what seemed to be another appendage is in fact an integral part of the main block and contains the upper portion of a stair hall, the most dramatic space within the building. The seemingly ad hoc character of the composition is enhanced by the array of materials: barnstorm and straight vertical-board siding in sections that are interspersed with walls of concrete blocks (fig. 10.11). To mitigate the "poisonous" effect of this cheap form of masonry construction, which was almost never left exposed save in service structures, Haskell insisted the vertical mortar joints be trowelled flush, allowing them to seep into irregular surfaces of the block, while the mortar in the horizontal joint be left to ooze beyond the surface—the combination forming a rough textural grid. Similarly, in the stair hall, colliding forms, enunciated by an array of materials, invoke surprise and a sense of pageantry, the curving stair with its balustrades of steel tubing and rope, occupying center stage (fig. 10.12). In a eulogy to his brother-in-law, Clark recalled that walking around the building felt like "moving through a massive, beautiful, delightful outdoor sculpture that is a superb blend of representational and abstract art."[21]

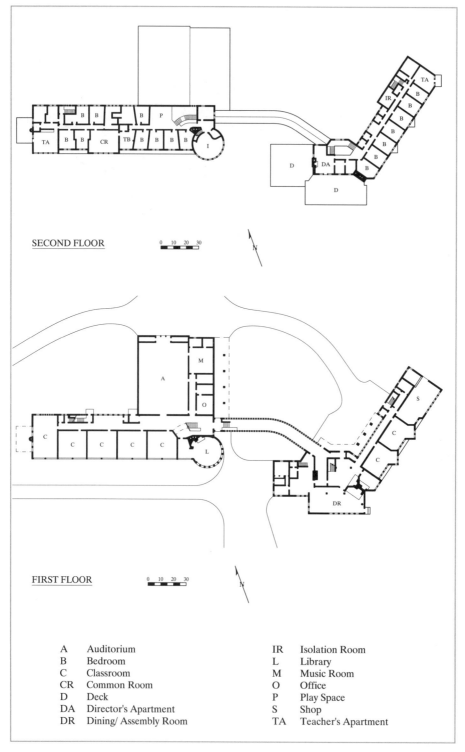

SECOND FLOOR   0   10   20   30   N

FIRST FLOOR   0   10   20   30   N

A	Auditorium	IR	Isolation Room
B	Bedroom	L	Library
C	Classroom	M	Music Room
CR	Common Room	O	Office
D	Deck	P	Play Space
DA	Director's Apartment	S	Shop
DR	Dining/ Assembly Room	TA	Teacher's Apartment

FIG. 10.8. North Country School, floor plans of main building, with original section to right and addition to left. (Drawing by Paul Davidson, 2013, after *Forms and Functions of Twentieth-Century Architecture,* ed. Talbot Hamlin, 3:618)

FIG. 10.9. Main building addition, converted Quonset hut interior in use as a gymnasium. (Photo ca. late 1940s/early 1950s; Haskell Collection, Avery Architectural and Fine Arts Library, Columbia University)

FIG. 10.10. Main building addition, northeast face. (Photo Richard Longstreth, 2010)

FIG. 10.11. Main building, aerial view looking east, with main building addition in center, and main entrance by parked cars. (Photo ca. late 1940s; Haskell Collection, Avery Architectural and Fine Arts Library, Columbia University)

Yet as with its predecessors, this building's components are rigorously practical. At the main level, the south elevation is lined with enormous windows, intended to maximize solar gain, given scale by iron grating that serves as an easily maneuvered fire escape and also as a screen for the summer sun (fig. 10.13; see also fig. 10.10). One side of the stair hall is comprised of what appears to be a giant, abstract bas-relief that functions as a climbing wall. The enclosed passage connecting the addition to the original building is lined with alcoves for the discrete storage of outdoor gear, which give scale and rhythm to an otherwise long, narrow passage (fig. 10.14). The dormitory rooms were each given their own shape to enhance a sense of individuality.

Over the first decade of its operation, North Country School's physical plant was largely Haskell's creation. He added to Little House in 1949, designing a simple but engaging quartet of carports, set in an open diamond pattern,

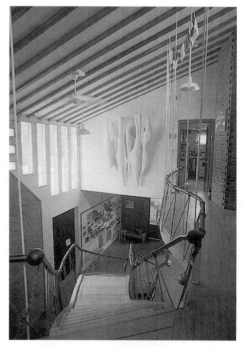

FIG. 10.12. Main building addition, stair hall. (Photo Richard Longstreth, 2005)

FIG. 10.13. Main building addition, classroom. (Photo ca. late 1940s/early 1950s; Haskell Collection, Avery Architectural and Fine Arts Library, Columbia University)

FIG. 10.14. Main building, interior of bridge connecting original section to addition, with alcoves for storage. (Photo Richard Longstreth, 2005)

enframed by woods. Other additions were made to Treetops and to the farm complex that served both institutions. Under the circumstances, the fact that the Clarks' own residence (known as Glass House), conspicuously positioned like a portal lodge at the approach to the school buildings, was designed in 1944 by the eminent California architect Harwell Hamilton Harris (1903-1990) seems curious. Harris, who with his wife had moved to New York in 1942 in search of intellectual stimulation and employment during the lean war years, may have needed the work. Conversely, Haskell may have been overwhelmed by editorial responsibilities, or may simply have wanted the campus to benefit from designs other than his own. Whatever the circumstances, Harris was a logical choice from Haskell's perspective. The Californian had not received the traditional academic training in architecture. After attending the Otis Art Institute in Los Angeles, he worked for five years (1928-32) in the office of Richard Neutra, who during that time was a rising, international leader in avant-garde modernism. While to many observers Neutra seemed the most European of American architects, his environmental and psychological concerns as well as his technical acuity all found favor with Haskell. Harris began his own practice immediately thereafter, developing a strong, personal approach

to design at an early stage. Harris was inspired not just by Neutra and European modernism, but also by Japanese traditions and the work of Frank Lloyd Wright. To Haskell, Harris's work must have epitomized the kind of synthesis he had been seeking to feature in his writings since the late 1920s.[22]

Harris's Glass House, which was also designed to include accommodations for several students, is indeed such a synthetic work (fig. 10.15). The form, vaguely reminiscent of a compact Wright Prairie house, is balanced by a dynamic composition of window banks and principal spaces with an interplay between expansiveness and enclosure likely drawn from Neutra's example. Haskell probably had direct input on the decision to have most of the glazing fixed, with natural ventilation integrated into the wall—an arrangement he believed could produce superior thermal results. Many facets of the plan reflect Haskell's and Clark's empathy for children's habits, while also introducing disciplines of the adult world.[23] But the scheme is very much Harris's own, without any of the seeming casualness of Haskell's work, its pervasively taut, purposeful forms softened by redwood siding. The Clarks, and no doubt the Haskells, were sufficiently pleased with the results that Harris was brought back, much later, to design a cluster of four dormitories (1967-68); while their

FIG. 10.15. Glass House. (Photo Richard Longstreth, 2005)

size afforded more student accommodations, in many ways they were variations on Glass House (fig. 10.16).

Haskell's concern for creating a total environment was manifested in the array of furniture selected for his and Harris's buildings. A number of chairs designed by Alvar Aalto and by Eero Saarinen (whose daughter attended the school and later became a counselor at Treetops) were acquired, as well as a table by Isamu Noguchi. Sculpture adorned the main building and grounds alike, including pieces by Harry Bertoia and a mobile by George Rickey (who, along with his two sons, was a counselor at various times at Treetops). In a number of cases works were donated by their creators, and in others by alumni. Hence, the settings for the vigorous programs in the fine, manual, and performing arts that were offered at both school and camp

FIG. 10.16. Bramwell House (part of a cluster of four dormitories), North County School, 1967–68, Harwell Hamilton Harris, architect. (Photo Richard Longstreth, 2005)

were places where art was an integral part of the scene.[24]

Landscape

As a loose-knit ensemble, school and camp buildings were greatly enhanced by their setting. From the start, Haskell saw the importance of manipulating the landscape to further the institutions' objectives. Prior to beginning work on the school he introduced 10,000 non-native pine, cedar, and spruce trees to form a wooded demarcation between it and the existing campus of the camp. Far from uniform, this plantation entails a series of differentiated clearings that would be used in summer months for the newly formed junior camp, which utilized the school's building, and later for the Harris-designed dormitories. An extension of these woods formed a cocoon-like shelter for the Glass House, interrupted only by the main drive, thus also becoming a verdant portal to the school's core area (fig. 10.17). The initial portions of the drive were punctuated by trees that shielded it from the parallel highway, framed aspects of the adjacent farm complex, and provided transition points between farm and fields. There are indeed few prospects from which a careful ordering of the landscape elements was not apparent upon close observation, although much of this "order" was attained by decisions as to what natural elements to leave in place and emphasize in vistas (fig. 10.18). And, like his buildings, Haskell's working with the land was intended to appear casual, as if things had simply happened. No evidence suggests that he ever developed a plan for the campus or conferred with a landscape architect. Instead, decisions appear to have been made on an incremental basis, responding to circumstance but with a consistent approach that led to a markedly understated whole. Unlike most landscape plans, it was not a design that was important, but rather the unobtrusive manipulation of, as well as building upon, what existed. In describing Haskell's contribution to the school's board of trustees, Clark wrote in 1975 that "all disturbances and intrusions upon the natural environment fell under his studied scrutiny of and

FIG. 10.17. Approach drive to North Country School, looking east, showing grove planted under Haskell's direction. Glass House (not shown) located in grove on left; grove on right destroyed by storm in 2010. (Photo Richard Longstreth, 2006)

FIG. 10.18. Approach drive to Camp Treetops, general view, looking northwest, showing elements of a natural vista—an open field brimming with boulders framed by trees—retained by Haskell. (Photo Richard Longstreth, 2006)

remarkable sensitivity to line, shape, color and texture."[25]

Douglas Haskell continued to spend the summer months codirecting Camp Treetops until he assumed his editorial duties at *Architectural Forum* in 1949. He appears to have remained thoroughly engaged with shaping the campus for many years thereafter, at least until he, his wife, and the Clarks all resigned their posts and sold their interests in the operation in 1970. Subsequent work was in keeping with the spirit he gave to the setting. In 1974, members of an advanced mathematics class, with supervision from their instructor, designed and built a sugarhouse that embodied a lively integration of utility and fantasy. Eleven years later, the Clarks' son Allan, one of a number of alumni who became architects, designed a residence for the camp's director that pays homage to the Glass House and to the early camp buildings. By far the most sophisticated addition was a pottery shop for Treetops (ca. 1972–73), designed by sculptor Paul Nowicki, then a member of the staff (fig. 10.19).[26] Perched on a promontory, the pavilion is at once sheltered and open, employing inexpensive materials with purpose and elegance, imbuing an order more reminiscent of the work of Louis Kahn than of Haskell, but fully in keeping with the latter's quest for creating a sense of adventure in the everyday environment of a child.[27]

For all his knowledge of architecture, building, planning, and landscape; for all his interests in the arts; for all the celebrated figures he knew; for all the renown he attained—Haskell was nowhere more engaged than in creating the North Country–Treetops campus in the Adirondacks. Clark recalled with admiration that his brother-in-law, when designing a building, "appeared to explore every aspect of its ultimate use in terms of the joy, stimulation, beauty, utility and practicality for those who would occupy it. Every door and window was studied in light of what would be seen and felt as one looked from the outside or the inside out. . . . Every element had to blend into a total integrated pattern." For Haskell, this process was far more than a cerebral exercise; he "loved to talk to children, teachers, and others about his plans and always listened attentively to their reactions." That balance between seriousness and play offered eloquent testament to the Clarks' aim of providing "a situation where children can be happy, creative, and natural, but where techniques are systematically taught, and where children are given a . . . well-organized introduction to important areas of human knowledge." The school was developed as a place that nurtured living and working with "a mixed group of people, professional and non-professional, colored and white, gentile and Jewish, church-going and non-church-going, more talented and less talented—in all cases with a feeling of oneness, of unity, of striving for a world of freedom and liberty and opportunity and happiness."[28] This eloquent testimonial to the institution is no less resonant in considering its programs today. In a distinctive and distinguished way Haskell understood how to manifest that spirit through architecture and landscape.

FIG. 10.19. Pottery "shed," Camp Treetops, ca. 1972, Paul Nowicki, designer. (Photo Richard Longstreth, 2004)

IV COMMONPLACE AND TAKEN FOR GRANTED

11 Assessing a Vernacular Landscape

A Community Garden in Washington, D.C.

The community garden lying to the rear of the apartment building, known by it street address, 3901 Connecticut Avenue, is not the kind of resource that normally comes before historic preservation review bodies, in part because very few examples have existed for more than a generation. In this case, however, the setting was created as a victory garden circa 1942 and has not experienced substantial changes since shortly after the end of World War II (fig. 11.1). Furthermore, while this is generally not regarded as a conventional type of landscape, it nevertheless must be considered as a closely related component of the larger property on which the apartment building stands, even though it has no small degree of historical significance in its own right. Indeed, by itself, the garden meets Criterion A.1 as the site associated with a movement—in this case the practices of creating victory and community gardens—that contributed significantly to the heritage and culture of Washington. It also meets Criterion A.2 for the same reasons (it exemplifies the significant social and historical heritage of the city); Criterion A.3 (it embodies a significant form of landscape); Criterion A.6 (it reveals a significant pattern of use of the landscape as well as the continuum of cultural attitudes, norms, and values); Criterion B (it possesses sufficient integrity); and Criterion C (sufficient time has passed to assess the property within a historical context).[1]

To understand a resource of this kind, we need to establish some parameters. First, while land-use issues are entailed in the concerns over this property—specifically, retaining open space adjacent to Rock Creek Park versus denser development undertaken in response to market demand—this is a preservation case based solely upon the historical attributes of garden and its setting. A second key matter is the kind of landscape this garden represents. It is not a designed landscape in the formal sense of that term. It was not laid out by a professional landscape architect, planner, or horticulturalist. Instead, it is *vernacular* in the full sense of that term—it embodies common patterns of shaping the land that have been practiced by a people over time. It is, in other words, part of a broad-based, popular tradition. A third matter is the time sequence. This garden was not an integral part of the original conception. When it was constructed in 1927–28, the apartment house did not boast highly embellished grounds as did Tilden Gardens (1927–29) across the street or the Westchester (1930–31) (fig. 11.2), to cite two of the most ambitious local examples of landscape design for apartment complexes realized during the interwar decades.[2]

Instead, like most other apartment houses of the period, 3901 Connecticut had a street orientation, and like many of those erected in then-outlying areas, it was set back from the sidewalk by a yard, with lawn and foundation

This chapter was originally drafted as testimony I delivered before the District of Columbia Historic Preservation Review Board in March 1996. It was published in Richard Longstreth, *History on the Line: Testimony in the Cause of Preservation* (Washington, D.C.: National Park Service, and Ithaca, N.Y.: National Council for Preservation Education, 1998), chapter 5. It is reprinted here with minor modifications. The review board granted landmark status to the apartment building, but did not include the garden, which was located on a separate land parcel and was destroyed the day after the hearing.

plantings. The space at the rear was considered a utility area. The community garden was an *addition* to the complex, which substantially modified the relationship between the building and its grounds. This addition was made when the building was less than twenty years old. The garden has been a part of the ensemble for over half a century [in 1996], more than twice as long. Now imagine for a moment that I am discussing a *building*. That building was constructed in the late 1920s. After about fifteen years, the owner created a substantial addition that by all estimates enhanced the character of the premises. Fifty years later, I doubt whether anyone familiar with the policies and practices of the national historic preservation program would have difficulty designating the property as a whole or would condone the removal of the addition, as is born out by the record of this Board in designation landmarks with significant additions. The community garden at 3901 Connecticut Avenue is in no way a different kind of case, only a different kind of resource.

. . .

A community garden is a coordinated enterprise with multiple parties responsible for its cultivation. The land may be owned by those parties collectively, leased from or lent by an outside party, or informally appropriated for the purpose. Normally each participating party has its own plot, although a few support functions such as the water supply are shared. The participating parties operate according to some ground rules, explicit or otherwise, which may include what can—or cannot—be grown, treatment of borders, and responsibility for upkeep of paths.

Community gardens are more than a century-old phenomenon in the United States.[3] This broader context is key to understanding the significance of the example at hand under criteria A.1, A.2, A.3, and A.6. The first examples were started during the depression of the 1890s to improve the plight of unemployed blue-collar workers in cities. Similar initiatives were launched during the early 1930s, but on a more limited basis. Far more prolific were the community gardens developed in cities during

the 1970s and 1980s. An outgrowth of both the civil rights and environmental movements, these gardens were primarily created by and for poor minority groups on land left fallow by the depopulation of blighted inner-city areas. In Washington, this phenomenon has attracted middle-class participants as well. The Newark Community Garden, created circa 1976, lies adjacent to the McLean Gardens apartment complex off Wisconsin Avenue. Friendship Community Garden exists in the middle of a single-family house district in American University Park. Other examples include the Fort Stephens, Emory, and Peabody community gardens in a predominantly single-family-house Brightwood neighborhood. Such tracts may be considered important for historical reasons in the future, for they have done much to foster a sense of togetherness in their neighborhoods. And, as the distinguished urban historian Sam Bass Warner has emphasized, these gardens revive a longstanding practice in the preindustrial city, where space was routinely used for growing plants to sustain the household.[4]

The most widespread development of community gardens, however, came during the two world wars, when gardening was championed as a patriotic duty to ensure adequate supplies of food for U.S. and Allied troops as well as for workers on the home front.[5] It is to this momentous period that 3901 Connecticut's garden owes its origins. Franklin Roosevelt declared in 1942 that "food is no less a weapon than tanks, guns and planes."[6] Gardening became a national pastime. A Washingtonian, Charles Lathrop Pack, organized the liberty garden initiative in 1917 and also coined the term victory garden, which became the official name of the World War II counterparts. The National Victory Garden Program, as it was called, was directed by a federal agency, the War Food Administration. In 1944, the program's third year, some 20 million victory gardens were yielding 40 percent of the nation's fresh vegetables.

Many victory gardens were planted by individuals on whatever space was available—in flower boxes and on tiny parcels of land as well as on house lots. Apartment dwellers contributed to the effort primarily by creating com-

FIG. 11.1. Community garden, 3901 Connecticut Avenue, N.W., Washington, D.C., ca. 1942; modified as flower garden ca. 1946; destroyed 1996. (Photo Richard Longstreth, 1995)

FIG. 11.2. Westchester apartments, 4000 Cathedral Avenue, N.W., Washington, D.C., 1929-31, Harvey H. Warwick, architect, Morris Cafritz and Gustave Ring, developers-builders. View of central garden. (Photo Richard Longstreth, 1995)

munity gardens, to which the abundant public open space permeating many of Washington's residential districts lent itself. The two major surviving examples on public land are the Sedgwick Community Garden (fig. 11.3), across the street from 3901 Connecticut, and the Glover Park Community Garden at Tunlaw Road and 42nd Street, N.W. Public land was similarly used by residents of row houses, as in the case of another rare surviving example, the Whitehaven Community Garden at 39th and W streets, N.W.[7]

The great majority of victory gardens disappeared after the war. They were never intended to be permanent. Often, the property reverted to a previous state or was developed. The continually changing residency of an apartment house posed additional challenges for maintaining a community garden on or near the premises. For all these reasons, the survival rate of victory gardens is very low. Among the more than thirty community gardens existing in Washington, the great majority are less than

twenty years old; only six are known to have originated during World War II.[8] The garden at 3901 Connecticut Avenue is of historical interest on these grounds alone, but there are additional aspects that contribute to its significance as an extremely unusual landscape in the District of Columbia.

First, this garden is an exception because it originated as a victory garden on privately held land that is part of an apartment complex. The one other known example is at the Kennedy-Warren, and there is perhaps a third, now neglected, at Cathedral Mansions. Both are smaller than that at 3901 Connecticut and are quite marginal to the spatial patterns of their respective complexes. The Kennedy-Warren's is tantamount to a secret garden in that it is almost impossible to find even when one knows it is there. By contrast, that at 3901 Connecticut functions much like the garden of a single-family house. It is a completely private space, shielded by foliage from public view at the rear of the apartment building. At the same

FIG. 11.3. Sedgwick Community Garden, Sedgwick Street, N.W., between Tilden Street and Connecticut Avenue, Washington, D.C., ca. 1942. (Photo Richard Longstreth, 1995)

time, it has always been a conspicuous space for that building's residents, and one that has been routinely a part of many of their lives. This relationship is also entirely different from that at Sedgwick and Glover Park gardens, where the plots lie in full public view beside the street.

The garden at 3901 Connecticut Avenue is further distinguished by the fact that for most of its life—since World War II—it has been cultivated primarily for ornamental rather than utilitarian purposes; it has been a flower garden, not a vegetable garden (fig. 11.4). Furthermore, related recreation spaces form an integral part of the ensemble, including a lawn for picnics, sitting, and other passive activities, and a terrace for outdoor cooking. These facets render the ensemble a much more visually coherent whole than most community gardens, where the size and configuration of plant materials tend to emphasize the individuality of allotments.

The siting of 3901 Connecticut Avenue's garden helps give it an important role in the complex as a whole. The garden effectively transforms the rear from a service space, common to apartment complexes of this period along Connecticut Avenue and in similar locations, to an actively used space. The garden has always functioned as a gathering place—a place to talk with neighbors, a place to take friends, a place in which to have one's photograph taken, as well as a place for individual contemplation, enjoyment, and exercise. Unlike the manicured grounds of the Westchester, for example, it is a place in which the residents assume the essential role in planning and maintenance. It is a personal creation, not an institutional one, and in this respect its significance is social, not just physical.

The differences between 3901 Connecticut Avenue's community garden and others of the period do not make either kind intrinsically more or less significant, but they do underscore the importance of the former as a virtually unique historic resource in this city. Unlike all the others, it combines the attributes of a community garden with those of a private garden.

FIG. 11.4. Community garden, 3901 Connecticut Avenue, N.W., general view. (Photo Richard Longstreth, 1995)

In so doing, it has markedly affected the living patterns of many of the apartment building's residents over the past half century. Since the mid-1940s, the grounds have evolved to a considerable extent, reflecting changes in horticultural taste as well as individual preferences in plant material. Yet those physical modifications have been gradual. The basic form, composition, and character of the landscape remain much the way they were two generations ago, a condition documented by vintage photographs and interviews with long-term residents. A sense of continuity has prevailed over one of change. Assessed as a landscape, which can never be static, the garden certainly meets criterion B in terms of possessing a sufficient degree of integrity for designation.

To take the garden away from 3901 Connecticut Avenue is no different from removing the backyard from a house. The *building* is not altered under those circumstances, but the character of the place and the routines of its occupants have been irrevocably changed.

As a phenomenon, the community garden represents a type of human activity—both individual endeavor and collective interaction—on the landscape that has contributed significantly to the heritage and culture of this and of many other cities. The nature of activity does not have to be extraordinary to be meaningful in this way. The garden at 3901 Connecticut Avenue is of unquestionable importance to those who live there, but it is an important object lesson for preservation, too. Such places are all too easily ignored because we take them for granted. This garden embodies a significant form of landscape design. "Design" can be a misleading term, for it is all too often associated with a structured undertaking among professionals for which there is a documentary record. Throughout the history of humankind, however, many things are not designed in this fashion. The significance of 3901 Connecticut Avenue's garden stems from its grassroots origins, in conception and in execution; that is, from the *absence* of professional procedures. It is a *vernacular* design, pure and simple. We do not always understand such places and may not take the time to get beyond superficial appearances to examine the important traditions they may represent. This garden is a singular historic resource in Washington and a valuable one to understanding the rich, multifaceted history of landscape in the nation's capital.

12   Nonconforming [?] Modernism

The Friendship Shopping Center in Washington, D.C.

Situated on Wisconsin Avenue, long a major route extending northwest from Georgetown, and drawing from a large, adjacent garden apartment complex as well as a series of affluent residential neighborhoods—most immediately, Cleveland Park—the Friendship Shopping Center (1953–54) is the largest complex of its kind ever built in Washington, D.C.[1] Encompassing some 80,000 square feet of commercial space, which included two large and fourteen small stores at street level and around sixteen offices above—all served by two parking lots with a combined capacity of approximately 300 cars—the sprawling complex at once became a major locus of business activity. At the same time, the design is not likely to elicit attention for its physical attributes. A pair of low-slung buildings, sheathed in a reddish-orange brick and large, plate-glass windows face the sidewalk in unassuming fashion as background for corporate signage and window displays (fig. 12.1). Rendered in a matter-of-fact modernism that characterizes countless examples of commercial architecture of the post–World War II period, the complex might seem striking solely for being so "ordinary." Surrounded by earlier residential and institutional buildings, many of them elegantly embellished in a spectrum of eclectic modes, the complex could even be construed as intrusive—a textbook case of a nonconforming property in a historic district.[2] In fact, the Friendship Shopping Center appears to have been developed very much with its setting in mind. Without historical allusions, the complex nonetheless was indeed likely tailored to the needs and physical characteristics of the neighborhood it served.

The Shopping Center

The shopping center as a type of business development—planned, constructed, owned, and managed by a single entity, with a selected mix of mutually reinforcing tenants whose goods and services are targeted to a specific audience—plays an important role in Washington's history. The city was the birthplace of the first successful integration of the neighborhood-oriented shopping center idea and the drive-in concept, whereby the site, size, configuration, and other basic attributes of the scheme are determined by the dictates of providing adequate off-street parking for customers. The pioneering example was the Park and Shop (1930), which lies a few blocks away on Connecticut Avenue near Cleveland Park's eastern edge (see fig. 6.2). Receiving much praise in professional and trade journals, the Park and Shop became a national model, but it also served as a defining precedent locally. Between 1935 and 1941 over thirty-five other examples were built in the metropolitan area, eighteen of them in the District alone—by far the largest number found in any metropolitan area in the country at that time. The nation's

This chapter is an expanded and refined version of testimony I drafted, but never delivered to, the District of Columbia Historic Preservation Review Board in 2002. The landmark nomination was withdrawn by the applicant following an agreement on the site's future density that suggested retention of the buildings. During protracted negotiations with subsequent property owners over the last decade, the allowable density has increased, paving the way for new construction. The shopping center was demolished in the latter months of 2012.

FIG. 12.1. Friendship Shopping Center, Wisconsin Avenue and Newark Street, N.W., Washington, D.C., 1953–54, David Baker, architect, Kass-Berger, developers; demolished 2012. General view of Wisconsin Avenue face. (Photo Richard Longstreth, 2010)

capital and its environs served as the principal incubator for the neighborhood shopping center at the formative stage of its development.[3]

These pre–World War II examples as well as the efforts of the Washington-based Urban Land Institute, founded in 1940 by an alliance of real estate developers seeking to raise standards of planning, design, and management in their field, were central factors in the drive-in neighborhood shopping center becoming a widespread national phenomenon after 1945. Examples proliferated in the counties surrounding the District no less than in other parts of the country, but few were now built in the city itself, owing to the fact that most areas were already developed and adequate land on which to build a low-density shopping center was scarce as well as generally expensive.[4] Less than a half dozen were realized; most of them were quite small and located in the still-developing neighborhoods east of the Anacostia River. The Friendship Shopping Center was the only example constructed in Northwest Washington and is in fact the last of its kind to be realized in the city—the final testament to a rich legacy over twenty years in the making.

One of the two principal tenants (or anchors) of the Friendship Shopping Center—Giant Food—also looms large in the history of Washington businesses. Established by N. M. Cohen (1890–1984), a butcher from Lancaster, Pennsylvania, with the financial backing of Sam Lehrman, a wholesale food distributor from Harrisburg, Giant opened its first store in 1936.[5] Cohen selected Washington for his new venture because of the city's relatively stable economy and the lack of local competitors who were committed to a new approach to food distribution manifested in the supermarket. During its early development in the 1930s, "supermarket" referred to not just a building, but also to an idea, one that was revolutionary in the retail field.[6] The basic objective of the supermarket was to turn over a large volume of goods at a high rate. The extent of sales kept prices low. Prices would attract customers, but so would the convenience of finding a great variety of items under one roof and paying for all of these goods at a single checkout stand. This system generated a selling space that also was a pronounced departure from the norm. Instead of having a confined area where the inspection and sale of a few goods were handled by one of the store's staff, customers were left to roam freely in a large, nondirectional, nonhierarchical space where they could select numerous goods on their own, paying for them at the end of the process. Eventually, this approach to merchandising transformed the retail field, affecting virtually all components in recent decades. In the mid-1930s, however, it was still a very new idea in the District, one that was met with considerable skepticism and some hostility.

From the opening of his first "Giant Food Shopping Center" on Georgia Avenue near Park Road, N.W., Cohen aggressively advanced the supermarket idea in the metropolitan area. The second store opened a year later, in December 1937, on Bladensburg Road, just north of H Street, N.E., next to the city's major Sears, Roebuck store. Encompassing some 20,000 square feet, this Giant supermarket was by far the largest of its kind in the city and ranked among the largest in the East, bringing the company national publicity in the process.[7] Six stores were in operation, all but one of them in the District, by the close of 1941. The immediate postwar years saw Giant expand at an even faster rate. Twelve units opened between 1945 and 1949, seven of them in the city. Seven more were completed prior to the one in the Friendship Shopping Center. By mid-1955, Giant had thirty-five supermarkets in Arlington, Fairfax, Montgomery, and Prince George's counties as well as in Washington and Alexandria.[8] Throughout this period, Giant was the industry's leader in the region. Much like Ralphs Grocery Company in Los Angeles, which contributed more than any other enterprise to develop the supermarket idea, Giant's example forced the local competition to follow its lead.

Remarkable as it may seem today, the supermarket was more the exception than the rule as part of a shopping center in the immediate postwar years. The supermarket had developed independently of the shopping center and often of other stores of any kind. One of the supermarket's strengths, industry leaders believed, was that it possessed sufficient draw to be a destination in its own right. Small grocery and other food stores were common to early neighborhood shopping centers, but supermarkets were not,

as many of the parties involved believed that the size of the supermarket and the large number of cars it drew did not make for a good fit. Only after World War II, and then only gradually and sometimes reluctantly, did the two components come together as the use of much larger tracts of land became the norm.[9]

Locally, Giant was the pioneer in integrating its expansion program with shopping center development. The first such coupling was the Minnesota Business Center (1946–47) at Minnesota Avenue and Benning Road, N.E., followed by the Arlandria Shopping Center near Alexandria, Virginia (1946–47), the Fillmore Gardens Shopping Center in Arlington (1947–48), and the Flower Avenue Shopping Center in Silver Spring, Maryland (1948–50).[10] In 1952, Giant stores opened simultaneously at Virginia Square, built next to the first branch of Kann's department store in Arlington, and nearby at Parkington, the Hecht Company development at Wilson Boulevard and Glebe Road, which was the area's first regional shopping center.[11] The following year, within two months of one another, additional Giant stores opened at the Friendship Shopping Center and as the first unit of the Chevy Chase Shopping Center farther north on Wisconsin Avenue in Maryland, just over the District line.[12] Soon thereafter, plans were unveiled for a Giant in a sizeable Prince George's County shopping center anchored by Lansburgh's department store.[13] Within a six-year period, Giant had established a presence in nearly all of the most important new shopping centers constructed in the metropolitan area.

The Friendship Shopping Center was not only the last of its kind to be built in the District, reflecting the relative small-scale, low-density, suburban character that many outlying sections of the city possessed as they evolved during the first half of the twentieth century, but it is also a unique example of its type in terms of both configuration and tenant mix. Beginning with the Park and Shop, Washington-area examples of the neighborhood shopping center were distinguished by having the car lot at the front, between the street and the building(s). The arrangement was extremely unusual at that time, but became the preferred one nationally within a few years after the Second World War. The Friendship Shopping Center broke with this pattern by placing the parking areas on each of the two occupied blocks at the rear (fig. 12.2). Several factors probably contributed to the decision to develop this layout, which had for the most part been rejected for shopping centers by the mid-1950s due to the inconvenience it posed for motorists in reaching the store entrances.[14] In all likelihood, the overriding factor was related to topography. With the land sloping to the west, stores placed at the rear of the property would scarcely be visible from Wisconsin Avenue. It also made sense to place the stores at the front property line to cater to the unusually large pedestrian trade that came from nearby apartments and well as customers who rode the public transit lines along Wisconsin Avenue. Furthermore, the complex did not stand alone, but was part of a small, street-oriented shopping area that had emerged before the Depression. Given the size of the parking lot that was deemed necessary by the early 1950s—three times the selling area of the stores and much larger than prewar examples—it also made sense to tie the shopping center into the existing commercial fabric rather than ignore it. In addition, the north building in the complex not only was designed for street-level businesses, but also for a full second floor of office space, mostly occupied by insurance agents and physicians, and an unusual component of postwar shopping centers (fig. 12.3). This mixing of functions did not make much

sense on the urban periphery, where space was adequate for separate office facilities, but it did work in what had become a close-in site where land was comparatively scarce in quantity and high in cost. Sequestering the offices at the rear of the property, with views of the car lot instead of the street, was not a sound planning strategy, again reinforcing the utility of a streetfront orientation. All these factors probably contributed to a solution that was closely tailored to the shape and location of the site, not only along Wisconsin Avenue but also at the rear, where the car lots are set back and screened so as to lessen the visual intrusion on the residential blocks beyond.[15]

The second anchor tenant, C. G. Murphy Company, was also an unusual tenant for a shopping center at that time. Throughout the country, variety store chains tended to avoid shopping center locations, which they considered too remote and poorly sited to attract the pedestrian trade they still saw as their core patronage. In outlying areas, traditionally structured business districts, such as those at Georgia Avenue and Colesville Road in Silver Spring and in the Clarendon district of Arlington County, were the magnets for variety stores.[16] Only as viable options outside the shopping center began to disappear during the 1950s did the variety store commit to a decisive change in course. Locally, the Murphy stores at the Minnesota Business Center, Parkington, and Friendship were among the first to break from the norm.

Nonetheless, the architectural character of

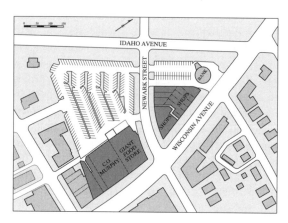

FIG. 12.2. Friendship Shopping Center, site plan, ca. 1954. (Drawing by Paul Davidson, 2013, after print in author's collection)

FIG. 12.3. Friendship Shopping Center, Newark Street face of north building. (Photo Richard Longstreth, 2001)

the Friendship Shopping Center is utterly typical for commercial work of its time. Such design is also decidedly out of fashion today, and discussing the issue warrants some background. With the recent rise of interest in popular culture of the 1950s and the post–World War II era more generally, we tend to focus on certain memorable images, which in turn provide the dominant framework for our perspective on and assessment of the period. In architecture, this has translated into an embrace of flashy forms, colors, and materials. Such work did exist, and some of it still does. But what Chester Liebs termed "exaggerated modern" and Alan Hess later popularized as "Googie" represents only one part, and not necessarily the dominant part, of the equation.[17] For every boomerang- or fin-shaped element, for every sputtering neon light display, for every spacecraft, beachcomber's shack, or other seductive allusion, many more examples were created in the commercial as well as institutional realms that embody more restrained and often pragmatic approaches to expression. This latter realm was arguably

the mainstream of postwar architecture, and it should not be dismissed as inconsequential, despite its absence of flash. It represents a very important current in American culture of that time, one premised on technical efficiency and on a level of social mobility that was markedly greater than in previous eras and one that was having a pronounced effect on life in this country. This approach was also especially appropriate to Washington, where under the purview of the National Capital Park and Planning Commission, architectural forms and signs deemed unduly conspicuous were not condoned.

We are only beginning to understand the decisive impact World War II had on the American outlook. The most gruesome armed conflict humankind had known was won with American technological and organizational prowess. Without pretense or fanfare we had introduced one innovation after another in matériel and in the systems to manage it that allowed the nation to overcome seemingly insurmountable odds. The "clean," logical, and efficient character of American design was an integral part of the story. GIs returned stateside not with visions of châteaux or other Old World splendors, as many of their forebears had in 1918, but of the ingenious virtuosity of U.S. military bases—the barracks, warehouses, airfields, and many other components that had been erected quickly, economically, and effectively thousands of miles from home, in a logistical transfer of a magnitude theretofore unimaginable.[18]

The war had a profound social impact on the nation as well. Hundreds of thousands of men and women of modest means, whose parents had been among the majority barely benefiting from the supposed economic boom of the 1920s, who grew up in the lean years of the Depression, and had matured on the front or in the factory, acquired a new level of skill and some financial security. These circumstances, coupled with the GI Bill and a booming economy, created a true mass consumer market, one far greater than in previous generations. With newfound and increasing prosperity, mobility, and choices, the vast new middle class had a significant impact in shaping tastes of the era. The physical record in all its dimensions makes very clear that neither aristocratic nor parvenu splendor was pursued, as it frequently was in popular culture before the war. But almost everything that might remind people of the world they left behind was summarily rejected as well. The new environment was decidedly not uptown, but it was not the old neighborhood either. Like wartime production, it was straightforward, no-nonsense, efficient, and exuded modernity.[19] The functionalist polemic of the modernist avant-garde, minus the artistically driven sophistication in the development of form, space, and detail, provided the architectural profession with a basis for departure. At the same time, the modernist mainstream—the vernacular, if you will—of the 1940s and 1950s was not rooted in ideology and certainly not in foreign examples, but rather in the way it addressed American preferences. To the consumer, who probably had more disposable income than her or his parents had enjoyed for most of their lives, and certainly much more than their European counterparts, this modernism was neat, orderly, efficient, economical, commodious, and convenient, catering to prac-

tical needs while eschewing indulgence—an environment that seemed wholly new, a proud legacy of wartime achievements.

The Friendship Shopping Center's design thus must be assessed on its own terms, not on those of other modernist strains. Its straightforward appearance should not be dismissed simply as plain—stripped to a minimum by economic expediency. Many buildings of this kind were admired in their day for the very qualities some now deride. Images in Giant's and Murphy's advertising make clear that the physical attributes of the complex were viewed as strong, positive ones for their target audience (fig. 12.4).

The Developer

The Friendship Shopping Center was also a major work of its developer, Garfield Kass (1889–1975). Kass's name may not loom large today, but from the late 1920s through the 1950s he ranked among the most prominent developers of commercial property in the metropolitan area. Born in the small town of Rockville, the seat of then-rural Montgomery County, Maryland, he was a nephew of Morris Cafritz, one of the Washington's largest residential real estate developers during the first half of the twentieth century. Kass's career, however, began in Newport News, Virginia, where his family had moved around 1900. After serving in the army, Kass embarked on large-scale house building in his adopted city, only to have the market evaporate once the boom in ship construction ended. In debt, Kass moved to Washington, where he worked for his uncle until he established his own real estate development and building firm in 1926.[20] Soon he made a specialty of catering to the needs of fast-growing chain store companies in outlying areas of the city and surrounding jurisdictions. The Great Atlantic & Pacific Tea Company (better known as A&P), Sanitary Grocery, F. W. Woolworth, and S. S. Kresge were among his clients. Kass also built store blocks tailored to the needs of a group of chain tenants, as with the 5900 block of Georgia Avenue (1937), which originally housed a small Sears outlet, a Superior Market, and a Pep Boys store as well as a beauty salon.[21] The firm was further known for building neighborhood movie theaters, such as the Beverly (1938–39; demolished) and the McArthur (1944–46).[22]

After Shannon & Luchs pioneered the drive-in neighborhood shopping center with the Park and Shop, Kass Realty Company was the first competing firm to adopt the model, beginning with Kass's Colonial Village Parking Stores in Arlington and Georgia Avenue Park and Shop Center in the District (both 1935–36). Kass then went on to develop three more complexes, at New Hampshire Avenue and First Street, N.W. (1936), in Clarendon (1937–38), and, perhaps best known, the Chevy Chase Park and Shop Stores (1938), which included a bowling alley and ice skating rink (fig. 12.5).[23] On the eve of World War

FIG. 12.4. Friendship Shopping Center, Giant Food Store opening advertisement. (*Washington Post*, 9 November 1953, 7)

II, no other developer had matched his commitment to this new and still experimental realm.

After the war, Kass constructed a twelve-story office building that bore his name in downtown Washington (1950–51), but his best-known projects remained retail facilities well removed from the city center.[24] The three major projects the firm undertook during this period were all larger and more ambitious in the array of tenants they housed than the prewar shopping centers, which tended to have ten or fewer units each. The Allen Shopping Center in Prince George's County, planned in 1946 and built four years later, had sixteen stores and a movie theater.[25] The Friendship Shopping Center, to which Kass and his new partner, son-in-law Irving Berger, relocated their offices, followed. The culminating venture of this kind was Seven Corners in Fairfax County, probably the most ambitious shopping center along the Eastern Seaboard south of the New York metropolitan area when it opened in September 1956 (fig. 12.6). Seven Corners was also among the first regional centers in the nation to secure two major department stores as anchors, and was a pioneering example of the dumbbell plan, which eventually became a standard configuration for the type.[26]

The architect for many of Kass's projects was James F. Hogan (1906–1979), who joined the firm in 1937 after several years of working for another prominent Washington developer, Waverly Taylor. Hogan received his training at Catholic University in Washington and the Beaux-Arts Institute of Design in New York. He was responsible for the plans of all the known retail and residential endeavors that Kass initiated prior to departing the company to open his own office in 1950.[27] For such buildings as the Beverly and the McArthur, Kass secured the services of two architects who specialized in designing movie theaters—John Eberson from New York, who was arguably then the nation's leading architect in that realm, and John Zink from Baltimore, who was preeminent in the greater region.[28] Though Kass was very much in control of the conceptualizing of his projects, he nonetheless depended upon well-qualified professionals, in-house or on a contractual basis, to develop these concepts effectively into three-dimensional form.

FIG. 12.5. Chevy Chase Park and Shop Stores, 4433-65 Connecticut Avenue, N.W., Washington, D.C., 1937-38, James F. Hogan, architect, Kass Realty Company, developer; since altered. (Photo ca. 1938; B. F. Saul Company, Bethesda, Maryland, courtesy James M. Goode)

FIG. 12.6. Seven Corners Shopping Center, Arlington Boulevard and Leesburg Pike, Falls Church, Virginia, 1954–56, Kass-Berger, designers and developers; since altered. (Photo Richard Longstreth, 1988)

The Architect

For the Friendship Shopping Center, Kass commissioned David Baker (1917–1980), who had recently entered private practice. After receiving his B.S. in architecture at the Illinois Institute of Technology in 1938, Baker was awarded a graduate scholarship under Ludwig Mies van der Rohe. He then transferred to Harvard's Graduate School of Design, studying under Walter Gropius. Having trained with two of the twentieth century's titans of architectural design and education, Baker entered active duty, moving to Washington, where he worked at the Naval Ordinance Laboratory and the Bureau of Ships. He stayed in the military after the war, designing hangers and other facilities at National Airport (fig. 12.7), as well as at Andrews and Bolling Air Force bases, and in 1952 established his own firm. The Friendship Shopping Center was among his first projects, followed by several other stores for Giant, including the one at Langley Park (fig. 12.8). He also designed or remodeled stores, including the Seven Corners branch of Jelleff's, a major apparel emporium. Finally, Baker produced a number of unsolicited proposals for development on the metropolitan periphery and for downtown, including a

pedestrianway for F Street.[29] Baker's practice never rivaled the major firms, and he remains a largely forgotten figure today. But whatever his reputation, it is evident from the record that his designs were the product of thought, care, and attention. His nearly ten years of service in the military no doubt had as significant an impact on his outlook as his training with the avant-garde masters. The evidence clearly shows that the Friendship Shopping Center was far from a hastily conceived and executed scheme. Indeed, both architect and developer appear to have devoted considerable energy to tailoring the design to the particulars of its setting, and to creating an emblem of modernity that was simultaneously dignified and respectful of its environs and a departure from most buildings on the Wisconsin Avenue and other commercial corridors.

In addition, the Friendship Shopping Center is a rare place in the metropolitan area where a retail complex of any kind from the late 1940s or early 1950s has survived more or less intact.[30] Other major shopping centers dating from the postwar period in greater Washington have been extensively remodeled or demolished, and extensive changes have been made to all but one of Kass's shopping centers and to most

FIG. 12.7. Aircraft hangers, National (now Reagan National) Airport, George Washington Parkway, Arlington, Virginia, 1950, David Baker, architect. Hanger on left since altered; other components demolished. (Photo Richard Longstreth, 1970)

FIG. 12.8. Giant Food Store at Langley Park Shopping Center, New Hampshire and University avenues, Langley Park, Maryland, 1955–56, David Baker, architect; since altered. (Photo Richard Longstreth, 1971)

of his store blocks from the prewar years. Even the capital's more run-of-the-mill store blocks from this period have, with few exceptions, had their character substantially modified. Despite efforts to preserve them, much of the fabric of the area's principal suburban postwar commercial districts, Clarendon and Silver Spring, has been lost. Indeed, the legacy of outlying commercial development from the postwar era throughout the region has for the most part vanished.

These circumstances make the condition of the Friendship Shopping Center highly unusual. Virtually all components of the exterior, including storefronts, remain in their original condition or only slightly altered. The most conspicuous changes are the remodeled entrance to the Giant and the replacement windows, dating to the 1980s, upstairs on the north building. Both these modifications, however, are comparatively minor, especially when one considers the

building type. In time and under the right circumstances, these are easily reversible.

In light of these details, and with the fabric of the complex in so remarkable a state of preservation, has sufficient time elapsed to assess this complex adequately from a historical context? The answer is a resounding "Yes." An extensive body of literature on postwar architecture generally and on retail architecture specifically has been published over the past quarter century.[31] Like so many things that we (or the previous generation) once took for granted, the Friendship Shopping Center can therefore be examined from a fresh perspective that lends new meaning and significance to mainstream patterns of another era—recent perhaps, but no less important given its dynamics and dimensions. We can ill afford to lose valuable testaments to this period, particularly when so very few of them are left.

13 The Continuous Transformation of Savannah's Broughton Street

For nearly a century—from the mid-1870s until the mid-1960s—Broughton Street served as principal retail center for Savannah and surrounding areas in South Carolina as well as Georgia. Department stores, apparel stores, jewelry stores, furniture stores, hardware stores, automobile supply stores, and stores purveying a spectrum of other consumable goods were quartered along a stretch of some eight blocks.[1] Major banking houses lay on or near Broughton Street, as did theaters and restaurants. Small-scale manufacturing and substantial wholesale operations also operated along Broughton in the nineteenth century. During the colonial and post-colonial periods, most commercial establishments hugged the bluff of the Savannah River, upon which the city's economy depended, on the south side of Bay Street. Three decades after Savannah's founding, the erection of the public market structure on Ellis Square, one of four such open spaces delineated in the city's original plan devised under the direction of James Edward Oglethorpe in 1733, which was located one short block south of Bay Street, ensured the area immediately around it would become a focus of commercial development as well.[2] Broughton was the next major east–west street south of the market. Broughton traversed most of Savannah, as the city expanded upon Oglethorpe's plan through much of nineteenth century, during which time the street served as a major connector from the heart of the burgeoning community to the railroad terminals that lined West Broad Street (now Martin Luther King Jr. Boulevard).

Broughton's transformation from street with a mélange of residential and some minor commercial and institutional functions, none of them housed in buildings of import, to a significant business thoroughfare began in the 1850s and exploded during the decades following the Civil War. Growth continued through the first three decades of the twentieth century and resumed with new vigor after World War II. The emergence of Broughton Street as a hegemonic regional retail spine for the city and its environs occurred as a result of Savannah's robust economic growth during the ante- and postbellum periods. Between 1840 and 1860, the city's population nearly doubled, reaching over 22,000 on the eve of the Civil War. By 1880, close to 31,000 people resided in Savannah. Growth continued into the early twentieth century, passing 83,000, and reaching 100,000 in 1920. At the core of Savannah's seventy-year run of prosperity, substantially interrupted only during the Civil War and, to a lesser degree, during the depression of the 1890s, was its large-scale exportation of cotton to domestic and foreign markets. Beginning in the 1840s, the Central of Georgia Railroad, soon followed by other carriers, developed what became within two decades a network of lines second only to Virginia's among Southern states. These routes tapped the vast yields of the cotton belt, propelling Savannah into third place, behind New Orleans and Mobile, in exports of the prized crop by 1860. Timber became a major source of export revenue as well. These industries spawned an array of other manufactories servicing them and

Research for this chapter began for a report I prepared for the Chatham County–Savannah Metropolitan Planning Commission, "Analysis of Selected Post-1937 Buildings in the Savannah National Historic Landmark District," in 1999.

the influx of people, many from the North and Europe, who were coming to the city.[3]

Savannah remained physically unscathed during the war, which contributed to its rapid resurgence. Rebuilt railroad lines and ongoing improvements to the ship channel in the Savannah River fostered the turnaround. By 1867, cotton exports exceeded those of 1859, and while annual fluctuations could be considerable, figures often ran significantly higher over the next two decades. By 1912 the city ranked second worldwide. Over the same period, Savannah began trading in naval stores (such as turpentine, pitch, and rosin oil), becoming the world's biggest distributor on the eve of World War I.[4] And though Savannah was no longer the largest city in Georgia, and did not become a major manufacturing center like Augusta and Columbus, it nonetheless reaped the benefits of a strong, stable economy that was amply manifested, decade by decade, in distinguished architecture.

Over the past half century, Savannah has become ever more renowned for its buildings and the embellished squares and tree-lined boulevards they help define. The antebellum period gave a particularly rich yield of institutional quarters and grand freestanding, semidetached, and row houses, which collectively form an urban landscape that has no counterpart. A somewhat less distinctive but scarcely less engaging enrichment of that landscape occurred between the 1870s and 1910s, with a panoply of buildings of all types.[5] That so much of this legacy remains is to a significant extent due to Savannah's role as a city of trade rather than of manufacture for much of its existence. The dissipation of that trade in the early 1920s, moreover, led to a hiatus in new construction at a time of major expansion in many other U.S. cities. Finally, as economic conditions improved during and after World War II, industry gravitated along an expansive stretch of the Savannah River, while the major thrust of other commercial and residential development occurred in outlying areas, some of them beyond the city limits. The prolonged lack of pressure for new development in Savannah's core, coupled with a conservative population, whose elite was

fiercely proud of the city's heritage, rendered the place as somewhat a physical time capsule in the mid-twentieth century, one that was ripe for the vigorous, innovative preservation efforts that were launched there at that time.[6] Not surprisingly, these circumstances were key in framing notions of what components of the landscape were determined to be historically significant.

During the 1950s and 1960s, preservationists' focus was on work realized before the Civil War. By the next decade, attention broadened to include the postbellum boom years, and by the 1980s, the early twentieth century was embraced as well. Development that occurred after the 1920s was generally considered antithetical to what had become a highly venerated heritage. Mid-twentieth-century changes, in particular, seemed to degrade the scene. Broughton Street was the most conspicuous example, with many nineteenth-century buildings refaced with plain veneers during the 1950s and 1960s, just as they were along Main Streets across the country. The fact that by 1970 Broughton's retail hegemony was being seriously challenged by shopping centers and other new establishments on the urban periphery only added to the sense of the street as a thorn in the middle of a city rejuvenating itself through historic preservation.

But examining Broughton Street's continually changing commercial character and the circumstances that contributed to those developments renders a very different view of the significance of its fabric. Until the locus of retail activity turned elsewhere in the late 1960s, the street was always one in which local business interests—and, by the 1920s, outside enterprises as well—made substantial investments (fig. 13.1).[7] The post–World War II era was in fact among the most significant periods of new development and one of the most important in the street's long history. The retail establishments and other commercial buildings erected during that time represented a major initiative to ensure that Broughton Street would remain the dominant place of business for the region. The fact that such efforts there, and in many small cities nationwide, ultimately failed

FIG. 13.1. 200 block of West Broughton Street, Savannah, looking east. Major buildings include, left to right: Chatham Furniture Co. store, ca. 1900; B. J. Sheppard Co. furniture store, 1905; S. H. Kress & Co. variety store, 1922–23, 1936–37; and, in the distance, Liberty National Bank & Trust Co., ca. 1905, demolished. (Foltz Photographic Studio, 1946; Georgia Historical Society, Savannah, 1360-10-15-03)

should not undermine the significance of such undertakings, which represent a largely forgotten episode in the evolution of American Main Streets. The significance of the postwar transformation of Broughton Street is best understood within the context of the corridor's long history of development.

In some respects Broughton Street in 1960 remained a product of the nineteenth century. Nearly half the commercial buildings standing on its blocks were constructed before 1900. Even while the local economy flourished, the pressures of growth were seldom so great as to warrant demolition of well-built, masonry-wall structures. As a result, Broughton then and today encompasses a complex layering of new construction and remodeling that extends from the 1840s to the present. Broughton Street is a palimpsest that encapsulates many stages of the

city's commercial growth and American commercial architecture.

Commercial Development, 1845–1945

Broughton Street's early commercial development began modestly, as an extension the growth around the market square. Soon, however, some projects became more ambitious in scope. Probably the earliest surviving buildings along Broughton's retail blocks is a speculative row of five units planned in 1845 and constructed between 1846 and 1853 for Alexander A. Smets, situated a block away from the public market.[8] Like many such projects developed in the eastern half of the United States during the second quarter of the nineteenth century, these retained vestiges of domestic character, derived from an earlier generation of party-wall houses that were rapidly converted to commercial purposes as well as buildings designed to accommodate shops at street level and living quarters above (fig. 13.2).[9] The nature of building continued to expand, with business blocks that were not only larger, but thoroughly commercial in character. A four-story speculative building, encompassing over 25,000 square feet, erected in 1854–55 for diplomat and planter William B. Hodgson and his sister-in-law, Mary Telfair, heiress to one of the city's great fortunes, was pivotal in setting a suave, urban tone (fig. 13.3). Equally important was its location, which lay at the corner of Bull Street, a key north–south axis that tied the City Hall on Bay Street to some of Savannah's most prestigious residential squares—a site that was also perceptually removed from the market square hub.[10] Not every attempt to transform Broughton's blocks succeeded, however. The Marshall House hotel, erected two blocks farther east in 1851, had no

impact on the development of its environs and never seems to have become the fashionable hostelry its promoters envisioned.[11]

Hodgson and Telfair's venture, in contrast, spawned a sizable neighbor, containing four store units, constructed right after the Civil War for commission merchant George W. Wylly and wholesaler Samuel Meinhard. The project, with over 40,000 square feet, among the largest commercial buildings in the city to date, was part speculative—Wylly's offices were elsewhere—but half the premises was occupied by Meinhard's operation, trading in apparel and footwear (see fig. 13.3). Concurrently, a large pile was erected one block farther west at 101–103 W. Broughton and occupied by two leading dry goods companies.[12] An ornate, three-unit building rose at 109–113 W. Broughton less than a decade later, while, across the street, the Lyons Block at 26–36 W. Broughton (1878) contained six stores, including Lyons's own sizable

FIG. 13.2. Store buildings for Alexander Smets, 102–108 W. Broughton Street, designed 1845, built 1846–53; various twentieth-century storefront alterations. (Photo ca. 1920s; Georgia Historical Society, Savannah, 1361-PH-9:2-1732)

FIG. 13.3. Hodgson Building, 1–3 W. Broughton Street, 1854–55 (center); commercial building constructed for George W. Wylly and Samuel Meinhard, 5–13 W. Broughton Street, 1866–68, Muller & Bruyn, architects (right); numerous later alterations. (Photo ca. late 1860s–1870s; author's collection)

grocery business.[13] These major projects were augmented by a number of other three-story buildings more modest in dimension, but no less embellished in their fronts.

Broughton Street experienced what was probably its most intensive development during the 1880s, with the construction of numerous two- and three-story commercial piles. The most consequential project of the decade was the new dry goods emporium of A. R. Altmayer, which opened in October 1885. Founded seven years earlier as a millinery store in one of the units of Meinhard's building, the business succeeded to the point that it could not only expand its lines significantly, but do so in quarters that far exceeded those of other retailers in the city (fig. 13.4). Purchased by and renamed after Altmayer's partner, Leopold Adler, in 1892, the store remained Savannah's preeminent mercantile house into the mid-twentieth century.[14] Altmayer's choice of location was also noteworthy, siting his emporium just west of Bull Street.

Like Hodgson and Telfair before him, Altmayer seems to have understood the strategic potential of this cross-axial location. Two of the city's leading hostelries—the venerable Pulaski and Screven houses—faced Johnson Square, a block to the north, and the Oglethorpe Club, the most elite in the city, occupied the building directly across the street. Soon after Altmayer's was completed, an even taller building, housing Ludden & Bates's Southern Music House, a prominent manufacturer of and dealer in music instruments, was erected next door.[15] Altmayer's remained on the retail edge, however. Decades would elapse before the blocks on East Broughton Street became important retail locations. The other two largest projects of the 1880s, four-story twin buildings constructed for a leading dry goods retailer, Daniel Hogan, and an investment partner (1883–84; rebuilt 1889) and for hardware merchant Joseph. D. Weed (1889–90), anchored the intersection of Barnard Street, two blocks to the west (fig. 13.5).[16]

The commercial functions found on Broughton Street encompassed a considerable range throughout the second half of the nineteenth century. Stores selling boots and shoes were the most numerous by 1881 (thirteen; eighteen in 1901). Dry goods houses probably dominated trade throughout (nine in 1866, twelve in 1881, ten in 1901), followed by furniture stores (five, seven, and nine, respectively). Jewelers became plentiful by 1881 (six), as did clothing stores (six; nine in 1901). Grocers dotted the street in 1866 (six), increasing by the century's end (nine). Other stores sold china and glass, books, cigars and tobacco, pharmaceuticals, hardware, liquor or beer, toys, candy, dairy products, fruit, trunks, stoves, and wallpaper. Two stores purveyed agricultural implements and/or guns in 1901; three specialized in saddles. A number of services were also provided by tailors, barbers,

dressmakers, an undertaker, an upholsterer, dentists and physicians, a gas fitter, photographers, a lock- and gunsmith, blacksmith, and notary public. Saloons grew from two in 1881 to nine in 1901; boarding houses from four to five. By 1881 a variety of light manufacturing businesses were established along Broughton, including a cabinetmaker, cigar maker, soda water manufacturer, two boot makers, and a maker of railings. By that time, too, several retailers included lucrative wholesale operations: three in dry goods, two in groceries. Only Meinhard's business was exclusively for the wholesale market. The number of combination wholesale and retail enterprises rose over the next two decades to eight in dry goods, three in clothing, three in groceries, and one in notions. At the turn of the twentieth century, Broughton Street was well poised not only to command the

FIG. 13.4. A. R. Altmayer & Co. dry goods store (later Leopold Adler) department store, 1–7 E. Broughton Street, 1884–85; Ludden & Bates's Southern Music House, 9–11 E. Broughton, ca. 1885–86, incorporated into Adler's ca. 1916, at right. Both buildings burned in 1958. (Foltz Photography Studio, 1930; Georgia Historical Society, Savannah, 1360-09-23-08)

FIG. 13.5. Daniel Hogan dry goods store and twin building, 125 and 123 W. Broughton Street, respectively, 1883–84; burned 1889; rebuilt with minor modifications 1889. To left, store block erected for E. E. Buckner, 1889, and occupied by F. W. Woolworth Co. variety store ca. 1912, 121 W. Broughton; store block erected for A. S. Cohen, 1889, and occupied by Schulte-United junior department store in 1929, 115 W. Broughton; three-store block erected for Edward Lowell, ca. 1873–74, and occupied by J. C. Penney Co. junior department store in 1934 and Schulte-United in 1929, 109–113 W. Broughton. (Photograph ca. 1934–40; Georgia Historical Society, Savannah, 1361-PH-9:2-1731)

immediate market, but to service retailers in a much larger hinterland.[17]

The number of new buildings constructed along Broughton Street during the opening two decades of the twentieth century nearly equaled that of the 1880s, but the nature of the work differed in several ways. Most new store blocks were modest affairs, rendered in a forthright manner without much embellishment, reflecting the restraint that was characteristic to the period. More conspicuous changes occurred with the expansion of furniture stores. In 1907, a hulking, three-story pile constructed in 1851 for the St. Andrew's Society was transformed into the quarters of the Rhodes-Haverty (later Haverty) Furniture Company, rendering it among the largest retail concerns on the street (fig. 13.6). Five years earlier, a mid-nineteenth-century building of nearly equal size that had accommodated the Savannah Carriage & Wagon

Company was purchased by the Walker-Mulligan Furniture Company, which remade it in 1912.[18] But by far the most ambitious project was the circa 1905 construction of the eleven-story office building for the Liberty National Bank & Trust Company at the northwest corner of Broughton and Bull streets. The tallest structure in the city at the time of its completion, the skyscraper tied the budding financial district just to the north to the retail spine, instantly becoming Broughton Street's most prominent landmark (fig. 13.7).[19] The presence of a major office building at this intersection may also have encouraged new commercial development along the two adjacent blocks of Broughton, where at least five new projects were realized between 1910 and 1920, the first such development since the mid-1880s.[20]

The fact that, unlike many other U.S. cities, major new construction was almost nonexistent in downtown Savannah during the 1920s was to a significant degree the result of the decimation of the cotton market caused by voracious boll weevil attacks in the state. However, sufficient diversification had occurred since the turn of the twentieth century for the city's economy to remain basically sound. Substantial new plants were erected for the manufacture of cottonseed oil and fertilizer, as well as the milling of timber—all concentrated along an ever-increasing stretch of the Savannah River, well removed from the city's heart. Aggressive pursuit of new industries during the Depression yielded further development, most notably with the Union Bag & Paper Company, which became the city's largest business.[21]

Under the circumstances, while Broughton Street continued to thrive as a focus of commercial activity, construction was, with a few noteworthy exceptions, limited to small-scale projects. Several substantial store blocks were erected to the east of Bull Street. One of these was for a prominent local enterprise, the Globe Shoe Company, which had occupied smaller quarters at 17 W. Broughton since at least 1890. Located near Adler's department store, the new outlet, opened in November 1929, had a stunning Art Deco design, reputedly inspired by recent stores in New York, with a two-story recessed entry enframed in etched glass (fig. 13.8).[22] Far more conspicuous than its dimensions might indicate, the front was a proclamation of the block's growth as a style center, a place where elegant specialty stores could complement Adler's venerable emporium.

Globe's owners may have been encouraged by the move even farther east made by Levy's department store four years earlier. Founded

FIG. 13.6. Haverty Furniture Co. store, 301–303 W. Broughton Street; built as St. Andrew's Hall, 1851; acquired by and modified for Haverty's, 1907. (Foltz Photography Studio, 1935; Georgia Historical Society, Savannah, 1360-10-17-05)

FIG. 13.7. E. Broughton Street, looking west from near the intersection of Drayton Street. Liberty National Bank & Trust Co. building (rising 11 stories in background center), with the former Oglethorpe Club in front of it; two new store blocks, at 30 and 32 E. Broughton (right); former Morrison House hotel, 102–108 E. Broughton, mid-nineteenth century, demolished ca. late 1940s (far right, below Liberty National Bank). On south side: former Marshall House hotel, 105–123 E. Broughton, ca. 1855 (left foreground); former house, 103 E. Broughton, late eighteenth/early nineteenth centuries (next to Marshall House); and Adler's department store. (Photograph ca. 1910; Georgia Historical Society, Savannah, VM-1361-PH-9-1-1707)

FIG. 13.8. Globe Shoe Company store, 17 E. Broughton, 1928–29, Levy & Clarke, architects; altered 1956. Detail of front. (Photo ca. 1929; courtesy John Sussman)

in 1871, B. H. Levy, Brother & Company rapidly grew into a major dry goods emporium, moving several times before establishing quarters in the pile formerly occupied by Meinhard at 5–9 W. Broughton in 1890. The addition of a fourth story to the premises circa 1905 proved insufficient to meet the store's needs; less than two decades later plans were begun for a new plant of some 53,000 square feet, twice the size of the existing quarters, two blocks to the east. Though not as fashionable as Adler's, Levy's was a strong second in local retailing. Visually that stature was expressed in the new building through its decorum and restraint (fig. 13.9). The exterior was indeed unusually chaste for a major retail establishment of the period, and appears to have been inspired by the reserved formality characteristic of a number of the city's elegant early-nineteenth-century buildings. Among department and dry goods stores, Levy's was also by far the most modern in its layout and appointments. Moreover, the location, away from the most congested blocks of the shopping district, facilitated access for a customer base increasingly reliant on automobiles for routine travel.[23]

No less important a change for Broughton Street was the emergence of chain stores. The trend began in the 1890s with small outlets of pioneering chain operations: the Great Atlantic & Pacific Tea Company (ca. 1892, better known as A&P) and Grand Union Tea Company (ca. 1898–1900). Another pioneer, the nation's largest variety store chain, F. W. Woolworth Company,

leased the building at 121 W. Broughton and the ground floor portion of Hogan's building next door around 1912. Rival S. H. Kress & Company established a unit down the street in 1913. The 1920s became the decade of major chain expansion in Savannah and nationwide. By 1932, the roster on Broughton Street boasted outlets of Lerner's (ca. 1929), Mangel's (ca. 1927), Miller's (1929), Rite's (1928), and Welco (1928) clothing stores; and G. R. Kinney (1929), Mack's (1926), and Thom McAn (ca. 1925) shoe stores. More diverse enterprises included a Schultz-United junior department store (1929), a Sears, Roebuck & Co. outlet (1929), and J. G. McCrory (1925) and W. T. Grant (ca. 1925) variety stores.[24]

All of these establishments occupied existing, mostly nineteenth-century buildings. In 1922, however, Kress embarked on a new project that was part of that company's initiative to erect distinctive, purpose-built stores—a program that set it apart from most chain variety busi-

FIG. 13.9. B. H. Levy, Bro. & Co. department store, 201–221 E. Broughton Street, 1924–25, Levy, Clarke & Bergen, architects; structure incorporated into new, larger building, 1952–54. (Foltz Photographic Studio, ca. late 1940s; Georgia Historical Society, Savannah, 1360-10-03-12)

nesses until at least the late 1930s. In an unusual move on Broughton Street, Kress demolished a substantial, three-story masonry building—albeit one about half a century old—and erected a new facility not much larger in size, but far more accommodating in layout. Business proved sufficiently strong to warrant doubling the building's size in 1936–37. To do so, the company acquired the still new (1927–28) and richly detailed clothing store of Blumberg Brothers and stripped it to portions of the frame to enable the exterior to match that of the existing store, while completely reconfiguring the interior of the older building to become an integral part of the expanded plant (fig 13.10).[25] With the exception of the new Levy's store, which was of equal dimensions, no comparably ambitious purpose-built retail facility had been constructed along Broughton Street since Altmayer's.

Savannah continued to be a good market in which to invest during the decade prior to World War II. J. C. Penney Company, the leading junior department store chain and since the 1920s one of the fastest growing retail operations in the United States, leased quarters at 109–111 W. Broughton in 1934 as part of its program to expand beyond the towns where its business had been so successful and into urban centers. Kress had probably made modifications to the circa 1875 building two decades previous; Penny's did the same in 1939. Concurrently, Sears moved into a larger building at 217–221 W. Broughton, more than doubling its floor space.[26]

For over a decade many independent merchants nationwide had feared chain store development, viewing it as a rapacious predator, fueled by unprecedented rates of expansion and profit margins.[27] Whatever Savannah retailers thought about chains, they managed to hold their own. While some stores such as Blumberg's fell victim to the Depression, most remained in operation. Well into the mid-twen-

FIG. 13.10. S. H. Kress & Co. variety store (right of center), 120–124 W. Broughton Street, 1922–23, E. J. T. Hoffman, architect. Blumberg Bros. clothing store (to the right of Kress), 114–118 W. Broughton, 1927–29; mostly demolished for expansion of Kress store, 1936–37, Edward W. Sibbert, architect. (Foltz Photographic Studio, 1936; Georgia Historical Society, Savannah, 1360-10-13-09)

tieth century, Broughton Street was marked by prominent establishments of considerable longevity. Hogan's began in 1868, three years before Levy's. Adler's dated to 1878; Haverty's to 1885. Globe Shoe Company opened in 1892; the Hub clothing store three years later. Thus, while the street's cumulative business operations were in a continuous state of flux, a substantial degree of mercantile stability existed as well. Patterns of both continuity and change reflected the narrowing of Broughton Street's functional range. Light manufacturing and wholesaling operations moved elsewhere or simply closed. Stores purveying food and other staples grew fewer in number due to both high downtown land prices and the advantages of neighborhood locations. Rooming houses disappeared. Broughton became a street devoted overwhelmingly to nonessential goods; department stores, variety stores, clothing stores, shoe stores, furniture stores, and jewelry stores provided virtually all the impetus for going there.

Between 1936 and 1941, remodeling dominated the construction sphere along Broughton Street, assuming a new dimension of importance in the process. Storefront remodeling had been commonplace locally and nationwide for many decades. During the 1930s, however, the practice became a crucial means for businesses to reinvent themselves in the public's mind, cleansing stores of any vestige of the past, advancing instead an image of progress through modernity.[28] Among the most ambitious of such projects locally was the transformation of the former Walker-Manigan Furniture Company building at 300–308 W. Broughton for a relatively new competitor, Maxwell Bros. & Asbill. B. Karpf, a women's clothing store which was founded in 1906, moved to 107 W. Broughton around 1922, and remodeled the lower stories at that time, now transformed the entire face, balancing élan with reserve (fig. 13.11). Perhaps the most arresting scheme was that for Morris Levy, a prominent clothier, whose phased project completely remade a small block of stores into an Art Deco billboard of structural and plate glass (fig. 13.12). More typical were new fronts of one or two stories, such as the Jones Company clothing store, which nevertheless

FIG. 13.11. B. Karpf clothing store, 107 W. Broughton Street, ca. late 1880s; remodeled for Karpf ca. 1922–24, Levy Clarke & Bergen, architects; extensively remodeled 1939, probably Levy & Clarke, architects. (Foltz Photographic Studio, ca. 1939; Georgia Historical Society, Savannah, 1360-10-12-03)

could have a sweeping effect (fig. 13.13). At street level, if seldom higher up, Broughton Street was bristling with exuberant expressions of newness by 1941.[29]

Commercial Development, 1945–1965

U.S. entry into World War II resulted in a massive influx of people and money to Savannah, with the construction of shipbuilding facilities, a major air base, and other military installations. The local economy continued to grow during the years that followed. A sizable military presence, with the reactivation of what was now Hunter Air Force Base in 1950 and the Parris Island Marine Corps Recruit Depot nearby, was a significant factor. Yet the most important source of increasing revenue remained the city's strategic port location and the ease with which industries could develop along the Savannah

FIG. 13.12. Morris Levy's Store for Men and Shop for Women, 8–12 E. Broughton Street, 1931, Cletus W. Bergen, architects, 1933, 1937, Levy & Clarke, architects, possibly using some structural components of earlier building on site; and store block (right), 14–16 E. Broughton, ca. 1918–20, incorporated into Levy's by 1946; buildings altered 1947 and late 1960s. (Foltz Photography Studio, 1946; Georgia Historical Society, Savannah, 1360-9-25-14)

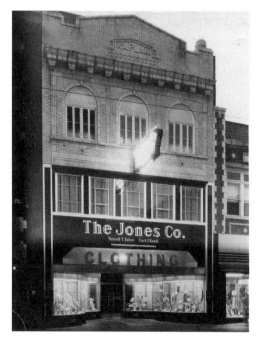

FIG. 13.13. The Jones Company clothing store, 18 E. Broughton Street, ca. 1920; storefront remodeled 1937, Cletus W. Bergen, architect; later alterations. (Foltz Photography Studio, 1937; Georgia Historical Society, Savannah, 1360-09-26-17)

River in an area that encompassed over 31 linear miles by 1958. Some $66 million was invested in new industrial plants and $60 million in existing facilities between 1946 and 1958. Manufacturing, wholesale, and retail businesses rose 24 percent between 1955 and 1958 alone. Prosperity brought an influx of newcomers. The county's population increased by 24.3 percent from 1950 to 1960, exceeding 188,000 in the latter year. The surge in county retail sales was even more dramatic, rising from $86.5 million in 1946 to $193.5 million in 1957.[30] Savannah boomed to an extent that it had not enjoyed since the late nineteenth century, a condition that had a significant impact on Broughton Street.

Even before the war's end, steps were initiated to make East Broughton Street the hub of motion picture exhibition. Modest movie houses had existed there since the 1910s, but the better establishments—the Savannah (ca. 1906-7) and the Lucas (1920-21) theaters—lay elsewhere.[31] Begun in 1946 and opened within a day of one another the following year, the Avon and Weis theaters, at 125 and 218–226 E. Broughton, respectively, ranked among the largest in the city as well as the first major local establishments designed for feature-length, sound films. Seating 1,400 people, the Avon was nearly as large as the Lucas and was developed by the same operation, the Savannah Theatre Company, to compete effectively for an expanding market. Similarly, the Weis Theatre was almost as large and built for Fred G. Weis, whose father had come in 1880 to run the Savannah Theatre and who still operated that facility. Overnight, Broughton Street became the magnet for first-run movies shown in exuberant Art Deco buildings. With its long streetfront, the Weis, especially, was a beacon at Broughton's eastern edge (fig. 13.14).[32]

The Avon and the Weis were the opening salvos of what would become a wholesale transformation of Broughton Street by the early 1960s, and, like them, the major projects that

FIG. 13.14. Weis Theatre, 218–226 E. Broughton Street, 1945–46, Tucker & Howell, architects. (Photo 1946; Georgia Historical Society, Savannah, 1961-PH-14:20-2968)

followed were all on the east side. One of the most prominent schemes was designed for the New York–based women's clothing chain, Lerner Shops, which had opened a modest unit at 17 W. Broughton circa 1929 and expanded into adjacent quarters some fifteen years later. The new building, opposite Adler's at Broughton and Bull, encompassed several times the floor area, with three levels for selling and an additional one for service functions.[33] Besides increasing the lines it carried, Lerner's erected a building that was probably the first retail establishment in the city to be planned as fully air-conditioned. Sealing the building this way, combined with refinements in the mixing of fluorescent and incandescent lighting, allowed the upper floors to be windowless. Above a nearly unbroken expanse of display windows on two sides at ground level, enunciated by a curving canopy of generous proportions, rose an unbroken mass faced in smooth plaster, relieved only by horizontal striations and two large signs bearing the company name (fig. 13.15). Having been the subject of experiments since the mid-1930s, windowless stores, now often sleekly detailed, proliferated after the war.[34] Lerner's Savannah outlet was part of the first wave of such work that gave a wholly new character to the nation's Main Streets. Locally, it must have seemed a radical departure indeed, one that made its neighbors appear old-fashioned irrespective of age.

Concurrently, Levy's was contemplating a major expansion. In 1945, the company's leadership envisioned the addition of two stories to the existing building; a year later, with the trebling of business over the interim period, the addition was planned eventually to have yet two more stories. Following the character established by the 1925 building, the remade plant would allude to local tradition, in this case two of the city's grand, early-nineteenth-century houses.[35] By the fall of 1950, however, the concept had been completely revised. The company would purchase the remainder of the block to expand laterally, a configuration that allowed for a far more efficient layout of selling floors and much easier customer circulation patterns than a multistory arrangement. The new scheme was also of a thoroughly modernist cut, with the existing plant somewhat simplified and tied by a canopy to a sleek, windowless addition. Over the next three years, further revisions were made that retained only the structure of the existing plant, wrapping the entire building in a great wall. The monolithic effect was to a degree mitigated by large corner window banks, sheathed in green granite and offering a hint of the reserve that characterized the older store (fig. 13.16).[36]

The progression in Levy's expansion plans was likely not the result of local decisions alone. In 1947 the business was purchased by Allied Stores, which had emerged as one of the nation's leading retail corporations over the previous decade and was now engaged in an aggressive development campaign. While Levy's management remained in the hands of the family, Allied's leadership would have in all likelihood been assisting to ensure implementation of the most current ideas both in store design and in merchandising. Part of that strategy entailed embracing the regional shopping mall as a supplement to downtown stores in the largest cities, but through the 1950s, the corporation also remained committed to improvements in the city center. Levy's was one Allied's few Southern stores and also one of a handful of its downtown plants nationwide to be so thoroughly remade. Encompassing over 100,000 square feet, it was now the largest emporium in the city. For Allied executives, no less than for Levy's, the new store was a showcase.[37]

Before plans were finalized for Levy's expansion, Woolworth executives committed to constructing a capacious new store next door at 129 E. Broughton, outfitted with self-service counters, a feature that the company was pioneering beyond the realm of the supermarket (fig. 13.17). Like Levy's, the building was fully air-conditioned and had escalators, still a novelty for stores beyond the major urban centers. Encompassing three times the area of the existing store, the new facility was part of a national campaign by the company to expand its downtown units in size and range of goods carried to the point where they would compete with those department stores that were oriented to pur-

FIG. 13.15. Lerner Shops clothing store (left), 2 E. Broughton Street, 1946–47, Cletus W. Bergen, architect, John Tassey Associate. (Photo ca. early 1960s; Chatham County–Savannah Metropolitan Planning Commission, courtesy Sarah P. Ward)

FIG. 13.16. Levy's department store, 201–229 E. Broughton Street, 1953–54, Levy & Kiley, architects. (Photo ca. early 1960s; Chatham County–Savannah Metropolitan Planning Commission, courtesy Sarah P. Ward)

FIG. 13.17. F. W. Woolworth Company variety store, 129 E. Broughton Street, 1953–54, Levy & Kiley, architects; vertical sign now removed. (Photo ca. early 1960s; Chatham County–Savannah Metropolitan Planning Commission, courtesy Sarah P. Ward)

veying low-cost merchandise.[38] In this respect Woolworth's was more a complement than a direct rival to Levy's. Siting the store near the eastern edge of Broughton's shopping district no doubt was determined in part by the availability of land at a time when business along the street was booming, but the decision was also likely affected by the desirability of being adjacent to Savannah's other most modern emporium.

Nearly on par with Levy's, the next most ambitious project in retail development along Broughton Street occurred on the same site where the thoroughfare's preeminence as a shopping district had been vouchsafed by the construction of Altmayer's over a century and a half before. Events were precipitated by the destruction of that building by fire in May 1958. Adler's had been remodeled inside at various times, but it had never had an extensive remaking, and from the street looked much the way it did in 1885, rendering it somewhat of an anomaly in retail facilities. An inherent conservatism, including the notion that updating was not necessary given the store's stature, may have been the root cause for avoiding more pronounced modernization. Now faced with rebuilding, company president Sam G. Adler decided to remove the business from downtown and relocate it as the anchor store in an outlying shopping center of modest size. Other Broughton Street retailers must have been shocked, especially since Adler's new emporium would be more specialized in nature and encompass less than a third of the space as the destroyed plant. The migration did not spawn a mass exodus. Less than four months after the plan was announced, J. C. Penney Company unveiled its project for a sizable store that would rise on the vacated downtown site.[39]

Opened in November 1962, the new Penney's emporium attracted widespread community acclaim. Paralleling the course taken by Woolworth's and some other variety stores, Penney's had been expanding its range of merchandise and its physical facilities to become competitive with full-line department stores. While lacking the elite associations of Adler's, the new Penney's store joined Levy's and Hogan's as downtown's retail anchors, assuring, in the eyes of many, a bright future for Broughton Street. The design followed company models, but was modified to be faced in Savannah grey brick and have other details vaguely suggestive of its setting. Rising four stories, the pile dominated its intersection and indeed offered a potent new visual landmark for the whole district (fig. 13.18).[40] As a retail destination, Penney's was complemented by an equally impressive financial center, the new quarters of the First Federal Savings & Loan Association, the first office building constructed in downtown Savannah since the early 1920s. The company was a relative newcomer, receiving its charter in 1935 and remaining a modest operation a decade later. Over the next fifteen years, however, it grew to be the largest institution of its kind in the region. President

J. D. McLamb, under whose tutelage First Federal had risen, was determined to have that success manifested in architecture. Over a three-year period, he toured new financial quarters nationwide to gather ideas. The six-story building he commissioned stood out, not simply by virtue of its height, but by its elements, most conspicuously three-tiered ranges of louvers that adjusted automatically to the movement of the sun to shield the office floors, enframed by walls sheathed in an aggregate made with Norwegian blue granite (fig. 13.19). In contrast to the reserve that marked Levy's and Penney's new stores, First Federal had a lively character more evocative of modernist work in south Florida than in staid Savannah. With a penthouse (housing civic meeting facilities) and the banking floors enveloped in glass, the premises was intended to be welcoming as well as providing the latest customer amenities.[41]

Collectively, Lerner's, Levy's, Woolworth's, Penney's, and First Federal represented the

FIG. 13.18. J. C. Penney Company department store, 1–5 E. Broughton Street, 1959–60; extensively remodeled 1992–94. (Photograph ca. early 1960s. (Chatham County-Savannah Metropolitan Planning Commission, courtesy Sarah P. Ward)

FIG. 13.19. First Federal Savings & Loan Association, 132 E. Broughton Street, 1959–61, Levy & Kiley, architects; louvers now removed. (Photograph ca. early 1960s; Chatham County–Savannah Metropolitan Planning Commission, courtesy Sarah P. Ward)

greatest density of new building on Broughton since the 1880s, and also the most concentrated embrace of modernity in Savannah. But by 1960, they no longer stood out from their neighbors as much as Lerner's had a dozen years earlier. During the interim period, Savannah's shopping corridor underwent a remodeling boom that encompassed most existing buildings. The great majority of projects were for storefronts, many of them removing the livelier Art Deco facades installed prior to World War II. Others entailed a redesign of the premises, as occurred with the quarters of Stanley Jewelers at 21–27 E. Broughton, Morris Levy across the street, and Ray Jewelry at 202 W. Broughton, all recast in 1946–47.[42]

Within a few years, such remodeling became more ambitious in scale, but also gradually less expensive and more expeditiously executed, reflecting retailers' wish to gain maximum effect for minimum expenditure. Haverty's Furniture Company received an entirely new face as well as extensively remodeled selling

spaces in 1952. The exterior effect was conservative to a degree, recalling Art Deco designs of over a decade earlier (fig. 13.20). At the same time, the sense of solidity and mass conveyed by the materials used suggested a wholly new building rather than merely the application of new veneers. Belk, a large department store chain with operations throughout much of the South, opened a unit in 1946, occupying Sears's former building at 217 W. Broughton. Within a decade, it, too, received a front that read as an entirely new piece of construction.[43] In both cases, the concept entailed bold simplicity, with an expansive, glazed face at street level and a mass of windowless wall above, offset by large signs bearing the company name—a concept that Lerner's had introduced locally.

Other attempts at transformation were less convincing. Hogan's embarked on a major face-lift in 1954, a project that included annexing the adjacent stores after Woolworth's had vacated them. Here, the great expanse of stucco panels that covered the upper stories conveyed no sense of architectural substance. Meinhard's building was similarly remade with an aluminum face in 1961 to accommodate the new home of the fast-growing Asher's clothing store (fig. 13.21). The extensive remodeling, the architect boasted, took less than two months to execute. The rest of Meinhard's building was similarly draped, this time in stucco cast in giant, thinly recessed arches, as part of the makeover for the new facility of Fine's, a prominent local clothing store (see fig. 13.21). Earlier, McCrory's had undertaken a more compromising facelift of the grand pile Hodgson and Telfair had commissioned a century before. While the brick fronts were embalmed with expanses of stucco, some of the original window openings, reduced in size, were retained, indicating that the upper floors were not air-conditioned and conveying more the appearance of a minor industrial plant than a major retail establishment (see fig. 13.21). A number of smaller stores received similar treatments, such that blank walls came to be commonplace on Broughton Street.[44]

For all the changes that occurred between the 1920s and the 1960s, much of the work done emanated, ultimately, from one architectural office. Founded in 1921, the firm of Levy, Clarke & Bergen had strong ties to the community. All three principals—Morton H. Levy (1890–1954), William B. Clarke (1890–1943), and Cletus W. Bergen (1895–1966)—were Savannah natives and graduates of the Georgia Institute of Technology. Their general practice quickly grew to include a wide range of religious, educational, and other institutional buildings as well as commercial ones. Bergen opened his own office in 1927, designing numerous residences, housing projects, military facilities, schools, and college buildings in addition to retail and other business facilities. From 1947 until his death in 1966, he worked in partnership with his son, William P. Bergen (1922–1972). In 1945, Walter F. Kiley (b. 1909), also from Savannah and a Georgia Tech alumnus, became Levy's partner. Levy's son, Henry (b. 1927), worked at the practice as a summer draftsman while he attended

FIG. 13.20. Haverty's furniture store, as remodeled, 1952; exterior facings since removed. (Photo Richard Longstreth, 1999)

FIG. 13.21. McCrory's variety store, as remodeled, ca. mid-1950s (left); Asher's clothing store, as remodeled, 1961, Gunn & Meyerhoff, architects (center); Fine's clothing store, as remodeled, 1962, Cletus and William Bergen, architects (right)— 1–3, 5–9, 11–13 W. Broughton Street, respectively. (Photo ca. 1970s; courtesy of Historic Savannah Foundation)

Georgia Tech and joined the firm in 1954, not long before his father's premature death.[45] The two resulting firms—Bergen & Bergen and Levy & Kiley—designed new quarters for, or alterations to, the buildings of numerous prominent Broughton Street businesses. Indeed, these architects seem to have dominated the commercial sphere locally for at least several decades. If they were continually adjusting the nature of their designs to reflect new general trends, they were also thoroughly familiar with the traditions and distinctiveness of their city.[46]

Decline and Renewal

Despite all the investment made in Broughton Street during the decade and a half after World War II—by local businesses and regional and national companies alike—its retail center failed to grow in the ensuing years. Some modernizing of facilities continued, but it was meager compared to previous years, and new construction was nonexistent. Even if it was stagnant, the retail corridor held its own through the 1960s, then began to experience a steady decline that lasted into the 1990s. The most obvious cause of this shift was the rise of business activity in outlying parts of the city. The initial out-migration began when representatives of Sears announced plans in January 1946 to build a store of nearly 95,000 square feet, several times the size of its existing facility and second only to Levy's, at Bull and Henry streets, some twenty blocks south of Broughton Street. Unlike earlier Sears outlets in Savannah, the new facility would be a full-line department store, and would include a large automobile service station. The siting of this new complex had been the norm for large Sears stores since the company entered the retail field in 1925. Placing stores away from existing businesses so that they would be free of traffic congestion, so that adequate land could be purchased at relatively low cost to allow a horizontal configuration as well as an extensive surface parking lot, and so that the premises were readily accessible to the neighborhoods of moderate-to-middle-income households that constituted the company's core market was a revolutionary practice when it was first implemented, but became a basis for large-scale shopping center development after World War II.[47] Even then, such siting was unprecedented in Savannah and seems to have had no immediate impact on the large investments made along Broughton Street.

Indeed, shopping center development, which began in Savannah during the early 1950s, had little effect on Broughton Street for well over a decade. Of the seven shopping centers of any consequence that opened between 1952 and 1959, six were quite modest, each including between eight and eighteen stores and encompassing no more than 90,000 square feet. The last to open was slightly larger, with twenty-two stores, but hardly represented a pronounced departure from earlier projects. Equally significant, the great majority of businesses in these complexes focused on purveying routine goods and services, not the specialized ones that distinguished Broughton Street. Woolworth's had units in three of these centers; Belk had a branch in one, as did Hogan's, but these were small stores that could not offer the array of merchandise of those downtown. Even Adler's decision to relocate in 1959 entailed downsizing its emporium to a mere 18,000 square feet, enlarging a shopping center that had previously consisted of twelve stores catering to everyday needs. Rather than enhancing Adler's prestige, the move to the suburbs appears to have helped diminish it over the ensuing years.[48]

Shopping center development patterns did not change until the opening of Oglethorpe Mall in 1969, a 550,00-square-foot behemoth that brought Savannah its first regional shopping center. With two anchor department stores—Belk and Sears—and space for a third, the fully enclosed complex embodied state-of-the-art practices in the design of retail complexes.[49]

Even though the development was heralded as a catalyst for expanding the city's market area, bringing in shoppers from some distance afield, it also was a significant competitor with Broughton Street. The Belk store, one of the company's largest and the first planned as part of a regional mall, replaced the much smaller downtown plant. Likewise, the Sears unit replaced its 1946 building. A host of Broughton Street's specialty businesses opened stores at the mall as well, including Desbouillon's, Globe Shoe, Harris-The Hub, Lerner's, Lesser's, McCrory's, Morris Levy, and Thom McAn. Adler's also had a unit. With a total of fifty-eight businesses trading in a broad spectrum of specialty, as well as everyday goods and services, Oglethorpe Mall was a downtown in itself.[50]

Over the next twenty years, nine additional shopping centers comprising over 130,000 square feet were constructed, five of which were anchored by discount stores, mainly Wal-Mart and K-Mart, and three others containing no major emporia. Only Savannah Mall, opened in 1990, rivaled Oglethorpe Mall, with three anchors—Belk and two newcomers to the area, J. B. White and Montgomery Ward—and over one hundred other stores. In response, work soon started on expanding Oglethorpe Mall. Completed in 1992, the enlarged complex had two additional department stores—Atlanta-based Rich's and Penney's, replacing its Broughton Street store—and 134 other outlets encompassing over 963,000 square feet, 80,000 more than its rival. Even before the expansion, sales at Oglethorpe were well over twice those along Broughton Street. Two regional malls, with four times the retail space of Broughton Street's buildings; eleven other shopping centers with more than twenty stores each, totaling more than three times Broughton Street's retail space; many more shopping centers of smaller dimensions; and an array of freestanding retail facilities were all more than Broughton Street could match as a primary commercial district.[51]

Competition from shopping centers was, of course, fueled by the new residential construction on the urban periphery, which catered to newcomers and increasing numbers of white households migrating from older areas of the city. African Americans had always had access to Broughton Street, but were less than welcome at many stores and could not partake of food services until the 1960s. During the Jim Crow era, West Broad Street (now Martin Luther King Jr. Boulevard) served as the primary commercial center for the black community. The successful boycott of Broughton Street businesses over lunch-counter segregation in 1960–61 bolstered black patronage, but decreased that of whites. Blacks were estimated to comprise two-thirds of the street's customer base by 1985. Security ranked second to the need for more convenient parking around Broughton Street among households surveyed that same year. Demographic changes, in turn, caused a number of merchants to replace their lines and other entrepreneurs to open stores catering to a less affluent market (fig. 13.22).[52]

Weathering poor sales in the 1970s, the leading Broughton merchants were optimistic with an upturn in business at the start of the next decade. The trend proved short-lived, however.

By the mid-1990s, all but a few stalwarts among the street's once-prominent businesses—most notably Levy Jewelers and Globe Shoe—had either moved or closed their doors. Chatham Furniture, Fine's, Hogan's, and Maxwell's were gone. So was Levy's after a brief takeover by another Allied Stores affiliate, Maas Brothers of Tampa, Florida. Among the national chains, Mangel's terminated business in 1983, followed by both McCrory's and Woolworth's in 1991. Kress was the last big store, closing its Broughton Street location and ending its run of nearly eighty-five years in October 1997.[53]

Well before that time, efforts to rescue Broughton Street's physical fabric were mounting. The fact that Savannah never became a center of finance or other major office-based business kept the pressure for more intense development at bay. Indeed, the Liberty National Bank building and two contiguous early-twentieth-century skyscrapers facing Johnson Square were demolished in the 1980s to make way for a financial institution of five stories

FIG. 13.22. Store buildings for Alexander Smets, 102–108 W. Broughton Street, showing deteriorated condition (compare with fig. 13.2). (Photo 1980s; Chatham County–Savannah Metropolitan Planning Commission, courtesy Sarah P. Ward)

FIG. 13.23. J. C. Penney Company building, as remade, 1992–94. (Photo Richard Longstreth, 1999)

and an adjacent parking garage. Concerns centered on what to do with empty buildings—the vacancy rate on first-floor space along Broughton ran nearly 40 percent in 1991, and upper floor vacancy was even higher. At least two undermaintained buildings burned in the late 1980s, leaving vacant lots behind. By then, however, the historic value of many of Broughton Street's buildings was becoming recognized by the city's seasoned preservationists and others as well. Bolstered by surveys by Historic Savannah Foundation and the Chatham County-Savannah Metropolitan Planning Commission, calls for reviving the street's rich architectural legacy were soon matched by a concrete program. Spearheaded by the newly elected mayor, Susan Weiner, the Savannah Development and Renewal Agency (SDRA) was created in 1993, with Broughton Street its initial focus. With citizen-based leadership, SDRA began to provide low-interest façade improvement loans, design assistance, and other resources to encourage a respectful rehabilitation of buildings, secure

new ground-floor tenants, and encourage occupancy of other floors as well. Municipal affiliation and the dispensation of monies aside, SDRA's approach bears affinity to that of the National Main Street Program, which has rescued the buildings of, and given new vitality to, hundreds of town centers since its inception in 1980.[54] The movement of numerous affluent households into much of Savannah's antebellum residential fabric nearby as a result of preservation efforts begun in the 1960s and the city's subsequent growth as a major tourist mecca helped create new markets for recreation-oriented downtown businesses. Regeneration has been boosted as well by the rise of the Savannah College of Art and Design (SCAD) as a major academic institution. Not only has SCAD's unorthodox program of having a city-wide campus composed of dozens of scattered sites helped save numerous buildings—Levy's and the Weis Theatre among them—but the student population has contributed to the vitality of the streets and the viability of at least some commercial enterprises. Between 2000 and 2005 alone, Broughton Street gained around one hundred new businesses.[55] By that decade's end, the corridor had regained much of the vibrancy and visual richness it had enjoyed in its heyday.

But what aspects of Broughton Street's physical fabric should be preserved, rehabilitated, or restored? During the 1980s and 1990s, the prevailing view among those who wanted to rescue its historical legacy was to strip away the ostensibly shoddy work added since World War II. The fact that new construction from that era represented one of the most important phases of Broughton's development was offset by a dislike of what was often characterized as undistinguished modernist architecture. The former Penney store, which was remade in the early 1990s into an office building with elevations that attempt to relate to some unspecified past, but are neither historicizing nor modernist in character, was symptomatic of a view that denied the real past in favor of a vaguely imagined one (fig. 13.23).[56] Besides the major buildings of the postwar era, substantive remodelings exist that are likewise potent reminders of a time when investment in the street's properties was at a peak level. Many postwar storefronts should clearly be retained rather than replaced in a misguided an attempt to create, on the basis of little or no documentation, what would be pseudo-historical at best. But there are other inexpensive, expeditious façade coverings that convey much less that is significant about Broughton's evolution than the fabric they mask. The removal of the Marshall House's 1963 covering in the late 1990s, and the subsequent restoration of the front to a state that predated its appearance in even the late nineteenth century and rehabilitation of an interior that

FIG. 13.24. Marshall House hotel, 105–123 E. Broughton Street, 1851; showing front as rehabilitated approximating mid-nineteenth-century condition, 1998–99. (Photo Richard Longstreth, 1999)

boasted a remarkable number of intact spaces, set an important precedent for work that has followed (fig. 13.24).[57] Given the rate of change in many urban commercial centers, Broughton Street has retained an unusual amount of its early fabric, but its buildings reflect construction and remodeling over a century along its eight blocks. A clear sense of that full spectrum should be preserved as the street continues to change.

14 Building Houses, Creating Community

Joseph Geeraert and the Development of Twinbrook

The quilt of suburban tracts called Twinbrook (1947–59), lying more than five miles northwest of the District of Columbia line in Montgomery County, Maryland, can easily be construed as a typical residential landscape of the post–World War II era (fig. 14.1).[1] Twinbrook's site plan was likely derived from the subdivision guidelines promulgated by the Federal Housing Administration (FHA) beginning in the late 1930s.[2] Twinbrook's houses, a number of them somewhat similar to the quasi-modernist ones built in the Levittowns of Nassau County, New York (1947–51), and Bucks County, Pennsylvania (1951–57), seem typical in size, configuration, and appearance. Twinbrook's acreage, containing approximately 1,543 dwellings, may have been somewhat larger than most in metropolitan Washington through the mid-1950s, but was far closer to the norm than the more than 17,000 dwellings erected in each of the Levittowns. The shopping facilities, houses of worship, schools, and recreation areas in Twinbrook can be seen as manifestations of a general trend by the 1950s where an increasing portion of middle-class residential development was undertaken as "community building."[3] Nothing about Twinbrook stands out as particularly new or markedly different. It is, one might conclude, like thousands of such tracts built nationwide during the period, the general characteristics of which have now been amply delineated in a number of historical studies.[4]

But "typical" can be a deceptive term. A close examination of Twinbrook's development suggests that it was unusual in the length of its construction, which extended over a dozen years and encompassed five contiguous tracts with a total of forty-nine subdivision plats.[5] Twinbook is certainly unusual in the range of its house designs, all probably the personal creations of one builder, Joseph Geeraert. While many volume housebuilders of the postwar era were strongly committed to their major projects, Geeraert seems unusually so at Twinbrook, since its development consumed the major portion of his professional career. Equally important, beyond its layout and landscaping, houses and support facilities, infrastructure and amenities, Twinbrook was, like any new residential area, a forming community. The people who came there and organized themselves in a variety of ways for a greater common good, as well as their own satisfaction, defined Twinbrook as much as did its physical attributes. Their story is one with parallels to many other places, but also with characteristics that made it distinct—certainly in their eyes and likely from a historical perspective as well.

The substantial literature that now exists on postwar suburban development provides an essential framework for further inquiry, but those studies are to a significant degree based on a small number of very large and perhaps somewhat unusual ventures: the Levittowns; Lakewood, California (begun 1950); and Park Forest, Illinois (begun 1946).[6] The danger of viewing all such work of the period in the same generic terms is obvious, for a common perspective is absent the myriad distinctions, however slight, that shape any individual form of human endeavor. Suburban tracts may have been developed over a short period of time utilizing standardized components to the greatest degree possible; however, like places that evolved over

This chapter draws in part from a class research projects done in one of my graduate courses held during the Spring 2008 semester.

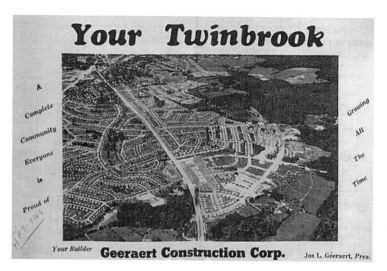

FIG. 14.1. "Your Twinbrook," Rockville, Maryland, Geeraert Construction Corporation advertisement (*Twinbrook Area Community Guide*, 1958, npp; courtesy John Tyner)

time as a result of many individual parties, often in uncoordinated ways, they can possess singular traits. A local perspective can inform inquiry into such places to a significant degree. The generalities go only so far. Indeed, they may perpetrate the unwarranted belief that postwar suburban development was as a more or less monolithic phenomenon. Moreover, the new residents of such places could play a major role in shaping their communities, perceptually and physically, personalizing them in many ways that could differentiate one place from another. Each place has its own history that entails not only the tangible and human dimensions, but also the impact each had on the other. The value of examining a tract such as Twinbrook lies with how much it can tell us about the individual characteristics of a place, and how many such places can collectively reveal the richness and variety often characterizing the vast, ostensibly homogeneous landscape that has profoundly affected American life for over sixty years.

The Builder

The announcement in September 1947 of plans for a "complete city" of six hundred houses that would be the "first" in the metropolitan area with its own "schools, stores, churches, amusements and public facilities," and with its own water and sewage treatment systems as well,

likely raised more than a few eyebrows among area real estate developers and homebuilders as well as with nearby residents. The acreage proposed for Twinbrook defined the outer fringe of the swelling number of housing tracts that were being built in metropolitan Washington.[7] In the county that had the highest incidence of major new residential tracts during the immediate postwar period, occupants of the new "city" would still feel isolated, with a fifteen-mile commute to downtown Washington, which remained the region's employment center. A scattering of federal entities such as the Naval Hospital in Bethesda, Maryland, lay closer at hand, but outlying areas had yet to become a major source for jobs. Rockville, the county seat, which had a population of around 6,000 in 1948, offered a very limited array of opportunities in business or government. Situated about a mile and a half from the center of Rockville, Twinbrook's site was perceptually cut off from most of that community by railroad tracks and open land. A scattering early-twentieth-century residences were situated about a mile away, and Rockcrest, a tract near that earlier development, had been started in 1940, but acres separated these places from Twinbrook. For his ambitious foray, Geeraert was initially branded "the fool of Rockville." The place was considered "too far out and too sleepy for development," he later recalled.[8]

Geeraert first noticed a two-hundred-acre farm that was for sale in 1945. Within a year he had formed a partnership with three cohorts, Twinbrook, Incorporated, that purchased the land for $94,000. Another eleven months were consumed making the preliminary plans; the first houses were ready for sale in August 1948.[9] The challenges entailed in launching a scheme that was so ambitious in scale and perceptually in so remote a setting were substantial. Both factors may have led to difficulties in securing financing. As president of the company, Geeraert was likely the driving force behind the vision, and he became the principal figure in executing a project that eventually grew to be more than twice its original projected size. At the same time, he had relatively little experience in the risk-laden field of real estate development.

Details of the life of Joseph Leivin Geeraert (1909–1979) are meager, yet enough information can be gleaned to suggest someone who was independent in spirit and entrepreneurial in inclination. He was also sometimes inclined to unorthodoxy. A native of Ghent, Belgium, Geeraert was raised in a prosperous but somewhat unstable household. He had a rigorous education bestowed by Christian Brothers and Jesuits. Besides being an avid sportsman, he nurtured hopes of becoming an artist, and, after graduating from St. Barbara's College in his hometown, entered art school. That education was cut short, however, when his father, Leon Geerhaert, abandoned the family to seek a new life in the United States. The eldest of six children, Joseph Geeraert was obliged to replace his father by running his maternal grandmother's family's company, which produced brass accouterments for churches, and for which his mother was a designer. Neither the burdens of that job nor those of becoming head of the household were endured for long. Around 1930, Geeraert, too, set sail for the United States, though not to reconnoiter with his father. Arriving in New York, he held a variety of odd jobs on the waterfront, but his newfound independence was sufficiently attractive that he returned to Belgium in order to secure a visa. En route he met Dorothy Howard (1912–2000) of Brooklyn, whom he married upon his return to the United

States circa 1933. What he did to sustain his family (daughters Rosanne and Dorothy were born in 1935 and 1940, respectively) during a time of economic uncertainty is unclear. By the close of the decade, however, he had accrued sufficient skills to be involved in the construction of a "hunting lodge" restaurant and nightclub at the New York World's Fair.[10]

It was perhaps from his various pursuits in New York that Geeraert met Harry Traver, who enlisted his assistance in developing Bonnie View, a nineteen-lot residential tract in Takoma Park, Maryland, just north of the District line. Apparently Traver overextended himself in this modest enterprise. Geeraert came to Washington to rectify its financial problems and soon was able to expand the project to thirty-four lots.[11] He seems to have acquired sufficient experience by this point to undertake the work of building himself. The modest, one-story houses that were erected, one of which became the family home, launched Geeraert into a career that would last over thirty years. Soon he was engaged in a bigger project, working on the completion of an eighty-house tract in Cheverly, Maryland, another Washington suburb. For the duration of World War II, he undertook repairs and remodeling for a number of embassies, as well as a small tract on Oakmont Avenue in Bethesda. Before the initial plans for Twinbrook were finalized, Geeraert was involved in developing Coquelin Terrace, an upscale enclave of twenty-three two-story houses adjoining Rock Creek Park in the northeastern corner of Chevy Chase, Maryland. Boasting four bedrooms, two and one half bathrooms, a den, and a breakfast room, as well as a carport (then a novelty in Washington), these ranked among the largest dwellings he would ever build (fig. 14.2). Geeraert's labors were sufficiently lucrative to allow him to move his family from the small abode in Bonnie View to 3211 Coquelin Terrace in 1949. Two of his neighbors were young members of Congress, George McGovern and Hubert Humphrey, with whom he became friends and remained in contact for many years.[12] Twinbrook represented a marked shift for Geeraert in its projected size and scope of facilities as well in its edge location.

FIG. 14.2. Houses, Coquelin Terrace, Chevy Chase, Maryland, 1946–48, Joseph L. Geeraert, designer and builder. (Photo Richard Longstreth, 2012)

Planning Twinbrook

While envisioning a "complete" community was by no means unprecedented when Twinbrook was announced in 1947, the idea was still quite new in its application to a mass market. A major reason why Geeraert may have set his sights on land so far afield from existing developments was not only because acquiring that land was far easier than the assembling of land necessary at a closer-in location, but also because its cost was much less. This factor may have been the decisive one, because at the start Twinbrook was envisioned as a development of modest dwellings, not much bigger than those Geeraert had built at Bonnie View. The initial group of houses, sold in 1948 (fig. 14.3), ran between $9,550 and $9,700 for each unit, which was in the lower price range for a freestanding, single-family residence in a metropolitan area where a "low-cost" house was then considered anything under $12,000, and less than half the $27,500 to $28,500 price tag of the Coquelin Ter-

race dwellings.[13] The target audience consisted of persons with enough means to become home-owners, but with only enough income to afford the basics—that is, those with an annual salary of around $4,100 to $4,200.

Yet Twinbrook was conceived to be more desirable than some forms of "minimal" market-rate dwellings. Semidetached houses, which had become a mainstay for the same audience in Washington during the 1920s, ran from $9,675 in 1947 to $11,250 two years later. Kay Construction Company introduced the type to Montgomery County in 1950 at its multiphased Connecticut Avenue Estates, just off Veirs Mill Road in Wheaton, two and a half miles southeast of Twinbrook. When this portion of the development opened, prices ranged from $9,250 for a two-bedroom unit to $10,950 for one with three. While of masonry construction, they were smaller than the Twinbrook houses and were organized in a regimental pattern along narrow and more or less straight streets (fig. 14.4).[14] Smaller freestanding houses could also be found, such as those selling for $8,500 to $9,500 in 1949 at Gregory Estates in Seat Pleasant, close to the District line in Prince George's County, Maryland; the equally modest dwellings of Glenmont Village in Wheaton, which were priced at $8,990 in 1950; or, not far from Twinbrook, at Viers Mill Village, which sold for $8,800 the previous year (fig. 14.5). At least some area residents considered Viers Mill Village an intrusion. Even while the dwellings were under construction, the local chamber of commerce branded them "hovels," and the president of the board of county commissioners regarded them as "potential slums." After approximately 200 houses of the projected 1,400-unit development were completed, a Montgomery County representative in the U.S. Congress launched an investigation, charging that they were substantially overpriced as well as poorly constructed.[15] Lined in rows along an orthogonal street grid, the houses met minimal FHA standards, but were cast as degrading among politicians and business leaders who held higher hopes for the evolving suburbanization of Montgomery County. With somewhat larger and more artfully designed houses facing curving streets, Twinbrook, by contrast, was widely seen as a welcome addition to the area. Geeraert sought a higher standard for his youthful, budget-conscious clientele.

To launch his enterprise, Geeraert seems to have depended on his more-experienced partners—Roland E. Simons and Wesley J. Sauter—at least to a degree. He was apparently already associated with Simons in 1946 when the idea of Twinbrook began to coalesce. Nothing is known of Simons save his ties with Geeraert, but he may have focused more on sales and running the office than on building. Geeraert met Sauter (1903-1959), a resident of Bethesda, who cofounded the Capitol Construction Company in 1933, at a Chicago real estate convention. Sauter not only had years of building experience, but was soon to become a member of the Montgomery County Council. Geeraert's idea proved sufficiently attractive to convince Sauter to join

FIG. 14.3. House, 1330 Ardennes Avenue, Twinbrook, 1948–49, Twinbrook, Inc., designer and builder. (Photo Richard Longstreth, 2012)

FIG. 14.4. Semidetached houses, 12112–12122 Andrew Street, Connecticut Avenue Estates, Wheaton, Maryland, 1949–50, Kay Construction Company, builder. (Photo Richard Longstreth, 2012)

FIG. 14.5. Houses, 12311–12315 Charles Road, Viers Mill Village, Wheaton, Maryland, 1947–49, Harris Construction Company, builder. (Photo Richard Longstreth, 2011)

forces along with one of his trusted younger associates, Donald E. Gingery (1913–1989). Before joining Sauter's company two years earlier, Gingery was in charge of construction for L. E. Breuninger & Sons, an esteemed residential building firm, from 1936 until 1941, and had studied engineering and law at George Washington University. He was active in the Metropolitan Washington Homebuilders Association and would shortly become a member of the Washington Suburban Sanitary Commission (in charge of the county's water and sewer systems) and the Maryland–National Capital Park & Planning Commission, serving on the latter for over a decade. During his dual career as a businessman and public servant, Gingery was an outspoken, often controversial, champion of ensuring that the county remain fertile ground for entry-level developments on the order of Twinbrook, and in this commitment, he and Geeraert no doubt found common ground.[16]

Though the partners of Twinbook, Incorporated, brought a spectrum of experience and talent to the project, the organization lasted only a little longer than three years. Simons and Sauter sold their interests to Geeraert and Gingery, but even before then, the parties appear to have worked in loose association. The first six plats, encompassing 269 house lots, were signed by Geeraert and Simons alone. In October 1950, Geeraert and his wife undertook three additional plats encompassing 64 lots; Sauter one plat with 21 lots; and Gingery and his wife one plat of 18 lots. The following year, Geeraert and his wife commissioned two plats with 64 lots, and Gingery and his wife three plats with 145 lots. Geeraert's projects were marketed under the company that bore his name, and Gingery's under the title of the Donley Construction Company, which he formed in Silver Spring, Maryland, then the county's major business center.[17] Gingery's work was based on designs that Geeraert had created and presumably allowed him to use so that the development would appear seamless, but the two builders seem to have had a serious parting of ways. Strong personalities as much as any business circumstances may have led to the fracture. Whatever the reasons, Gingery went on to do work in other parts

of the county as well as pursuing an ever more demanding life in the public realm.[18] Geeraert, in contrast, focused on expanding Twinbrook, working tirelessly to have it become the "complete city" he had conceived five years before.

To reach that goal, Geeraert proceeded in relatively small increments, much as he and his former partners had done and as many other Washington-area builders had worked as well. The "original" Twinbrook consisted of sixteen plats surveyed over nearly a six-and-a-half-year period, between March 1947 and July 1952 (fig. 14.6).[19] Collectively, this acreage held 541 houses, 348 of which were built by Geeraert, making it larger than most realized developments of its kind when the last dwellings were completed in the mid-months of 1953.[20] This assemblage covered a substantial area south of Veirs Mill Road. Well before these subdivisions were completed, however, Geeraert decided to acquire additional property across that artery (identified as "Geeraert's Addition to Twin-Brook" and "Geeraert's Addition to Broadwood Manor," respectively), increasing the overall development by a third, with 261 lots on eight plats surveyed between September 1951 and July 1952. The accelerated pace of development continued. An additional purchase made toward the end of the Korean War ("Twin-Brook Forest") was equally sizable, with 266 lots on five plats surveyed between July 1953 and October 1954. A year and a half later he acquired a third tract that nearly equaled the size of the two previous ones ("Geeraert's Addition to Twin-Brook Forest" or "Twinbrook Park"), which encompassed 446 lots on eighteen plats surveyed between January 1956 and February 1959.[21] By the decade's end, Twinbrook was more than twice its initially projected size.

However remote Twinbook may have seemed, Geeraert and his associates believed it could never function well in isolation as one of myriad unincorporated residential subdivisions that were beholden only to the county government. Although the great majority of settlements in Montgomery County, including its two major population centers, Bethesda and Silver Spring, were not legally constituted communities, the developers of Twinbrook thought that becoming part of Rockville, one of the county's few

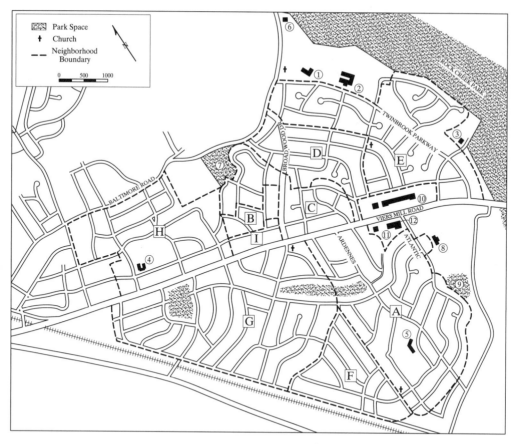

FIG. 14.6. Map of Twinbrook area, showing subdivisions and major facilities: A—original Twinbrook subdivision; B—Geeraert's Addition to Broadwood Manor; C—Geeraert's Addition to Twinbrook; D—Twinbrook Forest; E—Twinbrook Park; F—Rockland; G—Rockcrest; H—Silver Rock; I—Broadwood Manor; 1—Meadow Hall Elementary School; 2—Edwin Broome Junior High School; 3—Carl Sandburg Elementary School; 4—Lone Oak Elementary School; 5—Twinbrook Elementary School; 6—Park Forest Swimming Pool; 7—Calvin Park Recreation Area; 8—Twinbrook Swimming Club; 9—Twinbrook recreation area; 10—Twinbrook Shopping Center; 11—Twinbrook Shopping Mart. (Drawing by Paul Davidson, 2013, after *Twinbrook Area Community Guide*, 1962, 2)

independent municipalities, was far preferable. Annexation would permit the operation of Twinbrook's $60,000 water and sewer system to be taken over by the town and also bring fire and police protection close at hand. By mid-February 1949, the builders were pressing for an already sizable territorial expansion then being advanced to facilitate Rockville's growth to be enlarged yet further. Once that annexation was achieved several months later, it included all of the original Twinbrook as well as much of the land Geeraert would later acquire, increasing the square miles under Rockville's jurisdiction from one to six.[22] But Twinbrook Park, Geeraert's capstone development, lay beyond the expanded boundaries, and he began lobbying for its annexation, too, well before the first plat was surveyed. In April 1955, he offered the town an early-twentieth-century residential complex in the heart of the 220-acre tract as a civic and recreational center. Geeraert filed a petition the following month, but the matter took more than a year to resolve owing to the town's reluctance to expand its water system. In the midst of his campaign, the exasperated petitioner wrote of "annexation or chaos" to Twinbrook residents, predicting that newcomers "will find themselves an island, part of the county, yet set miles apart from the rest of the county," if Rockville failed to act.[23] Unstated, but implicit in his concerns was the fact that existing under two jurisdictions also would be detrimental to Twinbrook's coherence as a community.

Throughout Twinbrook's development, Geeraert and his associates appear to have followed FHA guidelines for subdivision layout rather closely. Streets were set in winding patterns that responded to the gently rolling terrain. Later components—Twinbrook Forest and especially Twinbrook Park—incorporated cul-de-sacs. Through traffic was discouraged by the overall configuration. Relatively few streets extend beyond the limits of the development. Only Twinbrook Parkway, situated near Twinbrook Park's northeast boundary, served as a ring road. Broadwood Drive was developed as a boulevard, with a wide, curving, tree-lined center median, connecting Veirs Mill and Baltimore roads, but was placed so that it would serve primarily as a feeder to a few cross streets and thus have light traffic (fig. 14.7). From the start, the development was oriented away from Veirs Mill Road, which, while zoned almost entirely for residential use in 1948, was becoming a major arterial in the county and during the mid-1950s was widened from 60 to 150 feet.[24] Although that project included secondary, feeder streets, few of Twinbrook's houses fronted them. Most of Twinbrook Park's frontage was occupied by a shopping center, which effectively served as a buffer from heavy traffic.

Public open space became an important factor in the development, and was at least as much the result of citizen activism as it was of Geeraert's planning. Though not a part of the plan, the northeastern portion of the original Twinbrook would soon be bounded by a swimming pool and recreation area. Connected by

FIG. 14.7. Broadwood Drive, Twinbrook, looking southwest. (Photo Richard Longstreth, 2008)

a curving creek bed enframed by natural vegetation, a second recreation area, which was
shared with an adjacent tract, Rockcrest, lay
to the east, while the expansive playing fields
and lawns of the Twinbrook Elementary School
were between the two to the south (see fig. 14.6).
Later tracts benefited from Rock Creek Park—
an enormous preserve that extended from the
Potomac River in Washington far into Montgomery County. The park defined Twinbrook's
northeastern perimeter, and was supplemented
by the expansive grounds of two elementary
schools and a junior high school situated along
part of that edge. In these tracts, too, lot sizes
tended to be larger than in their predecessors
in Twinbrook, so that with the maturation of
landscape, the effect was more one of a continuous park (fig. 14.8). Throughout the development, Geeraert retained a number of existing
trees, especially at the rear of lots, so that even
when tracts were new they did not appear barren (fig. 14.9). While Twinbrook's configuration
possessed no exceptional features as it evolved

through the 1950s, it did embody reasonably
high standards for large-scale, middle-market
residential developments.

Houses

Twinbrook's houses are among its most distinctive features, for they encompass not only
more than a decade's worth of design evolution
in tract dwellings, but in most cases embody the
somewhat individualistic inclinations of their
builder that make them readily discernable.
The initial eighty houses followed a conventional "Cape Cod" pattern used for countless
tract houses since the late 1930s, yet had dressier
fronts, which were slightly differentiated from
one another in veneers—some had brick, while
others had two-toned asbestos shingles—and
windows of varying sizes (see fig. 14.3). A small
extension to one side of the front emphasized
that these dwellings were somewhat larger
than many of their type. Probably inspired by
a practice best known through its use in Levit-

FIG. 14.8. McIntyre Road at Castlewood Road, looking south, Twinbrook Park, developed ca. 1959–60; view
showing "El Rancho" houses. (Photo Richard Longstreth, 2008)

FIG. 14.9. Twinbrook, view looking southeast from grounds of Twinbrook Elementary School, intersection of Okinawa Road and Ridgway Avenue in mid-ground. (Photo ca. 1952–53; courtesy Peerless Rockville Historic Preservation)

town, New York, the unfinished attic story was advertised as suitable for conversion into one or two additional bedrooms.[25]

Whether Geeraert was responsible for the design of the first houses at Twinbrook is unknown; however, by the mid-months of 1949 he had completed drawings for an entirely new scheme that had an unorthodox floor plan and was conspicuously more modernist in character. The public zones were essentially a single space, with the living room separated from the kitchen by cabinets and appliances on one side and a fireplace (then unusual for houses of this size) on the other (fig. 14.10). In many instances, the living room faced the rear yard, while the kitchen faced the street and also was the principal point of entry from an adjacent driveway (figs. 14.11 and 14.12; see also fig. 14.9). As with the earlier model, unfinished space for conversion was left on the upper level, but now that space was enhanced by a raised roof pitch across part of the front or by a large cross gable. In addition, Geeraert offered several different models from which prospective homeowners might choose.[26] The exteriors likewise departed from the norm, especially in the conservative Washington area where at least some allusions to "Colonial" precedent remained well ensconced into the mid-twentieth century. Here, floor-to-ceiling framed windows spanned the length of

the living room and other windows of unusual sizes worked together with the massing to give the houses a somewhat abstract quality. In all these aspects, Geeraert followed the models Alfred Levitt had designed for Levittown, New York, only a few months earlier. (It was likely during the intervening period when he visited Levittown, which provided inspiration for his designs for several years to come.[27]) The Maryland builder took pride in his work, signing his name as "designer" on the plans that he drew.[28]

Geeraert utilized the models he developed in 1949 for the rest of the original Twinbrook, introducing minor variations each year, and continued to rely on these patterns through the development of his first two "additions" north of Veirs Mill Road. Along the way, he expanded the range of designs as well. In 1951, prospective homeowners could select from five models; two years later, eight were available. As was often practiced by house builders of the period, the variations were relatively minor in order to retain the cost benefits of standardized components, yet the differences gave some sense of individuality to each dwelling as well as some measure of variety to the streetscape. As in the Levittowns, too, a range of exterior color schemes added to the differentiation. The houses cost slightly more than their Cape Cod predecessors, selling from $9,650 to $9,800 in

FIG. 14.10. Floor plan of 1949 model house, Twinbrook, Twinbrook, Inc., designer and builder. (Drawing by Paul Davidson, 2013, after *Washington Post*, 14, August 1949, R3)

FIG. 14.11. Twinbrook house, built according to Geeraert's 1949 design; rear elevation showing family posing by the living room window. (Courtesy Peerless Rockville Historic Preservation)

FIG. 14.12. House, 504 Dean Drive, Twinbrook, ca. 1952–53, Geeraert Construction Corporation, designer and builder. (Photo Richard Longstreth, 2011)

1949 and from $10,450 five years later, but were still a bargain in the under $12,000 category.[29] Geeraert remained wedded to his designs when he began Twinbrook Forest in 1953; there, however, the houses were noticeably larger, in all likelihood reflecting a rising market demand among young, middle-class families for more living space (fig. 14.13). While the main floor was billed as providing a greater sense of open-ness as well as efficiency, the upstairs remained "completely unhampered," as with all earlier models, so that purchasers could finish the area as and when they wished. Twinbrook Forest houses also included a carport, one of the few instances where Geeraert provided automobile shelter. The cost of these houses—$12,950—was relatively low given their size.[30]

Twinbrook Park's houses broke from Geer-

FIG. 14.13. Twinbrook Forest advertisement, showing 1954 model house, Geeraert Construction Corporation, designer and builder. (*Washington Post*, 12 December 1954, R9)

aert's established building patterns in several ways. Previous designs were abandoned. While still modernist in a generic way, the new plans shed all Levitt trappings. Over a four-year period, six basic designs were introduced, each of which entailed two or more variations and all of which bore their designer's distinctive imprint, distinguishing them from houses in other tracts. Three of these were split-level in configuration ("Meadow Hall," "Anniversary," and "El Dorado") (see figs. 14.14 and 14.16). An additional type had a two-story front and a lean-to rear ("Country Squire") (fig. 14.15). A fifth type had a compact two-story arrangement ("St. Regis") (see fig. 14.16), while the final design was a ranch house ("El Rancho") (see figs. 14.8 and 14.16). These models also varied in size and cost. The largest split-level type was in some cases rotated ninety degrees, with its one-story section facing the street. Several models were interspersed with one another. Finally, while Geeraert seems to have initiated a practice during the latter stages of Twinbrook Forest that the Levitts had helped pioneer years before, building houses only after they had been

purchased, this method was fully implemented at Twinbrook Park.[31] So that potential homeowners could get a clear sense of their choices, a range of the designs available were constructed as model homes (fig. 14.16). What propelled Geeraert to make such marked changes is unclear. Earlier houses may have been criticized as being monotonous by some observers; he may have sensed that a maturing market wanted a broader range of sizes and arrangements from which to choose.[32] As a designer, he may also have wanted to experiment more, relishing the circumstances that allowed him to do so now that his development was becoming well known and respected.

As Twinbrook grew, Geeraert also became more inclined to incorporate spectacle into his marketing strategy. While not appreciably different on the exterior, the 1954 variation on one of the 1953 models at Twinbrook Forest was encircled by a high fence and "protected" by Brinks uniformed guards for several weeks to heighten anticipation of its public unveiling. That model was dubbed the "Anniversary Home"—marking six years of occupied dwellings at Twinbrook—

FIG. 14.14. "Meadow Hall" houses, Marcia Road, Twinbrook Park, developed ca. 1956–57. (Photo Richard Longstreth, 2008)

FIG. 14.15. "Country Squire" houses, Meadow Hall Drive, Twinbrook Park, developed ca. 1956–57. (Photo Richard Longstreth, 2008)

FIG. 14.16. Twinbrook Park model homes, showing (left to right) the "El Rancho," the "St. Regis," and the "El Dorado." (Photo ca. 1958; courtesy Peerless Rockville Historic Preservation)

and subsequently presented as a potential Christmas "gift" for 1955. To promote the tract at the 1954 Washington Home Show, Geeraert had two young women, the "Twinbrook Twins," parade around on horses borrowed from the Cisco Kid, a well-known entertainer. Similarly, two young female pilots transported a model for a Twinbrook Park house in their plane at a local air show. As the site preparation of Twinbrook Forest was starting, Geeraert allowed purchasers to take a helicopter ride to see their lot in relation to the greater community.[33]

Support Facilities

Twinbrook Park represented more than just a substantial number of additional houses for its developer, for it was on portions of this land that he erected a shopping center, and he sold other parcels to the county as sites for three schools. Collectively, these were key physical components that defined Twinbrook as a community rather than just tracts of houses. As far as residents were concerned both the commercial and educational centers were vital resources to meet their basic needs. As late as 1954, even shopping of the most routine kind had to be done in the heart of Rockville or farther afield— well beyond easy walking distance. For many residents, the introduction of a shopping bus that ran to the town center during the early fall of that year was a godsend. One housewife explained what had been the plight of many: the family had one car, which was used by her husband to commute to work six days a week. She was thus stranded with two small children, and had to wait until the evening to run errands and keep medical appointments. One of her cohorts summed up what was likely a widespread sentiment: "I feel so independent now."[34]

Within months, plans for two competing shopping centers were underway. In February 1955, Donald Gingery, now on his own, submitted drawings for a six-store group, Twinbrook Shopping Mart, to the town council. Located at the eastern edge of Twinbrook at Veirs Mill Road and Atlantic Avenue, the complex was bolstered by a capacious parking lot and was clearly poised to attract customers from new

tracts beyond those in the immediate area. The project proceeded swiftly, with the first unit, an A&P supermarket, opening that November, followed by a unit of a Washington-based drug store chain and a post office.[35] Well before then, Geeraert unveiled plans for the much more ambitious Twinbrook Shopping Center directly across Veirs Mill Road (fig. 14.17). Planned for a customer base of 10,000 people, the $3 million complex was originally designed with an open pedestrian mall at its center. The plans underwent substantial revisions over the two years that followed, as Geeraert, who had no experience in building retail facilities, changed his mind about the optimal size the center would need to achieve dominance. As realized, the complex had a conventional linear arrangement, divided into three store blocks interspersed with short pedestrianways connecting front and rear parking lots. A variety store, C. G. Murphy Company, lay in the center; a second anchor, a Safeway supermarket, was located in a separate building to the west, while a third, a large drug store, terminated the complex on the eastern side. With twenty-one businesses, the Twinbrook Shopping Center ranked among the largest planned retail developments in Maryland, aside from metropolitan Baltimore, when it opened to much fanfare in early December 1957.[36] Geeraert did not enjoy dominance for long, however. Less than fifteen months later, Congressional Shopping Plaza opened a mile away on Rockville Pike. Besides being twice the size, with a department store (J. C. Penney Company), two variety stores, and a range of other specialty outlets, Congressional was just as convenient for many Twinbrook residents as Geeraert's center. A year later, Wheaton Plaza opened at the eastern terminus of Veirs Mill Road, five miles to the southeast. With eighty businesses, including a major branch of a prestigious downtown Washington department store (Woodward & Lothrop), Wheaton Plaza became the county's preeminent retail center. By 1960, too, increases in car ownership meant that driving to such places was becoming a much more common practice than only a few years previous. Twinbrook Shopping Center still attracted consumers for routine goods, but soon experienced an overall decline in sales, and was eventually sold by its once proud possessor.[37]

Given Twinbrook's size and proximity to Rockville, providing space for houses of worship was not as urgent a need. Two new churches were erected just on the edge of Geeraert's tracts in Rockcrest and Rockland: Crusader Lutheran Church (1953–56) and Faith United Church (Church of Chris; 1957). Three others lay slightly farther afield in earlier developed areas (Assembly of God Church, Free Methodist Church, and St. Mary's Catholic Church). Geeraert did not give land to the two dominations that built within his developments, but likely welcomed their presence as yet another community cornerstone. Both were built in prominent locations in Twinbrook Park. The Twinbrook Baptist Church purchased a corner property adjacent to the site of the Meadow Hall Elementary School in 1957, erecting the first part of its building two years later. As with many other fledgling churches in the area, with limited congregants and funds, the first component to be constructed was a modest parish hall that could serve as a makeshift worship space until more ample quarters could be erected. In contrast, St. Andrew's United Presbyterian Church (now Rockville United Church; 1960–62) was

the most ambitious undertaking in the area. Situated on the edge of a knoll, overlooking an array of recently completed houses, the church had a soaring sanctuary formed by a steeply pitched roof rising some three stories that made it one of the few landmarks of the community (fig. 14.18).[38]

In the eyes of those who had moved there, by far the most important nonresidential component of Twinbrook was the school. The great majority of families either arrived with young children or soon thereafter began to have them. Since most of these adults, too, were upwardly mobile, providing their offspring with a sound education was of paramount importance. Indeed, much of the appeal of places such as Twinbrook was as an environment conducive to child rearing. Moreover, the school was a key marker of community. Homeowners might work, shop, and worship in different places as well as pursue varying leisure activities, but everyone was tied to and identified with the school. The challenge of providing adequate facilities, however, remained constant throughout the 1950s. Like thousands of suburbanizing areas nationwide, Montgomery County's population growth outpaced its capacity to provide classrooms. County officials were well aware

FIG. 14.17. Twinbrook Shopping Center, Veirs Mill Road between Bradley Avenue and Meadow Hall drive, Twinbrook, preliminary design, 1955, John Samperton, architect. (*Twinbrook Life*, 25 May 1955, 5, courtesy John Tyner)

FIG. 14.18. St. Andrew's United Presbyterian Church, 355 Linthicum Avenue, Twinbrook Park, 1960–62, Clifton White, architect. (Photo Richard Longstreth, 2008)

of the problem and took aggressive actions to address it. Unlike many suburban jurisdictions in the United States, schools fell under the purview of Montgomery County, not local boards. This centralized system allowed for efficiencies in allocation of resources and operation; it also provided a more even field for places lacking the commercial and industrial properties that supplied a major portion of local tax revenues. Growth of the system was pronounced. The 1947–48 operating budget, for example, was increased by nearly $1.7 million, over twice the amount allocated the previous year. At the same time, estimates for new school construction ran nearly $8 million for 1947–49. The jump in students attending public schools during that time was 8,029, over a third of the total. By 1955, the total public school population was estimated at nearly 53,000.[39] Catching up was an ongoing challenge for the school board.

Twinbrook was contributing substantially to the demands of growth when funds were allocated for its first public school in the 1950–51 county budget. During its construction, the Twinbrook Elementary School was characterized as "a dream coming true for our little community," and when it opened for the fall 1952 session, the facility was enthusiastically received by residents. At the same time, many believed the county school board was less understanding of local needs than a municipal body would be. By then, Twinbrook's eight classrooms were already deemed insufficient, and an addition containing twelve classrooms, library, and all-purpose room was begun five months later. By 1954 the school population had trebled, from 212 to 645; over 1,000 students were projected for the fall of 1956. Staging classes and recreation periods in shifts, as well as relying on makeshift facilities, allayed a crisis. In 1955, frustrated school trustees registered "general public disgust, dissatisfaction, and in many cases anger at the [school board's] lack of vision." Mincing no words may have helped prompt action. Major additions were made to the building in 1956 and 1960 that addressed the need. With thirty-eight classrooms and 1,304 students, Twinbrook became the largest elementary school in the county.[40] While the merits of such size were now debated, students and their parents alike braved the overcrowding and the other challenges posed by a large institution to embrace the school as their own. Staging science fairs; publishing its own newspaper; establishing scholarships; and organizing schoolwide projects such as "How may we continue to make Twinbrook safe, healthy, and beautiful?" or "What experiences are common to all children in the world?" or "Are the needs and desires as revealed by growth in our community common to other communities in the world?"—all these factors contributed to making the place "one big happy family."[41]

By the mid-1950s, Geeraert's ongoing plans for expanding his development north of Veirs Mill Road made it clear that Twinbrook Elementary School could not address the community's education needs fully. That building was placed near the center of the original tract, within easy walking distance from all its sections. The now widened and heavily traveled Veirs Mill Road posed a substantial risk to pedestrians of all ages. By June 1955, adjacent sites for a second elementary school (Meadow Hall) and a junior high school (Edwin Broome) were selected along Twinbrook Parkway, on the northern perimeter of the yet-to-be-developed Twinbrook Park. Geeraert agreed to sell the ten- and twenty-acre parcels, respectively, for $3,200 an acre. When it opened in January 1957, Meadow Hall was, like Twinbrook Elementary before it, wholly inadequate in size, and an addition that would increase the number of classrooms from ten to twenty-two was started before the year's end. This measure still fell short, and a third primary school, Carl Sandburg, was erected in 1961–62. Situated off Twinbrook Parkway on a more secluded site, the school catered exclusively to young children (kindergarten through third grade) and operated on a markedly smaller scale than its predecessors (fig. 14.19). With 1,260 students by 1963, the junior high school boasted

FIG. 14.19. Carl Sandburg Elementary School, 451 Meadow Hall Drive, Twinbrook Park, 1961–62, Arthur L. Anderson, architect. (Photo Richard Longstreth, 2008)

an award-winning newspaper and magazine, a pioneering audiovisual center, and a heavily used library.[42] All three schools had extensive acreage for playing fields, providing the community with its largest recreation areas in the process.

Building Community

Whatever its merits or shortcomings, the physical environment created by Twinbrook's builders and public authorities highlights only one aspect of how the development took shape during its formative years. Equally important was the environment created by its residents, some components of which were manifested in three-dimensional forms, but much of which assumed the intangible elements of community building. The human dimension of postwar suburban development has usually been limited to generalities in historical accounts, if it is discussed at all. A dearth of documentation often precludes more detailed inquiry. Fortunately, an extensive record exists for Twinbrook, offering a valuable perspective on the extent to which its citizens involved themselves.[43] In some respects, this engagement may match that of numerous other new suburban tracts of the period; however, the evidence also suggests that Twinbrook may have been more the exception than the norm in the degree to which its residents took charge of their collective destiny.

The generation that initially populated places such as Twinbrook, men and women in their twenties and early thirties, differed from their forebears in the depth of their life experience and in the proportion who were upwardly mobile. Most men were veterans, who had experienced the ravages as well as the stern responsibilities of life in wartime. Many women, too, had held jobs during the war, acquiring a new sense of self-assurance in the process. The booming postwar economy combined with the emphasis that federal policy placed on education produced a new mass market of middle-class and prosperous blue-collar households. The outlying residential tracts to which this generation flocked in droves also differed from the majority of places developed during

the 1920s or earlier in the combination of factors: they were created de novo, on a large scale, and were, at least perceptually, removed from existing development. An established hierarchy—human and institutional—similarly did not exist. The postwar generation was on its own to create the communities it wanted.

In his unusual period examination of postwar suburban life, journalist Harry Henderson studied six new communities, including Levittown, New York, and Park Forest, Illinois, discovering many patterns that contradicted the stereotypical views of conformity, monotony, and malaise. "One rarely hears complaints about the identical character of the houses," he noted. The dwellings were a welcome release from the cramped apartment quarters that many residents had endured previously. "Gone are most rituals and ceremonies," he added, as residents "shed many of their parents' and hometown customs." While transience was common due to rising incomes and business transfers, Henderson found that the occupants of these places were conspicuous in "their friendliness, warmth, and lack of pretentious snobbery," and observed that "one does not find the indifference, coldness, and 'closed doors' of a long-established community." Group activities were pervasive, centering around worship and recreation. These were not places of isolation and ennui, but vibrant communities in the making that exhibited "rugged American collectivism." After reading Henderson's assessment, one Twinbrook resident concluded, "It was like seeing Twinbrook in a mirror." Maintaining enthusiasm for civic enterprises was hard, she admitted, but "for those who stay with organization work comes the reward of community esteem."[44]

A survey of 660 residents conducted by sixth graders at Twinbrook Elementary School in the fall of 1957 revealed a high proportion of professional occupations, but also a wide range of jobs, encompassing both white- and skilled blue-collar realms. Among the 420 employed, 40 worked in business offices, 37 were engineers, 36 were salesmen, 33 were mechanics, 30 were in the armed services, 28 were self-employed, 26 were scientists (including doctors and nurses), 17 worked for government, 12 were writers, and

10 were teachers. Nearly 17 percent of the men had two jobs, and paying jobs were held by 27 percent of the women. The great majority of respondents traveled an average of 12 miles to work, suggesting that Washington remained the primary place of employment; only a very small fraction worked in Rockville.[45] While higher-income households were probably more concentrated in those subdivisions where the houses were larger, there appears to have been a fair amount of mixing among people from various backgrounds and in differing lines of work through the plethora of civic and social organizations established both for adults and their children—a degree of association that may have been greater than in more established and stratified communities where the age range was also more varied.

Whatever the relationships among neighbors, Twinbrook had a critical mass of people who could bring their considerable experience and specialized talents to the community table. One resident remarked that the numerous college graduates in the development were "active people, eager to put in their two cents worth" in shaping their community's future, adding that their isolation from the entertainment and intellectual outlets of the city fostered channeling of talent toward local concerns. The elementary school's 1957 survey found that more than a third of the respondents (275 out of 660) volunteered for community work.[46] Profiles of officers and other key contributors to the Twinbrook Citizens Association (TCA) reveal no shortage of informed leadership. Many held positions in the federal government. A graduate of Harvard Law School, Leighton Dudley was a penal code advisor to the U.S. Air Force. John Robertson was with the U.S. Army Corps of Engineers; Harvey Pearce was assistant chief of personnel at the Bureau of Mines; Bert Sherman was chief of the Commodity Standards Section of the Department of Health, Education, and Welfare; Robert Bonham, chief of vocational rehabilitation facilities at the Navy Department; Kenneth Kasai an engineer at the Naval Ordinance Laboratory; Stanley Stein a tax analyst for the Internal Revenue Service; and Bernard Hasson Jr. an examiner at the Interstate Commerce Commission.

Others were educators: Edward Heine served as principal for a county school, and William Hall as vice principal to a county junior high. Some were in business: James Duffy was a tax lawyer in Washington, Durant Barton was a cartographer, Robert Rapp was city engineer for Rockville. While these individuals were all under forty, a few others were substantively older. In Washington state, Tom Rathbone had served as commander of Disabled Veterans and director of education and recreation for the Works Progress Administration (among other positions) before he became director of the Washington, D.C., Office of Vocational Rehabilitation. Henry Redkey was a pioneer in physical rehabilitation for the armed forces during the 1930s before he joined Rathbone's office as a consultant in 1949.[47]

The TCA served a dual purpose. Its concerns stemmed foremost from the immediate area (the original Twinbrook plats and those added by Geeraert north of Veirs Mill Road, as well as the tangent subdivisions of Rockland and, later, Halpine Village). At the same time, the organization sought to strengthen ties with the municipality of which Twinbrook was a part. It was all too easy, TCA's leadership intoned, for residents to think only of their immediate needs without involvement in the affairs of Rockville, which affected everything from taxation to libraries, land use to representation, traffic circulation to recreation opportunities. Just as Geeraert saw annexation as crucial to the long-term well-being of Twinbrook, the TCA strove to ensure its residents were full participants in municipal affairs. This commitment was conspicuously manifested at an early date by sweeping changes in local government. A casual style of municipal leadership that had proven adequate in Rockville prior to World War II failed to keep pace with the town's burgeoning growth, leading to an acute shortage in its water supply. For the well-educated newcomers, the problem seemed symptomatic of a government incapable of addressing change. In February 1954, the Citizens for Good Government was established to advance a reform slate of candidates. While the initiative was community-wide, Twinbrook residents played a central role: Frank Ecker was chairman of the citizens group, and Dickran

Hovsepian was elected mayor. Significantly, both the campaign and the administration that was subsequently voted into power were non-partisan. As a result, Hovesparian, a planner with the Army Map Service, could serve and call upon many other federal employees who resided in Rockville—engineers, lawyers, economists, and statisticians among them—for their expertise. A feature article on the subject in Washington's *Evening Star* estimated that "the Twinbrook influence in Rockville affairs [has been] incalculable." Writing for the *Montgomery County Sentinel*, a Twinbrook resident extolled, "Twinbrook has come of age. We are no longer an isolated community. . . . We need Rockville and Rockville needs us." After several years of urging citizen participation through the ballot, the TCA had an exemplary case to underscore the message.[48]

The TCA was also directly involved in municipal and sometimes county affairs through the numerous actions it took, weighing in on proposed rezoning of nearby land from residential to industrial use, opposing high-rise apartment projects on Twinbrook's periphery, lobbying for improved recreational facilities, pressing for sidewalks in areas where Geeraert had not provided them, arguing for stop signs at key intersections to slow traffic, repeatedly pushing for larger school budget appropriations, and pursuing myriad other projects. After the Twinbrook Elementary School's completion, the organization undertook an ambitious landscaping project, which included planting forty-eight trees and many more shrubs.[49] Towards the decade's end, the TCA launched a concerted campaign to secure a branch library for the community, which culminated after eighteen months with a facility in the Shopping Mart.[50] The organization's strength could in part be measured by its membership, which grew from an initial 40 people to 1,100 five years later, at the height of the drive for municipal reform.[51] Part of its effectiveness stemmed from an organizational structure that ensured community-wide representation, with a "block captain" appointed for every twenty houses who was charged with engaging his or her neighbors and with passing their concerns on to the TCA leadership. Besides

elected officials, the organization had as many as seven committees. As a result an estimated 200 to 300 members actively participated in TCA projects in 1954, an impressive number by any standard.[52]

The TCA's popularity was likely due in part to the fact that both its leadership and activities transcended the divides of gender and involved children at least as much as adults. That widespread appeal was bolstered by the numerous events that the organization sponsored. A picnic with softball games occurred each summer, attracting some 2,500 people by the decade's end. Just before Christmas, the TCA held a children's party, with a dance added for adults. In 1954, a caroling party was also organized, and a contest for the best decorated doorways was expanded to encompass all manner of holiday property embellishments. By 1957, there was a dance celebrating Valentine's Day, a square dance, an Easter parade, and an Easter egg hunt. Monthly meetings frequently included guest speakers addressing matters of public concern from education to civil defense. In 1953, the TCA began issuing a *Community Guide*, which contained a wealth of information on services, institutions, and businesses to which residents could avail themselves. The following year, it began issuing *Twinbrook Life*, a serial devoted "to help spread information on which our community spirit grows."[53] By the mid-1950s, the TCA leadership began calling for measures to address the fact that much of the community's youth population would be teenagers within a decade, and needed opportunities to channel their energies constructively. To support its operations, TCA relied on membership dues (generally kept to $1 per household) and fundraisers (picnics, dances, and other events), but the lion's share of work was accomplished through volunteers.

Volunteerism manifested itself most prominently in the TCA's ongoing campaign to develop recreational facilities. These projects were primarily for use by children, whose leisure pursuits have long proved one of the most effective ways to bring adults together. Although development of such places was being actively pursued by the Rockville Civic Association, the TCA took the matter into its own hands in July

1950, when it began to develop a playground area on the eastern edge of the original tract. Improvements continued the following year, when plans for a shelter were prepared, swings installed, and a sandbox built. By the summer of 1952, a preschool-age recreation program had developed, which culminated in a parade of 145 children. A circus was staged the next year.[54] In February 1954, a second playground area, Calvin Park, was set aside at the end of Gladstone Drive to serve residents of the fast-developing area north of Veirs Mill Road, including not only Geeraert's additions but also the adjacent tracts of Broadmoor and Silver Rock. The TCA's role was to initiate improvements and programs. Once the foundation was laid, the municipal government took over both further development and operations, while programs such as that for children under six were taken over by the Homemakers Club.[55] Without the TCA's proactive strategy, however, Twinbrook would likely have been less well positioned and boasted fewer resources by the decade's end. In hindsight, TCA's catalytic role proved overwhelmingly effective in spurring far more activity than the organization alone could support. The challenges of such unilateral action became evident to the organization's leadership when they began a two-year project to provide Twinbrook with its own swimming pool.

Having a place to cool off during the long, hot Washington summers was a top priority among Twinbrook residents. The idea of having a "swim club," owned by shareholders and operated through annual dues, was floated at the TCA's October 1954 meeting and proved so popular that it coalesced into a serious initiative within four months. By the following May, plans were afoot for an Olympic-sized pool as well as a wading pool and a bathhouse. The cost was formidable for a grassroots project. Land next to the Twinbrook recreation area was purchased from the Catholic archdiocese for $8,997; the facility itself cost around $13,000, even though much of the excavation and construction was done by volunteer labor. Still, 600 households contributed $150 each in membership dues toward the effort, and the project proceeded swiftly, opening just slightly behind schedule in September

1955.[56] Problems began to mount in the months that followed, however. Costs were somewhat higher than projected, exacerbated by a collapse of a retaining wall after a heavy rain in October. Loans were solicited from the membership. By spring, a request went out for more volunteers to help with finishing the facility and landscaping its grounds. By late August 1956, a deficit of $5,000, exacerbated by the failure to get the necessary health permit, spurred fears of an early closing. The membership agreed to a modest increase in dues, and monetary and in-kind contributions continued, so that the operation was finally deemed in the black by February 1957.[57] It was a more tortuous course than anyone involved had bargained for. Nevertheless, the popularity of the pool, coupled with Twinbrook's fast-growing population north of Veirs Mill Road, led some residents to press for a second facility near the Meadow Hall Elementary School in December 1956. Learning its lesson from the previous venture, the ad hoc citizens group formed to realize the project was assiduous in raising enough money up front and in hiring an architect to undertake the planning and supervision. What became known as the Park Forest Swimming Club progressed as rapidly as its predecessor, opening in August 1957.[58] Among new residential areas in Montgomery County, Twinbrook had perhaps the best range of such recreational facilities.

Aside from the TCA, Twinbrook's largest and arguably most influential organization was the Homemakers Club, which by June 1953 was comprised of three organizations, each with its own territory. First formed by mid-January 1950, the group initially focused on lectures, "lessons," and discussions about subjects that were important to first-time homeowners, including kitchen arrangement, using color inside the house, cleaning upholstery, and making slipcovers. Soon, however, the organization took over the preschool summer recreation program, which increased from 50 children in 1952 to 150 the following year, and sponsored picnics and other events—tours to see home improvements, such as how people were finishing their attics—to raise money. The group championed yard improvement as well. Around the same time, it led the campaign to petition the city for sidewalks.[59] The dual effort by the Homemakers Club and the TCA to promote care and embellishment of the community—personal and public property alike—fostered a sense of civic pride as well as self-achievement among residents.[60]

Many other groups were organized as well. By the summer of 1950 a baseball team had formed, and within four years five were playing regularly. There was a basketball team, three Cub Scout troops, a Boy's Club, Brownies, Camp Fire Girls, an adult bowling team, a sewing club, a modern dance group, a child-study group (where parents could discuss their children's developmental needs, sponsored by the County School Board), and the Twinbrook Twirlers, a dance troop that performed at the Washington Folk Festival in 1954. A Twinbrook 4-H chapter was frequently featured on area television programs. For children and for adults inclined to socialize, no shortage of options existed.[61] A chapter of the PTA was formed concurrent with the opening of the Twinbrook Elementary School, with 100 parents attending the second meeting when the school's teachers were introduced. Not surprisingly, this organization took an active role in pressing for adequate classroom space and other facilities. An annual fair was initiated in 1953 as a fundraiser for their efforts, and the progressive outlook of many Twinbrook residents was amply reflected in the PTA's involvement in community life. At a time when residents of many suburban communities—in the North as well the South—still resisted school desegregation, a large majority of Twinbrook PTA members voted for change in March 1955, over a half dozen years before the county's educational system was integrated.[62]

From an early stage, Geeraert appears to have been committed to fostering a sense of community, not just building houses. Otherwise, he could just as easily have moved on to other territory instead of buying additional acreage contiguous to the original site. Initially, Twinbrook was not nearly large enough to provide the amenities found in the Levittowns.[63] But as Twinbrook grew and Geeraert's profits increased accordingly, he did more to assist his clients' grassroots efforts toward civic improvement. His early donations, such as lumber for the first recreation area, were modest, but he subsequently gave the TCA the land for the Calvin Park Recreation Area, no doubt realizing that it would add to the appeal of houses in Twinbrook Forest and Twinbrook Park. He offered some assistance to the first Twinbrook pool and donated the land for the second facility. He also sponsored baseball, basketball, and bowling teams, as well as community parties. His interest in stemming juvenile delinquency was manifested not only through athletics, but also through teenage "havens" he displayed as part of his exhibit at the 1957 Washington Home Show.[64] As the Twinbrook subdivisions were nearing completion, Geeraert took pride in the place he had created. He wrote a public rebuke of John C. Keats's critique of new suburban housing tracts, *The Crack in the Picture Window* (1957), challenging the author to visit Twinbrook, to "see for himself the pride people have in their homes—their spirit of Americanism shown in their interest in good government, community activities, and above all, the homes and the home life they enjoy."[65]

Concurrent with Twinbrook's progress as a community, Geeraert gained increasing prominence among the metropolitan area's builders. In 1957, he served as president of the Suburban Maryland Homebuilders Association, an organization he cofounded that boasted 80 builders and 130 members of allied industries. In that capacity, he contracted to construct without profit a new treatment center for the Society for Crippled Children and Adults. The site was in Twinbrook Park, opposite the Meadow Hall Elementary School and near to the house he allowed the organization to occupy after it was forced to vacate its previous quarters.[66] At the same time, he chaired the Washington Suburban Sanitary Commission Committee of the Home Builders Association of Washington, which had elected him to their board in 1956. Geeraert became the association's vice president in 1959, president the following year, and regional vice president of the National Association of Home Builders the year after that.[67] He took advantage of his positions to speak out on a variety of issues, from a shortage of home financing funds to reform in site planning regulations, from home purchasing as an investment to needed changes in building codes.[68]

Aftermath

Even while he was at the height of his career, Geeraert began to encounter conflict with residents of the place he had spent over a decade building. At issue was his petition to rezone an edge portion of Twinbrook Park to permit construction of a garden apartment complex. As proposed in 1957, the plan was quite ambitious, calling for nearly thirty-eight acres to accommodate 400 units. In the face of opposition from some 200 neighborhood residents, the TCA, the city planning commission, and the Maryland–National Capital Park and Planning Commission, the city council tabled the petition. In an effort to find a viable compromise, Mayor Hovsepian proposed twenty-two acres for rezoning instead, to which Geeraert replied that he would use the fifteen remaining acres as a buffer zone. At the second hearing, Geeraert stated he would reduce the parcel further, but his petition was denied in January 1958.[69] Not one to accept defeat, Geeraert reapplied ten months later for a high-rise apartment building on a thirteen-acre parcel, with a pledge that "Meadow Hall," the sizable country house on the property, would be turned into a community center as part of the project. This proposal was considered over a period of several years, only to be denied in 1963.[70] Throughout, the TCA and residents focused on the estimated traffic burden as a basis for opposition, but it was also clear that many people felt that apartments of any kind would undermine the low-density character they had come to cherish. Apartment buildings seemed too urban and, perhaps, too subject to market changes that could lead to a demographic shift. Geeraert felt betrayed. In 1958, he lamented that "we were confronted with a well organized, vociferously objecting group, which frankly made me feel somewhat a criminal." He argued that it was important in such outlying areas to address the needs of people who chose to rent, to whom he was mak-

ing a long-term investment. Four years later, he told a reporter that his high-rise proposal would be a departure for Rockville, but he believed it would raise land values and make the place have "greater aesthetic appeal." After a long cooling-off period, Geeraert decided to erect thirty-three row houses on the site, a scheme that was subsequently reduced to two clusters totaling sixteen units. Set on a downward slope overlooking Rock Creek Park, completely removed from adjacent Twinbrook Park subdivisions, the development was as unobtrusive as it was modest. "I guess you could say that I am making a fresh start at the place where I had my greatest success," he admitted to a *Washington Post* reporter in 1967, shortly before the project got underway.[71]

Half a dozen years earlier, Geeraert could not have foreseen that Twinbrook would be the capstone to his career. He envisioned a new development in Fairfax County, Virginia, for which he began to amass land in the late 1950s, as a fitting sequel. Dubbed "Chandon"—conflating the names of the neighboring towns of Chantilly and Herndon—the tract would include 1,700 to 1,800 houses and a number of garden apartments. Houses were moderately priced (now at $16,000 to $18,000), as they had been in Twinbrook, and were to be built in a location then considered remote but nonetheless on the front lines of rapid growth, as Rockville had been a decade earlier. Geeraert believed that the construction of Dulles International Airport and the freeway that linked it to the Capital Beltway would accelerate that growth. In this case, however, he anticipated the future too soon. Securing access from the planned Dulles highway proved difficult and took longer than anticipated. Development was still occurring in the latter months of 1965, and earlier that year a "clearance sale" was staged for lower-price models, since by then homebuyers were requesting larger houses than originally projected.[72] But only about 150 houses were built over a five-year period, too few to include integrated support facilities such as a school or recreation center.

Whatever appeal the area had was in large part subsumed by Sterling Park, a much larger development several miles to the north which was begun in 1962. Developed by M. T. Broy-hill & Sons, one of the largest developers in the metropolitan area, this project boasted a population of some 5,000 people living in 924 houses and 272 apartment units by the close of 1966. Six schools, an athletic center, a swimming pool, a golf course, tennis courts, tot lots, baseball fields, a shopping center, police and fire stations, and an area for light industry were included in what ranked among the most ambitious residential developments to be realized during the decade.[73] By the 1970s, tracts started to appear closer to Chandon, but by then Geeraert was no longer involved.

Indeed, even when he still held high hopes for Chandon, Geeraert was at work on at least five other projects far afield in Prince George's County, Maryland. Never again would he focus on a single place the way he had at Twinbrook. The shift may have occurred because he now had adequate capital and credit to diversify. Perhaps, too, the rebuke Twinbrook residents gave him on the apartment project prompted a decision to avoid ever again becoming so involved with one of his developments. His Maryland undertakings were also much more modest in size—really subdivisions, without commercial or institutional facilities. Two of the new projects, Westgate in Lanham (1960–61) and Kenmoor in Landover (1961–62), encompassed a total of 173 single-family houses beginning at around $16,000 each. Two others, Highland Gardens (ca. 1961–62) and Holly Park North (1963) in Seat Pleasant included 192 and 116 semidetached houses, respectively, ranging from $14,000 to $16,400.[74]

Significantly, the Seat Pleasant tracts were built as "open occupancy" housing, meaning they carried no restrictions on race. At a time when African Americans had very few choices in new suburban housing and white prejudices remained widespread, the great majority of homebuyers there were black. Geeraert was far from the first white builder to construct houses for black homeowners, but he was among what appears to be a very small number who undertook such tract developments prior to the fair housing legislation of the mid-1960s. His adjacent developments also abutted Booker

T. Homes (1950–51), an earlier development for African Americans that was comprised of more modest semidetached houses, but Seat Pleasant was still a predominantly white community at that time, and its other postwar tracts were targeted to prosperous blue-collar and middle-class white families. Geeraert's last housing development was Fox Ridge (1964), several miles to the northeast in the historically African American community of Glenarden (fig. 14.20). Fox Ridge was something of a capstone to a series of house tracts that had been developed in the town since World War II, with 180 dwellings that cost from $18,760 to $24,000—the most expensive houses Geeraert had built since Coquelin Terrace. He was especially proud of this undertaking and asked his friend, Hubert Humphrey, by then a well-known U.S. senator and champion of civil rights, to attend the opening. Like many people who had been raised abroad, Geeraert did not understand the deep racial divides that existed in the United States during much of the twentieth century, and took special pleasure in providing houses for the black middle class who remained shut out from the vast majority of new suburban developments.[75] In Glenarden, too, Geeraert crusaded for an apartment complex aimed at middle-income households who could not afford the cost of a single-family residence. In this case he was successful. The proposal stirred some controversy, but the town's mayor was an ally, noting that that "ninety-eight percent of our young people move out . . . because they have no place to go" in the area, and adding that while there were many new apartment buildings in the county, "there are no apartments for Negroes."[76] In Seat Pleasant and Glenarden, Geeraert was again a pioneer, but the nearly 500-unit apartment complex in the latter community was the last major project he planned, and the realized complex was developed by others. The reward for such work may not have been equivalent to that derived from creating a larger community, but it was gratifying all the same. What he could not have anticipated is the catalytic role that Seat Pleasant and Glenarden would play during the 1970s in transforming much of the county into one of the nation's premier African America suburban areas.[77]

FIG. 14.20. Houses, 3600 block Tyrol Drive, Fox Ridge, Glenarden, Maryland, 1964, Geeraert Construction Corporation, designer and builder. (Photo Richard Longstreth, 2011)

During the last dozen years of his life, Geeraert spent much of his time was with family enjoying the fruits of his labor.[78] He never became a famous builder or a powerful one. A number of his colleagues, such as Broyhill, enjoyed longer careers, were responsible for many more houses, and had a much greater impact on the metropolitan area. Geeraert was never a cutting-edge developer, and despite his use of some of Levitt's design innovations, never embraced applying the ideas of the modernist avant-garde to the mass market, as did such firms as the Luira Brothers in Fairfax County, Virginia.[79] Twinbrook and his other developments remain largely unknown today, save among some of the people who reside there or close-by. But it nevertheless remains a special place. While reflecting broad patterns of the period, it is distinctive as well, bearing the indelible stamp of its builder and the imprint of its activist residents. Twinbrook, Fox Ridge, and Geeraert's tracts generally are places that thrive—well-maintained and vital enclaves that have now accommodated several generations—places that are reassuring sources of nourishment and havens of stability that are also conducive to engagement in community. In this regard, Geeraert's legacy in metropolitan Washington, and to a larger history, was hardly inconsequential.

A Note on Sources and Abbreviations

For purposes of brevity, titles of newspaper articles are shortened and their writers' names excluded except in cases where the individual is a noted critic or someone discussed in the text. Some titles of trade publication articles are also abridged for the same reason. Frequently cited periodicals are abbreviated, as noted below.

AF   *Architectural Forum*
AR   *Architectural Record*
CBM *Catholic Building and Maintenance*
CSM *Christian Science Monitor*
HBM *Home Builders Monthly* (Washington)
JSAH *Journal of the Society of Architectural Historians*
LA   *Landscape Architecture*
LtA *Liturgical Arts*
MCS *Montgomery County Sentinel* (Rockville, Maryland)
NYT *New York Times*
PA *Pencil Points/Progressive Architecture*
SEP *Savannah Evening Press*
SMN *Savannah Morning News*
TL *Twinbrook Life* (Rockville, Maryland)
TP *Times-Picayune* (New Orleans)
WP *Washington Post*

Introduction

1. Within a preservation framework, "recent past" is often used to refer to resources that are less than fifty years old. But the term has also come to mean resources dating from any time after the close of World War II, and by inference, embody characteristics of the various modernisms that have prevailed in architecture, landscape design, and urban development over that period. Within the latter framework, the years between 1945 and the early 1970s can be seen as a distinct period in American architecture, landscape architecture, and urbanism. It is also a period that continues to challenge the preservation realm.

For these reasons, "recent past" refers to that quarter century throughout this volume.

2. Among local organizations, the Los Angeles Conservancy has taken a leading role in raising public consciousness of post–World War II resources of many kinds, as revealed in the group's newsletter and website.

3. Some sense of the extent of preservation efforts addressing the recent past in the United States can be gleaned from Theodore H. M. Prudon, *Preservation of Modern Architecture* (New York: John Wiley, 2008), as well as from the newsletters and websites of DOCOMOMO/US (U.S. Chapter, International Committee for Documentation and Conservation of Buildings, Sites, and Neighborhoods of the Modern Movement) and the Cultural Landscape Foundation. I offer a brief historical overview of the preservation of twentieth-century resources in my "United States" entry for *Critical Encyclopedia for Restoration and Reuse of XXth Century Architecture*, ed. Bruno Reichlin and Roberta Grignolo, forthcoming.

4. Statewide and local surveys have been conducted even in places not generally associated with significant developments from the recent past. See, for example, Diana J. Painter, "Montana Post–World War II Architectural Survey and Inventory," Montana State Historic Preservation Office, Montana Historical Society, Helena, 2010; and Theresa B. Lachin, *Rockville's Recent Past* (Rockville, Md.: Peerless Rockville Historic Preservation, 2012).

5. David Gebhard and Robert Winter, *A Guide to Architecture in Southern California* (Los Angeles: Los Angeles County Museum of Art, 1965); Edward Teitelman and Richard Longstreth, *Architecture in Philadelphia: A Guide* (Cambridge, Mass.: MIT Press, 1974).

6. Some of the many images taken on those journeys will appear in Richard Longstreth, *Road Trip* (New York: Universe, 2015).

7. The two shopping centers, the Park and Shop (1930) and the Silver Spring Shopping Center (1937–38), are discussed in detail in Richard Longstreth, "The Neighborhood Shopping Center in Washington, D.C., 1930–1941," *JSAH* 51 (Mar. 1992): 5–34. Four of the other buildings are covered in Longstreth, *History on the Line: Testimony in the Cause of Preservation* (Wash-

ington, D.C.: National Park Service and Ithaca, N.Y.: National Council for Preservation Education, 1998), chapters 1–4.

8. I never wrote in detail on Silver Spring, but some of facets of my research can be found in Richard Longstreth, "Silver Spring: Georgia Avenue, Colesville Road, and the Creation of an Alternative 'Downtown' for Metropolitan Washington," in *Streets: Critical Perspectives on Public Space*, ed. Zeynep Celik et al. (Berkeley: University of California Press, 1994), 247–58, 294; Longstreth, "The Mixed Blessings of Success: The Hecht Company and Department Store Branch Development after World War II," in *Shaping Communities: Perspectives in Vernacular Architecture, VI*, ed. Carter L. Hudgins and Elizabeth Collins Cromley (Knoxville: University of Tennessee Press, 1997): 244–62; and Longstreth, *The American Department Store Transformed, 1920–1960* (New Haven: Yale University Press, 2010), 154–55, 167–68.

9. See Richard Longstreth, "The Significance of the Recent Past," *APT Bulletin* 23, no. 2 (1991): 12–24; Longstreth, "I Can't See It; I Don't Understand It; and It Doesn't Look Old to Me," *Historic Preservation Forum* 10 (Fall 1995): 6–15; Longstreth, "Midcentury Modernism at Risk," *AR* 220 (Sep. 2000): 59–61; and Longstreth, "Integrity and the Recent Past," in *Preserving the Recent Past 2*, ed. Deborah Slaton and William G. Foulks (Washington: National Park Service, Historic Preservation Education Foundation, and Association for Preservation Technology, 2000), 2–1 to 2–6.

10. Richard Longstreth, "The Levitts, Mass-Produced Houses, and Community Planning in the Mid-Twentieth Century," in *Second Suburb: Levittown, Pennsylvania*, ed. Dianne Harris (Pittsburgh: University of Pittsburgh Press, 2010), 123–74, 368–80; and Longstreth, "Brave New World: Southwest Washington and the Promise of Urban Renewal," in *Housing Washington: Two Centuries of Residential Development and Planning in the National Capital Area*, ed. Longstreth (Chicago: Center for American Places and University of Chicago Press, 2010), 255–80, 353–65.

11. See, for example, "Tucson Post World War II Residential Subdivision Development 1945–1973," Akros and College of Architecture and Landscape Architecture, University of Arizona, Tucson, October 2007; "Historic Context and Survey of Post-World War II Residential Architecture, Boulder, Colorado," Jennifer Bryant and Carrie Schomig, TEC, Boulder, April 2010; "The Ranch House in Georgia: Guidelines for Evaluation," New South Associates, Tucker, Ga., n.d. (ca. 2011); "Tract Housing in California, 1945–1973: A Context for National Register Evaluation," California Department of Transportation, Sacramento, 2011; and "A Model for Identifying and Evaluating the Historic

Significance of Post–World War II Housing," National Cooperative Highway Research Program Report 723, Transportation Research Board of the National Academies, Washington, D.C., 2012.

12. For a sampling of accounts, see "Holy Cross Announces Plans," *Clarion Herald*, Archdiocese of New Orleans, 17 Dec. 2005, 1, 11; "Cabrini Parishioners OK Holy Cross Talks," *Clarion Herald*, 29 July 2006, 3; "It's Gentilly for Holy Cross," *Clarion Herald*, 14 Oct. 2006, 1, 7; "Now You Tell Us?" *TP*, 12 Nov. 2006; "In Katrina's Wake," *TP*, 21 Nov. 2006, 5; Mark Schleifstein, "Church Is Designated as Historic by FEMA," www.nola.com, 21 Nov. 2006; and "In Tale of Church vs. School," *NYT*, 19 Dec. 2006, A18. A detailed chronicle of the whole episode is found in Stephen Verderber, *Delirious New Orleans: Manifesto for an Extraordinary American City* (Austin: University of Texas Press, 2009), chapter 6.

13. "Christian Science Church Wins," *Northwest Current* [Washington], 13 Mar. 2013, 4, 19.

14. For background, see Grace Gary, "It's Time to Evaluate *Our Past*," *Historic Preservation News*, Dec. 1990, 4; Benjamin Forgey, "Thoroughly Modern History," *WP*, 11 Jan. 1992, G1, G5; "This Is No Way to Preserve History," *Wall Street Journal*, 13 May 1993, A14; "A Place Unfit," *WP*, 1 Nov. 2007, B1, B5; Roger K. Lewis, "Deciding the Fate of Modern Buildings," *WP*, 10 Nov. 2007, F5; Sarah McCann, "Brutal, or Just Plain Ugly?" *Medill Reports*, 14 Nov. 2007 (http://news.medill.northwester.edu/washington/news.aspx?id=69467); Deborah A. Dietsch, "Modernism Worthy of Preserving," *Washington Times*, 1 Dec. 2007, B1, B4; "Church Awarded," *WP*, 7 Dec. 2007, B3; "Church, Builder Battle," *Dupont Current* [Washington], 12 Dec. 2007, 1, 23; "City Preservation Board," *InTowner* [Washington], Dec. 2007, 1, 6; Tersh Boasberg, "Why We Landmarked the Third Church," *Northwest Current*, 6 Feb. 2008, 11; Kim A. O'Connell, "Church Landmarking Offers a Brutal Lesson," *Inform*, 2008, no. 1: npp.; "Church Sues," *NYT*, 8 Aug. 2008, A17; Marc Fisher, "D.C.: Church May Not Decide Its Own Fate" (http://blog.washingtonpost.com/rawfisher/2008/07/dc_chruch_may_not_decide_its_o.html); Lewis, "Congregation vs. Preservation," *WP*, 13 Sep. 2008, F6; Dwight Young, "The Brutal Truth," *Preservation* 60 (Nov.–Dec. 2008): 72; "A Congregation Fights," *Wall Street Journal*, 24 Nov. 2008, W13; Larry Van Dyne, "Tear It Down! Save It!" *Washingtonian* 44 (Mar. 2009): 48–57, 82–86; "Preservation Board's Order," *InTowner*, Apr. 2009, 1, 7; "Developers Are Proceeding," *WP*, 22 No. 2010, 4; and "After Four Years of Controversy," *InTowner*, May 2011, 1, 6. One can only hope that the upbeat coverage following the filing of the landmark nomination and the markedly less

enthusiastic, often vituperative accounts some fifteen years later do not indicate an undercurrent of public disaffection with preservation more generally.

15. "Demolition Progress," *WP*, 11 Mar. 2014, B4.

16. For background, see "The Second Battle of Gettysburg," *WP Magazine*, 29 Dec. 1996, 12–16, 21; Allen Freeman, "Unwelcome Centers," *Preservation* 49 (July-Aug. 1997): 16–17; "Gettysburg's Development Battleground," *WP*, 28 Oct. 1997, A20; "Gettysburg Renovation," *WP*, 7 Nov. 1997, A3; Dion Neutra, "Gettysburg Visitor Center: Too Old to Be Chic, Too Young to Be Revered," *AIA Architect*, Feb. 1998, 5; "Cyclorama Has Legions," *Gettysburg Times*, 12 Mar. 1998, A1, A6; Michael Davis, "A Civic Dispute," *Central PA*, Apr. 1998, 39–45; Deborah Fitts, "Some Say Save the Cyclorama," *Civil War News*, July 1998, 19a; "Gettysburg's Cyclorama Faces Demolition," *Preserving Pennsylvania* 11:4 (1998): 1, 7; Thomas Hine, "Which of All Pasts to Preserve," *NYT*, 21 Feb. 1999, 48; "Giving Historic Gettysburg a New Look," *Philadelphia Inquirer Magazine*, 4 July 1999, 10–15; "Cyclorama Center's Future," *Gettysburg Times*, 3 Dec. 1999, A1, A12; Christine Madrid, "Neutra's Cyclorama: No Safe Ground," *LA Architect*, June-Aug. 2000, 11; Margaret Loftus, "Rescuing the Relics of Modern Times," *U.S. News & World Report*, 5 June 2000, 56–57; John Beardsley, "Another Battle at Gettysburg," *LA* 91 (Sep. 2000): 128; "Who Chooses History," *Los Angeles Times Magazine*, 27 June 2004, 14–17; "Richard Neutras Cyclorama in Gefahr," *tec21*, nos. 33–34 (2004): 30; "Neutra's Cyclorama Holds Its Ground," *DOCOMOMO*, summer 2004, 8; "Neutra in the News," *DOCOMOMO/US*, Fall 2004, 2, 7; "Professor Wants to Save," *Gettysburg Times*, 27 Apr. 2005, A5, A12; "What's Ugly, Round and Out There?" *Evening Sun* [Hanover, Pa.], 1 Dec. 2006; "The Past Imperfect," *Evening Sun*, 20 Jan. 2007; Herbert Muschamp, "Martial Place: The Enduring Relevance of a Modern Masterpiece," *NYT Style Magazine*, Summer 2007, 60, 61; and "Battle Rages to Save Neutra's Cyclorama Center," *AR* 195 (Oct. 2007): 44.

17. "Neutra Cyclorama Building," *Philadelphia Inquirer*, 10 Jan. 2013; Editorial, *York Daily Record* [Pennsylvania], 6 Mar. 2013; "The Death of the Gettysburg Cyclorama Building," *Evening Sun*, 9 Mar. 2013; "The Gettysburg Cyclorama," *Philadelphia Inquirer*, 12 Mar. 2013; Richard Longstreth, "The Loss of a Major Monument at Gettysburg," *Newsletter*, Society of Architectural Historians, Apr. 2013. See also Christine Madrid French, "The Visitor Center as Monument: Recontextualizing Richard Neutra's 1962 Cyclorama Center within the Commemorative Landscape of the Gettysburg Battlefield," in *Public Nature: Scenery, History, and Park Design*, ed. Ethan Carr et al. (Charlottesville, University of Virginia Press, 2013), 728–44.

18. For background, see "Board Delays," *Northwest Current*, 1–14 Nov. 1995, 1, 6; "Board Approves," *Northwest Current*, 3 Apr. 1996, 3, 28; "Gardens, Bitter and Sweet," *WP*, 18 Apr. 1996, J1; "Community Dirt—Garden Is Barren," *Northwest Side Story* [Washington], 30 (May 1996): npp.

19. The case was extensively covered in the *Northwest Current*: "Group Files," 7 Nov. 2001, 1, 22; "Giant Vows Battle," 14 Nov. 2001, 4, 26; "Landmark Status," 21 Nov. 2001, 11; "Landmark Proponents," 5 Dec. 2001, 1, 14; "Giant Landmark Bid," 19 Dec. 2001, 3, 29; "War of Words," 23 Jan. 2002, 2, 18; "Talks on Giant," 24 Apr. 2002, 3, 20; "Giant, Neighbors," 1 May 2002, 11; and "Giant, Neighbors Sign Agreement," 8 May 2002, 1, 14. See also "A Nice Little Giant," *WP*, 14 Feb. 2002, DW3, 13; "Giant, Neighbors," *WP*, 7 May 2002, B2; and Tersh Boasberg, "Preservation Pleasing to All Parties," *WP*, 19 May 2002, B8.

Chapter 1. The Problem with "Style"

1. The concept was introduced in embryo by Fred B. Kniffen, in "Louisiana House Types," *Annals of the Association of American Geographers* 26 (Dec. 1936): 179–93; and in more developed form in "Folk Housing: Key to Diffusion," *Annals of the Association of American Geographers* 55 (Dec. 1955): 549–57. It was further refined by a disciple, folklorist Henry Glassie, in *Pattern in the Material Folk Culture of the Eastern United States* (Philadelphia: University of Pennsylvania Press, 1968); and in "Eighteenth-Century Cultural Process in Delaware Valley Folk Building," *Winterthur Portfolio* 7 (1972): 29–57. For a more recent study that broadens the scope of houses covered, see John A. Jakle et al., *Common Houses in America's Small Towns: The Atlantic Seaboard to the Mississippi Valley* (Athens: University of Georgia Press, 1989).

2. William L. Lebovich, *America's City Halls* (Washington, D.C.: Preservation Press, 1984); Andrew Gulliford, *America's Country Schools* (Washington, D.C.: Preservation Press, 1984); Diane Maddex, *Built in the U.S.A.: American Buildings from Airports to Zoos* (Washington, D.C.: Preservation Press, 1985).

3. Yet the classifications based on structure that is commonly used for bridges is hardly an arcane one. See, for example, Richard Cleary, *Bridges* (Washington: Library of Congress, and New York: W. W. Norton, 2007).

4. Marcus Whiffen, *American Architecture since 1780: A Guide to the Styles* (Cambridge, Mass.: MIT Press, 1969), vii. Although Whiffen was likely unaware of the fact, his guide did have a predecessor, which was targeted to real estate brokers so that they might seem to speak with greater "authority" on houses

they sought to sell: A. Rowden King, *Realtors' Guide to Architecture: How to Identify and Sell Every Kind of House* (New York: Prentice-Hall, 1954). King divided his subject into four basic categories: "The Colonials," "English Architecture in America," "Latin [including French!] Architecture in America," and "The Contemporaries." He appended a miscellaneous category ("How to Sell Houses You Cannot Identify")—a harbinger of the "other" category in style lexicons.

5. Letters, *Historic Preservation* 28 (Oct.-Dec. 1976): 47. The series to which the writer was referring, "What Style Is It?" appeared in the magazine in four installments (28 [Apr.-June 1976]: 10-19; [July-Sep. 1976]: 34-43; [Oct.-Dec. 1976]: 14-23; and 29 [Jan.-Mar. 1977]: 14-23). Written by John Poppeliers, then chief of the Historic American Buildings Survey, and two of his lieutenants, S. Allen Chambers and Nancy Schwartz, the series was issued as a book of the same name and published by the National Trust's Preservation Press in 1977. It has gone through three subsequent editions, the latest in 2003.

6. The provision was implemented not long after this chapter was originally written.

7. Meyer Shapiro, "Style," in *Anthropology Today*, ed. A. L. Kroeber (Chicago: University of Chicago Press, 1953), 287-312 (quotes on p. 287).

8. Henry-Russell Hitchcock and Philip Johnson, *The International Style*, 1932; reprint ed. (New York: W. W. Norton, 1966), vii, ix.

9. Letters, *Historic Preservation* 28 (Oct.-Dec. 1976): 47. The problems art historians were having with methodologies based on style is amply reflected in *The Concept of Style*, ed. Berel Lang, 1979; revised ed. (Ithaca: Cornell University Press, 1987).

10. John J.-G. Blumenson, *Identifying American Architecture: A Pictorial Guide to Styles and Terms*, 1977; revised ed. (New York: W. W. Norton, 1981), 34-37; Whiffen, *American Architecture*, 68-82; Blumenson, *Identifying American Architecture*, 40-41, 66-69.

11. "More Local Sites Recognized as Historic," *Historic Kansas City News* 3 (Feb.-Mar. 1979): 7; "Revolving Fund Rescues House," *Historic Kansas City News* 4 (Feb.-Mar. 1980): 1. Despite its propensity to invent odd terms, the sponsoring group, the Historic Kansas City Foundation, did exemplary work in saving both buildings and neighborhoods and in advancing its cause to the public.

12. Lester Walker, *American Homes: The Illustrated Encyclopedia of Domestic Architecture*, 1981; reprint ed. (New York: Black Dog & Leventhal, 1996), 114-15, 120-21, 126-27, 142-43, 202-9, 224-25, 228-33, 242-45, 250-51; Mary Mix Foley, *The American House* (New York: Harper & Row, 1980), 194-95, 208-10, 239, 242-43, 236-39, 299-300, 264-65.

13. "How to Complete the National Register Form," *National Register Bulletin* 16A (1991): 24-26. While institutionalizing "style" has indeed curbed wretched excess in the use of nomenclature, it also has done much to perpetuate a flawed system.

14. John C. Poppeliers and S. Allen Chambers Jr., *What Style Is It? A Guided to American Architecture*, 1977; revised ed. (New York: John Wiley & Sons, 2003), 46-53; Whiffen, *American Architecture*, 172-77. Blumenson, *Identifying American Architecture*, ignores the medieval-inspired work of Cram's generation altogether. Concerning that generation of architects' outlook toward style and revival, see Richard Longstreth, "Academic Eclecticism in American Architecture," *Winterthur Portfolio* 17 (Spring 1982): 55-82.

15. Poppeliers and Chambers, *What Style Is It?* 20-25.

16. Virginia McAlester and Lee McAlester, *A Field Guide to American Houses* (New York: Alfred A. Knopf, 1984), 5-12, 321-497.

17. Whiffen, *American Architecture*, 83-86; Blumenson, *Identifying American Architecture*, 48-49; McAlester and McAlester, *A Field Guide*, 234-37; Foley, *The American House*, 158-59, 40-41; 56-57.

18. J. C. Loudon, *Encyclopedia of Cottage, Farm, and Villa Architecture and Furniture*, 1833; reprint ed. (London: Longman, Brown, Green & Longmans, 1846), 75-79. Davis quoted in Alan Gowans, *Images of American Living: Four Centuries of Architecture and Furniture as Cultural Expression* (Philadelphia: J. B. Lippincott, 1964), 303. An insightful analysis of the concept of style beginning with the rise of eclecticism in the late eighteenth and early nineteenth centuries is afford by J. Mordaunt Crook, *The Dilemma of Style: Architectural Ideas from the Picturesque to the Post-Modern* (London: John Murray, 1987).

19. Richard Longstreth, "Architectural History and the Practice of Historic Preservation in the United States," *JSAH* 58 (Sep. 1999): 327-28.

20. McAlester and McAlester, *A Field Guide*, 12-19.

21. Ibid., 308-17.

22. Carole Rifkind, *A Field Guide to American Architecture* (New York: New American Library, 1980), part IV.

23. Sir Banister Fletcher, *A History of Architecture on the Comparative Method*, 1896; 11th revised ed. (New York: Charles Scribner's Sons, 1943), 888.

Chapter 2. Taste versus History

1. See chapter 1, this volume.

2. The warehouse in question was built for the Woodward & Lothrop department store in 1937-38 and was designated a city landmark in 1992. For discussion, see Richard Longstreth, *History on the Line: Testimony in the Cause of Preservation* (Washington,

D.C.: National Park Service, and Ithaca, N.Y.: National Council for Preservation Education, 1998), chapter 3.

3. See chapter 6, this volume, and Ronald Lee Fleming, "Saving Shopping Centers: An Owlish View, or, Give a Hoot for Enhancement," *Forum*, Society of Architectural Historians, Committee on Preservation, 21 (Apr. 1993), whole issue.

4. A number of other "histories" can be added to this roster, including agricultural history, business history, and landscape history.

Chapter 3. The Difficult Legacy of Urban Renewal

1. For background, see Marc A. Weiss, "The Origins and Legacy of Urban Renewal," in *Urban and Regional Planning in the Age of Austerity*, ed. Pierre Cavel et al. (New York: Pergamon Press, 1980), 53–80, which offers an excellent overview of the subject.

2. Herbert J. Gans, *The Urban Villagers: Group and Class in the Life of Italian-Americans* (New York: Free Press, 1962).

3. Concerning the Waldorf-Astoria and its replacement, see Robert A. M. Stern et al., *New York 1900: Metropolitan Architecture and Urbanism 1890–1915* (New York: Rizzoli, 1983), 254–55, 261; Stern et al., *New York 1930: Architecture and Urbanism between the Two World Wars* (New York: Rizzoli, 1987), 611–15; and John Tauranac, *The Empire State Building: The Making of a Landmark* (New York: Scribner, 1995). For discussion of twentieth-century redevelopment of Fifth Avenue more broadly, see Max Page, *The Creative Destruction of Manhattan, 1900–1940* (Chicago: University of Chicago Press, 1999), chapter 2. Concerning Crown Hall and the Mecca, see Daniel Bluestone, "Chicago's Mecca Flat Blues," in *Giving Preservation a History*, ed. Max Page and Randall Mason (New York: Routledge, 2004), 207–56.

4. Concerning Central Park, see Roy Rosenzweig and Elizabeth Blackmar, *The Park and the People: A History of Central Park* (Ithaca, N.Y.: Cornell University Press, 1992). Concerning lofts, see Andrew Dolkart, "The Fabric of New York City's Garment District: Architecture and Development in an Urban Cultural Landscape," *Buildings & Landscapes* 11 (Spring 2011): 14–42. Concerning the landscape of slavery, see John Michael Vlach, *Back of the Big House: The Architecture of Plantation Slavery* (Chapel Hill: University of North Carolina Press, 1993); and Vlach, *The Planter's Prospect: Privilege and Slavery in Plantation Paintings* (Chapel Hill: University of North Carolina Press, 2002).

5. This subject is discussed in several essays in Charles A. Birnbaum et al., eds., *Preserving Modern Landscape Architecture II: Making Postwar Landscapes Visible* (Washington, D.C.: Spacemaker Press, 2004).

6. The extent of such writings is vast. Basic works include Martin Anderson, *The Federal Bulldozer* (Cambridge, Mass.: MIT Press, 1964); Scott Greer, *Urban Renewal and American Cites* (New York: Bobbs Merrill, 1965); *Urban Renewal: The Record and the Controversy*, ed. James Q. Wilson (Cambridge, Mass.: MIT Press, 1966); and Jeanne R. Lowe, *Cities in a Race with Time: Progress and Poverty in America's Renewing Cities* (New York: Random House, 1967).

7. Most notably Mark I. Gelfand, *A Nation of Cities: The Federal Government and Urban America, 1933–1965* (New York: Oxford University Press, 1975); and Jon C. Teaford, *The Rough Road to Renaissance: Urban Revitalization in America, 1940–1985* (Baltimore: Johns Hopkins University Press, 1990). Substantive analyses are also found in broader studies such as Robert M. Fogelson, *Downtown: Its Rise and Fall, 1880–1950* (New Haven: Yale University Press, 2001), chapter 7; and Alison Isenberg, *Downtown America: A History of the Place and the People Who Made It* (Chicago: University of Chicago Press, 2004), chapter 5. A useful retrospective examination that considers both process and product is found in Alexander Garvin, *The American City: What Works, What Doesn't*, 1996; revised ed. (New York: W. W. Norton, 2010), Chapter 6.

8. David Schuyler, *A City Transformed: Redevelopment, Race, and Suburbanization in Lancaster, Pennsylvania 1940–1980* (University Park, Pa.: Penn State University Press, 2002). My discussion is in no way intended to dispute the findings of Schuyler's meticulous study. For other case studies, see Richard Longstreth, comp., "A Historical Bibliography of Architecture, Landscape Architecture, and Urbanism in the United States Since World War II," http://www.preservenet.cornell.edu.

9. Unlike architects, planners and real estate developers have received little scholarly attention. A noteworthy exception is Miles L. Berger, *They Built Chicago: Entrepreneurs Who Shaped A Great City's Architecture* (Chicago: Bonus Books, 1992). A detailed autobiographical account of his urban renewal work in Baltimore and elsewhere is given in David A. Wallace, *Urban Planning My Way* (Chicago: Planners Press, American Planning Association, 2005). Zeckendorf also produced an autobiography, *Zeckendorf* (New York: Holt, Rinehart & Winston, 1970), but such works are also the exception.

10. For background, see Lowe, *Cities in a Race*, chapter 9; C. William Domhoff, *Who Really Rules? New Haven and Community Power Reexamined* (New Brunswick, N.J.: Transaction Books, 1978), chapter 9; Mandi Isaacs Jackson, *Model City Blues: Urban Space and Organized Resistance in New Haven* (Philadelphia: Temple

University Press, 2008), chapters 6-7; and Richard Longstreth, *The American Department Store Transformed, 1920-1960* (New Haven: Yale University Press, 2010), 231-33.

11. Since this chapter was first published, the Macy's store has also been demolished and new construction was underway on the site on the site as of March 2013.

12. Period sources include "Financing Set," *Women's Wear Daily,* 2 Feb. 1960, 6; "Hartford: Renewal in the Round," *AF* 113 (Dec. 1960): 72-76; "Ellipse for Hartford," *PA* 42 (Mar. 1961): 59; and "Planning the Downtown Center," *AR* 135 (Mar. 1964): 177-85. For recent discussion, see Bernard J. Frieden and Lynn B. Sagalyn, *Downtown, Inc.: How America Rebuilds Cities* (Cambridge, Mass.: MIT Press, 1989), chapter 13; and Garvin, *American City,* chapter 6.

13. Period sources include Jane Jacobs, "New Heart for Baltimore," *AF* 108 (June 1958): 88-92; Archibald C. Rogers, "Charles Center, Baltimore," *AIA Journal* 31 (Mar. 1959): 30-40; "Baltimore's Charles Center: A Case Study in Downtown Renewal," ed. Martin Milspaugh, *Urban Land Institute Technical Bulletin* 51 (Nov. 1964): whole issue; "Charles Center in Baltimore: How the Plan Didn't Get Compromised," *LA* 59 (Jan. 1969): 122-27; John Morris Dixon, "Charles Center," *AF* 130 (May 1969): 48-57. Recent analyses include Katharine Lyall, "A Bicycle Built-for-Two: Public-Private Partnership in Baltimore," *National Civic Review* 72 (Nov. 1983): esp. 546-51; Garvin, *American City,* 129-32; Mary Ellen Hayward and Frank R. Shivers Jr., eds., *The Architecture of Baltimore: An Illustrated History* (Baltimore: Johns Hopkins University Press, 2004), 278-85; and Wallace, *Urban Planning,* chapters 1-3.

14. Longstreth, *The American Department Store,* 233-36.

15. Contemporary accounts include Walter McQuade, "Toughness before Gentility Wins," *AF* 117 (Aug. 1962): 96-101; "Boston City Hall," *Casabella* 271 (Jan. 1963): 17-27; "Another Major Project for Boston," *PA* 45 (Feb. 1964): 62-64; "A Great Plaza for Boston," *AR* 135 (Mar. 1964): 190-200; "Boston's City Hall," *AF* 130 (Jan. 1969): 38-53; "The New Boston City Hall," *AR* 145 (Feb. 1969): 133-44; "Boston's Open Center," *AF* 132 (June 1970): 24-31; James Marston Fitch, "City Hall Boston," *Architectural Review* 147 (June 1970): 398-41; Diana Ford and Geoffrey Collins, "Boston City Hall Government Center Plaza, USA," *Landscape Design* 101 (May 1973): 8-10; and Carl John Black, "A Vision of Human Space," *AR* 145 (July 1973): 105-16. Retrospective accounts include Jane Holtz Kay, "Saving a Modern Masterpiece," *PA* 69 (Apr. 1988): 25, 30; David A. Crane, "The Federal Building in the Making of Boston's Government Center," and Norman Fletcher, "The John F. Kennedy Federal Office Building," in *Fed-*

eral Buildings in Context: The Role of Design Review, ed. J. Carter Brown (Washington: National Gallery of Art, and Hanover, N.H.: University Press of New England, 1995), 21-38, 39-43, respectively; Gretchen Schneider, "The Never Ending Story: City Hall Plaza," *Architecture Boston* 4:5 (2001): 16-19; and Gerhard Kallman and Michael McKinnell, "Original Thinking: Reflections on the Genesis of Boston City Hall," *Architecture Boston* 8 (May-June 2005): 33-35. For a historical critique of the project, see Daniel A. Gilbert, "'Why Dwell on a Lurid Memory?' Deviance and Redevelopment in Boston's Scollay Square," *Massachusetts Historical Review* 9 (2007): 103-33.

16. An early indication of the name change is "The 'Town House' Replaces the Row House in Jeffrey Manor," *NAHB Correlator* 3 (Sep. 1949): 28-31. Most examples built through the mid-1950s were targeted to moderate-income households. Toward that decade's end, however, some costlier designs began to be developed. See, for example, "The Patio Town House," *House & Home* 12 (Oct. 1957): 129-40A; "Town Houses: Planned-Unit Development," *Urban Land* 22 (Sep. 1963): 3-7; and Jacqueline Davidson, "The Row House Comes Back to Life," *AIA Journal* 48 (Sep. 1967): 56-65. Washington-area projects are discussed in: "Town Houses Regain Vogue," *WP,* 27 July 1963, C1, C15; "Town House Concept Looks Great," *WP,* 25 Apr. 1964, C1; Wolf Von Eckardt, "The Row House Revival," *WP,* 24 July 1966, G7; and "Town House Comes Back," *WP,* 10 May 1969, C1, C18, C19.

17. For a sampling of accounts, see Howard Davis, "Portland Center, Portland, Oregon," *Center* 5 (1989): 128-29; Judith A. Martin, "Recycling the Central City: The Development of a New Town-In Town" (Ph.D. dissertation, University of Minnesota, 1976); Jane King Hession et al., *Ralph Rapson: Sixty Years of Modern Design* (Afton, Minn.: Afton Historical Society Press, 1999), 192-201; Lisa Newman, "Lafayette Park, Detroit," *Center* 5 (1989): 124-27; and Charles Waldheim, *Case: Hilberseimer/Mies van der Rohe, Lafayette Park, Detroit* (Munich: Prestel, 2004).

18. Richard Longstreth, "Brave New World: Southwest Washington and the Promise of Urban Renewal," in *Housing Washington: Two Centuries of Residential Development and Planning in the National Capital Area,* ed. Longstreth (Chicago: Center for American Places and University of Chicago Press, 2010), chapter 12.

19. The urban renewal program actually funded a number of historic preservation endeavors, including the seminal College Hill and Vieux Carre surveys in Providence and New Orleans, respectively. For brief discussion, see "Interview with Dorn C. McGrath, Jr.," *CRM Journal* 2 (Winter 2005): 16-18.

20. For background, see Valerie Sue Halverson

Pace, "Society Hill, Philadelphia: Historic Preservation and Urban Renewal in Washington Square East" (Ph.D. dissertation, University of Minnesota, 1976); and Marietta Harte Barbour, "Overcoming Urban Renewal: Preservation in Society Hill, Philadelphia" (M.A. thesis, George Washington University, 2005). The significance of Society Hill in preservation and as a Modern landscape is discussed in chapter 4, this volume. Period sources include Stephen J. Thompson, "Philadelphia's Design Sweepstakes," *AF* 109 (Dec. 1958): 94–99; Edmund N. Bacon, "Pei in the Sky and Other Aspects of the Philadelphia Story," *Architectural Association Journal* 79 (Nov. 1963): 103–12; Philip Herrera, "Philadelphia: How Far Can Renewal Go?" *AF* 119 (Aug.-Sep. 1964): 179–93; and William L. Rafsky, "Success Comes to Society Hill," *Historic Preservation* 18 (Sep.-Oct. 1966): 194–95.

Chapter 4. The Last Landscape

1. I chose "The Last Landscape" as the title of the paper from which this chapter was developed simply because it was an engaging and economical way to introduce the ideas presented below. Only later did I recall that this was also the title of a once well-known book by William H. Whyte (1968), which advanced a much praised, but largely unheeded, call for reform in the design of outlying portions of the metropolis. The fact that this book has been forgotten in many quarters only underscores the tenuous position of things from the recent past.

2. For background, see Richard Longstreth, *The American Department Store Transformed, 1920-1960* (New Haven: Yale University Press, 2010), chapter 9; and Longstreth, *City Center to Regional Mall: Architecture, the Automobile, and Retailing in Los Angeles, 1920-1950* (Cambridge, Mass.: MIT Press, 1997), chapter 10.

3. Sidney Nichols Shurcliff, *The Day It Rained Fish and Other Encounters of a Landscape Architect* (Gloucester, Mass.: Pressroom, 1991), 151ff. For contemporary accounts, see Shurcliff, "Shopper's World: The Design and Construction of a Retail Shopping Center," *LA* 42 (July 1952): 144–51; and Robert L. Zion, "The Landscape Architect and the Shopping Center," *LA* 43 (Oct. 1957): 6–12.

4. Longstreth, *The American Department Store*, 203–5; "Garden Setting Lends Charm to Suburban Center: Old Orchard," in *Stores and Shopping Centers*, ed. James S. Hornbeck (New York: McGraw-Hill, 1962), 131–38.

5. Louise A. Mozingo, *Pastoral Capitalism: A History of Suburban Corporate Landscapes* (Cambridge, Mass.: MIT Press, 2011).

6. Ibid., 119–36; Jayne Merkel, *Eero Saarinen* (London: Phaidon, 2005), 95–101. Contemporary accounts

include "Rural Insurance Plant," *AF* 100 (Sep. 1954): 104–7; "Insurance Sets a Pattern," *AF* 106 (Sep. 1957): 113–27; "John Deere's Sticks of Steel," *AF* 120 (July 1964): 77–85; "Bold and Direct, Using Metal in a Strong, Basic Way," *AR* 136 (July 1964): 135–41; and Donald Canty, "Evaluation: The Wonders and the Workings of Saarinen's Deere & Co. Headquarters," *AIA Journal* 60 (Aug. 1976): 18–21.

7. *Hollin Hills, Community of Vision: A Semicentennial History 1949-1999*, ed. Scott Wilson (Alexandria, Va.: Civic Association of Hollin Hills, 2000); Mark A. Klopfer, "Theme and Variation at Hollin Hills: A Typological Investigation," in *Daniel Urban Kiley: The Early Gardens*, ed. William S. Saunders (New York: Princeton Architectural Press, 1999), 47–64.

8. Donlyn Lyndon et al., *The Sea Ranch*, 2004; revised ed. (New York: Princeton Architectural Press, 2014). Contemporary accounts include "Second-Home Communities," *AR* 138 (Nov. 1965): 152–55; and "Ecological Architecture: Planning the Organic Environment," *PA* 47 (May 1966): 120–35.

9. Barbara M. Kelly, *Expanding the American Dream: Building and Rebuilding Levittown* (Albany: State University of New York Press, 1993); Cynthia L. Girling and Kenneth I. Helphand, *Yard, Street, Park: The Design of Suburban Open Space* (New York: John Wiley & Sons, 1994), chapter 4; *Second Suburb: Levittown, Pennsylvania*, ed. Dianne Harris (Pittsburgh: University of Pittsburgh Press, 2010). See also chapters 5 and 14, this volume.

10. Concerning the former, see "Landscape Design: Works of Dan Kiley," *Process Architecture*, no. 33 (1982): 106–8; and Dan Kiley and Jane Amidon, *Dan Kiley: The Complete Works of America's Master Landscape Architect* (Boston: Bulfinch Press, 1999), 42–43; and *Dan Kiley Landscapes: The Poetry of Space*, ed. Reuben M. Rainey and Marc Treib (Charlottesville: University of Virginia School of Architecture and Richmond, Calif.: William Stout Publishers, 2009). Concerning the latter, see Ann Komara, *Lawrence Halprin's Skyline Park* (New York: Princeton Architectural Press, 2012).

11. "Fresno Downtown: Pedestrian Preserve," *Architect & Engineer* 220 (Mar. 1960): 12–13; "Heart of Gruen's Fresno Plan," *PA* 46 (Jan. 1965): 184–86; "Upgrading Downtown," *AR* 137 (June 1965): 175–90; George W. Wickstead, "Critique: Fresno Mall's First 12 Months," *LA* 56 (Oct. 1965): 44–45, 48; Alex Wall, *Victor Gruen: From Urban Shop to New City* (Barcelona: Actar, 2005), 151–58.

12. "When Shoppers Walk Away," *NYT*, 5 Nov. 1996, D1; Joe Bower, "Kalamazoo Keeps Stalled Mall," *Preservation* 49 (Jan.-Feb. 1997): 18–19; "A Mall Out of Season?" *Wisconsin State Journal* [Madison], 1 Mar. 1997, 1A. The mall was retained, but redesigned; see

Michael Cheyne, "No Better Way? The Kalamazoo Mall and the Legacy of Pedestrian Malls," *Michigan Historical Review* 36 (Spring 2010): 103-28. Concerning the decline of urban malls generally, see Lawrence O. Houstoun Jr., "From Street to Mall and Back Again," *Planning* 56 (June 1990): 4-10; and Kent A. Robertson, "The Status of the Pedestrian Mall in American Downtowns," *Urban Affairs Quarterly* 26 (Dec. 1990): 250-73.

13. For background, see "Profile of a City: Atchison, Kansas," *Urban Renewal Notes*, Sep.-Oct. 1965, 4-10; Roberto Brambilla et al., *American Urban Malls: A Compendium* (Washington: U.S. Government Printing Office, 1977), 16-17; and G. E. Kidder Smith, *The Architecture of the United States: The Plains and the Far West* (Garden City, N.Y.: Anchor Press, 1981), 327-28.

14. For background, see Harvey M. Rubenstein, *Central City Malls* (New York: John Wiley, 1978), 125-29; and Sanita M. Herman, "A Pedestrian Mall Born Out of Urban Renewal: Lawrence Halprin Associates and Harland Bartholomew & Associates in Charlottesville, VA," *Magazine of Albermarle County History* 68 (2010): 79-110. The Halprin design became the object of preservation in recent years; see Daniel Jost, "Mall Brawl," *LA* 98 (Oct. 2008): 60, 62-71.

15. The literature on cultural landscape is now, of course, extensive and historians of the built environment have argued for a more integrative approach for some years; see, for example, Dell Upton, "Architectural History or Landscape History," *Journal of Architectural Education* 44 (Aug. 1991): 195-99. To my knowledge, however, the discussion of how landscape design can enrich a broader view of landscape history has been minimal.

16. For background on the project, see Angela Danadjieva, "Seattle's Freeway Park," *LA* 67 (May 1977): 399-406; Sally Woodbridge, "Green for I-5," *PA* 58 (June 1977): 86-87; and Alison Hirsch, "Lawrence Halprin's Public Spaces: Design," *Studies in the History of Gardens & Designed Landscapes* 26 (Jan.-Mar. 2006): whole issue.

17. Chester H. Liebs, *Main Street to Miracle Mile: American Roadside Architecture*, 1985; reprint ed. (Baltimore: Johns Hopkins University Press, 1995) is the pioneering scholarly book on the subject; see also *Roadside America: The Automobile in Design and Culture*, ed. Jan Jennings (Ames: Iowa State University Press, 1990). More detailed studies have been published in subsequent years. Among the most prolific authors in this realm, John A. Jakle and Keith A. Sculle, have recently issued a volume addressing preservation issues: *Remembering Roadside America: Preserving the Recent Past as Landscape and Place* (Knoxville: Uni-

versity of Tennessee Press, 2011), which begins to broaden the focus beyond buildings.

18. For background, see Marc Treib, "J. B. Jackson's Home Ground," *LA* 78 (Apr.-May 1988): 2-5, 7.

19. The importance of landscape for Neutra is evident in his presentation of the Kaufmann house; see *Richard Neutra: Buildings and Projects*, vol. 1, ed. W. Boesinger (Zurich: Editions Ginsburg, 1951), 70-79. See also Richard Neutra, *Mysteries and Realities of the Site* (Scarsdale, N.Y.: Morgan & Morgan, 1951). For an exception in scholarly assessment, see Pamela Burton and Marie Botnick, *Private Landscapes: Modernist Gardens in Southern California* (New York: Princeton Architectural Press, 2002), 30-87.

Chapter 5. The Extraordinary Postwar Suburb

1. Throughout this essay, "postwar suburb" is loosely defined to encompass a variety of particular forms. I use it to include large areas of new development in a metropolitan area to which a number of builders contributed—such as Wheaton in Montgomery County, Maryland, north of Washington, D.C., or Southfield, in Oakland County, Michigan, north of Detroit—and also individual developments, ranging from around one hundred to several thousand houses—erected during the quarter century after World War II.

2. Most notably in William H. Whyte, *The Organization Man* (New York: Simon & Schuster, 1956); and John Keats, *The Crack in the Picture Window* (New York: Houghton-Mifflin, 1957).

3. General surveys include Gwendolyn Wright, *Building the Dream: A Social History of Housing in America* (Cambridge, Mass.: MIT Press, 1981); Joseph B. Mason, *History of Housing in the United States, 1930-1980* (Houston: Gulf Publishing, 1982); Kenneth T. Jackson, *Crabgrass Frontier: The Suburbanization of the United States* (New York: Oxford University Press, 1985); Clifford Edward Clark Jr., *The American Family Home, 1800-1960* (Chapel Hill: University of North Carolina Press, 1986); Robert Fishman, *Bourgeois Utopias: The Rise and Fall of Suburbia* (New York: Basic Books, 1987); Rosalyn Baxandall and Elizabeth Ewen, *Picture Windows: How the Suburbs Happened* (New York: Basic Books, 2000); and Robert A. Beauregard, *When America Became Suburban* (Minneapolis: University of Minnesota Press, 2006).

More specialized writings include Barry Checkoway, "Large Builders, Federal Housing Programmes, and Postwar Suburbanization," *International Journal of Urban Regional Research* 4 (March 1980): 21-45; Ned Eichler, *The Merchant Builders* (Cambridge, Mass.: MIT Press, 1982); Marc A. Weiss, *The Rise of the Com-*

munity Builders (New York: Columbia University Press, 1987); Richard L. Florida and Marshall M. A. Feldman, "Housing in US Fordism," *International Journal of Urban and Regional Research* 12 (June 1988): 186–210; Peter G. Rowe, *Making a Middle Landscape* (Cambridge, Mass.: MIT Press, 1991); Cynthia L. Girling and Kenneth I. Helphand, *Yard, Street, Park: The Design of Suburban Open Space* (New York: John Wiley & Sons, 1994); and Christopher Gramp, *From Yard to Garden: The Domestication of America's Home Grounds* (Chicago: Center for American Places, 2008).

In recent years, several detailed case studies have been published: Barbara M. Kelly, *Expanding the American Dream: Building and Rebuilding Levittown* (Albany: State University of New York Press, 1993); Greg Hise, *Magnetic Los Angeles: Planning the Twentieth-Century Metropolis* (Baltimore: Johns Hopkins University Press, 1997); Gregory C. Randall, *America's Original GI Town: Park Forest, Illinois* (Baltimore: Johns Hopkins University Press, 2000); Allison Baker et al., *The Lakewood Story: History, Tradition, Values* (Lakewood, Calif.: City of Lakewood, 2004); and *Second Suburb: Levittown, Pennsylvania*, ed. Dianne Harris (Pittsburgh: University of Pittsburgh Press, 2010). One of the most valuable period studies, which began to challenge conventional perspectives on the postwar suburb, is Herbert J. Gans, *The Levittowners: Ways of Life and Politics in a New Suburban Community* (New York: Vintage Books, 1967).

4. This genre of residential development has yet to receive the scholarly attention it deserves, particularly from a national perspective. Valuable case studies exist: Roberta M. Moudry, "Gardens, Houses, and People: The Planning of Roland Park, Baltimore" (M.A. thesis, Cornell University, 1990); and William S. Worley, *J. C. Nichols and the Shaping of Kansas City: Innovation of Planned Residential Communities* (Columbia: University of Missouri Press, 1990). See also Robert M. Behar and Maurice G. Culot, *Coral Gables: An American Garden City* (Paris: Editions Norma, 1997).

5. Little in-depth examination of this subject has been published. For exceptions, see Kelly, *Expanding the American Dream*, esp. chapters 5 and 6; and, for earlier dwellings, Alice Gray Read, "Making a House a Home in a Philadelphia Neighborhood," in *Perspectives in Vernacular Architecture, II*, ed. Camille Wells (Columbia: University of Missouri Press, 1986), 192–99; Chris Wilson, "Spatial Mestizaje on the Pueblo-Hispanic-Anglo Frontier," *Mass*, Journal of the School of Architecture, University of New Mexico, 10 (Fall 1994): 40–49; and Paul Groth and Marta Gutman, "Workers Houses in West Oakland," and Marta Gutman, "Five Buildings on One Corner and Their Change

Over Time" in "Sights and Sounds: Essays in Celebration of West Oakland," ed. Suzanne Stewart and Mary Praetzellis (Anthropological Studies Center, Sonoma State University, Robert Park, Calif., 1997), 31–84, 113–32, respectively.

6. The subject is discussed in relation to substantially different forms of housing stock in Deborah Marquis Kelly and Jennifer Goodman, "Conservation Districts as Alternatives to Historic Districts," *Historic Preservation Forum* 7 (Sep.-Oct. 1993): 6–14. A premise for the authors' argument, however, is that the fabric in question lacks sufficient historical significance for district designation, a point with which a number of historians of vernacular architecture and urbanism would disagree.

7. What real estate appraisers refer to as the "physical life" of a house—the period for which it will remain standing without significant repairs or improvements—is around fifty years. A house's "economic life"—the period for which it can remain useful—can be extended over many times that period with proper maintenance and improvements, a process to which preservation has contributed in a very substantial way. I am grateful to Eugene Pasymowski, M.A.I., for his insights on the appraisal process.

Chapter 6. The Lost Shopping Center

1. Concerning the precinct, see Mary Rose Szoka, "Nob Hill Study," Economic Development Department, City of Albuquerque, New Mexico, 1985.

2. For background on the building and its impact on shopping center development, see Richard Longstreth, "The Neighborhood Shopping Center in Washington, D.C., 1930-1941," *JSAH* 51 (Mar. 1992): 5–34; and Longstreth, *The Drive-In, the Supermarket, and the Transformation of Commercial Space in Los Angeles, 1914-1941* (Cambridge, Mass.: MIT Press, 1999), 148–61.

3. Richard Longstreth, "J. C. Nichols, the Country Club Plaza, and Notions of Modernity," *Harvard Architecture Review* 5 (1986): 120–35; William S. Worley, *J. C. Nichols and the Shaping of Kansas City: Innovation of Planned Residential Communities* (Columbia: University of Missouri Press, 1990), chapter 8.

4. For historical background, see Richard Longstreth, *City Center to Regional Mall: Architecture, the Automobile, and Retailing in Los Angeles, 1920-1950* (Cambridge, Mass.: MIT Press, 1997), 139–75; and Longstreth, "The Diffusion of the Community Shopping Center during the Interwar Decades," *JSAH* 56 (Sep. 1997): 276–79.

5. Most historical accounts of the regional shopping mall are case studies. See, for example, Mer-

edith Clausen, "Northgate Regional Shopping Center—Paradigm from the Provinces," *JSAH* 43 (May 1984): 144-61; Lizabeth Cohen, "From Town Center to Shopping Center: The Reconfiguration of Community Marketplaces in Postwar America," *American Historical Review* 101 (Oct. 1996): 1050-81; Stephanie Dyer, "Designing 'Community' in the Cherry Hill Mall," in *Constructing Image, Identity, and Place: Perspectives in Vernacular Architecture, IX*, ed. Alison K. Hoagland and Kenneth A. Breisch (Knoxville: University of Tennessee Press, 2003), 263-75. For an overview, see Richard Longstreth, *The American Department Store Transformed, 1920-1960* (New Haven: Yale University Press, 2010), chapter 8. See also Alex Wall, *Victor Gruen: From Urban Shop to New City* (Barcelona: Actar, 2005), 56-113.

6. See, for example, Francesca Yurchiano, "The (Un)Malling of America," *American Demographics* 12 (Apr. 1990): 36-39; Robert Goodman, "The Dead Mall," *Metropolis* 13 (Nov. 1993): 44-47, 61, 63; and "The Aging Shopping Mall," *Wall Street Journal*, 16 Apr. 1996, B1, B16. A long list of moribund shopping centers is posted on http://www.deadmalls.com.

7. Concerning the building, see Susannah Harris Stone, *The Oakland Paramount* (Berkeley: Lancaster-Miller, ca. 1980); and *Oakland Paramount*, ed. Steven Levin, Theatre Historical Society of America, *Annual Number 18*, 1991.

8. I am grateful to the late Steven Levin, one of a triumvirate responsible for the Paramount's restoration and former president of the Theatre Historical Society of America for his many insights on the subject. Concerning Heinz Hall, see Donald L. MacLachlan, "Heinz Hall for the Performing Arts," *Marquee* 3:4 (1971): 1-7.

9. For background, see Longstreth, *The American Department Store*, 184-86.

10. For background, see Longstreth, *City Center to Regional Mall*, 286-300. Concerning the Los Alamos complex, see Geoffrey Baker and Bruno Funaro, *Shopping Centers: Design and Operation* (New York: Reinhold, 1951), 242-45.

11. The complex remains extant, but has apparently experienced further remodeling since my visit in 1991.

12. Concerning that complex, see "Supermall," *AF* 136 (Apr. 1972): 30-33; Louis G. Redstone, *New Dimensions in Shopping Centers and Stores* (New York: McGraw Hill, 1973), 174-75; and Robert E. Witherspoon et al., *Mixed-Use Developments: New Ways of Land Use* (Washington, D.C.: Urban Land Institute, 1976), 148-53.

13. At present (2013), efforts to "recycle" retail facilities of the recent past have focused on pronounced physical transformation to accommodate other uses. See, for example, Julia Christensen, *Big Box Reuse* (Cambridge, Mass.: MIT Press, 2008). While in many such cases preservation may be unwarranted or, at the very least, premature, there are many other retail developments of the period worthy of serious historical evaluation.

Chapter 7. New Orleans New and Old

1. Among the most important historical studies focusing on the intentions of this phenomenon remain Peter Collins, *Changing Ideals in Modern Architecture 1750-1950* (London: Faber & Faber, 1965); and Reyner Banham, *Theory and Design in the First Machine Age* (New York: Praeger, 1967). Early histories of the postwar period include Henry-Russell Hitchcock, *Architecture: Nineteenth and Twentieth Centuries* (Baltimore: Penguin, 1958); and John Jacobus, *Twentieth-Century Architecture: The Middle Years, 1940-65* (London: Thames & Hudson, 1966).

2. Alfred H. Barr Jr. et al., *Modern Architecture: International Exhibition* (New York: Museum of Modern Art, 1932); Henry-Russell Hitchcock and Philip Johnson, *The International Style*, 1932; reprint ed. (New York: W. W. Norton, 1966). For historical accounts, see Terence Riley, *The International Style: Exhibition 15 and the Museum of Modern Art* (New York: Rizzoli, 1992); Franz Schulze, *Philip Johnson: Life and Work* (Chicago: University of Chicago Press, 1994), 74-86; John Elderfield et al., *Philip Johnson and the Museum of Modern Art* (New York: Museum of Modern Art and Harry N. Abrams, 1998).

3. The exportation of Modern architecture abroad as an embodiment of American values is the subject of Jane C. Loeffler, *The Architecture of Diplomacy: Building America's Embassies*, 1998; 2nd rev. ed. (New York: Princeton Architectural Press, 2011); and Annabel Jane Wharton, *Building the Cold War: Hilton International Hotels and Modern Architecture* (Chicago: University of Chicago Press, 2001).

4. Among period sources, see, for example, John Peter, *Masters of Modern Architecture* (New York: George Braziller, 1958); Ian McCallum, *Architecture USA* (New York: Reinhold, 1959); and *Form Givers at Mid-Century* (New York: Time and American Federation of the Arts, 1959).

5. For a listing of such literature, see Richard Longstreth, comp., "A Historical Bibliography of Architecture, Landscape Architecture, and Urbanism in the United States Since World War II," posted on http://www.preservenet.cornell.edu.

6. Dale Woolston Dowling, "For God, For Family, For Country: Colonial Revival Church Buildings in the Cold War Era" (Ph.D. dissertation, George Washington University, 2004).

7. "Boundaries Established for Two New Parishes," *Catholic Action of the South* [New Orleans], 3 July 1952, 1; "Temporary Church for New Parish," *New Orleans States,* 5 July 1952; "Concrete Floor Poured for St. Cabrini Church," *Catholic Action of the South,* 31 July 1962, 5; "Cabrini School Unit Dedicated," *TP,* 2 Nov. 1953, 40; St. Frances Cabrini Church file, Archdiocese of New Orleans, New Orleans.

8. "World to See Cabrini School," *TP,* 21 July 1958. See also "Classrooms Open to the Breeze," *AF* 105 (Oct. 1956): 146–47. I am grateful to the late Arthur Davis for sharing his recollections on how Father Frey commissioned Curtis & Davis and on his role as client; telephone interview, 13 Dec. 2006.

9. Nathaniel Cortlandt Curtis [Sr.] file, American Institute of Architects Archives, Washington, D.C.,http://public.aia.org/sites/hdoaa/wiki/ (hereafter AIA Archives). Among his many designs were those of the Union Indemnity Building, American Bank Building, Feibelman's (Sears) department store, the library and science building at Tulane, Audubon Park Zoo, and the Magnolia Street housing project. His books included *Architectural Composition* (Cleveland: J. H. Jansen, 1923) and *Architectural Graphics* (Cleveland: J. H. Jansen, 1926). See also note 28 below.

10. "Questionnaire for Architects' Roster," 22 Oct. 1947, Curtis & Davis file, AIA Archives; *American Architects Directory,* ed. George S. Koyl (New York: R. R. Bowker, 1957), 121, 126; Abbye A. Gorin, "A Master Architect Remembered," *TP,* 25 June 1997, B-6; Gorin, "The Design Architect: Nathaniel Curtis, FAIA (1917–1997)," in Gorin et al., "The Rivergate (1868–1995): Architecture and Politics No Strangers in Pair-a-Dice," chapter 3, Howard Tilton Memorial Library, Tulane University (http://www.tulane.edu/~rivrgate); "Famed Architect's Home," *TP,* 4 Dec. 2004; Nomination statement for Nathaniel Curtis to receive AIA Louisiana Medal of Honor, Apr. 2005, AIA New Orleans archive. Many additional details can be found in a recently published autobiography: Arthur Q. Davis, *It Happened by Design: The Life and Work of Arthur Q. Davis* (New Orleans: Ogden Museum of Southern Art, University of New Orleans, and Oxford: University Press of Mississippi, 2009).

11. For a good case study, see Ernest H. Wood III, "The Opportunities Are Unlimited: Architects and Builders since 1945," in Catherine W. Bishir et al., *Architects and Builders in North Carolina: A History of the Practice of Building* (Chapel Hill: University of North Carolina Press, 1990), chapter 7. A major exception, of course, could be found in large Florida centers, especially Miami and Miami Beach.

12. "New Orleans Modern," *Fortune* 52 (Apr. 1955): 172. See also "The Architect and His Community: Curtis & Davis, New Orleans," *PA* 41 (Apr. 1960): 142.

13. "Libraries for People," *NYT,* 5 Jan. 1969, R1, R5. Concerning the building, see "Public Use: Design Award," *PA* 38 (Jan. 1957): 116–17; "P/A Design Awards Seminar IV," *PA* 38 (Oct. 1957): 101–4; "Book Showcase," *AF* 110 (Apr. 1959): 128–29; Clinton H. Cowgill and George E. Pettengill, "The Library Building, Part 2," *Journal of the AIA* 31 (June 1959): 106–11; "The Architect and His Community," 152–55; "Bibliotheque, Nouvelle Orleans, États-Unis," *Architecture d'aujourd'hui* 32: 96 (June–July 1961): 92–93; and Karen Kingsley, *Buildings of Louisiana* (New York: Oxford University Press, 2003), 100.

14. Useful compilations of the firm's work include "The Architect and His Community," 141–55; and "Design Firm Case Study," *Interiors* 126 (Feb. 1967): 101–47. A number of works were cited in Samuel Wilson Jr., *A Guide to the Architecture of New Orleans—1699-1959* (New York: Reinhold, 1959), 57, 59, 61, 63, 64, 67, 69, 71, 73, 74, 77, 79, and 80; in Albert C. Ledner et al., *A Guide to New Orleans Architecture* (New Orleans: New Orleans Chapter of the American Institute of Architects, 1974), 30–31, 38, 47, 48–49, 64, 103, 119, 132, and 141; and in Kinglsey, *Buildings of Louisiana,* 67, 96–97, 100–101, 118–19, 132, 142–43, and 155. Curtis & Davis received by far the most coverage among those firms featured in Edward Waugh and Elizabeth Waugh, *The South Builds: New Architecture in the Old South* (Chapel Hill: University of North Carolina Press, 1960), 32–33, 36–37, 46–47, 76, 93–95, 98–99, 112–13, 121, 126–27, suggesting the firm's preeminence in the greater region.

15. "New Multi-Purpose Arena," *TP,* 5 Nov. 1999; "Famed Architect's Home"; Letters to AIA Louisiana Board from Creed W. Brierre (18 Apr. 2005) and from Raymond G. Post (13 Apr. 2005), Nomination file for Nathaniel Curtis, AIA Archives.

16. Nomination file for Nathaniel Curtis; Nathaniel Cortlandt Curtis [Jr.] and Arthur Quentin Davis files, AIA Archives. See also "What the Architects Dream for Tomorrow," *Business Week,* 19 Jan. 1957, 106–8; and "Off Beat—and Award-Winning," *Newsweek* 52 (21 July 1958): 72–73.

17. Among the nationally prominent architects supporting Curtis's nomination were William Caudill, O'Neil Ford, Lawrence Perkins, and Harry Weese. For Davis, nominators included Pietro Belluschi, Marcel Breuer, Gordon Bunshaft, Walter Gropius, and Hugh Stubbins.

18. Loeffler, *Architecture of Diplomacy,* 238–39; "Jeunes architects dans le monde," *Architecture d'aujourd'hui* 28:73 (Sep. 1957): 82–85; "Medical Center for Free Berlin," *AF* 112 (Feb. 1960): 132–37.

19. "Cast-in-Place in Two Finishes," *PA* 45 (Sep. 1964): 166–71; "Planning the Downtown Center," *AR* 135

(Mar. 1964): 177–85; "Hotel Takes Part in Downtown Renewal," *AR* 136 (Oct. 1964): 166–67.

20. "Design Firm Case Study," 101, 102, 105.

21. "No-Corridor School," *AF* 98 (Apr. 1953): 132–33; "School on Stilts," *Newsweek* 43 (15 Mar. 1954): 98; "A Reason for Smiles in 'Back-of-Town,'" *Life* 36 (29 Mar. 1954): 59, 60, 62; "School on Stilts," *AF* 101 (Nov. 1954): 148–51; James F. Redmond, "Thomy Lafon—The School on Stilts," *American School and University* 27 (1955–56): 161–64; John Ferguson, "The Architecture of Education: The Public School Buildings in New Orleans," in Donald Devore and Joseph Logsdon, *Crescent City Schools: Public Education in New Orleans, 1841–1991* (Lafayette: University of Southwestern Louisiana, Center for Louisiana Studies, 1991), 340–41.

22. "A New Kind of Prison," *AF* 101 (Dec. 1954): 148–51; Reed Cozart, "Should Prisons Be Merely Dungeons?" *AR* 119 (Apr. 1956): 203–8; Cozart, as told by Edward W. Stagg, "Our Prisons Need Not Fail," *Saturday Evening Post* 228 (8 Oct. 1955): 17–18, 121–22; "An Argument for the One-Story Hospital," *AF* 105 (Nov. 1956): 120–22.

23. "Classrooms Open to the Breeze"; "Space for Worship—Cloistered and Exalted," *PA* 39 (June 1958): 120–23; "Louisiana Church Gathers Honor," *CBM* 11 (Jan.-Feb. 1959): 36–38, 96–99, 111.

24. Concerning the IBM Building, see "Design Firm Case Study," 108–9; "Steel Skeleton Is Also a Sheath," *NYT*, 24 June 1962, 251; "Building's Lattice Wall Carries Beams, Resists Wind," *Engineering News-Record* 169 (6 Sep. 1962): 34–36, 41; Franklin Toker, *Pittsburgh: An Urban Portrait* (Pittsburgh: University of Pittsburgh Press, 1986), 28; and "1960s: IBM Building," *Pittsburgh Post-Gazette*, 18 Dec. 2005, G-7. Concerning the World Trade Center and Skilling's role in its design, see "Twin Towers Engineered to Withstand Jet Collision," *Seattle Times*, 27 Feb. 1993, A-1; Angus Kress Gillespie, *Twin Towers: The Life of New York City's World Trade Center* (New Brunswick: Rutgers University Press, 1999), esp. 78–82; and Robert A. M. Stern et al., *New York 1960: Architecture and Urbanism between the Second World War and the Bicentennial* (New York: Monacelli Press, 1995), 198–206, and references cited therein. Concerning Skilling, see "Structural Engineer Skilling Dies," *Seattle Times*, 6 Mar. 1998, A-1.

Frank Lloyd Wright, of course, had broken from the skeletal frame earlier in his towers for Johnson Wax Company in Racine, Wisconsin (1943, 1947–50) and H. C. Price Company in Bartlesville, Oklahoma (1952–56), in which concrete floors were cantilevered from a core. These were, however, buildings with much smaller floor plates.

25. "Exterior Columns Support Building," *NYT*, 6 Feb. 1966, R6; "Spatial Drama in Baton Rouge," *Interiors* 128 (Jan. 1969): 102–7.

26. "Humpbacked Barrel Arches Cover 4-Acre Hall," *Engineering News-Record* 179 (3 Aug. 1967): 58–60; "A New Face for 'Old' New Orleans," *NYT*, 18 Feb. 1968, 382; Michele Melaragno, *An Introduction to Shell Structures: The Art and Science of Vaulting* (New York: Van Nostrand Reinhold, 1991), 163, 165; "Saving a Significant Building," *TP*, 10 Aug. 1994, B-6; "Requiem for the Rivergate," *TP*, 11 Dec. 1994, A-1, A-4; Nathaniel Curtis [Jr.], "The Design Process," in Gorin et al., "The Rivergate," chapter 4.

27. "Louisiana Superdome," *NYT*, 4 Nov. 1971, 61; "World's Largest Steel Dome Spans 680 ft over Superdome," *Engineering News-Record* 190 (22 Mar. 1973): 66–67; *The Builders: Marvels of Engineering* (Washington, D.C.: National Geographic Society, 1992), 156–59.

28. Nathaniel Cortland Curtis [Sr.], *New Orleans: Its Old Houses, Shops and Public Buildings* (Philadelphia: J. B. Lippincott, 1933); Nathaniel Cortlandt Curtis [Sr.] file, AIA Archives. According to Karen Kingsley, this book long served as a standard text for architecture students at Tulane in order to sensitize them to the special qualities of the city (telephone conversation, 18 Dec. 2006). See also Curtis's foreword to William Woodward, *French Quarter Etchings of Old New Orleans* (New Orleans: Magnolia Press, American Academy of History, 1938).

29. "The Architect and His Community," 142. See also "A New Face."

30. For examples, see "Modern Interpretation Reminiscent of Old French Quarter," *AR* 112 (Oct. 1952): 174–78; "Louisiana House Combines Privacy, Open Plan," *AR* 118 (Nov. 1955): 172–75; "To Achieve Complete Outdoor Privacy," *House & Home* 10 (Oct. 1956): 136–37; "Walled-In Plan for a City Lot," *AR, Houses of 1957* 121 (mid-May 1957): 180–83; "This Big and Handsome House," *House & Home* 13 (June 1958): 84–89; "Split-Level Opens Vistas in Confined Lot," *AR, Houses of 1959* 125 (mid-May 1959): 124–27; "Honor Award" and "Merit Award," *House & Home* 15 (June 1959): 116–17, 122–23, respectively; "A 'Walled-In' House in New Orleans," *Journal of the AIA* 33 (Jan. 1960): 58–59; "New Orleans House Designed for Easy Expansion," *AR, Houses of 1960* (mid-May 1960): 144–49; "Patios and Pavilions Are Combined," *AR, Houses of 1964* 135 (mid-May 1964): 116–19; "Patio Life Behind Walls," *Life* 58 (12 Mar. 1965): 92–95, 97, 98; and "A Two-Part Steel House," *House & Home* 29 (Feb. 1966): 106–7.

31. "Medical Office Area," *TP*, 15 Feb. 1959, 1; "Gardens on a Garage," *AF* 116 (Jan. 1962): 79–81 (Medical Plaza); "Four-Story Office Building," *TP*, 16 June 1957, V-1; "Clay Tile Screens Shade Offices," *AR* 127 (Feb. 1960): 192–94 (Caribe Building). Concerning the Lakewood Hospital and New Orleans Library, see notes 22 and 13 above, respectively.

32. For background, see Peter Hammond, *Liturgy and Architecture* (New York: Columbia University Press, 1961), chapters 2 and 4. See also Frederic Debuyst, "Church Architecture and Christian Celebration," *LtA* 32 (Nov. 1963): 3. A useful discussion of Catholic beliefs and practices and how these can be manifested through design is found in Paul Thiry et al., *Churches & Temples* (New York: Reinhold, 1953), 3C-79C. For a more general discussion, see Edward A. Sovik, "Church Design and the Communication of Religious Faith," *AR* 128 (Dec. 1960): 137-40.

33. Edward J. Sutfin and Maurcie Lavanoux, "Contemporary Catholic Architecture," in Albert Christ-Janer and Mary Mix Foley, *Modern Church Architecture: A Guide to the Form and Spirit of 20th Century Religious Buildings* (New York: McGraw-Hill, 1962), 1; Otto Spaeth, "Worship and the Arts," in *Religious Buildings for Today*, ed. John Knox Shear (New York: F. W. Dodge, 1957), 36, 38, 40 (quote on p. 38); Robert J. Dwyer, "Art and Architecture for the Church in Our Age," *LtA* 27 (Nov. 1958): 4; Debuyst, "Church Architecture," 4. See also Edward D. Mills, *The Modern Church* (London: Architectural Press, 1956); and Hammond, *Liturgy and Architecture*, chapter 6.

34. Sutfin and Lavanoux, "Contemporary Catholic Architecture," 2. See also "Diocesan Building Directives," *LtA* 26 (Nov. 1957): 7-9 and (Feb. 1958): 43-44.

35. Dwyer, "Art and Architecture," 5, 6; Patrick J. Quinn, "Real Determinants of Significant Church Building," *LtA* 30 (Nov. 1962): 2, 3; James Cardinal Lercaro, "Building the House of God," *LtA* 28 (Nov 1959): 2. See also Marvin Halverson, "On Getting Good Architecture for the Church," in *Religious Buildings for Today*, ed. Shear, 3-7; and Aelred Tezels, "The Church Building as a Symbol of New Jerusalem," *LtA* 30 (Nov. 1962): 8-9.

36. Debuyst, "Church Architecture," 4, 3, 5.

37. Brenda Bettinson, "Patron of the Living Arts," *LtA* 32 (Nov. 1963): 25; Christ-Janer and Foley, *Modern Church Architecture*, 82; M. A. Couturier, "Religious Art and the Modern Artist," *Magazine of Art* 44 (Nov. 1951): 269-70; Maurice Lavanoux, "Catholic Tradition," in *Religious Buildings for Today*, ed. Shear, 47; Debuyst, "Church Architecture," 8; Quinn, "Real Determinants of Significant Church Building," 3. See also Robert H. Mutrux, "The Architect and Church Appointments," *CBM* 14 (Nov.-Dec. 1962): 30-32, 44, 50; and "Liturgical Furnishings," *CBM* 16 (Jan.-Feb. 1964): 63-70.

38. "A Benedictine Monastery," *AF* 101 (July 1954): 148-55; Whitney Stoddard, *Adventure in Architecture: Building the New St. John's* (New York: Longmans, Green, 1958); Marcel Breuer, *Buildings and Projects 1921-1961* (New York: Frederick A. Praeger, 1962), 36-55; "A School in Praise of God," *AF* 107 (Jan. 1957):

122-27; "Design of St. Louis Priory and School," *LtA* 26 (Feb. 1958): 50-61; "P/A Design Awards Seminar IV," *PA* 39 (Oct. 1958): 129-32; "Belluschi Designs a Church and Monastery," *AR* 129 (June 1961): 116-21; Christ-Janer and Foley, *Modern Church Architecture*, 281-307; Maurice Lavanoux, "The Reality of a Dream," *LtA* 20 (Nov. 1962): 4-7, 12-25; Lavanoux, "The Past Is Prologue," *LtA* 31 (May 1963): 40-52; Meredith L. Clausen, *Spiritual Space: The Religious Architecture of Pietro Belluschi* (Seattle: University of Washington Press, 1992), 81-85; Clausen, *Pietro Belluschi: Modern American Architect* (Cambridge, Mass.: MIT Press, 1994), 226-33; Isabelle Hyman, *Marcel Breuer, Architect: The Career and the Buildings* (New York: Harry N. Abrams, 2001), 218-22.

39. Examples published in the New York-based *CBM* appear to be a good indication of mainstream views. See, for example, "Most Modern Unit," 1 (Dec. 1949): 31-35; "A Notable Example of Construction," 2 (Mar. 1951): 15-18; "In Classic Style," 3 (Mar. 1952): 31-33, 52; "Church of Striking Beauty," 5 (Dec. 1953): 36-39-72; "Cruciform Church," 6 (June 1954): 40-44; and "Parish Church in Virginia," 6 (Dec. 1954): 38-41, 66. Modernist church designs of any sort do not begin to appear in the journal until the mid-1950s.

40. George W. Tucker, *America's Church: The Basilica of the National Shrine of the Immaculate Conception* (Huntington, Ind.: Our Sunday Visitor, 2000); Rev. J. Joseph Gallagher, *The Cathedral of Mary Our Queen* (Baltimore: By the Cathedral, ca. 1959).

41. "Contemporary with the Times," *CBM* 14 (Nov.-Dec. 1962): 53-59, 121-24 (quote on p. 124); Robert Mutrux, *Great New England Churches: 65 Houses of Worship That Changed Our Lives* (Chester, Conn.: Globe Pequot Press, 1982), 214-17; Robert C. Broderick, *Historic Churches of the United States* (New York: Wilfred Funk, 1958), 220-21. See also "Monumental Tower Incorporates Ancient Custom," *CBM* 10 (July-Aug. 1956): 31-34. A good example of the complaint against "modernistic" designs is found in Thiry et al., *Churches & Temples*, 17-19.

42. This is evident in the contents of the Catholic Art Association's journal, *Catholic Art Quarterly* (later *Good Work*); see, for example, Mary Jeanne, "Artistic Freedom, Part II," and Graham Carey, "Distortion," 22 (Pentecost 1959): 77-80, 81-88, respectively.

43. For examples of the former, see Resurrection of Our Lord Church, St. Louis (1952-53) in *Modern Architecture in St. Louis: Washington University and Postwar American Architecture, 1948-1973*, ed. Eric Mumford (St. Louis: Washington University School of Architecture, 2004), 35-36; St. Ann's Church, Normandy, Missouri (ca. 1953-54) in *CBM* 7 (Mar.-Apr. 1955): 51-54; and St. Joseph's Church, Fort Atkinson, Wisconsin (ca. 1954-55) in *Religious Buildings for Today*, ed. Shear, 14-17.

44. Roughly a third (pp. 4–121) of Christ-Janer and Foley, *Modern Church Architecture* is devoted to Catholic churches and cathedrals. A few examples were used in a similar volume: *Religious Buildings for Today*, ed. Shear, 14–17, 48–49, 96–99.

45. See illustrations of the Church of Saints Peter and Paul, Tulsa, Oklahoma, and St. Patrick's Church, Oklahoma City (*LtA* 30 [Aug. 1962]: 125–27 and 133–35, respectively). For comparisons, see Christ-Janer and Foley, *Modern Church Architecture*, 6–69; and Mills, *Modern Church*, 35–39. A few more adventurous, central-plan churches followed; see *LtA* 31 (May 1963): 84–95; and 33 (Nov. 1964): 20.

46. Among prominent Modern architects in the United States, only Belluschi, Eliel Saarinen, and Barry Byrne had much of a track record in this sphere. Byrne's several Catholic churches of the late 1940s had little impact on work a decade later.

47. Robert H. Mutrux, "A Post-Vatican Perspective," *PA* 52 (Dec. 1971): 45–53 (quote on p. 50). Some concise accounts of how the Second Vatican Council's measures would affect church design can be found in Robert F. Hayburn, "On the Sacred Liturgy Constitution," *CBM* 16 (Jan.–Feb. 1964): 53–56, 119–20; "The Sanctuary, Church Design, and the Constitution on the Sacred Liturgy," *CBM* 16 (Sep.–Oct. 1964): 53, 72, 172; and "Liturgical Design—A Symposium," *CBM* 17 (Jan.–Feb. 1965): 55–67. See also Theodor Filthaut, *Church Architecture and Liturgical Reform*, trans. Gregory Roettger (Baltimore: Helicon, 1968).

48. St. Frances Cabrini file, Archdiocese of New Orleans; "Striking New Cabrini Church to Be Erected," *Catholic Action of the South*, 8 May 1960, 1A, 3A.

49. As quoted in "Authority and Simplicity of Cabrini Church Cited," *Clarion Herald* [New Orleans], 25 Apr. 1963, 14.

50. Other contemporary accounts include "N.O. Church Gets Architectural Award," *TP*, 23 Mar. 1962, 2; "New Look in Churches," *TP, Dixie* magazine, 22 Apr. 1962, 3–4; "Church Blaze Damage Heavy," *TP*, 23 May 1962, I-1; "Cabrini Church Dedication Set," *Clarion Herald*, 18 Apr. 1963, 1; "New St. Frances Cabrini Church," *TP*, 20 Apr. 1963, 21; "St. Frances Cabrini Church," *New Orleans States-Item*, 19 Apr. 1963, 25; "New Cabrini Church Gets Cody's Praise," *New Orleans States-Item*, 22 Apr. 1963, 2; "Church Construction Active," *TP*, 26 Jan. 1964, V-23; and "Visible Expressions of Man's Faith," *Fortune* 70 (Dec. 1964): 124–25. Concerning Immaculate Conception, see note 23 above.

51. Davis interview. The descriptive analysis that follows in the text below is based on site inspections of 20 Apr. 1995 (with Nathaniel Curtis), 17 Oct. 2006, and 20 Dec. 2006; period and recent photographs, and

working drawings, dated 27 Mar. 1961, in the Curtis papers at the Southeastern Architectural Archive, Special Collections, Tulane University. Prints of the latter were kindly made available through the Archdiocese of New Orleans.

52. Jeanne Halgren Kilde, *When Church Became Theatre: The Transformation of Evangelical Architecture and Worship in Nineteenth-Century America* (New York: Oxford University Press, 2002).

53. Two unusual precursors to St. Frances Cabrini's plan were by Seattle-based architect Paul Thiry for the Church of Christ the King in Seattle and St. Anthony's Church in Missoula, Montana; see Thiry et al., *Churches & Temples*, 92C–98C. Curtis respected this book, as noted in "Louisiana Church Gathers Honor," 37.

54. Melaragno's *Introduction to Shell Structures* includes a useful survey of noteworthy examples of all types. Exceptions of utilitarian applications included Eero Saarinen's Kresge Auditorium at MIT (1952–55), Minoru Yamasaki's Lambert–St. Louis Air Terminal (1952–55), and I. M. Pei's May-D&F department store in Denver (1955–58). A few additional, lesser-known examples are in Jurgen Joedicke, *Shell Architecture* (New York: Reinhold, 1963). See also Leonard Michaels, *Contemporary Structure in Architecture* (New York: Reinhold, 1958), 102–25; Carl W. Condit, *American Building Art: The Twentieth Century* (New York: Oxford University Press, 1961), 177–85; David P. Billington, *Thin Shell Concrete Structures* (New York: McGraw-Hill, 1965), chapter 1; and Maria E. Moreya et al., *Felix Candela: Engineer, Builder, Structural Artist* (New Haven: Yale University Press, 2008).

55. Eduardo Torroja, *The Structures of Eduardo Torroja* (New York: F. W. Dodge, 1958), 2–18. See also Torroja, *Philosophy of Structures* (Berkeley: University of California Press, 1967), 186–87; Peter, *Masters of Modern Architecture*, 102–3, 222; and Ivan Margolius, *Architects + Engineers = Structures* (London: Wiley-Academy, 2002), 38–39.

56. Davis interview.

57. Nathaniel Curtis [Jr.] manuscript, undated, p. 71, in possession of Mrs. Nathaniel Curtis, New Orleans.

58. "New Iberian—Carving a Reputation," *TP, Dixie* magazine, 28 Mar. 1968, 10–11; "Visible Expressions of Man's Faith," 125.

59. Davis interview.

60. A similar defiance of readily perceived structural logic was embraced in a very different way by Frank Lloyd Wright in Florida; see Joseph M. Siry, *Beth Shalom Synagogue: Frank Lloyd Wright and Modern Religious Architecture* (Chicago: University of Chicago Press, 2012), chapter 4.

61. "Editor's Diary, LXVI," *LtA* 33 (Feb. 1965): 55, 57.

62. Curtis, *New Orleans*, 7.

63. Sheri Olson, "Lauded and Maligned: The Cadet Chapel," in *Modernism at Mid-Century: The Architecture of the United States Air Force Academy*, ed. Robert Bruegmann (Chicago: University of Chicago Press, 1994), 156–68; Robert Allen Neuman, *On the Wings of Modernism: The United States Air Force Academy* (Urbana: University of Illinois Press, 2004), chapter 5.

64. "Wayfarer's Chapel, Palos Verdes, California," *AF* 95 (August 1951): 153–55; Alan Weintraub et al., *Lloyd Wright: The Architecture of Frank Lloyd Wright Jr.* (New York: Harry N. Abrams, 1998), 156–59; Thomas S. Hines, *Richard Neutra and the Search for Modern Architecture: A Biography and History*, 1982; 4th ed. (New York: Rizzoli, 2006), 281, 284–87; "3 New Projects by Marcel Breuer," *AR* 131 (Mar. 1962): 132–36; "A Bold Geometric Image for a Church," *AR* 142 (Nov. 1967): 130–36; Hyman, *Marcel Breuer*, 227.

65. Victoria Newhouse, *Wallace K. Harrison, Architect* (New York: Rizzoli, 1989), 167–73; "Saarinen's Church," *AR* 136 (Sep. 1964): 185–90; Jayne Merkel, *Eero Saarinen* (London: Phaidon, 2005), 158–61; Jennifer Komar Olivarez, "Churches and Chapels: A New Kind of Worship Space," in *Eero Saarinen: Shaping the Future*, ed. Eeva-Liisa Pelkonen and Donald Albrecht (New Haven: Yale University Press, 2006), 266–75.

66. "Chapel: Interdenominational," *AR* 119 (Jan. 1956): 154–57; "Theological School and Chapel," *PA* 38 (Feb. 1957): 148–52; "Central Plan for a College Chapel," *PA* 39 (June 1958): 132–37; Merkel, *Eero Saarinen*, 170–74, 180–81; David B. Brownlee and David G. De Long, *Louis I. Kahn: In the Realm of Architecture* (Los Angeles: Museum of Contemporary Art and New York: Rizzoli, 1992), 66–69, 192–201; Sarah Williams Goldhagen, *Louis Kahn's Situated Modernism* (New Haven: Yale University Press, 2001), 148–61.

67. Curtis, *New Orleans*, chapter 9 (quote on p. 238). For background on the buildings, see Betty Swanson, "Brick Churches in the Lower Garden District," in Samuel Wilson and Bernard Lemann, *New Orleans Architecture, Volume I: The Lower Garden District* (Gretna, La.: Pelican Publishing, 1971), 58–63, 124, 132; Samuel Wilson, *The Church of St. Alphonsus* (New Orleans: Friends of St. Alphonsus, 1996); George Gurtner and Frank Methe, *Historic Churches of New Orleans* (New Orleans: Friends of St. Alphonsus, 1996), 48–51; Charles E. Nolen, *Splendors of Faith: New Orleans Catholic Churches, 1727–1930* (Baton Rouge: Louisiana State University Press, 2010), 94–102; and Kingsley, *Buildings of Louisiana*, 114–15.

68. Curtis, *New Orleans*, chapter 10. For background, see Leonard Huber, *New Orleans Architecture, Volume III: The Cemeteries* (Gretna, La.: Pelican Publishing, 1974).

69. Schulze, *Philip Johnson*, 281–83.

70. Mutrux, "A Post-Vatican Perspective," 46–57; Kingsley, *Buildings of Louisiana*, 299, 300.

71. Wilson, *Guide to the Architecture of New Orleans*, 65–67; Ledner et al., *Guide to New Orleans Architecture*; Kingsley, *Buildings of Louisiana*, 55–168.

72. An early indication of broadening recognition among scholars came with Hitchcock, *Architecture: Nineteenth and Twentieth Centuries*, 333, pl. 146. The first detailed examination of the building was in Esther McCoy, *Five California Architects* (New York: Reinhold, 1960), 24–35. Accounts that followed include William H. Jordy, *American Buildings and Their Architects, Volume 3: Progressive and Academic Ideals at the Turn of the Twentieth Century* (Garden City, N.Y.: Doubleday, 1972), chapter 6; Kenneth H. Cardwell, *Bernard Maybeck: Artisan, Architect, Artist* (Santa Barbara, Calif.: Peregrine Smith, 1977), chapter 6; Sally Woodbridge, *Bernard Maybeck: Visionary Architect* (New York: Abbeville Press, 1992), 88–98; and Edward R. Bosley, *First Church of Christ, Scientist, Berkeley: Bernard Maybeck* (London: Phaidon, 1994).

Chapter 8. The Power of Reserve

1. Period accounts of the complex include "Christian Scientists Break New Ground," *WP*, 7 Oct. 1969, C5; Wolf Von Eckardt, "New Church Design," *WP*, 28 Nov. 1970, B1; and "Edifice Reflects Simple Faith," *WP*, 11 Dec. 1971, B6. A detailed examination of the property is provided in Sue A. Kohler and Jeffrey R. Carson, *Sixteenth Street Architecture*, vol. 2 (Washington: U.S. Commission of Fine Arts, 1988), 106–19. See also Pamela Scott and Antoinette J. Lee, *Buildings of the District of Columbia* (New York: Oxford University Press, 1993), 221–22; and G. Martin Moeller, *AIA Guide to the Architecture of Washington, D.C.*, 5th ed. (Baltimore: Johns Hopkins University Press, 2012), 164.

2. Among Cossutta's major realized independent projects are the forty-two-story Crédit Lyonaise Tower in Lyon, France (1973–77); Harbour Tower Apartments in Portsmouth, Virginia (1979–83); the Long Wharf Marriott Hotel in Boston (1980–82); Greenhouse Apartments, Boston (1980–83); and Cityplace Center East in Dallas (1987–90). The latter was to be part of an extensive, mixed-use complex that fell victim to recession. See William Marlin, "Araldo Cossutta's New Look-Out," *AR* 163 (Mar. 1978): 87–94; and "For Boston: A Harborfront Hotel," *AR* 171 (Mar. 1983): 100–107.

3. For a sampling of assessments, see Arthur Herzog, "He Loves Things to Be Beautiful," *NYT Magazine*, 14 Mar. 1965, 34–35, 98–100; Ada Louis Huxtable, "Mr. Pei Comes to Washington," *NYT*, 11 July 1971, D24; Stanley

Abercrombie, "Pei's Place," *Architecture + Urbanism,*
no. 61 (Jan. 1976): 99-100; Paul Goldberger, "Winning
Ways of I. M. Pei," *NYT Magazine,* 20 May 1979, 24-27,
116, 118, 121-22, 124; and Andrea O. Dean, "Conversations: I. M. Pei," *AIA Journal* 68 (June 1979): 61-67.

4. Cobb was (and remains) a design partner. He had
known Pei as a fellow student at Harvard's Graduate School of Design, and left Hugh Stubbins's office,
where Pei had also worked, to join Webb & Knapp in
1950. Pei hired Leonard three years later to manage
the operation.

5. Both Carter Wiseman, *I. M. Pei: A Profile in American Architecture* (New York: Henry N. Abrams, 1990)
and Philip Jodidio and Janet Adams Strong, *I. M. Pei:
Complete Works* (New York: Rizzoli, 2008) focus on the
work for which Pei was the principal designer. A historical study that examines the firm's work as a whole
and analyzes the internal dynamics that significantly
contributed to its distinguished output has yet to be
undertaken.

6. Whatever the stigma of working for a developer,
Pei was still considered a rising star by 1960. Besides
extensive coverage in architectural journals, the
firm's work was featured in John Peter, *Masters of
Modern Architecture* (New York: George Braziller,
1958), 194-95; and Ian McCallum, *Architecture USA*
(New York: Reinhold, 1959), 191-96.

7. A detailed account of the firm's operating practices
is given in Peter Blake, "I. M. Pei & Partners," *Architecture Plus* 1 (Feb. 1973): 52-59 and (Mar. 1973): 21-25.
Pei was quoted on the subject in Barbaralee Diamondstein, *American Architecture Now* (New York: Rizzoli,
1980), 156. Years later, the firm was reorganized as
Pei Cobb Freed & Partners; see Andrea Oppenheimer
Dean, "Changes for Survival," *AR* 79 (Feb. 1990): 56-61.

8. During these years, some design associates were
given charge of projects as well, with some guidance
from Pei.

9. The major exceptions were Cobb's Place Ville
Marie and John Hancock Tower.

10. Biographical information supplied to me by the
architect was supplemented by an interview, New
York, 31 January 2011, and a lengthy telephone interview, 8 March 2011. Janet Adams Strong, who served
as the firm's director of communications from 1986 to
2003, provided additional insights on Cossutta's contribution to the office dynamics; interview, Cranford,
N.J., 30 January 2011; electronic communication, 10
March 2011.

11. Concerning Lurçat, see Pierre Joly, *Architecte
André Lurçat* (Paris: Picard, 1995). Concerning Perret, see Peter Collins, *Concrete: The Vision of a New
Architecture, A Study of Auguste Perret and His Predecessors* (London: Faber & Faber, 1959); and Karla Brit-

ton, *Auguste Perret* (London: Phaidon, 2001). See also
Antoine Picon, "Architecture and Technology: Two
Centuries of Creative Tension," Jean-Louis Cohen,
"Modern Architecture and the Saga of Concrete," and
Adrian Forty, "Concrete: The Material without a His-
tory," in *Liquid Stone: New Architecture in Concrete,* ed.
Cohen and G. Martin Moeller Jr. (New York: Prince-
ton Architectural Press, 2006), 8-19, 20-33, and 34-45,
respectively.

12. For background, see Anthony Alofsin, *The Struggle for Modernism: Architecture, Landscape Architecture,
and City Planning at Harvard* (New York: W. W. Norton,
2002), chapters 5 and 6; and Jill Pearlman, *Inventing
American Modernism: Joseph Hudnut, Walter Gropius,
and the Bauhaus Legacy at Harvard* (Charlottesville:
University of Virginia Press, 2007).

13. For background on the firm and its Honduran
projects, see Jane C. Loeffler, *The Architecture of Diplomacy: Building America's Embassies* 1998; 2nd rev. ed.
(New York: Princeton Architectural Press, 2011), 157-
58, fig. 51. See also "Architecture to Represent America Abroad," *AR* 117 (May 1955): 189.

14. A preliminary design (by Franzen?) is illustrated in "Original Plan Enlarged," *Denver Post,* 23 Jan.
1955, 1A. Cossutta's scheme is depicted in "Final Plans
Okayed," *Denver Post,* 7 June 1956, 1; and "Hotel and
Store Scheduled for Denver," *PA* 38 (Apr. 1957): 96.

15. Truman Sparks, "Building Faced with 4,000 Pre-
cast Window Frames," *Concrete* 66 (Aug. 1958): 22-23;
"Precast Window Frames Cover Denver Hotel," *Engi-
neering News-Record* 163 (22 Oct. 1959): 38-40; "Grand
Hotel—1960 Style," *AF* 113 (Aug. 1960): 94-99; "A New
Idiom of Strength and Texture," *Western Architect and
Engineer* 220 (Aug. 1960): 16-23; "I. M. Pei et Associes
et la Recheche d'une Architecture en Beton Arme,"
Architecture d'Aujourd'Hui, nos. 91-92 (Sep.-Nov.1960):
63-65; A[ra]ldo Cossutta, "From Precast Concrete to
Integral Architecture," *PA* 47 (Oct. 1966): 196.

16. This assessment in no way negates the very
important urbanistic aspects of both projects, which,
certainly in the case of Place Ville Marie, render them
major projects of the era. Concerning the former, see
Wiseman, *I. M. Pei,* 57-58; and Jodidio and Strong,
I. M. Pei, 36-39. Concerning the latter, see Jan C.
Bowen, "The Story of Place Ville Marie," *PA* 41 (Feb.
1960): 123-35; "Place Ville Marie," *AF* 118 (Feb. 1963):
74-89; "Plaza and Tower Combine," *AR* 133 (Feb. 1963):
123-36; and Frances Vanleath and Isabelle Gournay,
"A Long-Term Perspective on Place Ville-Marie," *Journal of the Society for the Study of Architecture in Canada*
24:1 (1999): 6-15.

17. For a fuller discussion of the firm's key role in
using concrete, see Bejean Legault, "I. M. Pei's East
Building and the Postwar Culture of Materials," in

A Modernist Museum in Perspective: The East Building, National Gallery of Art, ed. Anthony Alofsin (Washington: National Gallery of Art and New Haven: Yale University Press, 2009), 81–92. See also Legault, "The Semantics of Exposed Concrete," in *Liquid Stone,* ed. Cohen and Moeller, 46–56; "The Changing Face of Concrete," *Concrete Construction* 4 (Aug. 1959): 1–6; "Concrete . . . and the Revolution in Architecture," *Concrete* 68 (July 1960): 14–21; "Concrete: The Material That Can Do Almost Anything," *AF* 117 (Sep. 1962): 78–96; and "Concrete: Where Do We Go from Here?" *PA* 47 (Oct. 1966): 172–95.

If Cossutta's claim that the design for the Denver Hilton was first in its extensive exterior use of exposed concrete (Cossutta, "From Precast Concrete," 196) seems exaggerated, one would be hard-pressed to find a scheme as ambitious as his at the time of its design in 1956, save, of course, for Frank Lloyd Wright's Guggenheim Museum in New York (built 1956–59). Cossutta was aware of a few prototypes in this country but, like most architects in the mid-1950s, knew nothing about the many imaginative uses of exposed concrete in both Northern and Southern California during the first four decades of the twentieth century or about the innovative work, manifested mainly in resort hotels, of Philadelphia-based William Price in the 1900s and 1910s.

18. Cossutta interview. Concerning the buildings, see "Big Hyde Park Redeveloping Plan," *Chicago Tribune,* 19 Jan. 1957, 17; "Record Price Bid," *Chicago Tribune,* 21 July 1957, S1; "New Forming Techniques," *Concrete Construction* 5 (Oct. 1960): 307; "Rapid Progress in Hyde Park-Kenwood," *AR* 128 (Nov. 1960): 140–43; and "High-Rise, Low-Rise," *AR* 131 (Apr. 1962): 163–67.

19. Kips Bay and subsequent Pei residential projects for Zeckendorf in Philadelphia, Washington, and Chicago, were all intended for middle-income households as part of the urban renewal program's agenda to attract them back to the city. Although the budget was a key consideration in the design, these complexes were (and continue to be) erroneously branded as low-cost housing.

20. "East Side Housing Revamped," *NYT,* 26 Apr. 1958, 21; "Kips Bay Project in Line for Start," *NYT,* 24 Mar. 1959, 24.

21. "Cast-in-Place Technique Restudied," *PA* 41 (Oct. 1960): 158–77, affords the most detailed information from a technical perspective. See also "Architect Uses New Technique," *NYT,* 23 Apr. 1961, R1, R13; Walter McQuade, "Pei's Apartments Round the Corner," *AF* 115 (Aug. 1961): 106–14; "Concrete: The Material," 86; James Marston Fitch, "Housing in New York, Washington, Chicago and Philadelphia," *Architectural Review* 134 (Sep. 1963): 192–200; Paul Heyer, *Architects on Architecture: New Directions in America* (New York: Walker, 1966), 315, 317; Wiseman, *I. M. Pei,* 62–64; Jodidio and Strong, *I. M. Pei,* 48–53; and Robert A. M. Stern et al., *New York 1960: Architecture and Urbanism between the Second World War and the Bicentennial* (New York: Monacelli Press, 1995), 286–88. Pei discussed the project in Gero von Boehm, *Conversations with I. M. Pei: Light Is the Key* (Munich: Prestel, 2000), 53–54.

22. Concerning Society Hill, see "Philadelphia Redevelopment Becomes Design Competition," *PA* 39 (Nov. 1958): 36–37; Stephen J. Thompson, "Philadelphia's Design Sweepstakes," *AF* 109 (Dec. 1958): 94–99; Edmund N. Bacon, "Downtown Philadelphia: A Lesson in Design for Urban Growth," *AR* 129 (May 1961): 135; "Society Hill, Philadelphia/USA," *Baumeister* 61 (Apr. 1964): 361–69; Wiseman, *I. M. Pei,* 64–66; and Jodidio and Strong, *I. M. Pei,* 60–63. A more sculptural and vigorous variation was developed for University Plaza in New York (1964–66); see "Bright Landmarks on a Changing Urban Scene," *AF* 125 (Dec. 1966): 21–29; and Jodidio and Strong, *I. M. Pei,* 72–75. The same structural system was employed for the Washington Plaza apartments in Pittsburgh (1960–64); see "Eggcrate Frames Support Towers," *Engineering News-Record* 168 (28 June 1962): 24; "Apartment Framing to Resist Wind," *AR* 133 (Jan. 1963): 161; and "Plastic Forms Give Smooth Finish to Building's Concrete Façade," *Engineering News-Record* 171 (12 Dec. 1963): 44–46.

23. According to Cossutta, though Pei was involved with the project, the design was principally his (telephone interview, 8 March 2011). The two are cited as collaborating partners in period accounts.

24. Concerning that complex, see Mark M. Jarozombek, *Designing MIT: Bosworth's New Tech* (Boston: Northeastern University Press, 2004).

25. Cossutta, "From Precast Concrete," 200–203 (quote on p. 200); "A Tower Built Like a Bridge," *AF* 113 (Aug. 1960): 100–103; "First Tower at M.I.T.," *AR* 136 (Oct. 1964): 135–38; "New Landmark for M.I.T.," *PA* 46 (Mar. 1965): 156–63; Jodidio and Strong, *I. M. Pei,* 64–67. For a different perspective, see O. Robert Simha, *MIT Campus Planning 1960–2000: An Annotated Chronology* (Cambridge, Mass.: MIT Press, 2001), 30–31. The tower was designed as the centerpiece of a three-building complex, the other components of which were later realized in modified form. Cossutta and Pei designed a tower for the Pan-Pacific Center in Honolulu (1960–63), which was a much larger variation on the MIT building. Its structure was comprised of L-shaped walls at the corners and a service core. See Heyer, *Architects on Architecture,* 315, 318.

26. Several of these projects are diagrammed in Cossutta, "From Precast Concrete," 197, 205. According to

Cossutta, he was asked by Pei to refine the structural and systems configurations of both the Wilmington and Hartford buildings (telephone interview, 8 March 2011). Concerning the buildings themselves, see Jodidio and Strong, *I. M. Pei*, 100–103; "Bushnell Plaza Group," *Hartford Courant*, 25 July 1963, 33; "Bushnell Plaza Was Designed," *Hartford Courant*, 24 Dec. 1967, 11D; "High Rise Opens," *Hartford Courant*, 25 May 1969, 1D; "No Whipped Cream, But It Vibrates," *Evening Journal* [Wilmington], 14 Oct. 1947, 21; "Occupancy Slates May 15," *Evening Journal*, 17 Jan. 1970, 4; "Harbor Project Design," *Sun* [Baltimore], 13 Apr. 1968, B16, B8; "A Graceful Symbol of Renewal," *Sun*, 26 Dec. 1976, D1; and "World Trade Center," *Sun*, 25 Sep. 1977, PB17.

27. "Pei's New Washington Complex," *PA* 43 (Aug. 1962): 56; "L'Enfant Plaza Starting," *WP*, 17 Dec. 1966, E1, E8; "Freshness in Capital Skyline," *CSM*, 15 Nov. 1968, 3; "From Module to Mall," *PA* 49 (Nov. 1968): 94–101. Subsequently, Cossutta's master plan guided the design of a hotel and an additional office building by a locally based architect, Vlastimil Koubek, but these components were noticeably less refined in detail. Concerning the original Zeckendorf scheme, see Richard Longstreth, "Brave New World: Southwest Washington and the Promise of Urban Renewal," in *Housing Washington: Two Centuries of Residential Development and Planning in the National Capital Area*, ed. Longstreth (Chicago: Center for American Places and University of Chicago Press, 2010), 261–63.

28. Cossutta, "From Precast Concrete," 203–5 (quote on p. 203); and as quoted in "Buildings that Breathe," *CSM*, 17 Apr. 1967, 9. In discussing the American Life Insurance Company Building, Pei remarked: "Whipped cream, the material used to cover a building's inner structure is absent . . . just poured concrete" ("No Whipped Cream").

29. Components of the plan designed for the church were realized. Development of surrounding properties on land the church had assembled was either modified in execution or never undertaken.

30. Christian Scientists use "Mother Church" to refer both to the church edifice and to the managing organization. The most detailed and insightful account of the project is William Marlin, "Formed Up in Faith," *AF* 139 (Sep. 1973): 24–39. See also Walter McQuade, "A Church Center for Boston," *Fortune* 72 (Sep. 1965): 179–80; "Action Phase of Church Center," *CSM*, 7 July 1966, 5; "A Case History: Church-Sponsored Community Renewal," *PA* 47 (June 1966): 154–57; "Plan for Progress," *CSM*, 5 June 1967, 13; "Development Plans Take Shape," *CSM*, 21 Dec. 1968, 4; "A Symbolic New Center," *NYT*, 10 June 1973, 56; and Melanie Simo, *Sasaki Associates: Integrated Environ-*

ments (Washington, D.C.: Spacemaker Press, 1997), 158–50. Additional material can be found in "Christian Science Center Complex, Study Report," Boston Landmarks Commission, draft, 2011, a copy of which David Fixler kindly provided me.

In preparing the plan, Cossutta closely collaborated with planner Vincent Ponte, who was a member of the Pei firm and became Cossutta's partner when they established an independent practice in 1973. Some years later Cossutta designed twin apartment buildings on adjacent land that were substantially different from those called for in his master plan of 1966. See "Huntington Avenue Complex," *CSM*, 26 Oct. 1978, 7; and "'Greenhouse' Apartment Complex," *CSM*, 29 Aug. 1980, 6.

31. "Plan for Progress"; Marlin, "Formed up in Faith," 31, 34.

32. "Christian Science in Washington, D.C., An Historical Sketch," D.C. Office of the Christian Science Committee, 1982, typescript, Historical Society of Washington, D.C., 41–43; Kohler and Carson, *Sixteenth Street Architecture*, vol. 2, 92–105, 107.

33. "Christian Science in Washington," 18–20, 41; Kohler and Carson, *Sixteenth Street Architecture*, vol. 2, 107. The Mother Church had decided upon this course well before the Third Church sold its building; see "Church to Raze Gray-Payne House," *WP*, 29 June 1966, B5. The union came less than a year later; see "D.C. Landmark Is Raised," *WP*, 23 May 1967, B2.

34. The phenomenon is analyzed in detail in Paul Eli Ivey, *Prayers in Stone: Christian Science Architecture in the United States* (Urbana: University of Illinois Press, 1999). The First Church in Washington (1911–12) was rendered in this vein; see "Scientists to Build," *WP*, 11 June 1911, C3; and "Christian Science Church Starts Worship," *WP*, 6 Oct. 1912, E6.

35. Dale Woolston Dowling, "For God, For Family, For Country: Colonial Revival Church Buildings in the Cold War Era" (Ph.D. dissertation, George Washington University, 2004), affords a detailed investigation of the subject. The Christian Science predilection for work of this type is amply reflected in Charles Draper Faulkner, *Christian Science Church Edifices* (Chicago: By the author, 1946). I was fortunate enough to procure a copy of this volume, which had previously been in the library of Leon Chatelain Jr., the architect whom the Third Church had initially hired, as noted in the text below.

36. Namely, the Second Church in Ranier Highlands (1949–53), the Fifth Church in Georgetown (remodeled 1956–57), and the Sixth Church in American University Park (1960–62, 1976–77), as well as the First Church in Chevy Chase, Maryland (1949–50) and Second Church in Arlington, Virginia (1952–53).

37. Kohler and Carson, *Sixteenth Street Architecture*, vol. 2, 108. This account was gleaned from a 1980 interview with David Williams, chair of the building committee.

38. Milton L. Grigg, "A Guide for Planning Buildings for Christian Science," *AIA Journal* 40 (Oct. 1963): 92–96 (quote on p. 95). During his long career, Grigg designed some 400 churches. He was not a Christian Scientist, but did design the First Church in Alexandria, Virginia (1945)

39. Cossutta interview. The architect emphasized that Rechner was really the person in charge of the project and his principal church contact during the course of its realization.

40. Cossutta interview.

41. Cossutta interview, and telephone interview, 29 October 2007.

42. For illustration, see Krisztina Passuth, *Moholy-Nagy* (New York: Thames & Hudson, 1985), pls. 60, 124–25, 137, 141–43, 147. Gropius brought Moholy-Nagy with him to the GSD, but the latter died in 1946, five years before Cossutta arrived.

43. Concerning the design, see "I. M. Pei's Master Plan," *AR* 135 (May 1964): 176–77; James Bailey, "Academic Center at Fredonia," *AF* 130 (May 1969): 36–47.

44. Grigg, "A Guide for Planning," 94–96 (quote on p. 95).

45. A ca. 1970 promotional brochure on the new church edifice entitled "Other Foundation Can No Man Lay . . . ," subtly infers an expansionist mode for the congregation (copy in author's collection).

46. Cossutta interview. Concerning Unity Temple, see Joseph M. Siry, *Unity Temple: Frank Lloyd Wright and Architecture for a Liberal Religion* (New York: Cambridge University Press, 1996). That building's intricate circulation paths are also discussed in Richard Longstreth, "Afterword: A Case for Collaboration," in *The Charnley House: Louis Sullivan, Frank Lloyd Wright, and the Making of Chicago's Gold Coast*, ed. Longstreth (Chicago: University of Chicago Press, 2004), 206–8.

47. Herzog, "He Loves Things," 98.

48. The church as a social center is discussed at length in Dowling, "For God, For Family, For Country."

49. While this facet of the firm's work is often noted in accounts of the period, detailed discussion of the steps taken by those actually involved with the designs is rare. For an exception, see a lengthy quote from A. Preston Moore in "Bushnell Plaza Was Designed."

50. Pei discussed his concern with the site's physical context in Diamondstein, *American Architecture Now*, 146, 148. Concerning the building, see *A Modernist Museum in Perspective*, ed. Alofsin.

51. Benjamin Forgey, "The D.C. Pei List" *WP*, 5 Oct.

2003, N1, N7, focuses on the firm's earlier work. The majority of the firm's buildings postdate the early 1980s and were designed under the direction of either Cobb or Freed. The former's were all office buildings, including: National Place (now Columbia Square) (1985–87), 2099 Pennsylvania Avenue, N.W. (1997–2001), the International Monetary Fund Headquarters 2 (completed 2005), and the American Association for the Advancement of Science Building (completed 1996). Besides the Reagan Building and Holocaust Museum noted in the text, Freed designed the Warner Building (1989–93), 1700 K Street, N.W. (completed 2005), and Potomac Tower (1987–89) in the District of Columbia, and the Air Force Memorial (2003–6) and Waterview (1999–2007) in Arlington, Virginia. A more or less complete list can be found on the firm's website, www.pcfandp.com.

52. For background, see Robinson & Associates, *Growth, Efficiency, and Modernism: GSA Buildings of the 1950s, 60s, and 70s* (Washington: General Services Administration, 2003). For discussion of individual buildings, see Wolf Von Eckardt, "New 'Federal' Style Is Emerging," *WP*, 22 Oct. 1964, A22; Von Eckardt, "We Can Be Proud of 'Little Pentagon,'" *WP* 29 Nov. 1964, G8; "New Federal Architecture," *AR* 137 (Mar. 1965): 135–46; "New Direction, Patience + Fortitude = Rejuvenated Architecture for Washington, D.C.," *PA* 46 (Mar. 1965): 188–95; "Headquarters for HUD," *AR* 144 (Dec. 1968): 99–106; Ada Louise Huxtable, "J. Edgar Hoover Builds His Dreamhouse," *AF* 36 (Apr. 1972): 44–45; Von Eckardt, "Hirshhorn Enclave," *WP*, 28 Sep. 1974, B1, B3; Mary E. Osman, "After a 36-Year Wait," *AIA Journal* 62 (Nov. 1974): 44–45; Von Eckardt, "New FBI Building," *WP*, 12 July 1975, B1, B3; Von Eckardt, "Space, Time and Architecture," *WP*, 27 June 1976, E1, E3; "Modernism and the Monolith," *PA* 57 (July 1976): 70–75.

53. Talbot Hamlin, *Benjamin Henry Latrobe* (New York: Oxford University Press, 1955), 462–63; Richard F. Grimmett, *St. John's Church, Lafayette Square: The History and Heritage of the Church of Presidents, Washington, D.C.* (Minneapolis: Mill City Press, 2009), chapter 1.

54. Several of these buildings were surveyed in Kohler and Carson, *Sixteenth Street Architecture*, vol. 1 (Washington: U.S. Commission of Fine Arts, 1978), 194–231, 510–43; and vol. 2, 395–415, 520–43.

55. Isabelle Hyman, *Marcel Breuer, Architect: The Career and the Buildings* (New York: Henry N. Abrams, 2001), 140–44, 218–28.

56. For a sampling, see Editors of Architectural Record, *Religious Buildings* (New York: McGraw-Hill, 1979), chapter 5.

57. Concerning the former, see "An Architecture Strongly Manipulated in Space and Scale," *AR* 141

(Feb. 1967): 137–141. Concerning the latter, see "Plan to Build," *Chicago Tribune*, 2 Jan. 1965, W1; John Morris Dixon, "Church in a Grove of Skyscrapers," *AF* 130 (June 1969): 42–45; and Robert Bruegmann, *The Architecture of Harry Weese* (New York: W. W. Norton, 2010), 138–41.

58. Jeanne Halgren Kilde, *When Church Became Theatre: The Transformation of Evangelical Architecture and Worship in Nineteenth-Century America* (New York: Oxford University Press, 2002).

Chapter 9. A Modernist's Tribute to Lincoln and Remembrance of the Civil War

1. Generally, the building was referred to as the Visitor Center, but because it accommodated the range of functions associated with that designation for less than fifteen years, it is referred to as the Cyclorama Building in this chapter.

2. For detailed examination of the building, see Sara Allaback, *Mission 66 Visitor Centers: The History of a Building Type* (Washington: National Park Service, U.S. Department of the Interior, 2000), chapter 3; "Cyclorama Building," Historic American Buildings Survey Report, 2004 (HABS PA-6709); and Christine Madrid French, "The Visitor Center as Monument: Recontextualizing Richard Neutra's 1962 Cyclorama Center within the Commemorative Landscape of the Gettysburg Battlefield," in *Public Nature: Scenery, History, and Park Design*, ed. Ethan Carr et al. (Charlottesville: University of Virginia Press, 2013), 228–44.

3. The official dedication did not occur until November 1962, marking the ninety-ninth anniversary of Abraham Lincoln's Gettysburg Address.

4. Ethan Carr, *Mission 66: Modernism and the National Park Dilemma* (Amherst: University of Massachusetts Press and Library of American Landscape History, 2007), 4. For discussion of the program, see also Christine L. Madrid, "The Mission 66 Visitor Centers, 1956–1966: Early Modern Architecture in the National Park Service" (M.A. thesis, University of Virginia, May 1998).

5. Carr, *Mission 66*, chapters 2–3. For a summary overeiw of Wirth's career, see Carr's entry, "Conrad Louis Wirth," in *Shaping the American Landscape: New Profiles from the Pioneers of American Landscape Design Project*, ed. Charles A. Birnbaum and Stephanie S. Foell (Charlottesville: University of Virginia Press, 2009), 383–85.

6. Bernard DeVoto, "Let's Close the National Parks," *Harper's* 207 (Oct. 1953): 49–52; see Carr, *Mission 66*, 54–56.

7. "Statement by Conrad L. Wirth, Public Services Conference," 20 Sep. 1955, and "Public Services,"

agenda, 20 Sep. 1955, both Conrad L. Wirth Collection, American Heritage Center, University of Wyoming, boxes 4 and 6, respectively; Conrad L. Wirth, "Mission 66," *American Forests* 61 (Aug. 1955): 16–17—all quoted in Carr, *Mission 66*, 105–8.

8. Letter from Ronda Mason to National Park Service, 27 July 1959, Revised Prospectuses, Mission 66, 1960–61, Record Group 79, National Archives, quoted in Madrid, "Mission 66 Visitor Centers," 14. Later known as the Rosensteel Building, the facility was purchased by the Park Service. It began to supplement the Cyclorama Building in 1974 and eventually became the main visitor center. It was demolished after the new visitor center opened in 2008.

9. Relatively little attention has been accorded to this component of the TVA's complexes. See Christine Macy, "The Architect's Office of the Tennessee Valley Authority," and Todd Smith, "Almost Fully Modern: The TVA's Visual Art Campaign," in *The Tennessee Valley Authority: Design and Persuasion*, ed. Tim Culvahouse (New York: Princeton Architectural Press, 2007), 43–45 and 111–13, respectively. This book and Walter L. Creese, *TVA's Public Planning: The Vision, the Reality* (Knoxville: University of Tennessee Press, 1990), provide the best discussions of the agency's architecture and planning.

10. Carr, *Mission 66*, 142–44. See also Allaback, *Mission 66 Visitor Centers*, 17–21, 24–25, 29. For a complete list of these facilities, see Allaback, *Mission 66 Visitor Centers*, 255–61.

11. For further discussion, see Allaback, *Mission 66 Visitor Centers*, 10–24; and Carr, *Mission 66*, 136–41.

12. Jonathan Searle Monroe, "Architecture in the National Parks: Cecil Doty and Mission 66" (M.A. thesis, University of Washington, 1986), 82; quote in Allaback, *Mission 66 Visitor Centers*, 12; and Carr, *Mission 66*, 139.

13. Only three other visitor centers cost more than $400,000, those at Death Valley and Paradise, as well as the complex, including the Arch, at the Jefferson National Expansion Memorial in St. Louis; see Carr, *Mission 66*, 155.

14. For background on the cyclorama phenomenon, see John L. Marsh, "Drama and Spectacle by the Yard," *Journal of Popular Culture* 10 (Winter 1976): 581–89; Harold Holzer and Mark E. Neely Jr., *Mine Eyes Have Seen the Glory: The Civil War in Art* (New York: Orion, 1993), chapter 5; and Bernard Comment, *The Painted Panorama* (New York: Henry N. Abrams, 1999). Concerning the painting, see Dean S. Thomas, *The Gettysburg Cyclorama: A Portrayal of the High Tide of the Confederacy* (Gettysburg, Pa.: Thomas Publications, 1989).

15. Allaback, *Mission 66 Visitor Centers*, 25–26; Carr, *Mission 66*, 147–48, 153.

16. Namely, Anshen & Allen's Quarry Visitor Center, Dinosaur National Monument, Jensen, Utah (1957–58), and Lodgepole Visitor Center, Sequoia National Park, Three Rivers, California, (1963–66); Giurgola's Wright Brothers National Memorial Visitor Center, Kill Devil Hills, North Carolina (1958–60); and Taliesin's Administration Building, Beaver Meadows Visitor Center, Rocky Mountain National Park, Estes Park, Colorado (1965–67); see Allaback, *Mission 66 Visitor Centers*, chapters 1, 2, and 5.

Anshen & Allen was a well-respected architectural firm in the San Francisco Bay Area where it was based. Romaldo Giurgola was then just beginning independent practice, which would propel him into the national and then international limelight during the following decade. After Frank Lloyd Wright's death in 1959, the successor firm, Taliesin Associated Architects, ceased to attract much attention in architectural circles save among those who continued to bear allegiance to Wright himself. Neutra & Alexander also designed the Painted Desert "community," which included the visitor center and staff housing; see Allaback, *Mission 66 Visitor Centers*, chapter 4.

17. John B. Cabot, "Creative Park Architecture," in *Park Practice Guidelines*, Department of the Interior, National Park Service, July 1963, 55, as quoted in Carr, *Mission 66*, 147; Conrad L. Wirth to Richard J. Neutra, 3 May 1957, box 14, Thaddeus Longstreth Papers, Architectural Archives, University of Pennsylvania, as quoted in "Cyclorama Building," 18.

18. Richard J. Neutra, "Gettysburg—Shrine of One Free World," in *Richard Neutra 1950-60: Buildings and Projects*, vol. 2, ed. W. Boesinger (Zurich: Ginsburg, 1959), 192–93. The piece was reprinted in a somewhat expanded form in Neutra's autobiography, *Life and Shape* (New York: Appleton-Century-Crofts, 1962), 302–14.

19. Frederick Tilberg, park historian, revision of museum prospectus, 1956; quoted in Madrid, "Mission 66 Visitor Centers," 13. Philippoteaux's painting, one of four that he completed, was originally housed in a building that has been preserved as part of the Boston Center for the Arts; see Keith Morgan et al., *Buildings of Massachusetts: Metropolitan Boston* (Charlottesville: University of Virginia Press, 2009), 133.

20. Carr, *Mission 66*, 193–95; Allaback, *Mission 66 Visitor Centers*, 26–28.

21. For illustration of the Park Service scheme, see Allaback, *Mission 66 Visitor Centers*, 100.

22. Neutra, "Gettysburg."

23. For discussion, see John S. Patterson, "A Patriotic Landscape: Gettysburg, 1863-1913," *Prospects* 7 (1982): 315–33; Reuben M. Rainey, "The Memory of War: Reflections on Battlefield Preservation," in *The Year-book of Landscape Architecture: Historic Preservation*, ed. Richard Austin et al. (New York: Van Nostrand Reinhold, 1985), 69–89; John S. Patterson, "From Battle Ground to Pleasure Ground: Gettysburg as a Historic Site," in *History Museums in the United States*, ed. Warren Leon and Roy Rosenzweig (Urbana: University of Illinois Press, 1989), 128–57; Edward Tabor Linenthal, *Sacred Ground: Americans and Their Battlefields* (Urbana: University of Illinois Press, 1991), chapter 3; Jim Weeks, "Gettysburg: Display Window for Popular Memory," *Journal of American Culture* 21 (Winter 1998): 41–56; Weeks, *Gettysburg: Memory, Market, and an American Shrine* (Princeton: Princeton University Press, 2003); and Timothy B. Smith, *The Golden Age of Battlefield Preservation: The Decade of the 1890s and the Establishment of America's First Five Military Parks* (Knoxville: University of Tennessee Press, 2008), chapter 6. See also Ronald F. Lee, *The Origin and Evolution of the National Military Park Idea* (Washington: U.S. Department of the Interior, National Park Service, 1973).

24. Kirk Savage, *Standing Soldiers, Kneeling Slaves: Race, War, and Monument in Nineteenth-Century America* (Princeton: Princeton University Press, 1997). Amanda Holmes, "Gettysburg National Military Park Tour Roads," Historic American Engineering Record, National Park Service, 1998 (HAER PA-485) affords detailed documentation of infrastructural development.

25. For discussion of the monuments, see Wayne Craven, *The Sculpture at Gettysburg* (New York: Eastern Acorn Press, 1982); Frederick W. Hawthorne, *Gettysburg: Stories of Men and Monuments as Told by Battlefield Guides* (Gettysburg: Association of Licensed Battlefield Guides, 1988); and Judith Dupre, *Monument: America's History in Art and Memory* (New York: Random House, 2007), 32–45. Good pictorial coverage of the park's development during the nineteenth century is afforded by Garry B. Adelman, *The Early Gettysburg Battlefield* (Gettysburg: Thomas Publications, 2001); Timothy H. Smith, *Gettysburg's Battlefield Photographer—William H. Tipton* (Gettysburg: Thomas Publications, 2005); and John S. Salmon, *Historic Photos of Gettysburg* (Nashville: Turner Publishing, 2007).

26. Thomas S. Hines, *Richard Neutra and the Search for Modern Architecture: A Biography and History*, 1982; 4th ed. (New York: Rizzoli, 2006), remains the essential biography.

27. See, for example, John Peter, *Masters of Modern Architecture* (New York: George Braziller, 1958); and Ian McCallum, *Architecture USA* (New York: Reinhold, 1959).

28. Thomas S. Hines, "Richard Neutra, AIA's 1977 Gold Medalist," *AIA Journal* 66 (Mar. 1977): 53–54;

Richard Guy Wilson, *The AIA Gold Medal* (New York: McGraw-Hill, 1984), 216–17; Arthur Drexler and Thomas S. Hines, *The Architecture of Richard Neutra: From International Style to California Modern* (New York: Museum of Modern Art, 1982).

29. Neutra's office training with Mendelsohn, who was the first and remained one of the few members of the European avant-garde to receive numerous commissions for sizable commercial and institutional buildings, then with the large Chicago firm of Holabird & Roche, set him apart from most of his avant-garde colleagues.

30. The most extensive coverage of Neutra's work, built and unrealized, is in the three-volume series, *Richard Neutra*, 1951, 1959, and 1966, ed. W. Boesinger. The most significant of these designs are discussed in Hines, *Richard Neutra*, and realized examples are also covered in Barbara Mac Lamprecht, *Richard Neutra: Complete Works* (Cologne: Taschen, 2000).

31. One indication is afforded in a news item announcing that Neutra had won a prestigious medal in his native Austria, which was to be presented to him by the chancellor. While he always relished the limelight, Neutra was sufficiently enveloped in the Gettysburg project not to attend. The American ambassador accepted in his stead. See "Personalities," *PA* 4 (Feb. 1960): 75.

32. Neutra and Alexander proved as different in temperament as they were in their approach to design. After recovering from a heart attack, Neutra hoped that Alexander would manage the office in addition to securing new business. But Alexander had considerable design interests of his own and refused to be a second-tier associate. The partnership was beginning to unravel when the Gettysburg commission was received. Evidence strongly suggests that Neutra had full or nearly full charge of the building's design; see Allaback, *Mission 66 Visitor Centers*. My father, Thaddeus Longstreth, who Neutra asked to be the office's site representative, also noted, on numerous occasions, Neutra's intimate connection to every aspect of the design.

33. "Cyclorama Building," 33–34.

34. See, for example, Richard Neutra, *Mysteries and Realities of the Site* (Scarsdale, N.Y.: Morgan & Morgan, 1951); Neutra, *Survival Through Design* (New York: Oxford University Press, 1954); Neutra, *Building with Nature* (New York: Universe, 1971); and Neutra, *Nature Near: Late Essays by Richard Neutra*, ed. William Marlin (Santa Barbara, Calif.: Capra Press, 1989).

35. Neutra, who was an avid observer of the built environment, may well have been familiar with this common Pennsylvania barn type, but no evidence has been found to indicate it was an inspiration here. On

the other hand, taking advantage of a sloping site in this way was often done during the post–World War II period with retail and other buildings where ample public circulation on two floors was desirable.

36. The account in Allaback, *Mission 66 Visitor Centers*, 116–17, 123–24, is based on notes my father compiled while directing this project (T. Longstreth Papers). He had lived in Bucks County, Pennsylvania, from 1936 to 1941 and again from 1947 to 1958, and was an ardent admirer of the region's stone barns, many of which dated to the early nineteenth century.

37. Allaback, *Mission 66 Visitor Centers*, 121–22.

38. Ibid., 122–23. The cascading of water does not appear to have been kept for long. Later, the reflecting pool was removed.

39. Additional insight on Neutra's intentions was relayed by my father to his eldest nephew, George B. Longstreth III, for a term paper at Yale ("The Visitor's [*sic*] Center at Gettysburg," 11 May 1960), a copy of which is in the Longstreth Papers. While the accuracy of such a document might be questioned, I recall my father, who never indulged in idle praise, making a point of how well my cousin had presented the subject. My father's only source for discussion of design intent would have been Neutra himself.

40. G. Longstreth, "The Visitor's Center."

41. The situation began to change in the 1960s. See Robinson & Associates, *Growth, Efficiency, and Modernism: GSA Buildings of the 1950s, 60s, and 70s* (Washington: General Services Administration, 2003).

42. See Jane C. Loeffler, *The Architecture of Diplomacy: Building America's Embassies*, 1998; 2nd rev. ed. (New York: Princeton Architectural Press, 2011).

43. *Richard Neutra*, ed. Boesinger, 2:158–61, 3:224–33.

44. George A. Dudley, *A Workshop for Peace: Designing the United Nation's Headquarters* (New York: Architectural History Foundation, and Cambridge, Mass.: MIT Press, 1994); Victoria Newhouse, *Wallace K. Harrison, Architect* (New York: Rizzoli, 1989), chapter 12.

45. *Modernism at Mid-Century: The Architecture of the United States Air Force Academy*, ed. Robert Bruegmann (Chicago: University of Chicago Press, 1994); Robert Allen Nauman, *On the Wings of Modernism: The United States Air Force Academy* (Urbana: University of Illinois Press, 2004).

46. Antonio Roman, *Eero Saarinen: An Architecture of Multiplicity* (New York: Princeton Architectural Press, 2003), 110–23; Jayne Markel, *Eero Saarinen* (London: Phaidon, 2005), 216–29.

47. William Graebner, "Gateway to Empire: An Interpretation of Eero Saarinen's 1948 Design for the St. Louis Arch," *Prospects* 18 (1993): 367–99; Roman, *Eero Saarinen*, 124–41; Markel, *Eero Saarinen*, 194–203.

48. "Gettysburg's Gain," *NYT*, 6 May 1962, 15; "A Date

to Recall," *NYT*, 9 June 1963, 19. See also "A New Look at Gettysburg," *Evening Star* [Washington], *Star Magazine*, 11 Feb. 1962, 4–5.

49. Wolf Von Eckardt, "The Park Service Dares to Build Well," *WP*, 29 Mar. 1964, G6; James D. Van Trump, "Circular History: The Visitor Center and Cyclorama at Gettysburg, Pa.," *Charette* 42 (Oct. 1962): 21–23 (quote on p. 23).

50. Richard Neutra issue, *Vitrum* [Milan] 131 (May–June 1962): 12; Richard Neutra number, *Arquitectura* [Madrid] 7 (Sep. 1965): 48–49; "Richard Neutra: His Thoughts and Architectural Works," *Column* [Tokyo] 16 (ca. 1962), 93–95. The building received passing note in Esther McCoy, *Richard Neutra* (New York: George Braziller, 1960), 19, pl. 120; and in "West Coast Architects I: Richard Neutra," *Arts & Architecture* 81 (Mar. 1964): 19. The only coverage I have found in national architectural journals is a brief "bulletin" in the "P/A New Report": *PA* 40 (Mar. 1959): 161.

51. "Two Visitor Centers Exemplify New Park Architecture," *PA* 40 (Feb. 1959): 87; Jan C. Rowan, "Wanting to Be: The Philadelphia School," *PA* 42 (Apr. 1961): 150–55; Rowan, "Kitty Hawk Museum," *PA* 44 (Aug. 1963): 112–19. For historical coverage, see Allaback, *Mission 66 Visitor Centers*, chapter 2; and "Wright Brothers National Memorial Visitor Center: Historic Structure Report," ed. Tommy H. Jones (Atlanta, Cultural Resources Southeast Region, National Park Service, 2002), part 1. Ironically, the scheme was soon marginalized in accounts of Giurgola's work.

52. Robert E. Koehler, "Our Park Service Serves Architecture Well," *AIA Journal* 60 (Jan. 1971): 18–25.

Chapter 10. Douglas Haskell's Adirondack Legacy

1. A detailed chronicle of Haskell's family and background is provided in Robert Alan Benson, "Douglas Putnam Haskell (1899–1979): The Early Critical Writings" (Ph.D. dissertation, University of Michigan, 1987), chapter 1.

2. Benson, "Haskell," analyzes his writings until his employment at *Architectural Record*. For a condensed version focusing on the earliest work, see Benson, "Douglas Haskell and the Modern Movement in American Architecture," *Journal of Architectural Education* 36 (Summer 1983): 2–9.

3. See, for example, "Shells," *New Student* 4 (25 Apr. 1925): supplement; "Organic Architecture: Frank Lloyd Wright," *Creative Art* 3 (Nov. 1928): li–lvii; "Building or Sculpture?" *AR* 67 (Jan. 1930): 46–47; "Chrysler's Pretty Bauble," *Nation* 131 (Oct. 1930): 450–51; "The Architectural League and the Rejected Architects," *Parnassus* 3 (May 1931): 12–13; "Modern Architecture, Occupied," *Architecture* 66 (Aug. 1932): 77–84; "Houses Like Fords," *Harper's Monthly* 168 (Feb. 1934): 286–98; "Bringing Shelter Up to Date," *Nation* 138 (16 May, 23 May, 30 May 1934): 555–57, 586–88, 614–15, respectively; "Architecture on Routes U.S. 40 and 66," *AR* 81 (May 1937): 15–22; "Architecture of the TVA," *Nation* 152 (17 May 1941): 592–93; "The Revolution in House-Building," *Harper's Monthly* 185 (June 1942): 47–54

4. Haskell's writings on the subject in *Architectural Forum* include "The Value of Used Architecture," 106 (Apr. 1957): 107–8; "Save Grand Central, Save Robie," 117 (Nov. 1962): 138; "Instinct for Preservation," 118 (Mar. 1963): 75; and "The Lost New York of the Pan American Building," 119 (Nov. 1963): 106–11.

5. Benson, "Haskell," 361–63; Haskell to Edmund Purves, 10 Oct. 1950, record group 803, box 261, folder 1, American Institute of Architects Archives, Washington, D.C., http://public.aia.org/sites/hdoaa/wiki/ (hereafter AIA Archives). Benson (pp. 161–62) noted that Frank Lloyd Wright invited Haskell and his wife to join his office at Taliesin in 1930. Benson also documented Haskell's friendship with fellow critic Lewis Mumford.

6. Henry Kamphoefner and Chloethiel Woodard Smith to College of Fellows, AIA, 4 Sep. 1961 and 25 Oct. 1961, respectively, record group 803, box 261, folder 1, AIA Archives; "AIA Will Present a 1979 Medal to Douglas Haskell," press release, 2 Mar. 1979, Baldwin files, AIA Archives.

7. Correspondence between Haskell and Churchill between June and October 1938 (Haskell Collection, Avery Architecture and Fine Arts Library, Columbia University; hereafter, Haskell Collection) suggests that Churchill's role was to review Haskell's drawings, advise him on technical and procedural matters, and prepare working drawings and specifications. The two men were good friends.

8. For background, see Harvey H. Kaiser, *Great Camps of the Adirondacks* (Boston: David R. Godine, 1982); and Craig Gilborn, *Adirondack Camps: Homes Away from Home, 1850–1950* (Blue Mountain Lake, N.Y.: Adirondack Museum, and Syracuse: Syracuse University Press, 2000).

9. A good analysis of the camp's development during the interwar decades is provided in Stephen Burry, "Creating a 'Child's World': An Early History of Camp Treetops" (senior thesis, Amherst College, 1992), a copy of which was kindly provided to me by the staff at North Country School and Camp Treetops. Concerning Helen Haskell, see Benson, "Haskell." Concerning Dewey, Kilpatrick, and progressive education of the period, see Gregory Fernando Pappas, *John Dewey's Ethics: Democracy as Experience* (Bloomington: Indiana

University Press, 2008); *John Dewey: Between Pragmatism and Constructivism*, ed. Larry A. Hickman et al. (New York: Fordham University Press, 2009); Melvin L. Rogers, *The Undiscovered Dewey: Religion, Morality, and the Ethos of Democracy* (New York: Columbia University Press, 2009); and John A. Beineke, *And There Were Giants in the Land: The Life of William Heard Kilpatrick* (New York: P. Lang, 1998). Children's camps in the Adirondacks are explored more broadly in Hallie E. Bond et al., *"A Paradise for Boys and Girls": Children's Camps in the Adirondacks* (Blue Mountain Lake, N.Y.: Adirondack Museum, and Syracuse: Syracuse University Press, 2005), and Leslie Paris, *Children's Nature: The Rise of the American Summer Camp* (New York: New York University Press, 2008).

10. Burry, "Creating a 'Child's World'"; interview with Helen Haskell by Dick Wilde and Joan Dumont, Lake Placid, 11 Feb. 1982, North County School Archives (hereafter NCS Archives). Helen Haskell, "Camp Life," in Barbara Morgan, *Summer's Children: A Photographic Cycle of Life at Camp* (Scarsdale, N.Y.: Morgan & Morgan, 1951), 10–17, delineates her views on how such an institution should be run. Morgan's photographic essay, using images she had taken entirely at Treetops, affords a vivid picture of daily life there. Concerning the Clarks, see "'Rugged, Resourceful, and Resilient': North Country School 1938–1988," North Country School, Lake Placid, New York, Spring 1989, 6–9.

11. "'Rugged, Resourceful, and Resilient,'" 11.

12. Douglas Haskell, "Boarding Schools," in *Forms and Functions of Twentieth-Century Architecture*, 4 vols., ed. Talbot Hamlin (New York: Columbia University Press, 1952), 3:617–18.

13. Douglas Haskell, "Filing-Cabinet Building," *Creative Art* 10 (June 1932): 447–49; Benson, "Haskell," 320–22. Concerning Hessian Hills School, see Robert A. M. Stern, *George Howe: Toward a Modern American Architecture* (New Haven: Yale University Press, 1975), 98–101, figs. 65–68; and Lorraine Welling Lannon, *William Lescaze, Architect* (Philadelphia: Art Alliance Press, 1987), 76–77. Haskell did utilize one distinctive aspect of Hessian Hills's plan: having an "activity area" as an adjunct space to each classroom, which he believed to be one of the few innovations private institutions contributed to recent school design; see Haskell, "Boarding Schools," 603–4.

14. "School in the Adirondacks," *AR* 92 (Dec. 1942): 28–35. The tone of the piece, coupled with the fact that Haskell had recently joined the magazine's staff, suggest he was the author. See also "Work to Start," *Lake Placid News*, 1 July 1938, 1; and "Article Describes," *Lake Placid News*, 22 Jan. 1943, 1.

15. "School in the Adirondacks"; remarks by Wal-

ter Clark at memorial gathering for Douglas Haskell, North Country School, 16 Aug. 1979, typescript, NCS archives.

16. "'Rugged, Resourceful, and Resilient,'" 14, 15. Liability issues led to the eventual removal of this distinctive feature as well as of the crow's nest in the earlier building. The building was designed in 1942. Whether the four-year delay in its construction was due to materials shortages during the war or the Clarks' need to amass sufficient capital for its construction—or both—is unknown.

17. "Simple Frame," *House & Home* 2 (Dec. 1952): 108–10; "Article Describes."

18. For background, see Mary B. Hotaling, "Ben Muncil, Master Builder," *Newsletter*, Adirondack Architectural Heritage, 6 (June 1997): 1, 3.

19. Douglas Haskell, "Flexibility under the Roof," *AR* 94 (Nov. 1943): 61–65 (quote on p. 63); Haskell, "They Never Spoke Latin," *PA* 24 (June 1943): 37–43. Concerning Quonset huts, see Julie Decker and Chris Chiel, *Quonset Hut: Metal Living for a Modern Age* (New York: Princeton Architectural Press, 2005).

20. Henry Churchill likely served as consulting architect on this portion of the building as well. Haskell needed an architect of record for so sizable and costly a building and still did not have the capacity to develop the working drawings and specifications such work required. In a letter of 5 July 1945, Haskell wrote Churchill about what appears to have been a collaborative venture for a building at Camp Treetops. Soon thereafter, they entertained collaborating on the design of some cottages at the Grand View Hotel in Lake Placid, but nothing appears to have come of that project. In a letter to Churchill of 16 October 1958, he asked if Churchill would like "to continue in your capacity as architect for North Country School," in this case reviewing Haskell's documents for a second-story addition to Little House (Haskell Collection).

21. Remarks by Walter Clark (16 Aug. 1979). Unlike his previous work, Haskell did not publish this ambitious scheme, except for a floor plan in his boarding school essay. Perhaps he thought it a bit unseemly to do so given his ever more prominent role as an editor, or perhaps he feared it would be judged too eccentric by his peers.

22. Lisa Germany, *Harwell Hamilton Harris* (Austin: University of Texas Press, 1991), provides abundant details on the architect's career, although the connections with Haskell and North Country School are not discussed. Haskell's correspondence with Harris indicates the two were good friends. In Harris's 1964 nomination for fellowship in the AIA, Haskell indicated he had known him since the late 1930s, writing

that "those who have learnt how do better architecture and to pursue a higher standard of conduct [by his example] have been legion" (Haskell Collection).

23. "North Country House for Many Children," *AR* 103 (Feb. 1948): 106–11; "Designs for All-Year Sun Control," *NYT*, 7 Aug. 1949: SM64; Haskell, "They Never Spoke Latin," 38–39. The ventilating system proved insufficient for countering the substantial amount of sun the house received during the summer months. Haskell's correspondence with Harris indicates that some details were left up to the former (Haskell Collection).

24. Don Rand, "Doug . . . the Aesthetic Legacy," *Organic Roots*, North Country School and Camp Treetops Alumni Bulletin, Spring 2002, 10–11. According to Paul Nowicki, who served as a counselor at Treetops for some twenty years, Helen Haskell asked Rickey to join the staff ca. 1950–52 and gave him studio space in the garage adjacent to the farmhouse where she and her husband lived. Interview with Paul Nowicki, Keene, New York, 20 July 2010.

25. "'Rugged, Resourceful, and Resilient,'" 15. Remarks by Walter Clark (16 Aug. 1979), and Walter Clark, "Douglas Haskell" eulogy at memorial service, National Arts Club, New York, 27 Sep. 1979, typescript, NCS archives, also credit Haskell with landscaping the property.

26. Nowicki recently recalled that both Haskell's work and Glass House were key sources of inspiration for this building (Nowicki interview).

27. The sculptor's father was Matthew Nowicki, an architect of unusual distinction, whose career was tragically cut short just as it was taking shape. See Lewis Mumford, "The Life, the Teaching and the Architecture of Matthew Nowicki," *AR* 114 (June–Sep. 1954): 139–49, 128–35, 169–76, 153–59, respectively; and Bruce Harold Schafer, *The Writings and Sketches of Matthew Nowicki* (Charlottesville: University Press of Virginia, 1973). Not surprisingly Haskell was a friend.

28. Remarks by Walter Clark (16 Aug. 1979); Clark, "Douglas Haskell" eulogy; "'Rugged, Resourceful, and Resilient,'" 12, 33.

Chapter 11. Assessing a Vernacular Landscape

1. These, of course, are criteria for historic landmark and district designation in the District of Columbia, but they are similar to those of many, perhaps most, other local jurisdictions as well as to those of the National Register of Historic Places.

2. See James Goode, *Best Addresses: A Century of Washington's Distinguished Apartment Houses*, 1988; rev. ed. (Washington: Smithsonian Books, 2003), 256–62, 300–306.

3. The most detailed historical account of the subject at the time of the preparation of this testimony was Thomas J. Bassett, "Vacant Lot Cultivation: Community Gardening in America, 1893–1978" (Ph.D. dissertation, University of California, Berkeley, 1979), which appeared in highly condensed form as Bassett, "Reaping on the Margins: A Century of Community Gardening in America," *Landscape* 25: 2 (1981): 1–8. Since then, a comprehensive history has been published: Laura J. Lawson, *City Bountiful: A Century of Community Gardening in America* (Berkeley: University of California Press, 2005).

4. Sam Bass Warner, *To Dwell Is to Garden: A History of Boston's Community Gardens* (Boston: Northeastern University Press, 1987). See also "Community Gardening," *Plants & Gardens*, Brooklyn Botanic Garden Record, 35 (May 1979): whole issue; *A Handbook of Community Gardens*, ed. Susan Naimark (New York: Scribner, 1982); Tom Fox et al., *Struggle for Space: The Greening of New York City, 1970–1984* (New York: Neighborhood Open Space Coalition, 1985); and Lawson, *City Bountiful*, chapters 7, 8.

5. In addition to pertinent chapters in Lawson, *City Bountiful*, and Bassett, "Vacant Lot Cultivation," see Joachim Wolschke-Bulmann, "From the War-Garden to the Victory Garden: Political Aspects of Garden Culture in the United States during World War I," *Landscape Journal* 11 (Spring 1992): 51–57; R. E. Gough, "Gardening for Victory," *Country Journal* 20 (May–June 1993): 22–24; and *The New Garden Encyclopedia*, ed. E. L. D. Seymour (New York: Wm. H. Wise & Co., 1943), Victory Garden Supplement, 1349–80.

6. *The New Garden Encyclopedia*, 1353.

7. Ruth H. Landman, director, "Community Gardens in Washington: An Anthropological Study," Washington, American University, Spring 1989, and Landman, *Creating Community in the City: Cooperatives and Community Gardens in Washington, D.C.* (Westport Conn.: Bergin & Garvey, 1993), provide detailed coverage of the subject.

8. Since the preparation of my testimony in 1996, from which this chapter is adapted, two of these gardens have been lost: the one on the grounds of the Kennedy-Warren apartment building, which was destroyed to make room for an addition, and the garden at 3901 Connecticut, after the parcel on which it was located failed to be included in the landmarked property.

Chapter 12. Nonconforming [?] Modernism

1. "Shop Center Planned Near McLean Gardens," *WP*, 21 June 1953, 1R; "Room for Expansion Here," *Evening Star* [Washington], 30 January 154, B-4. The shopping

center was named after Friendship, the house of Robert and Evalyn Walsh McLean, which had been torn down to accommodate the 724-unit McLean Gardens constructed during World War II.

2. When the nomination for the Cleveland Park historic district was prepared in the mid-1980s, the property was excluded in part because Wisconsin Avenue made a logical western boundary, but also due to fears that it would seem far too new and "plain" to pass the review process. Including commercial properties developed for the most part during the interwar decades along Connecticut Avenue proved controversial enough.

3. For background, see Richard Longstreth, "The Neighborhood Shopping Center in Washington, D.C., 1930-1941," *JSAH* 51 (Mar. 1992): 5-34.

4. For brief discussion, see Richard Longstreth, "Building for Business: Commercial Architecture in Metropolitan Washington," in *Capital Drawings: Architectural Design for Washington, D.C., from the Library of Congress*, ed. C. Ford Peatross (Washington: Library of Congress, and Baltimore: Johns Hopkins University Press, 2005), 142-45.

5. For background, see *1936-1961: Progress through Customer Satisfaction* (Washington, D.C.: Giant Food Stores, 1961); Scott Sedar et al., *Fifty Years of Caring: Giant Food Stores* (Washington, D.C.: Giant Food Stores, 1987); "N. M. Cohen, 93 Founder of Giant Food Stores, Dies," *WP*, 6 June 1984, B10; and "Giant Store Co-Founder Dies in Miami," *WP*, 14 Jan. 1949, B2. I am grateful to Lisa Pfueller Davidson for bringing these and other pertinent sources to my attention.

6. For background, see Richard Longstreth, *The Drive-In, the Supermarket, and the Transformation of Commercial Space in Los Angeles, 1914-1941* (Cambridge, Mass.: MIT Press, 1999), chapter 3; James Mayo, *The American Grocery Store: The Business Evolution of an American Space* (Westport, Conn.: Greenwood Press, 1993), chapters 4 and 5; and Tracey Deutsch, *Building a Housewife's Paradise: Gender, Politics, and American Grocery Stores in the Twentieth Century* (Chapel Hill: University of North Carolina Press, 2010), chapter 5.

7. "Capital Surrenders to Super Market," *Super Market Merchandising* 3 (May 1938): 12-13.

8. "Alexandria Gets $500,000 Giant," *WP*, 14 Jan. 1951, 2R; "Two Giant Stores to Open," *Evening Star*, 24 Feb. 1952, A-9; "Giants Food Stores," *WP*, 31 Jan. 1954, R2; "Giant Opens 29th," *WP*, 19 June 1955, D14; "Giant Opens Unit," *WP*, 24 July 1955, C13.

9. Longstreth, *The Drive-In*, 176-80.

10. "New Shopping Center Opens in Northeast," *WP*, 13 Apr. 1947, 2R; "Alexandria, Nearby Maryland Units Set," *WP*, 20 July 1947, R1; "Work to Begin Soon on Big Trade Center," *WP*, 6 July 1947, C7 ; "Action on a Long Dormant Front," *Maryland News* [Silver Spring], 4 June 1948, B-1; "New Shopping Center Opens," *WP*, 17 Jan. 1950, R3; "Neighboring Shopping Centers," *Maryland News*, 20 Jan. 1950, B-1.

11. "Two Giant Stores to Open"; Richard Longstreth, "The Mixed Blessings of Success: The Hecht Company and Department Store Branch Development after World War II," in *Shaping Communities: Perspectives in Vernacular Architecture, VI*, ed. Carter L. Hudgins and Elizabeth Collins Cromley (Knoxville: University of Tennessee Press, 1997), 252-55; Longstreth, *The American Department Store Transformed, 1920-1960* (New Haven: Yale University Press, 2010), 175-76.

12. "New 'Giant' Store," *Record of Montgomery County*, 1 May 1953, 1; "Bethesda Busy Building," *WP*, 11 Oct. 1953, 1R; "New Chevy Chase Shopping Center," *WP*, 16 Sep. 195439; "Throngs See Opening," *Evening Star*, 16 October 1954, A-R.

13. "Lansburgh's Soon to Build," *WP*, 21 Nov. 1954, M1, M10.

14. Given the tradition of front-lot parking areas in Washington shopping centers, there is no indication that the Friendship Shopping Center's layout was predicated on merchants resisting removal from the sidewalk, as remained common in Los Angeles, among other cities, well into the postwar period. See Richard Longstreth, *City Center to Regional Mall: Architecture, the Automobile, and Retailing in Los Angeles, 1920-1950* (Cambridge, Mass.: MIT Press, 1997), chapters 7 and 9.

15. As realized, the complex was scaled down from the original conception, which included a department store branch, several chain stores, a bowling alley, a roller skating rink, and a legitimate theater, but no indication of how this complex was to be configured has been found; see "Shopping Center to Be Built," *WP*, 2 July 1948, 1; and "Theater Planned," *WP*, 27 Aug. 1948, B4. Later Kass opened an outdoor skating rink on the property, but this appears to have been removed when the shopping center was constructed; see "Skating Rink to Open," *WP*, 7 Aug. 1950, B1.

16. Longstreth, *The Drive-In*, 170-80.

17. Chester H. Liebs, *Main Street to Miracle Mile: American Roadside Architecture*, 1985; reprint ed. (Baltimore: Johns Hopkins University Press, 1995); Alan Hess, *Googie Redux: Ultramodern Roadside Architecture* (San Francisco: Chronicle Books, 2004). See also Jim Heimann, *California Crazy and Beyond: Roadside Vernacular Architecture* (San Francisco: Chronicle Books, 2001).

18. For discussions of the impact that World War II had on architecture, design, and urbanism in subsequent decades, see *World War II and the American Dream: How Wartime Building Changed a Nation*, ed.

Donald Albrecht (Washington: National Building Museum, and Cambridge, Mass.: MIT Press, 1995); *Cold War Hothouses: Inventing Postwar Culture from Cockpit to Playboy*, ed. Beatriz Colomina et al. (New York: Princeton Architectural Press, 2004); Andrew M. Shanken, *194X: Architecture, Planning, and Consumer Culture on the American Home Front* (Minneapolis: University of Minnesota Press, 2009); and Jean-Louis Cohen, *Architecture in Uniform: Designing and Building for the Second World War* (Montreal: Canadian Centre for Architecture, and Paris: Éditions Hazan, 2011).

19. A countertendency in design of the period is the subject of Alice T. Friedman, *American Glamour and the Evolution of Modern Architecture* (New Haven: Yale University Press, 2010).

20. For background, see "Garfield I. Kass, Builder 20 Years," *WP*, 21 Mar. 1937, R3; "7 Corners Builder Undaunted," *WP*, 3 Oct. 1956, 42; "'7 Corners' Marks Peak," *WP*, 15 Sep. 1957, C9; "Kass Is Disposing of Properties," *WP*, 15 Apr. 1960, B6; and "Garfield Kass Dies," *WP*, 27 Feb. 1975, B8.

21. "Shannon, Luchs Firm Reports," *WP*, 20 June 1937, R2; "Store Center Erected," *WP*, 25 Apr. 1937, R10. For a sampling of other accounts, see "Improvement Seen," *WP*, 13 Oct. 1929, R3; "Lot Sold Leased," *WP*, 3 May 1931, R1; "Building Values for 1936 Set," *WP*, 6 Dec. 1936, R1; and "Stores Built and Leased," *WP*, 21 Nov. 1937, R7. The Kass Realty Company also constructed a number of gasoline stations, motion picture exchanges, and warehouses during this period.

22. For a sampling of accounts, see "New Motion Picture Theater," *WP*, 29 May 1938, R7; "Beverly Theater is Modernistic," *WP*, 25 Dec. 1938, R3; "Garfield Kass Plans Movie Chain," *WP*, 9 Jan. 1944, R9; and "Movie Palace Being Built," *WP*, 5 Aug. 1945, R3. See also note 28 below. A detailed inventory of the building type in the metropolitan area is found in Robert K. Headley, *Motion Picture Exhibition in Washington, D.C.* (Jefferson, N.C.: McFarland, 1999).

23. Longstreth, "Neighborhood Shopping Center," 19, 21–22, 33. For period accounts, see "Kass Project Ready," *WP*, 29 Mar. 1936, R14; "Company Seeks Permit," *WP*, 12 Apr. 1936, R8; "Many Permits Are Granted," *WP*, 28 June 1936, R8; "Architect Asks for Estimates," *WP*, 9 Aug. 1936, R6; "Kass Realty Co. Plans," *WP*, 11 July 1937, R4; "Park and Shop," *American City* 52 (Oct. 1937): 71–72; "Chevy Chase Sports Center Opens," *WP*, 20 Nov. 1938, R11; "'Park and Shop' Building for the Suburbs," *National Real Estate Journal* 60 (Mar. 1939): 42–43; and "Park and Shop Building," *AR* 87 (June 1940): 119–20. Another shopping center was planned at Minnesota Avenue and Benning Road, N.E., which was later realized, according to a new

plan by other parties; see "Kass Realty Co. Plans," *WP*, 16 Mar. 1941, R2.

24. "Kass Building to Be Ready," *WP*, 14 Aug. 1949, R4; *AF* 96 (Feb. 1952): 58.

25. "Plans for Million Dollar Shopping Center," *Takoma Journal* [Maryland], 13 Sep. 1946, 1; "Rezoning Petition Approved," *Takoma Journal*, 21 Feb. 1947, 1; "Shopping Centers," *Takoma Journal*, 25 Mar. 1947, 1; "New 'Hampshire' Theater," *Takoma Journal*, 20 Jan. 1950, 1; "Building Plans, Home and Store," *Takoma Journal*, 28 Apr. 1950, 1; "Plans Completed," *WP*, 10 Dec. 1950, R3; "Two New Shopping Centers," *Takoma Journal*, 15 Dec. 1950, 1.

26. For background, see "Plans for Seven Corners," *WP*, 13 Mar. 1955, G4; *WP*, 3 Oct. 1956, Seven Corners Section; and *Evening Star*, 3 Oct. 1956, Seven Corners Section.

27. For background, see Thomas M. Cahill, "This Week in Real Estate," *WP*, 4 Apr. 1937, 45; "Village Site," *WP*, 11 Apr. 1937, R1, R7; and "Realty Roundup," *WP*, 7 May 1950, R8. Hogan's application for membership in the American Institute of Architects differs somewhat from earlier newspaper accounts, in that he lists himself as a partner in an architectural firm with Taylor from 1932–35 and in independent practice thenceforth (AIA Archives). In seeking professional standing, Hogan may have been reluctant to portray himself as a developer's architect.

28. Concerning Eberson, see Jane Preddy et al., *Glamour, Glitz, and Sparkle: The Deco Theatres of John Eberson* (Chicago: Theatre Historical Society of America, 1989). Concerning Zink, see *The Architecture of Baltimore: An Illustrated History*, ed. Mary Ellen Hayward and Frank R. Shivers Jr. (Baltimore: Johns Hopkins University Press, 2004), 264; and Robert K. Headley, *Motion Picture Exhibition in Baltimore* (Jefferson, N.C.: McFarland, 2006), 155–57.

29. Application for membership, 10 November 1944, AIA Archives; "Architect David Baker Dies," *WP*, 9 Mar. 1980, B6. I am grateful to David S. Hammond of Washington for supplying me with a copy of a promotional booklet issued by Baker ca. 1966, which gives many additional details of his career.

30. The observations made in the text below are based on fieldwork that I conducted in the early 1970s and from the mid-1980s on.

31. See Richard Longstreth, comp., "A Historical Bibliography of Commercial Architecture in the United States," http://www.sah.org and http://www.preservenet.cornell.edu; and Longstreth, comp., "A Historical Bibliography of Architecture, Landscape Architecture, and Urbanism in the United States Since World War II," at http://www.preservenet.cornell.edu.

Chapter 13. The Continuous Transformation of Savannah's Broughton Street

1. The focus of this study are those blocks of Broughton that comprised the city's principal shopping district through the mid-twentieth century, extending from West Broad Street (now Martin Luther King Jr. Boulevard), itself long an important part of the commercial center catering to the less affluent of the consumer market, east to Lincoln Street, beyond which neighborhood commercial and residential functions have always been interspersed.

2. Concerning the Oglethorpe Plan, see Thomas D. Wilson, *The Oglethorpe Plan: Enlightenment Design in Savannah and Beyond* (Charlottesville: University of Virginia Press, 2012). See also John W. Reps, *The Making of Urban America: A History of City Planning in the United States* (Princeton: Princeton University Press, 1965), 185-92, 195-203; Stanford Anderson, "Savannah and the Issue of Precedent: City Plan as Resource," in *Settlement in the Americas: Cross Cultural Perspectives,* ed. Ralph Bennett (Newark: University of Delaware Press, 1993), 110-44; and Louis De Vorsey, "The Origin and Appreciation of Savannah, Georgia's Historic City Squares," *Southeastern Geographer* 52 (Spring 2012): 90-99. The first public market was constructed in 1763; the third was built in 1870 and demolished in 1953.

3. Walter S. Fraser Jr., *Savannah in the Old South* (Athens: University of Georgia Press, 2003), chapter 6. Useful period accounts from the turn of the twentieth century include J. Dean Enslow, *Savannah, Illustrated* (Savannah: Presses of the Morning News, 1899), 31-36, 41-42; *Savannah: A City of Opportunity* (Savannah: Savannah Morning News, 1904), 25-35; and William Harden, *A History of Savannah and South Georgia,* 1913; reprint ed. (Atlanta: Cherokee, 1969), 325-31, 420-24, 471-72.

4. Harden, *History of Savannah,* 472-76.

5. Remarkably, Savannah has yet to benefit from substantive, detailed historical analyses of its built environment. *Historic Savannah: Survey of Significant Buildings in the Historic and Victorian Districts of Savannah, Georgia,* ed. Mary L. Morrison, 1968; updated ed. (Savannah: Historic Savannah Foundation and Junior League of Savannah, 1979) provides basic data on many buildings, but now is quite dated in format and scope. Savannah figures prominently in Frederick Doveton Nichols, *The Early Architecture of Georgia* (Chapel Hill: University of North Carolina Press, 1957), and a similar, updated study, Mills Lane, *Architecture of the Old South: Georgia* (Savannah: Beehive Press, 1986)—both antiquarian in tone. See also *Antiques* 41 (Mar. 1967): whole issue; and *Savannah Revisited: A*

Pictorial History (Athens: University of Georgia Press, 1969). The most detailed study currently in print is unfortunately difficult to find: "Savannah and the Lowcountry," ed. Marisa C. Gomez and E. G. Daves Rossell, Field Guide for the 28th Annual Meeting, Vernacular Architecture Forum, 2007; a Buildings of the United States volume focusing on Savannah, by Robin Williams et al., will be published in 2015.

6. For background, see Nathan Weinberg, *Preservation in American Towns and Cities* (Boulder, Col.: Westview Press, 1979), 95-107; Preston Russell and Barbara Hines, *Savannah: A History of Her People since 1733* (Savannah: Frederic C. Beil, 1992), 174-88; Elizabeth A. Lyon, "Savannah: The Preservation of a Unique Historic Environment for Today," *Historic Preservation Forum* 13 (Fall 1998): 37-44. Lee Adler and Emma Adler, *Savannah Renaissance* (Charleston: Wyrick, 2003) is an insightful, firsthand account of preservation efforts. Leopold Adler II, grandson of the owner of Adler's department store, was arguably the key figure in devising a series of innovative strategies that transformed many of Savannah's nineteenth-century residential blocks and made the city a national showcase for preservation as well as a major tourist destination. See also Beth Lattimore Reiter et al., *Preservation for People in Savannah* (Savannah: Savannah Landmark Rehabilitation Project, 1983).

7. Useful pictorial coverage of Broughton Street can be found in Luciana M. Spracher, *Lost Savannah* (Charleston: Arcadia, 2002), and Justin Gunther, *Historic Signs of Savannah* (Charleston: Arcadia, 2004).

8. Unless otherwise indicated in the notes, data on the buildings discussed in this chapter was gleaned from historic resource surveys conducted by the Historic Savannah Foundation and the Chatham County-Savannah Metropolitan Planning Commission during the last three decades of the twentieth century, as well as city directories (examined generally at ten-year intervals: 1866, 1871, 1881, 1891, 1901, 1911, 1921, 1932, 1941, 1951, and 1961), Sanborn fire insurance maps (1884, 1888, 1898, 1916, and 1916-50), extensive collections of photographs in the archives of the Georgia Historical Society and the Planning Commission, and firsthand examination of the buildings themselves.

9. For discussion of the type, see Richard Longstreth, *The Buildings of Main Street: A Guide to American Commercial Architecture,* 1987; reprint ed. (Walnut Creek, Calif.: Alta Mira Press, 2000), 24-29; and Howard Davis, *Living Over the Store: Architecture and Local Urban Life* (London: Routledge, 2012).

10. Hodgson left the diplomatic corps when he married Mary's sister, Margaret Telfair, and devoted much of his time managing the Telfair family's

plantations. See Thomas A. Bryson, *An American Consular Officer in the Middle East in the Jacksonian Era: A Biography of William Brown Hodgson, 1801–1871* (Atlanta: Resurgens, 1979). The Telfair name is best remembered for the extraordinary house that Mary's brother, Alexander, commissioned from architect William Jay (1819–20).

Square footages for Broughton Street buildings are estimates derived from the Sanborn fire insurance maps. The gross figures include basements as well as above-ground space, and encompass both leasable space and space devoted to support functions.

11. The Pulaski and Screven houses were probably the most fashionable, superseded by the De Soto (1890), which lay outside the commercial district.

12. Throughout the text, street numbers used are current ones, not those of the nineteenth century.

13. Completed in 1866, the building at 101–103 W. Broughton was occupied by Rogers & Dasher and Gray & O'Brien dry goods stores; the group at 109–113 W. Broughton was built ca. 1873–74. For illustration of the Lyons Block, see Gunther, *Historic Signs*, 45.

14. "Adler Store Has Honorable History," *SEP*, 19 Nov. 1936, 13A; "Adler Store Is Sixty Years Old," *SMN*, 1 May 1938, 20, 38.

15. In 1870, the year of its formation, the Oglethorpe Club occupied a grand building constructed in 1851 as the Solomons Lodge, the third-oldest Masonic lodge in the country. The club remained there until it moved to Gaston and Bull streets in 1914. Ludden & Bates's building first appears in the 1887 city directory, suggesting 1886 as its construction date. In 1885, the operation was listed nearby on Congress Street. Adler's expanded into the building ca. 1915.

16. "A Palatial Dry Goods House," *SMN*, 17 Sep. 1884, 4; "In the Burnt District," *SMN*, 6 Sep. 1889, 16. Hogan's building at 123–125 W. Broughton was divided between his establishment and other merchants probably until the first decades of the twentieth century, when his operation took over the upper floors of number 123. The Weed Building was never occupied by its client, but appears to have been a speculative venture, initially occupied by Lindsay & Morgan, a leading furniture store. Weed was also president of the Savannah Bank & Trust Company and the Savannah Rice Mill Company in 1889.

17. Supplementing data gleaned from city directories are period accounts such as *Savannah, Illustrated*, 37, and *Savannah: A City of Opportunity*, 37.

18. "New Building for Walker-Mulligan Company," *SMN*, 14 July 1912, 12; Gunther, *Historic Signs*, 33–34. St. Andrew's Hall probably always had businesses at its ground level. The 1866 city directory lists A. Myers & Co., a large wholesale and retail operation purveying dry goods, clothing, boots and shoes, millinery, and notions. During the 1920s a similar conversion was made to a four-story pile constructed ca. 1900 for Mohr Bros. wholesale notions company at 230–234 W. Broughton for Philip Levy & Company furniture store, which became quarters for the Chatham Furniture Company by the eve of World War II (see fig. 13.1).

19. Adjacent to the building on Bull Street lay the eight-story Germania Bank (ca. 1904). Within a few years, construction began on the fourteen-story Savannah Bank & Trust Company building, which was completed in 1911 across Johnson Square.

20. Namely, two-story buildings probably first occupied by the Manhattan Restaurant at 124–126 (ca. 1910) and the J. S. Pinkussohn Cigar Company at 32–34 (ca. 1910); a one-story building with two store units at 110–112 (ca. 1900–1910), the two-story Lamas Building at 202–208 (1917), and a three-story block at 14–16 (ca. 1918–20).

21. Robert M. Hitch, "Modern Savannah," *Georgia Historical Quarterly* 13 (Sep. 1929): 301–37; "Industrial Committee Has Vitally Affected Advance" and "Union Bag & Paper Corp. Is City's Largest Industry," *SMN*, 27 Oct. 1938, 4, 10, respectively; and untitled paper delivered by Thomas Gamble to Savannah Rotary Club, ca. 1934, in "Savannah—Economic Conditions, 1950–59," pamphlet file, Georgia Room, Savannah Public Library. See also Edward Chan Sieg, *Eden on the Marsh: An Illustrated History of Savannah* (Northridge, Calif.: Windsor, 1985), 95, 97, 103, 105.

22. "Globe Shoe Co.," *SMN*, 21 Nov. 1929, 2D. For illustration of the previous store, see Gunther, *Historic Signs*, 23. Other new East Broughton buildings included the three-story edifice soon to be occupied by the Jones Store at 32 (ca. 1920), additions to a second Lamas Building at 24–30 (1921), the Moylan Building at 21–27 (ca. 1923), and the Arthur Lucas Building at 116–120 (1928), all of them two stories.

23. *SMN*, 6 Sep. 1925, Levy Section; "1871–1971: One-Hundred Happy Years," *SMN*, 12 Feb. 1971, 16F. Early-nineteenth-century references were pursued in the preliminary scheme for the store's addition; see "Levy's Reveals," *SEP*, 27 Nov. 1946. The store may have encouraged others to plan for a five-story department store and adjacent twelve-story hotel directly across the street, but nothing came of the venture; see "To Erect 5-Story Building," *Women's Wear Daily*, 5 Aug. 1926, 8. For illustration of the older Broughton Street store, see Gunther, *Historic Signs*, 11.

24. For a sampling of accounts, see "Mack's Boot Shop," *SMN*, 16 Oct. 1926, 9; "Rites Clothes," *SMN*, 31 Aug. 1928, 16; and "New Stores Open Today," *SMN*, 7 June 1929, 1B. Haverty's was a chain in embryo. The company, based in Atlanta, opened its second store

in Savannah, and the two units were run, somewhat independent of one another, for many years. Only in recent decades has the store grown into a major national chain operation. A junior department store, a term long out of use, entailed a more limited array of lines than a full-fledged department store and, like the variety store, generally catered to a bargain-conscious clientele. The Sears store was of the "C" type, modest in size and in choice of merchandise. Not until after World War II did the company open a full-line, "A" store in the city. Another variety store, Silver's, started in Savannah in 1901, occupying the lower portion of the Weed Building, and had become a substantial chain by the late 1920s. For illustrations, see Gunther, *Historic Signs*, 13–15, and 19.

25. "Kress Has Formal Opening Today," *SMN*, 28 Sep. 1937, 9; Bernice L. Thomas, *America's 5 & 10 Cent Stores: The Kress Legacy* (Washington, D.C.: National Building Museum and Preservation Press, and New York: John Wiley & Sons, 1997); Richard Longstreth, "Sears, Roebuck and the Remaking of the Department Store, 1924–42," *JSAH* 65 (June 2006): 252–53. Concerning the Blumberg store, see "Blumberg Bros. Formal Opening," *SMN*, 27 Mar. 1929, 20.

26. "J. C. Penney Is Among Leaders," *SMN*, 27 Oct. 1938, 15; "J. C. Penney Co. Is Modernized," *SMN*, 31 Oct. 1939, 56; "Sears, Roebuck and Company's New Savannah Store," *SMN*, 25 June 1936, 9.

27. Concerning chain store growth and competition, see Richard Longstreth, *The American Department Store Transformed, 1920–1960* (New Haven: Yale University Press, 2010), 9–10, 34–35; and Geoffrey Lebhar, *The Chain Store in America, 1859–1962* (New York: Chain Store Pub. Corp., 1963), esp. chapters 6–8. For a concise period account, see Paul H. Nystrom, *Economics of Retailing* (New York: Ronald Press, 1930), chapter 8.

28. For background, see Gabrielle Esperdy, *Modernizing Main Street: Architecture and Consumer Culture in the New Deal* (Chicago: University of Chicago Press, 2008); and Alison Isenberg, *Downtown America: A History of the Place and the People Who Made It* (Chicago: University of Chicago Press, 2004), esp. chapter 4. For an informative period account, see Kenneth Kingsley Stowell, *Modernizing Buildings for Profit* (New York: Prentice-Hall, 1935).

29. *SEP*, 19 Nov. 1936, 5C (Maxwell Brothers); "B. Karpf Store Steady Growth," *SMN*, 19 Nov. 1936, 13A; "B. Karpf Opening," *SMN*, 23 Sep. 1938, 5 (B. Karpf); "Black and Silver Adorn New Store," *SMN*, 23 Sep. 1931, 12; "Morris Levy's Fine New Store Addition," *SMN*, 7 Nov. 1937, 23 (Morris Levy). For other examples, see "Stanley & Company Remodeling," *SMN*, 18 Feb. 1927, 2; "Improvements for the Jones Company," *SMN*, 20 Feb. 1937, 3; "The Jones Company Formal Opening,"

SMN, 27 June 1937, 19; "New Minkowitz Store Opening," *SMN*, 15 Oct. 1937, 12; and "Levy Jewelers," *SEP*, 8 Apr. 1938, 17.

30. "The Savannah Marketplace," *SMN*, 7 Sep. 1958; "Introduction," Savannah City Directory, 1958, xi–xiii; "Summary" (ca. 1960) and "Statistical Information Section" (ca. 1958), "Savannah—Economic Conditions, 1950–59," pamphlet file, Georgia Room, Savannah Public Library.

31. The second Savannah Theatre became a full-fledged movie house in 1931. The Lucas was the city's premier house. On Broughton, the Arcadia, Bijou, and Folly all opened before 1916, probably as nickelodeons. The larger Odeon Theatre also predated 1916, but was a more decorous house designed for live performances. See Gunther, *Historic Signs*, 96, 98–99, 101. The Lucas stands just off Broughton; the Savannah, rebuilt in the 1950s, several blocks away.

32. "Avon Theatre," *SEP*, 8 Sep. 1944, 14; "'Road to Utopia' Opens" and "Maximum Ease and Fun," *SMN*, 13 Feb. 1946, 11, 17, respectively; "Plans Announced," *SMN*, 13 Apr. 1945, 10; "New Movie House," *SMN*, 13 Jan. 1946, 32; "Beautiful New Weiss," *SMN*, 14 Feb. 1946, 11–15. The Avon's lobby replaced the former Folly.

33. "Lerner to Erect," *SMN*, 22 Sep. 1946, 16; "New Lerner Store," *SMN*, 21 Mar. 1947, 12. For illustration of the previous store, see Gunther, *Historic Signs*, 19.

34. Department stores set the pace for such work during the 1930s, beginning with Sears, Roebuck's Englewood store in Chicago (1933–34). For discussion, see Longstreth, "Sears, Roebuck," 256–60; and Longstreth, *The American Department Store*, chapter 2.

35. "B. H. Levy Plans," *SMN*, 8 Nov. 1945; "Levy's Reveals."

36. "Levy's to Expand," *SEP*, 10 Nov. 1950, 24; *SMN*, 12 Sep. 1954, 45–60.

37. "1871–1971." Concerning Allied, see Longstreth, *The American Department Store*, 50–51, 162, 185–86, 187–88, 247. See also "Puckett of Allied Stores," *Fortune* 35 (Mar. 1947): 122–25, 162, 164, 166–70.

38. "Woolworth Announces," *SEP*, 30 July 1953, 40; "Woolworth's New Store," *SMN*, 6 Oct. 1954, 3. Concerning national trends among variety stores of the period, see Richard Longstreth, *The Drive-In, the Supermarket, and the Transformation of Commercial Space in Los Angeles, 1914–1941* (Cambridge, Mass.: MIT Press, 1999), 171–74.

39. "Downtown Department Store," *SEP*, 20 May 1958, 1, 2, 24; "Two Savannah Stores," *Women's Wear Daily*, 21 May 1958, 1, 14; "Adler's Will Open," *SMN*, 17 May 1959, 1B; "Adler's Opens," *SMN*, 25 Oct. 1959, 1B, 8B; "Penney's Plans Big Store," *SEP*, 13 June 1959, 18.

40. "Design of Penney Store," *SMN*, 13 June 1959, 11B; "New J. C. Penney Department Store," *SEP*, 26 Oct.

1960, 22; "Shopping Crowds Pack," *SEP*, 3 Nov. 1960, 40.

41. "First Federal Building" and "Building Reflects," *SMN*, 14 May 1961, 4, 11, respectively.

42. "Work Progresses," *SEP*, 7 June 1947, 12; "Plans for Morris Levy's," *SMN*, 18 May 1947, 8; "New Jewelry Store," *SMN*, 8 Nov. 1947, 4.

43. "New Haverty's," *SMN*, 18 Sep. 1952, 9. "Belk-Parrott Co. Opens," *SEP*, 31 Dec. 1946, 20. The Belk store is illustrated in the 1962 City Directory, p. 48.

44. "Customer Convenience Theme," *SMN*, 28 Mar. 1954, 10; "New Building Is 4th Expansion," *SMN*, 3 Aug. 1961, 2C; "Open House Set," *SMN*, 12 Mar. 1962, 10A. For another example, see "Michelle's Grand Opening," *SEP*, 23 Sep. 1961, 7. First used at Thalheimer's department store in Richmond, Virginia (1953–55), the aluminum curtain wall was considered a major breakthrough in terms of quick, low-cost exterior remodeling. See Longstreth, *The American Department Store*, 56–57. It became widely used for retail buildings in cities and towns alike nationwide by the late 1950s. The remaking of stores during the postwar era has received little scholarly attention in print. For an exception, see Richard Mattson, "Store Front Remodeling on Main Street," *Journal of Cultural Geography* 3 (Spring–Summer 1983): 41–55.

45. Concerning the Levy firm, see "Local Architects Planned Building," *SMN*, 6 Sep. 1925, 4D; "Morton Levy Funeral," *SMN*, 1 Dec. 1954, 2; Henry F. Withey and Elsie Rathburn Withey, *Biographical Dictionary of American Architects (Deceased)*, 1956; reprint ed. (Los Angeles: Hennessey & Ingalls, 1970), 124; and *American Institute of Architects' Directory* (New York: R. R. Bowker), 298, 320 (1955 ed.); 417–18 (1962 ed.); and 487–88, 540 (1970 ed.). On the Bergens, see "Father-Son Leave Imprint," *SMN*, 8 July 1973, 1B; "Noted Savannah Architect Dies," *SMN*, 30 Oct. 1972, 1B; and *American Institute of Architects' Directory*, 39 (1956 ed.) and 50 (1962 ed.). Additional material was gleaned from the American Institute of Architects Archives in Washington, D.C.

46. The Levy office's work included new buildings for Levy's department store (1924–25), Arthur Lucas Building (1928), Globe Shoe Company (1928–29), Morris Levy's Shop for Women (1937), F. W. Woolworth Co. (1953–54), Levy's Department Store (1953–54), and First Federal Savings & Loan Association (1959–61); and alterations for B. Karpf (ca. 1922–24), Lady Jane Shop (ca. 1922–25), Miller & Miller (ca. 1922–25), J. D. Weed Company (ca. 1922–25), Jones Company (1937), and Friedman Jewelers (1938). Bergen's work included new buildings for Morris Levy's Store for Men (1931) and Lerner Shops (1946–47); and alterations to buildings for Morris Levy's Store for Men and Shop for

Women (1946), Ray Jewelers (1947), Stanley Jewelers (1947), and Fine's (1962). In all likelihood, both offices were responsible for numerous other remodeling projects along Broughton Street as well.

47. "Sears Shopping Center," *SMN*, 12 Jan. 1946; "Opening of Sears," *SMN*, 1 Nov. 1946, 18; "Hundreds Work Hard," *SMN*, 12 Nov. 1946, 14, 7. Concerning the company's development practices, see Longstreth, "Sears, Roebuck," 238–79.

48. Woolworth's had branches at Crossroads, Habersham, and West Side shopping centers (opened 1953, 1955, and 1959, respectively). Crossroads also had branches of Belk and Friedman's Jewelers, and West Side of Hogan's. Remler's Corner, later named Victory Drive Shopping Center (opened 1952) became home to Adler's and, concurrently, to a second unit of Grant's. These two stores, coupled with the expansion of the center's supermarket, added 45,000 square feet to the complex, which previously had encompassed 31,000 square feet. Data culled from *Directory of Shopping Centers in the United States and Canada* (Chicago: National Research Bureau, 1958, 1962, 1972, 1996). Concerning Grant's, see "W. T. Grant Co. Will Build," *SMN*, 24 May 1959, 2B.

49. For background on the regional mall's development, see Longstreth, *The American Department Store*, chapter 8.

50. "Giant New Complex," *SEP*, 29 May 1967, 1, 2; "Oglethorpe Mall to Open," *SMN*, 28 Jan. 1969, 17; *SMN*, 13 Apr. 1969, Oglethorpe Mall Section. Concerning Belk, see Howard E. Covington Jr., *Belk: A Century of Retail Leadership* (Chapel Hill: University of North Carolina Press, 1988), 10–11.

51. *Directory of Shopping Centers* (1996); "Broughton Street Market Analysis and Development Plan," E. L. Crow, Lafayette Hill, Pa., June 1985, II-22, II-2, III-1. Total square footage suitable for retail use in Broughton Street buildings was estimated at 420,000.

52. "Broughton Street Market Analysis," II-9, II-36, III-1, III-2. "Broughton Street: The Circle of Economic Life," *SMN*, 24 Mar. 2010, 23. Concerning Martin Luther King Jr. Boulevard, see Ellis Garvin, *A Guide to Our Two Savannahs* (Savannah: Garvin, 2009), 36–45; and Gomez and Rossell, "Savannah and the Lowcountry," 90–94, 100–101, 154–56, 187–88. Most of the street's commercial buildings have been demolished.

53. "Downtown, Mall Retail Shops," *SMN*, 29 Oct. 1981, 8A; "Broughton Blues," *SMN*, 25 Aug. 1996, 1E, 2E; "Broughton Landmark," *SMN*, 11 Oct. 1997, 8B.

54. A concise overview of SDRA's program is found in Susan S. Weiner, "If They Build It, They Will Come," *Places* 10:2 (Winter 1996): 12–19. Extensive additional information on the agency was kindly provided by its director, Lise Sundrla, and senior program manager,

Peter Featheringill. SDRA was established as an alternative to a proposal that called for high-end retail development similar to that found in a regional shopping center; see "Broughton Street Redevelopment Plan, Savannah, Georgia," Terranomics Development Corporation, Washington, D.C., and Cooper Carey & Associates, Atlanta and Washington, 1991.

55. "Broughton Street: The Circle." Concerning SCAD, see Andrea Oppenheimer Dean, "School of Redesign," *Historic Preservation* 44 (Nov.-Dec. 1992): 34-41, 87; and Connie Capozzola Pinkerton and Maureen Burke, *The Savannah College of Art and Design: Restoration of an Architectural Heritage* (Charleston: Arcadia, 2004).

56. [Leopold Adler II], "Back to Broughton," typescript, ca. 1984, copy provided to author by SDRA, makes an eloquent plea for the street's revitalization, an initiative that, by his admission, was unsuccessful. See also Adler and Adler, *Savannah Renaissance*, 77-78.

57. "Something Old, Something New," *SMN*, 6 Aug. 1999, 1A, 10A. For illustrations of the Marshall House, see Gunther, *Historic Signs*, 106-7.

Chapter 14. Building Houses, Creating Community

1. For some years, the "Twinbrook" that has been an official planning area of the City of Rockville (the municipality within which it resides), and that has been popularly known among area residents, has encompassed a considerably larger area than the "Twinbrook" that is the focus of this study. The latter Twinbrook consists of tracts within that larger area developed by builder Joseph Geeraert, several of them in conjunction with three early partners. Initially, tracts were platted as "Twin-Brook"; "Twin Brook" was another common spelling. By the mid-1950s, "Twinbrook" became the most widely used form and is employed throughout the text here. See "Let's Get Together on Our Town's Name," *MCS*, 27 Feb. 1959, A6. Subdivision plats made throughout the state are available through the Maryland State Archives at http://www.plats.net.

Other subdivisions in the Twinbrook area include Rockcrest (platted 1946-48, 63 lots), Broadwood Manor (platted 1950-51, 61 lots), Rockland (platted 1951-55, 342 lots), Burgundy Estates (platted 1955-58, 125 lots), and Halpine Village (platted 1955-56 and 1960-61, 110 lots).

2. See, for example, Federal Housing Administration, *Successful Subdivisions*, Land Planning Bulletin No. 1 (Washington: U.S. Government Printing Office, 1940).

3. Marc A. Weiss, *The Rise of the Community Builders* (New York: Columbia University Press, 1987). For a period account, see "Yesterday's Small Home Builder Is Today's Community Developer," *HBM* 8 (Aug. 1951): 19-20. The number of dwellings erected in Twinbrook is based on counting lots in the subdivision plats filed by Geeraert and his partners. Period estimates of the extent of this work run substantially higher—from 2,200 to 2,500—and may be derived from the builder's interest in dramatizing his achievement.

4. Gwendolyn Wright, *Building the Dream: A Social History of Housing in America* (Cambridge, Mass.: MIT Press, 1981), chapter 13; Kenneth T. Jackson, *Crabgrass Frontier: The Suburbanization of the United States* (New York: Oxford University Press, 1985), chapter 13; Clifford Edward Clark Jr., *The American Family Home, 1800-1960* (Chapel Hill: University of North Carolina Press, 1986), chapters 7, 8; Rosalyn Baxandall and Elizabeth Ewen, *Picture Windows: How the Suburbs Happened* (New York: Basic Books, 2000); Robert A. Beauregard, *When America Became Suburban* (Minneapolis: University of Minnesota Press, 2006), chapters 5-6.

5. If the subdivision plats give any indication, Geeraert appears to have been responsible for the great majority of houses (1,350). One partner, Donald Gingerly, built 145 houses; another, Wesley Sauter, built 21.

6. These are also now the subject of detailed case studies; see Barbara M. Kelly, *Expanding the American Dream: Building and Rebuilding Levittown* (Albany: State University of New York Press, 1993); Greg Hise, *Magnetic Los Angeles: Planning the Twentieth-Century Metropolis* (Baltimore: Johns Hopkins University Press, 1997); Allison Leslie Baker, "The Lakewood Story: Defending the Residential Good Life in Postwar Southern California Suburbia, 1950-1999" (Ph.D. dissertation, University of Pennsylvania, 1999); Gregory C. Randall, *America's Original GI Town: Park Forest, Illinois* (Baltimore: Johns Hopkins University Press, 2000); Allison Baker et al., *The Lakewood Story: History, Tradition, Values* (Lakewood, Calif.: City of Lakewood, 2004); Chad M. Kimmel, "Levittown: Pennsylvania: A Sociological History" (Ph.D. dissertation, Western Michigan University, 2004); and *Second Suburb: Levittown, Pennsylvania*, ed. Dianne Harris (Pittsburgh: University of Pittsburgh Press, 2010). Among scholarly studies of popular housing forms of the postwar period, James A. Jacobs, "'You Can't Dream Yourself a House': The Evolving Postwar Dwelling and Its Preeminent Position within a Renewed Consumer World, 1940-1970" (Ph.D. dissertation, George Washington University, 2005), stands apart in its focus on the changing nature of domestic space and its relation to consumerism of the period.

7. "600-Home City Set for Maryland," *WP*, 21 Sep. 1947, R1; "Viers Mills Road to Get Many New Homes," *MCS*, 25 Sep. 1947, 1. Maps published in the *Washington Post* charting subdivisions with houses for sale provide a useful indication of the geography of residential growth in the metropolitan area. See, for example, "How to Reach the 'Homes of '49,'" 11 Sep. 1949, F3; and "Here Is Location Map," 9 Sep. 1951, F3. See also *HBM* 10 (Oct. 1953): 11–49. Such concern for developing a "complete" place appears to have been rare in the metropolitan area at that time, and not until the 1960s did the situation begin to change; see "Total Planned Community Finding More Acceptance," *WP*, 28 July 1962, D1, D-19.

8. "Airport Opening Spotlights Chandon," *WP*, 17 Nov. 1962, B1, B7.

9. The farm was purchased 18 October 1946, the same day the partnership was incorporated; see Gladys L. Cross, "This Is Twinbrook," *TL* 2 (27 Jan. 1955): 7; and "Twinbrook Plans," *WP*, 14 Aug. 1949, R3. Cross's piece was reprinted from two installments in the *MCS*: "It Wouldn't Admit to Selling or Dividing," 19 Aug. 1954, C1; and "200-Acre Home for 1,000 Families," 26 Aug. 1954, C1.

10. This may have been the Ballantine Three-Ring Inn, illustrated in Larry Zim et al., *The World of Tomorrow: The 1939 New York World's Fair* (New York: Harper & Row, 1988), 174. Whatever the nature of Geeraert's involvement, it was probably as part of the construction team. For the information on Geeraert's career I have relied on the recollections of his younger daughter, Dorothy Patterson: interview, Rockville, Maryland, 3 Nov. 2011, and correspondence, 2 Apr. 2012; and Gladys L. Cross, "The Spotlight," *TL* 2 (15 Mar. 1955): 5.

11. Patterson interview; Cross, "The Spotlight." The original plat was made by Traver in October 1940. A portion was re-platted in January 1942 in association with Geeraert. Three months later, Geeraert filed a new plat consisting of fifteen additional lots. Aside from his name appearing on the plat maps, I have yet to find any information regarding Traver.

12. Patterson interview; Cross, "The Spotlight"; "Geeraert Real Sportsman," *WP*, 15 July 1953, 14. Concerning Coquelin Terrace, see "Home Building Boom," *WP*, 12 Oct. 1947, R1; "Car Port, Storage 'Heaven,'" *WP*, 18 July 1948, R1; "That Sleek '49 Car," *WP*, 8 May 1949, F5; and advertisements, *WP*, 26 Sep. 1948, R17, and 3 Oct. 1948, R5. The development was also called Rock Creek Knolls. It contains twenty-eight lots on Coquelin Terrace and the tangent east side of Jones Mill Road; however, five of those lots contain one-story houses that appear to be of later vintage.

13. "Low Cost Homes," *WP*, 28 Aug. 1949, R4, R11. See also "Housing Check Shows," *WP*, 23 Jan. 1949, R1;

"New Housing Projects," *WP*, 26 Mar. 1950, R1, R3; and "Camera Covers," *WP*, 26 Feb. 1950, R1, R6.

14. "Low Cost Homes"; "Montgomery Home Project," *WP*, 5 Jan. 1949, B3; "County Heads Rezone Land," *MCS*, 6 Jan. 1949, 1; advertisements, *WP*, 29 June 1947, R4; 14 Aug. 1947, R3; 11 Sep. 1949, R7; and 29 Jan. 1950, R8.

15. Concerning Gregory Estates, see "Work Starts Soon," *WP*, 1 Sep. 1949, 15; and advertisement, *WP*, 2 Oct. 1949, R15. Concerning Glenmont Village, see "New Housing Projects," R1. Concerning Viers Mill Village, see "A Preview of Viers Mill Village," *MCS*, 11 Dec. 1947, 1; "Weather's a Nuisance," *WP*, 25 Jan. 1948, C4, C6; advertisement, *WP*, 8 Feb. 1948, R5; "Probe Sought," *WP*, 2 Mar. 1948, B2; "FHA Appraisal," *WP*, 7 Mar. 1948, R1, R2; "Viers Mill Village," *WP*, 7 Apr. 1948, 1, 7; "Viers Mill Homes," *WP*, 19 June 1948, B1; and advertisements, *Evening Star* [Washington], 7 Aug. 1948, B6, and *WP*, 28 Aug. 1949, R12. Not all the 1,400 projected units were built. Platted lots number 936, and a site visit suggests substantially fewer houses were realized. No matter how disparaged at the time, Viers Mill Village remains intact and provides an important enclave of affordable housing, now occupied primarily by recent immigrants, in an affluent county.

The correct spelling of the millwright after whom the road was named is "Veirs." During the mid-twentieth century it was misspelled "Viers" for the road and places along it such as Viers Mill Village.

16. Cross, "This Is Twinbrook," 7. She notes (p. 9) that by 1955 Simons and Sauter had retired. Concerning the latter, see "Wesley Sauter," *WP*, 24 June 1959, B2. Concerning Gingery, see Cross, "The Spotlight"; "Meeting Set," *WP*, 10 Jan. 1948, B5; "Don Gingery Saves," *HBM* 5 (Feb. 1948): 25–26; "Builders Charge High," *WP*, 13 Mar. 1949, B1; "Lane Appoints Browning," *WP*, 12 May 1949, B1; "Montgomery Group Formed," *WP*, 24 Feb. 1950, 18; "Montgomery County Builders," *HBM* 7 (Mar. 1950): 20, 47; "Cost-Cutting Building Code," *WP*, 29 Apr. 1951, R1, R3; "Interest in Planning," *WP*, 17 May 1957, B1; and "Gingery Leads," *WP*, 1 June 1960, B2. Founded in 1891, the Breuninger firm was responsible for many of the high-end residential developments in Shepherd Park and other portions of the upper Sixteenth Street corridor in Washington.

17. Cross, "This Is Twinbrook," 9. For samples of Gingery's advertisements, see *WP*, 9 Mar. 1952, R7; 18 May 1952, R7; and 17 May 1953, R1.

18. Early ventures were developed on a small scale; see "Silver Spring Units," *WP*, 22 Jan. 1950, R6; "20 Silver Spring Dwellings," *WP*, 5 Nov. 1950, R2; "14 Silver Spring Apartment Houses," *WP*, 26 Nov. 1950, R3; "15 Houses Okayed," *WP*, 15 Apr. 1951, R2. By mid-decade, Gingery was undertaking larger tracts, including

Hungerford Towne (begun 1954) in Rockville and Kingswell (begun 1958) and Wheaton Woods (begun 1959) in Wheaton. The early Hungerford Towne houses drew considerable inspiration from Geeraert's work, to the point that they are often thought to be by the same designer.

19. An earlier plat with forty-three lots, surveyed in December 1946, was re-platted in March 1947 with eighty lots.

20. Several miles to the east, Kay Construction Company's three contiguous developments, Connecticut Avenue Estates, Kenwood, and Wheaton Hills, totaled over 1,400 houses by November 1954 (see *HBM* 11 [Nov. 1954]: 38). An average of 88 houses were erected in the original Twinbrook each year, placing its builders near the top of what was locally considered a "medium"-sized operation (25 to 99 houses per year). See Christopher T. Martin, "Tract-House Modern: A Study of Housing Design and Consumption in the Washington Suburbs, 1946–1960" (Ph.D. dissertation, George Washington University, 2000), 67.

21. All these purchases were made of land owned by the Silver Spring–based Bullis School, which had acquired the site in 1949 for a new campus that never materialized. The first was purchased from Broadwood Manor Housing Corporation, which had developed a small tract (61 lots) adjacent. The two subsequent purchases were from the school. See "Settlement Near," *WP*, 21 May 1949, B2; and Cross, "This Is Twinbrook," 9.

22. "Rockville Plans," *MCS*, 17 Feb. 1949, 1, 8; "Bill for Expansion," *WP*, 18 Feb. 1949, 18; "Twinbrook Will Be Included," *MCS*, 24 Feb. 1949, 1, 8.

23. "Rockville Appoints Five," *WP*, 12 Jan. 1955, 29; "Rockville to Get," *MCS*, 21 Apr. 1955, 1, 4; "Annexation Fight," *TL* 2 (Nov. 1955), 2, 8; "Annexation Bid," *WP*, 14 Dec. 1955, 41; "TCA Review," *TL* 2 (Dec. 1955): 3; "Geeraert Asks," *MCS*, 16 Feb. 1956, A1; "City Agrees," *MCS*, 1 Mar. 1956, 1, 6; "City Near Annexation," *MCS*, 5 Apr. 1956, A1, A5; "Twinbrook Park Still Outside," *MCS*, 12 Apr. 1956, A1, A6; "Twinbrook Park Tract," *MCS*, 19 Apr. 1956, A1, A6.

24. "Viers Mill Road Section," *WP*, 15 Oct. 1948, B2.

25. These models were advertised as "expandable homes"; see *Evening Star*, 31 July 1948, B4; *WP*, 15 Aug. 1948, R9, and 22 Aug. 1948, R2. That the practice was widespread is suggested in "Converting Attics into Bedrooms," *American Builder* 73 (Apr. 1951): 172–74.

26. "Twinbrook Plans"; "Easier, Cheaper," *WP*, 18 Dec. 1949, R1.

27. "Easier, Cheaper," notes that members of Twin-Brook, Inc., "made a detailed study of the Levitt development, later incorporating some of what they saw into model homes at Twinbrook." Geeraert's daughter

confirmed that he frequently mentioned Levittown during the period (Patterson interview). For comparisons, see "Levitt's New Home Models Accelerate Sales," *American Builder* 71 (Mar. 1949): 78–81; and "4,000 Houses Per Year," *Architectural Forum* 90 (Apr. 1949): 84–93.

28. Plans for several of Geeraert's models survive in the archives of Peerless Rockville Historic Preservation. Many of these are signed by him as "designer"; others also list John Samperton as architect, but the sequence suggests Geeraert was behind the conceptions. His daughter confirmed that the designs were essentially his, Samperton assisting only to a limited degree (Patterson interview).

29. "Camera Tour," *WP*, 19 Feb. 1950, R1; "More 'Homes of '51,'" *WP*, 29 July 1951, R1, R2; advertisement, *WP*, 9 Sep. 1951, F26; "Twin-Brook Homes," *HBM* 8 (Sep. 1951): 33–34; "Builders Hasten," *WP*, 2 Mar. 1952, R1; "New Section of Twinbrook," *WP*, 30 Mar. 1952, R13; *WP*, 28 Sep. 1952, R15; "Homes for a Lifetime," *HBM* 9 (Sep. 1952): 12; *WP*, 12 Apr. 1953, R11.

30. "Prospective Buyer," *WP*, 30 Aug. 1953, R1. See also *WP*, 13 Sep. 1953, H28; *HBM* 10 (Oct. 1953): 7; advertisement, *WP*, 27 June 1954, R13; "Twin-Brook Offers," *WP*, 12 Sep. 1954, H19.

31. "Geeraert Plans," *TL* 2 (26 Apr. 1955): 1; "A New Twin Brook," *HBM* 13 (Feb. 1956): 48; "Twinbrook Park Opening Up," *TL* 3 (May 1956): 2; advertisement, *WP*, 30 June 1956, 41; "The Meadow Hall," *WP*, 30 June 1956, 42; *WP*, 8 Sep. 1956, H34; *WP*, 22 June 1957, C6; "Twinbrook Park," *WP*, 7 Sep. 1957, E23; *WP*, 27 Sep. 1958, C1; "El Rancho Sells," *WP*, 4 Oct. 1958, C1; *WP*, 12 Sep. 1959, B11. Known costs ranged from $16,762 ("Anniversary" in 1957) to $17,750 ("Meadow Hall" in 1956). The "St. Regis" may have been cheaper, and only a few were built.

32. Martin, "Tract-House Modern," 84. For period discussion of national trends, see Gilbert Burck and Sanford S. Parker, "The Changing Market for Housing," *House & Home* 5 (Mar. 1954): 130–33, 193, 198; and "What Do People Want?" *House & Home* 5 (May 1954): 123–37.

33. "Twinbrook Exhibit," *WP*, 26 Sep. 1954, R4; "'Anniversary Home' Unveiled," *WP*, 10 Oct. 1954, R2; "Everyone's Ready," *WP*, 12 Dec. 1954, R7; advertisement, *WP*, 12 Dec. 1954, R9; "A Fireplace Fit," *WP*, 19 Dec. 1954, G2; advertisement, *WP*, 26 Dec. 1954, G3; "Twinbrook Homes," *WP*, 12 June 1955, G4; "Imaginative Promotion Pays," *HBM* 12 (Nov. 1955): 15–16; *HBM* 14 (June 1955): 44; "A Portrait of 'Mr. G,'" *HBM* 17 (July 1960): 18, 42.

34. "10c Shoppers' Bus," *MCS*, 2 Sep. 1954, A1, A4; "Shoppers' Bus Praised," *MCS*, 9 Sep. 1954, B4.

35. "Shopping Center Considered," *TL* 2 (25 Feb. 1955):

1; "Twinbrook Enjoys," *MCS*, 17 Nov. 1955, A4; "People's Drug Opens," *MCS*, 21 Feb. 1957; advertisement, *TL* 4 (Feb. 1957): 10. Concerning the post office, see "Bidding Asked," *MCS*, 16 Aug. 1956, 1; "Twinbrook PO," *MCS*, 3 Jan. 1957; and "Twinbrook P.O.," *MCS*, 21 Nov. 1957, A1. When completed, the complex also contained a barber shop, a beauty shop, a laundry, a clothing store, a Montgomery Ward catalogue store, a gas station, and a dance studio.

36. "$3 Million Twinbrook Center," *WP*, 15 May 1955, G2; "Geeraert Announces," *MCS*, 26 May 1955, A8; "Geeraert Appoints," *WP*, 14 Aug. 1955, G3; "Fourteen Set," *MCS*, 10 May 1956, A6; "Contractors Rush," *MCS*, 26 Sep. 1957, B3; "Twinbrook Opening," *MCS*, 28 Nov. 1957, A1, A-5; advertisement, *WP*, 30 Nov. 1957, B12; "Christmas Unofficial," *MCS*, 5 Dec. 1957, B3; "$4,000,000 Twin-Brook Shopping Center," *HBM* 14 (Dec. 1957): 15. Besides a host of entertainers at the opening, spectators were treated to remarks by Geeraert's former neighbor, Senator Hubert Humphrey.

Other businesses included a clothing shop, dry cleaners, a bank branch, a children's clothing store, a gift shop, a dairy products outlet, a jewelry store, a hardware store, a shoe store, a music and arts store, a sports and hobby center, a barber shop, a beauty shop, a bakery, a television store, a restaurant, a bowling alley, and a service station.

37. "Business Is Booming," *MCS*, 26 Mar. 1959, A1; "Geeraert Sells," *TL* 10 (Jan. 1963): 4. Figures on Maryland shopping centers taken from *Directory of Shopping Centers in the United States and Canada* (Chicago: National Research Bureau, 1962), 177–86. Concerning Congressional Shopping Plaza, see "2 More Area Stores," *WP*, 13 Oct. 1955, 32; "New Rockville Shop Center," *WP*, 1 May 1958, C14; "Opening Ceremonies," *WP*, 12 Mar. 1959, B4; "Sparkling New Plaza" and "Penney's Design," *MCS*, 12 Mar. 1959, B6, B10, respectively; and advertisement, *MCS*, 12 Mar. 1959, B16. Concerning Wheaton Plaza, see "Woodward & Lothrop Plan," *WP*, 27 Mar. 1958, B8; "Wheaton Plaza," *WP*, 30 Nov. 1958, A22; "First Section," *WP*, 29 Jan. 1960, C6; and *Evening Star*, 30 Mar. 1960, section H. In 1962 a large discount center opened on Rockville Pike south of Congressional Plaza; see "Giant Discount Store," *MCS*, 1 Nov. 1962, A1, B4. Concerning changes in family shopping habits, see Lizabeth Cohen, *A Consumer's Republic: The Politics of Mass Consumption in Postwar America* (New York: Alfred A. Knopf, 2003), 267–70; and Richard Longstreth, *The American Department Store Transformed, 1920–1960* (New Haven: Yale University Press, 2010), 139–40, 197–98.

38. "Twinbrook Baptist Chapel," *MCS*, 1 Mar. 1956, A2; "New Church," *TL* 3 (Mar. 1956): [5]; "Baptists Buy," *MCS*, 10 Jan. 1957, A2; "New Church Slated," *WP*, 11 July 1959, D6; "Church Lays Cornerstone," *TL* 9 (June 1962): [7]; "St. Andrews Proudly Dedicates," *MCS*, 20 Sep. 1962, B9.

39. "School Budgets," *MCS*, 13 Mar. 1947, 1; "School Needs," *MCS*, 6 Jan. 1949, 1; "School Census," *MCS*, 10 Feb. 1949, 1; "Montgomery Faces," *WP*, 11 Sep. 1949, L4; "Swift Growth," *WP*, 11 Dec. 1949, B1, B3; "Upper County," *MCS*, 16 Mar. 1950, 1; "Montgomery 5-Year Plan," *WP*, 12 Mar. 1950, B1; "County Council," *MCS*, 15 June 1950, 1; "Most County Schools," *MCS*, 14 Sep. 1950, 1; "County Sees," *WP*, 13 Mar. 1955, B1; "County Asks $9 Million for Schools," *WP*, 31 Mar. 1955, 37.

40. "Twin Brook," *MCS*, 22 May 1952, 7; "Twin Brook," *MCS*, 9 Oct. 1952, 8; "Twin Brook PTA," *MCS*, 8 Jan. 1953, 6; "Twin Brook," *MCS*, 18 June 1953, 3; "Crowding in Schools," *MCS*, 10 Sep. 1953, 1; "A Day at Twinbrook," *MCS*, 22 Oct. 1953, 1, 2; "Twin Brook," *MCS*, 19 Nov. 1953, 8; "Twinbrook," *MCS*, 3 June 1954, B4; "Twinbrook," *MCS*, 17 June 1954, A4; "Record Breaking 800," *TL* 1 (15 Sep. 1954): 3; "Norris Promises," *MCS*, 13 Jan. 1955, A5; "Twinbrook Says Future," *MCS*, 12 May 1955, A8; "County Plan," *WP*, 16 May 1955, 21; "Double-Time Plan," *MCS*, 4 Aug. 1955, A8; "Half-Day Schooling," *MCS*, 8 Sep. 1955, A1, A4; "School-Community Ties," *MCS*, 28 Nov. 1957, B7; "Twinbrook Addition," *MCS*, 2 July 1958, A1; "Twinbrook Addition," *MCS*, 23 Oct. 1958, B7; "Schools Hard Put," *MCS*, 12 Mar. 1959, B7; "Half-Day Classes," *MCS*, 3 Sep. 1959, 1; "Big Elementary Schools," *WP*, 15 Jan. 1961, B1; "Twinbrook Elementary School," *TL* 10 (Nov. 1963): 4.

41. "A Day at Twinbrook"; "Twinbrook," *MCS*, 16 Sep. 1954, C4; "Twinbrook's Science Fair," *MCS*, 3 Feb. 1955, A8; "Twinbrook Teachers," *MCS*, 16 June 1955, A8; "Blazing School," *MCS*, 27 Oct. 1955, A6; "Twinbrook Elementary," *MCS*, 19 Apr. 1956, A2; "Scholars Benefit," *WP*, 20 Oct. 1956, D2; "School-Community Ties"; "Smaller Schools," *WP*, 10 Aug. 1960, B4.

42. "Twinbrook," *MCS*, 27 May 1954, A5; "Area Schools," *MCS*, 2 June 1955, A1; "County School Addition," *WP*, 14 Sep. 1955, 24; "Montgomery School," *WP*, 4 Oct. 1955, 18; "Board Action," *MCS*, 20 Oct. 1955, A1; "School Board," *MCS*, 27 Oct. 1955, A4; "PTA Takes," *TL* 3 (Mar. 1956): 1, 8; "Board Awards," *WP*, 31 July 1956, 14; "240 Children," *TL* 4 (Apr. 1957): 5; "Community Now Cloaked," *MCS*, 12 Sep. 1957, B4; "Meadow Hall," *TL* 10 (Oct. 1963): 2; "Edwin Broom," *TL* 11 (Jan. 1964): 2; Justin Kockritz, "Carl Sandburg Elementary School," *Peerless Rockville* 27 (Sep. 2008): (3).

43. The *Montgomery County Sentinel* focused on its home base of Rockville, and from an early date had a Twinbrook column, chronicling local activities, in each of its weekly issues. Begun in 1954, the Twinbrook Community Association's publication, *Twinbrook Life*, was issued as often as ten times annually.

It provides not only a wealth of information about its sponsoring group, but also about the community in general. While copies of this periodical are almost impossible to find, a longtime resident, John Tyner, has amassed a collection of issues over a period of many years, and kindly shared them and other scarce materials with me.

44. Harry Henderson, "The Mass-Produced Suburbs," *Harper's Magazine* 207 (Nov. 1953): 25–32; (Dec. 1953): 80–86 (quotes on pp. 26, 29, 31–32, and 80); Doris Neumann, "Suburbia," *TL* 1 (15 Oct. 1954)" 2, 7. See also Betty Hannah Hoffman, "The Big Move," *Ladies Home Journal* 70 (Mar. 1953): 151–54, 164–65, 167. The best-known period study of this genre is Herbert J. Gans, *The Levittowners: Ways of Life and Politics in a New Suburban Community* (New York: Vintage Books, 1967). See also Sylvia Fleis Fava, "Suburbanism as a Way of Life," *American Sociological Review* 21 (Feb. 1956): 34–37. Alan Ehrenhalt, *The Lost City: Discovering the Forgotten Virtues of Community in the Chicago of the 1950s* (New York: Basic Books, 1995), part 4, is a pioneering study in this sphere. Other valuable case studies are found in Baker, "The Lakewood Story," and Kimmel, "Levittown," chapter 4. See also Mark Clapson, *Suburban Century: Social Change and Urban Growth in England and the United States* (Oxford: Berg, 2003), chapter 7.

45. "Sixth Graders Conduct," *MCS*, 21 Nov. 1957, B6.

46. "Rockville Citizens Watch," *Evening Star*, 5 June 1955, A22; "Sixth Graders Conduct."

47. "TCA Officers," *TL* 1 (15 Oct. 1954): 3; Gladys Cross, "The Spotlight," *TL* 2 (25 Feb. 1955): 5, *TL* 2 (25 May 1955): 6, and *TL* 5 (29 June 1955): 5; "Candidates for TCA's Executive Committee," *TL* 2 (Oct. 1955): 2; 3 (Oct. 1956): 2; "The Bert Sherman Story," *TL* 4 (Feb. 1957): 3, 8; "Neighbors Behind," *TL* 4 (May 1957): 3; "Three Candidates Vie," *TL* 5 (Oct. 1958): 1, 5.

48. "Rockville Forms," *WP*, 5 Feb. 1954, 23; "Rockville Citizens Watch"; "City Heads," *WP*, 16 May 1954, M20; "Proud of Its Part," *MCS*, 20 Jan. 1955, A8; "Rockville Honored," *WP*, 2 Feb. 1955, 24. See also "Twinbrook," *MCS*, 18 Mar. 1954, B6; editorial, *TL* 2 (Nov. 1955): 3. For a historical overview, see Eileen S. McGuckian, *Rockville: Portrait of a City* (Franklin, Tenn.: Hillsboro Press, 2001), 137–40. See also McGuckian, interview with Dickran Hovsepian, 2 Aug. 1984, typescript, Peerless Rockville archives. To a degree, the matter of identity was an ongoing issue; see "We're All Rockvillians," *TL* 10 (Nov. 1963): 3. A somewhat similar transfer of political power happened in Pennsylvania under the initiative of the Levittown Civic Association; see Craig Thompson, "Growing Pains of a Brand-New City," *Saturday Evening Post* 220 (7 Aug. 1954): 26–27, 71–72.

49. "Twinbrook," *MCS*, 1 July 1954; "Beautification

About to Become a Reality," *TL* 1 (15 Oct. 1954): 2, 7; "Operation School Beautification," *TL* 1 (25 Nov. 1954): 3.

50. "Twinbrook Fights," *MCS*, 20 Mar. 1958, A1; "Library Committee," *TL* 5 (Mar. 1958): 8; "Library Committee," *TL* 5 (Apr. 1958): 8; "Twinbrook to Get," *MCS*, 23 Dec. 1958, A1; "New Twinbrook Library," *TL* 6 (Feb. 1959): 1, 5; "Library Will Open," *TL* 6 (Apr. 1959): 1; "Library Going," *TL* 7 (May 1961): 2.

51. Useful synopses of the group's efforts can be found in "History of the Twin-Brook Citizens Association," *Twin-Brook Community Guide* (Rockville: By the association, 1954), 5–6, Tyner collection; "TCA Completes Year of Growth," *TL* 1 (25 Nov, 1954): 1, 2; "A Year's Work Ahead," *TL* 2 (Nov. 1955): 6; "Twinbrook Community," *MCS*, 21 Nov. 1957, B6; and "The Twinbrook Citizens' Association, Inc.," *Twinbrook Area Community Guide* (Rockville: By the association, 1958), 10–18, Tyner collection.

52. "TCA in 15 Area Plan," *TL* 4 (Apr. 1957): 1, 6; "Introducing Your Block Organization," *TL* 5 (May 1958): 6, 7, 8; "The Twinbrook Citizens' Association, Inc.," 10–11. Committees in 1949 included programs and entertainment, playgrounds and health, civic representation, local governance, and beautification and decoration. In 1954 they included recreation, traffic and streets, beautification, telephone, directory, nominating, and block organization. See "Twin Brook News," *MCS*, 27 Oct. 1949, 2; and "Working Together: Annual Report of the Twinbrook Citizens Association, 1953–1954," typescript, Tyner collection.

53. "Community Newspaper Debuts," *MCS*, 23 Nov. 1954, B4. The *Community Guide* was a joint venture with the Twinbrook PTA and Homemakers Club; see "Twin Brook," *MCS*, 26 Mar. 1953, 9.

54. "Rockville Civic Association," *MCS*, 21 Aug. 1947, 7; "Town Recreation Survey," *MCS*, 4 Dec. 1947, 1; "Recreation Bd. Scheduled," *MCS*, 27 Jan. 1949, 1; "Twin Brook News," *MCS*: 16 Mar. 1950, 6; 13 July 1950, 4; 22 Feb. 1951, 2; 19 July 1951, 3; 16 Aug. 1951, 2; 19 July 1952, 11; 11 Sep. 1952, 2; 9 July 1953, 2; 20 Aug. 1953, 4.

55. "Twinbrook Parents," *MCS*, 25 Feb. 1954, A2; "Summer Programs," *TL* 2 (25 May 1955): 2; "A Full Summer Program," *TL* 3 (June 1956): 1–2; "Miller Is for Togetherness," *TL* 4 (Jan. 1957): 1; "Latest Developments," *TL* 6 (Oct. 1953): 5; "Development of Recreation Areas," *City of Rockville Newsletter* 7 (Aug. 1963): npp.

56. "Swimming Pool Referendum," *TL* 1 (15 Oct. 1954): 1; "Twinbrook Weighs," *MCS*, 24 Feb. 1955, A5; "TCA Kicks Off," *TL* 2 (25 Feb. 1955): 1; "Let's Swim," *TL* 2 (18 Mar. 1955): 1–2; "Twinbrook Reveals," *MCS*, 19 May 1955, A8; "We Proudly Present," *TL* 2 (18 May 1955): 1–2; "Enthusiastic Twinbrook Response," *MCS*, 26 May 1955, A8; "Dedicate Twinbrook's 'Dream Pool,'"

MCS, 21 June 1955, A1; "Area's Biggest Pool," *TL* 2 (29 June 1955): 1–2; "Work on Pool," *MCS*, 7 July 1955, B8; "Twinbrook Pool Has Troubles," *MCS*, 11 Aug. 1955, B6; "Twinbrook Pool," *MCS*, 1 Sep. 1955, A5; "Community 'Do It Yourself' Pool Completed," *TL* 2 (14 Sep. 1955): 1. Membership was opened to residents of Twinbrook, Rockcrest, Rockland, Silver Rock, and Broadmoor.

57. "Rains Bring Collapse," *MCS*, 20 Oct. 1955, A2; "Twinbrook's Pool," *MCS*, 3 Nov. 1955, A6; "New Swimming Pool," *TL* 2 (Dec. 1955): 1; "Twinbrook Pool," *MCS*, 19 Jan. 1956, A3; "Operation Bootstrap," *TL* 3 (Jan. 1956): 1, 10; "Spring Brings," *MCS*, 5 Apr. 1956, A2; "Things Brighten," *TL* 3 (April 1956): 1; "Twinbrook Pool," *MCS*, 26 July 1956, A2; "Twinbrook Pool," *MCS*, 2 Aug. 1956, A2; "Twinbrook, with No Pool Permit," *MCS*, 9 Aug. 1956, A1, A4; "Twinbrook Pool," *MCS*, 16 Aug. 1956, A2; "Twinbrook Pool Opens," *TL* 4 (Feb. 1957): 3.

58. "Twinbrook," *MCS*, 29 Nov. 1956, B4; "New Swimming Pool," *TL* 4 (Jan. 1957): 4, "Twinbrook," *MCS*, 18 Apr. 1957, B2; "Park-Forest Memberships Grow," *TL* 4 (Apr. 1957): 7; "Twinbrook Will Be," *MCS*, 13 June 1957, A2; "New Pool Symbolizes," *MCS*, 22 Aug. 1957, B5.

59. Much of this information was gleaned from the weekly *MCS* "Twin Brook" column; see, for example: 23 Oct. 1952, 8; 6 May 1954, 4. See also "Twin Brook Club," *MCS*, 25 Sep. 1952, 1; "Twinbrook Attic Tour," *MCS*, 4 June 1953, 1; and "Sidewalk Construction," *MCS*, 11 Feb. 1954, B6.

60. See, for example, columns in *TL*: "How It's Done," 1 (25 Dec. 1954): 4 and 2 (18 May 1955): 5; "Have Fun with Your Basement," 1 (25 Nov. 1954: 5 and (25 Dec. 1954): 3; "Design for Living," 2 (25 Feb. 1955): 4 and (25 Apr. 1955): 4; "Design for Outdoor Living," *TL* 2 (25 May 1955): 4 and (29 June 1955): 9; "Have Fun with Your Attic," *TL* 2 (29 June 1955): 7; "Twinbrook Decorator Awards," *TL* 4 (Jan. 1957): 6; and "How to Grow a Good Lawn," *TL* 4 (May 1957): 6.

61. Among the many notices in the *MCS* "Twin Brook" column, see 19 Mar. 1953; 7 May 1953, 3; 29 Oct. 1953, B8; 15 Apr. 1954, B3; and 22 Apr. 1954, B6. See also "General Assembly Visit," *MCS*, 4 Mar. 1954, A2; "Twinbrook Twirlers," *MCS*, 29 Apr. 1954, A6; "Twinbrook Child Study," *MCS*, 10 Feb. 1955, A5; "Twinbrook Youngsters," *MCS*, 3 Mar. 1955, A6; "Litz Is New Cubmaster," *MCS*, 1 Mar. 1956, A6; and "Twinbrook Twirlers," *MCS*, 21 May 1956, A3.

62. For a sampling of accounts, see "Twin Brook PTA," *MCS*, 2 Oct. 1952, 1; "Twin Brook," *MCS*, 16 Oct. 1952, A8; "Twin Brook Bazaar," *MCS*, 18 Dec. 1952, 1; "Twinbrook P-TA Meeting," *MCS*, 5 Oct. 1953, 1; "Twin Brook," *MCS*, 10 Dec. 1953, B6; "Twinbrook," *MCS*, 20 May 1954, A2; "Twinbrook Fair," *MCS*, 5 May 1955, A8, "Twinbrook PTA," *MCS*, 11 Oct. 1956, A3; and "PTA News Items," *TL* 5 (Mar. 1958): 5. Concerning deseg-

regation, see "Integration: Tolerance or Intolerance," *TL* 2 (25 Feb. 1955): 3; "Looking Forward," *TL* 2 (15 Mar. 1955): 6; "Segregation to End," *MCS*, 22 Jan. 1959, C5; and "Teacher Integration," *MCS*, 1 July 1959, A1. I have yet to ascertain the date that Twinbrook began to assume the racial diversity it now possesses.

63. For discussion, see Richard Longstreth, "The Levitts, Mass-Produced Houses, and Community Planning in the Mid-Twentieth Century," in *Second Suburb*, ed. Harris, 151–53, 155–56, 161–63.

64. "Twin Brook," *MCS*, 19 June 1952, 11; 9 July 1953, 2; 29 Oct. 1953, B8; "Twinbrook Parents"; Cross, "The Spotlight"; "Twinbrook Pool Has Troubles"; "The Letter Box," *MCS*, 22 Dec. 1955, A2; "Twinbrook Grows," *HBM* 13 (Feb. 1956): 26; "Teen-age Haven," *WP*, 9 Feb. 1957, C6; "New Swimming Pool" (Dec. 1955); "Park-Forest Pool," *HBM* 14 (Aug. 1957): 14.

65. "Builder Geeraert Reviews," *MCS*, 14 Feb. 1957, A4.

66. "Builders Elect," *WP*, 17 Nov. 1956, B2; "Distinguished Members," *HBM* 13 (Dec. 1956): A5; "Geeraert Heads," *WP*, 12 Jan. 1957, D5; "Md. Builder Group," *WP*, 30 Nov. 1957, B1; "Treatment Center," *WP*, 17 May 1959, C7.

67. *HBM* 14 (Apr. 1957): 14; "HBA Gets Strong Leadership," *HBM* 16 (Jan. 1959): 5; "Regional Veep," *WP*, 18 Feb. 1961, B6; "NAHB Names Two to Posts," *WP*, 4 May 1963, B8.

68. "Lack of Financing," *WP*, 12 Jan. 1957, D1; "Competition Spurs Maryland Builders," *WP*, 18 May 1957, C1, C6; Joseph L. Geeraert, "Land Scaping: The Builder's View," letter to the editor, *WP*, 22 May 1957, A12; "Builders Look to Plans," *WP*, 8 June 1957, C1, C3; Geeraert, "Home Values Listed," *WP*, 10 May 1958, C1, C2; Geeraert, "The Builders Story," *HBM* 17 (June 1960): 10, 37; Geeraert, "Growth in Value," *WP*, 10 Sep. 1960, B2; "Home Builders Can Still Smile," *WP*, 22 Oct. 1960, B1; Geeraert, "N.A.H.B.'s Accomplishments," *HBM* 17 (Oct. 1960): 10.

69. "Apartment at Rockville," *WP*, 31 July 1957, B2; "Meadows [sic] Hall Rezoning," *WP*, 25 Sep. 1957, B2; "Geeraert Renews," *MCS*, 26 Sep. 1957, A1; "Pros and Cons Listed," *MCS*, 10 Oct. 1957, C4; "Rockville Defers," *WP*, 30 Oct. 1957, B2; "Big Apartment Job," *MCS*, 31 Oct. 1957, A1, A6; "Twinbrook Residents," *MCS*, 28 Nov. 1957, A6; "Rezoning Plea Denied," *WP*, 8 Jan. 1958, B10. Opposition to such proposals was by no means uncommon in the county; see, for example, "Apartment Plans Banned," *WP*, 13 July 1948, B1.

70. "Rockville Apartment Plan," *WP*, 16 Dec. 1959, D7; "Geeraert Apartment Plan," *MCS*, 17 Dec. 1959, A1, A6; "T.C.A. Says 'No'" and "TCA Review," *TL* 10 (Jan. 1963): 1, 3, respectively; "Bullis Rezoning Decision," *TL* 10 (March 1963): 1.

71. Joe Geeraert, "Quote and Misquote," *MCS*, 13 Feb. 1958, A8; "Airport Opening Spotlights," B2; "Choice of Townhouses," *WP*, 15 July 1967, C1, C14.

72. "Chandon Expected," *WP*, 25 June 1960, B15; "Geeraert's Whirlwind Promotion," *HBM* 17 (July 1960): 16–17; "Builder Ready," *WP*, 6 Aug. 1960, B1, B12; "Airport Opening Spotlights"; "Herndon Mayor Works," *WP*, 2 Feb. 1963, D4; advertisement, *WP*, 29 May 1965, D7; "Space the Key," *WP*, 2 Oct. 1965, E6; Patterson interview.

73. "Broyhill Firm Getting Ready," *WP*, 21 Apr. 1962, D1, D3; "Broyhills Offer School Fund," *WP*, 13 June 1962, B3; "Model Homes Shown," *WP*, 28 July 1962, D1, D18; "Sterling Park Pace Is Fast," *WP*, 13 Oct. 1962, D11; "Sterling Park Moves," *WP*, 14 Sep. 1963, D8; "Sterling Park Takes," *WP*, 12 Nov. 1966, D1, D19.

74. "Geeraert Readying Subdivision," *WP*, 1 July 1961, B8; "Westgate Model," *WP*, 16 Sep. 1961, B19; *WP*, 22 Sep. 1962, B8; "7-Room Homes," *WP*, 29 Apr. 1961, B6; "Open Occupancy Project Shown," *WP*, 25 Nov. 1961, B3; "New Section Opened," *WP*, 27 July 1963, C6; advertisement, *WP*, 18 Jan. 1964, E6.

75. "Geeraert Pioneers Again," *WP*, 18 July 1964, E1, E2; advertisements, *WP*, 1 Aug. 1964, E15, and 17 Apr. 1965, E10; Patterson interview. A slightly earlier development was Glen Arden Woods (1960–63),

which was planned for 400 houses, not all of which were built. See "Negroes Buy," *WP*, 22 Oct. 1960, B19; "Street Scene," *WP*, 10 Dec. 1960, B7; advertisements, *WP*, 11 Aug. 1962, B14; 23 Feb. 1963, D12; and 9 Mar. 1963, D7. Area builders were divided on the subject of open occupancy as national policy; see "Area Builders Spurn," *WP*, 21 Aug. 1963, D1; "Broyhill Firm Opens," *WP*, 22 Aug. 1963, C1; "3000 Homes," *WP*, 23 Aug. 1963, C1; "Negro Ban Reaffirmed," *WP*, 30 Aug. 1963, D1; and "Suburbs Opening Up," *WP*, 17 Oct. 1963, A1, A8.

76. "Glenarden Apartment Plan Sought," *WP*, 22 May 1965, B2; "Negro Housing Project," *WP*, 21 Aug. 1965, A8; "Low Income Homes," *WP*, 16 June 1966, B3.

77. For background, see Valerie C. Johnson, *Black Power in the Suburbs: The Myth or Reality of African-American Suburban Political Incorporation* (Albany: State University of New York Press, 2002); and Karyn R. Lacy, *Blue-Chip Black: Race, Class, and Status in the New Black Middle Class* (Berkeley: University of California Press, 2007).

78. Patterson interview. See also "Joe Geeraert, Built Twinbrook Homes," *WP*, 24 Nov. 1979, B10.

79. M. T. Broyhill & Sons built 1,465 houses in five subdivisions during 1955 alone; see Martin, "Tract-House Modern," 68. Martin's dissertation focuses on the work of the Luria Brothers.

Curtis & Davis, 71–77, 81, 88; branch offices of, 74; Caribe Building, 76; Curtis house, 77; Forrestal Building, 108; Free University, Berlin, 73; Hotel America, Constitution Plaza, 32, 74; IBM Building, Pittsburgh, 74, 76; IBM offices, Mobile, Shreveport, and Trenton, 73–74; Immaculate Conception Church, 74, 81, 90; Lakewood Hospital, 74, 76; Louisiana National Bank, 74; Louisiana State Penitentiary, 74; Louisiana Superdome, 72, 75; Medical Plaza, 76; New Orleans Public Library, 72, 73, 74, 77; Our Lady of Queen of Heaven Church, 90; Rivergate exhibition hall, 72, 74–75, 76; St. Frances Cabrini Church, 5, 6, 9, 69, 70, 71, 77, 80, 81–90, 83, 84, 85, 86, 87; St. Frances Cabrini School, 70, 71, 74; Thomy Lafon School, 74, 75; U.S. Embassy, Saigon, 73; Worcester Public Library, 74

Dallas, Texas: Cityplace Center East, 237n2; Highland Park Village, 61
Davenport, Robert, Hollin Hills residential development, 44
Davis, A. J., 17, 18; Llewellyn Park, 18
Davis, Arthur Quentin, 71, 81. See also Curtis & Davis
Delano & Aldrich, 17
Denver, Colorado, 28; Hilton Hotel, 94–95, 94; May-D&F department store, 236n54; Miles High Center, 95; Skyline Park, 45, 46
Detroit, Michigan, 28, 230n1; Lafayette Park, 4, 37, 37, 38
Dewey, John, 136
Dinosaur National Monument, Quarry Visitor Center, 243n16
DOCOMOMO (International Committee for Documentation and Conservation of Buildings, Sites, and Neighborhoods of the Modern Movement), 223n3
Donley Construction Company, Twinbrook, 201. See also Gingery, Donald E.
Doty, Cecil, 116
Douglass, Lathrop, Chapel Square, 31, 31–32

Eames, Charles, 70
Eberson, John, 166
Eckbo, Garrett, 41; Fulton Mall, 45, 46, 47
École des Beaux-Arts, Paris, 93, 100
Eddy, Mary Baker, 103
Eggers & Higgins, Cathedral of St. Joseph, 80, 80
Eidlitz, Leopold, 17
Eisenhower, President Dwight D., 113
Esherick, Joseph, Sea Ranch, 42, 43, 44
Evantash & Friedman, Parole Plaza, 61–62, 63

Fairfax County, Virginia, 161, 219, 221; Chandon, 219–20; Chantilly, 219; Dulles International Airport, 1, 130, 219; Herndon, 219; Hollin Hills, 42, 44; Jelleff's apparel store, 167; Seven Corners Shopping Center, 166, 167; Sterling Park, 219–20
Featheringill, Peter, 254n54
Federal Aviation Administration, 97, 130

Federal Housing Administration (FHA), 53–55, 199, 203
Fletcher, Sir Banister, History of Architecture, 19
Foley, Mary Mix, Modern Church Architecture, 80
Folse, Sidney, St. Frances Cabrini Church, 81, 84
Ford, O'Neil, 233n17
Fortune magazine, 72, 81
Framingham, Massachusetts, Shopper's World, 41, 43, 62–63
Franzen, Ulrich, 94
Fredonia, New York, Academic Center, SUNY, 102
Freed, James Ingo, 107, 241n51. See also Pei, I. M., & Associates
French, Christine Madrid, 111
Fresno, California, Fulton Mall, 45, 46, 47
Frey, Monsignor Gerard, 71, 80
Friedberg, Paul, 41
Fuller, Buckminster, 4, 70
Furness, Frank, 17

Gallier, James (Senior and Junior), 72
Gans, Herbert, 29
Garden Grove, California, Community Church, 86
Gebhard, David, 2
Geeraert, Dorothy, 197
Geeraert, Dorothy Howard, 197, 201
Geeraert, Joseph (Geeraert Construction Corporation): Bonnie View, 197, 198, 255n11; Chandon, 219; Coquelin Terrace, 197, 198, 255n12; early career of, 196–97, 255n7, 255n11; Fox Ridge, 220, 221, 221; Highland Gardens, 220; Holly Park North, 220; Kenmoor, 220; partners of, 199, 201; Twinbrook, 195, 196, 198–214, 218, 219, 254n1, 254n3 (see also Twinbrook, Rockville, Maryland); Westgate, 220
Geeraert, Leon, 197
Geeraert, Rosanne, 197
Gehry, Frank, 4
General Services Administration, 107–8
Georgetown University, Lavinger Library, 108
George Washington University, 201
Georgia Historical Society, 250n8
Georgia Institute of Technology, 189
Gettysburg, Pennsylvania, Gettysburg National Military Park, 111, 113–14, 116–17, 118, 128, 131; Cemetery Ridge, 117, 124, 125; Little Round Top, 124, 125; original cyclorama building, 117, 117; Pennsylvania State Memorial, 124, 125; road system, 123, 124; Rosensteel Building (National Museum), 112, 114, 242n8; Visitor Center and Cyclorama Building, 2, 3, 5, 7, 8, 111–12, 112, 113–14, 116–25, 119, 120, 121, 122, 126, 127, 128–31, 128, 129, 242n1, 242n8; Ziegler's Grove, 117, 128
Gettysburg, Battle of, 116, 123; Pickett's Charge, 112, 117
Gettysburg Address, 118
Gettysburg Battlefield Memorial Association, 123
Gill, Irving, 17
Gingery, Donald E., 201, 254n5; 255–56n18; Hungerford Towne, 256n18; Kingswell, 256n18; Twinbrook

Wolfflin, Heinrich, 15
Works Progress Administration, 113
World War II, impact of on architecture and culture,
   163–64, 248–49n18
Wright, Frank Lloyd, 1, 17, 21, 70, 125, 128, 129, 134, 135,
   146, 236n60, 243n16, 245n5; Guggenheim Museum,
   126, 129–30, 239n17; Johnson Wax Company research
   tower, 234n24; Price Tower, 234n24; Robie house, 135;
   Taliesin, 245n5; Unity Temple, 105, 107
Wright, Henry, 135, 136; *Rehousing Urban America*, 136
Wylly, George W., 173

Yale University: Art and Architecture Building, 1;
   School of Architecture, 32

Yamasaki, Minoru, 70; Lambert-St. Louis Air Terminal,
   236n54
Yosemite National Park, 114

Zeckendorf, William, 31, 91, 92, 107, 239n19; Hilton Hotel,
   Denver, 94; Kips Bay Plaza, 95; L'Enfant Plaza, 96–97,
   98, 240n27; Society Hill Towers, 95, 239n19. *See also*
   Webb & Knapp
Zenner Boyd, 3
Zink, John, 166
Zion, Robert, 38, 41

.